THE OCCUPATION
OF JAPAN
1945-1952

THE OCCUPATION OF JAPAN
1945-1952

Tokyo, Washington, and Okinawa

FUKUNAGA Fumio

Japan Publishing Industry Foundation for Culture

PUBLISHER'S NOTE

This book follows the Hepburn system of romanization of Japanese words. Japanese personal names are written in the conventional Japanese order: family name followed by given name. The use of macrons for rendering of extended vowels in Japanese has been employed throughout the text. However, in some cases, macrons are absent in documents from American sources; for the sake of faithfulness to the source, we have presented the quotations as they were written (often without macrons). Paraphrased translations (for unlocatable source texts) generally employ macrons.

The Occupation of Japan 1945–1952: Tokyo, Washington, and Okinawa
Fukunaga Fumio. Translated by the Japan Institute of International Affairs (JIIA).

Published by
Japan Publishing Industry Foundation for Culture (JPIC)
2-2-30 Kanda-Jinbocho, Chiyoda-ku, Tokyo 101-0051, Japan

First English edition: March 2021

Originally published in Japanese under the title *Nihon senryōshi 1945–1952: Tōkyō, Washinton, Okinawa* by CHUOKORON-SHINSHA, INC., in 2014.
English publishing rights arranged with the author.

This publication is the result of a collaborative effort between the Japan Institute of International Affairs (JIIA) and Japan Publishing Industry Foundation for Culture (JPIC).

Jacket and cover design: Miki Kazuhiko, Ampersand Works
Front jacket and cover photographs © Kyodo News and the U.S. Coast Guard Historian's Office

Printed in Japan
ISBN 978-4-86658-125-5
https://www.jpic.or.jp/

Preface

Memories and Records of the Occupation

Following its defeat in the Asian-Pacific War, Japan was placed under the Occupation of the Allied Powers, and the United States in particular, between August 1945 and April 1952.

By accepting the Potsdam Declaration issued by the United States, the United Kingdom, and China, Japan was forced into a period of political, economic, social, and psychological transformation that was equal to, if not more dramatic than, what the nation had experienced during the Meiji Restoration. Beginning at the end of the war, this period of upheaval and transformation lasted nearly seven years until the San Francisco Peace Treaty went into effect and Japan regained its independence. It is no exaggeration to say that the foundations of contemporary Japanese law and politics were laid during this period.

As Supreme Commander of the Allied Powers, General Douglas MacArthur would rule over the vanquished nation. Of the power and authority that he wielded, MacArthur would later say that no colonial governor, conqueror, or military commander in history equaled the power that he had over the Japanese people. As testified to by this comment, MacArthur challenged and endeavored to transform the virtually impregnable systems and institutions of the Empire of Japan that had been reinforced over the decades that followed the Meiji Restoration.

At the outset of the Occupation, MacArthur's primary objective was to forestall Japan's return to militarism, and a thorough program of democratization was implemented to achieve that goal. However, a further objective was added to the Occupation as the face-off between the United States and the Soviet Union intensified during the Cold War. The creation of a democratic "pacifist country" no longer sufficed as Japan was prodded in the direction of emerging as a "pro-U.S. and anti-communist" country. How did Japan and the Japanese people cope with these two different faces of the Occupation?

Now that more than seven decades have elapsed since the end of the war, the events of the Occupation appear to be rapidly receding into the distant past. The generations that experienced Japan's defeat and occupation are also disappearing and the great majority of Japan's present population was born after the war.

What comes to the minds of the Japanese people when they are asked about the Occupation? Do they see the faces of the principal actors, such as General MacArthur and Yoshida Shigeru? Or do they associate it with such events as the promulgation of the Constitution of Japan, the Tokyo Tribunal, the Korean War, and the San Francisco Peace Conference? Perhaps memories of the Occupation of Japan are being increasingly partitioned, fragmented, and re-constituted according to each observer's particular understanding of history before, during, and after the war or according to their political perspective.

The most fundamental elements of Japan's contemporary framework—the Constitution of Japan and the Japan-U.S. Security Treaty—were both established under the Occupation of Japan. The Constitution of Japan was drafted less than six months after Japan's defeat. It was promulgated only a year and three months after the end of the war and came into effect in less than two years. The Security Treaty was concluded after approximately one year of bilateral negotiations and was signed concurrent to the San Francisco Peace Treaty.

Assessments of the Constitution of Japan and other reforms implemented in the name of democratization are currently in a state of flux. Similarly, there is no firm and established assessment of the occupation of Okinawa, which was cut off from the Japanese mainland immediately after the war and placed under continuous U.S. administration. Moreover, the task of properly positioning the Occupation in the context of Japan's postwar era as created by the Constitution of Japan and the Security Treaty has yet to be completed.

Seventy years after the end of the war, more than sixty years after the San Francisco Peace Treaty and the independence of Japan and a quarter of a century after the end of the Cold War, Japan has now arrived at a critical crossroads. The vital questions being asked pertain to the Constitution of Japan and the Security Treaty, which defined postwar Japan, and the unsettled matter of postwar

Okinawa.

When considering Japan's postwar experience, two very important things must be kept in mind. First is the structure and reality of the Occupation that stood at the point of origin of the postwar era. Second is an accurate awareness must be developed of the trajectory of events that culminated in the conclusion of the Occupation.

The purpose of this book is to present the reality of the Occupation of Japan by wading into this extremely dense seven-year period of history, to take a fresh look at the records left by both the occupiers and the occupied while standing above any specific perspective of history and politics.

Contents

Introduction

The Occupiers and the Occupied: Tokyo, Washington, and Okinawa

A Long Occupation

On August 15, 1945, Japan accepted the Potsdam Declaration and surrendered to the Allied Powers. On August 30, General Douglas MacArthur, Supreme Commander of the Allied Powers, landed at Atsugi Airfield. Later, Japan's instrument of surrender was signed and exchanged on September 2, formally marking the start of the Occupation.

Having misjudged international relations and entered into a war that would end in defeat, Japan was now temporarily ejected from the international community. Thus, in a sense, the Occupation was the price that Japan had to pay in order to be allowed back into the international community and it afforded the exhausted nation a preparatory period for building a new nation.

The Allied Powers (but effectively the United States) sought to destroy Japan's military capability so that Japanese militarism would never again threaten world peace. But the occupiers did not stop there, for they landed in Japan with a grand vision for transforming Japan into a democratically constituted "pacifist country."

Once in place, General Headquarters, Supreme Commander for the Allied Powers (GHQ/SCAP: hereinafter, GHQ) implemented in rapid succession a series of policies and measures for demilitarizing and democratizing Japan, effectively taking a sledgehammer to Japan's political, economic, and social structures. Demilitarization—featuring disarmament, the seizure of munitions industries, and related measures—was essentially completed by the end of 1945. Following these were reforms for democratization, and ultimately the challenge of writing and promulgating a new constitution. These initiatives were also for the most part completed during the early phase of the Occupation in the years 1946 and 1947.

Having more or less accomplished the two primary objectives of the Occupation, MacArthur announced on March 17, 1947 that the Occupation was now ready to move on to a new set of objectives, principal among which was economic reconstruction and recovery. Identifying the conclusion of a peace treaty as a requirement for realizing this goal, MacArthur stated that the time had now arrived for forging a peace with Japan.

However, negotiations on the peace treaty quickly became entangled in the Cold War that pitted the United States against the Soviet Union. As a result, the treaty required an additional five years to be consummated. As the twin challenges of forging a peace and achieving economic recovery became caught in the cross currents of the Cold War, the issue of Japan's independence was thrown into the crucible of international politics. Meanwhile, the Japanese economy was subjected to the draconian prescriptions of the "Dodge Line," and the general policies of the Occupation underwent a sharp re-direction popularly referred to as the "reverse course."

In any case, Japan remained under the Occupation of the Allied Powers until April 1952 when the San Francisco Peace Treaty came into force, thus ending the long Occupation that lasted nearly seven years. What narratives and interactions did this Occupation engender between the victor and the vanquished, and how did this long Occupation influence and characterize the formation of postwar Japan?

The Dynamism of the Occupation

An occupation unfolds within the confines of an asymmetrical relation between the victor (the occupiers) and the vanquished (the occupied). Needless to say, occupation denotes domination by the victor where the victor exerts its will upon the vanquished through military might as an apparatus of force.

This is not to say, however, that the formation of postwar Japan was the product solely of the policies implemented by MacArthur and the United States. It is simply unrealistic to think that an occupying force can take a nation endowed with its own rich history and culture and change it overnight.

The vanquished are never reduced to merely passively observing the actions and behavior of the victor. Because the Occupation of the Japanese mainland took the form of indirect rule, the nation was left with two governments—GHQ and the Japanese government. While there is a tendency to view Japan as being generally acquiescent in character, the reality of the Occupation was that the Japanese people themselves were keenly aware of the need for some form of dramatic change that would carry the nation from its wartime regime to a peacetime system and thereby facilitate the "construction of a new Japan." Some of the most seminal reforms of the Occupation years—women's suffrage, the Labor Union Law, and farmland reform—have been referred to as "MacArthur's gifts." However, a lesser known truth is that these specific reforms had been pending since before the war and were actually pursued under the initiative of the vanquished well before being instructed by GHQ.

For instance, even Yoshida Shigeru, who was known for his lack of enthusiasm for reform, wrote the following about farmland reform.

> The reason why this radical reform took root was that the groundwork for farmland reform had already been laid in Japan.... It was Wada Hiroo who as Minister of Agriculture and Forestry was responsible for postwar farmland reforms. As a prewar bureaucrat of the Ministry of Agriculture and Forestry, Wada had already spent many years surveying and investigating Japanese agriculture and had put considerable time planning for farmland reform. He had conducted serious research and had thoroughly surveyed the conditions on the ground. Thus, the Japanese side presented its program for farmland reform before being instructed by the Occupation forces. Of course, some voiced their opposition. Because the voices of opposition were quite strong, perhaps farmland reform would not have been implemented without the boost given by the Occupation forces.... In other words, the government of Japan took the initiative in farmland reform and the Occupation forces came from behind to give it a boost. Finally, the Occupation forces went beyond the initial plan of the government of Japan and directed the implementation of far more thorough reform. Another important factor was that farmer movements that existed from before the war continued to campaign for the liberation of tenant farmers. They were elated to know that farmland reforms were to be introduced and enthusiastically assisted in their implementation. Moreover,

many low-level agriculture bureaucrats and village officers favored farmland reform and devoted their energies to realizing them.[1]

As Yoshida points out, various reforms had been formulated before the war by bureaucrats with jurisdiction and had been supported by a broad range of social movements. Thus, it can be said that the Occupation's program for democratization threw open the doors for these long-standing initiatives. While it is important to consider the significance of the "boost" given by the Occupation forces, the reforms should be assessed in the context of a continuum that starts in prewar Japan and extends through the war and the postwar years.

On the other hand, the Occupation also functioned to decisively sever and detach the postwar from the war years. It should be borne in mind that the postwar prime ministers—Shidehara Kijūrō, Yoshida Shigeru, Katayama Tetsu, and Ashida Hitoshi—had all been hounded by the military during the war years and had been reduced to living sequestered lives. For them, Japan's defeat signified personal liberation and the war years represented a period of history that needed to be negated. These leaders had matured and completed their personal development in prewar Japan. This makes it necessary to examine how they re-invented themselves as they emerged from the war and embarked on new personal journeys of the postwar era.

The Occupation was a period pregnant with possibilities and a period in which various competing visions for the postwar rebirth of Japan were debated between Japan and the United States.

These visions for the future were drawn from the past experiences of the respective countries, and any discord or friction that arose between the two during the Occupation was essentially a product of the pasts. Ultimately, Japan's rebirth was realized through a constant give and take between conflicting and harmonious visions. Thus, the Occupation can be seen as the product of a certain dynamism that was animated by the constant interaction between the occupiers and the occupied.

---

1 Yoshida Shigeru, *Gekidō no hyakunenshi: Waga ketsudan to kiseki no tenkan* [History of a turbulent hundred years], Shirakawa Shoin, 1978, pp. 123–126.

Two Occupations: The Occupation and Postwar Politics

As indicated by its subtitle, this book attempts to depict the Occupation of Japan from the three perspectives of Tokyo (the Japanese mainland), Washington, and Okinawa.

While the Japanese mainland and Okinawa experienced occupation at approximately the same time, the treatment they received was fundamentally different. In most instances, however, discussions of the Occupation of Japan focus almost exclusively on the Occupation of the Japanese mainland. Okinawa was placed under the direct rule of the U.S. military and was left out of the democratization reforms that culminated in the promulgation of the Constitution of Japan. Similarly, Okinawa was excluded from the peace treaty and the return of sovereignty and independence. New light can be shed on the Occupation of Japan by contrasting the occupations of the Japanese mainland and Okinawa. Juxtaposing the two experiences brings different overall pictures into focus, making it possible to relativize and integrate the Occupation as a whole.

The purpose of this book is to develop a granular picture of the Occupation of Japan through a presentation of the occupations of the Japanese mainland and Okinawa, and to place all of this in the context of postwar political history. At the same time, this book represents an attempt to escape the orbit of the conception of Japan's postwar as something that was "forced upon the Japanese." In addition, the book focuses on the following three questions.

First, the book attempts to determine the reality of U.S. and GHQ Occupation policies and goes on to ask two sets of related questions. Did these policies achieve their objectives? And how did these policies change and not change in the course of negotiations with the Japanese side?

Second, how were the reforms of the Occupation connected to and disconnected from the prewar and war years?

Third, how did the Occupation influence the formation of Japan's postwar systems and institutions?

The book is structured as follows. Chapters 1 through 3 cover the Occupation of Japan and its reforms. Chapters 4 and 5 trace the course of the Occupation of Japan through discussions of economic recovery and the peace treaty, respectively.

Chapter 1 addresses the period between the final year of the war and the establishment of GHQ, and examines the "demilitarization" policies of GHQ and the responses of the Japanese side.

Chapter 2 starts by considering the friction that occurred between the Japanese and U.S. sides and within the domestic scene in connection with the "democratization" reforms as observed through the process of the drafting and enactment of the Constitution of Japan. The latter part of the chapter focuses on the resurrection of political parties and traces political maneuvering by GHQ and the Japanese government in pursuit of democratization and economic recovery.

Chapter 3 is given to a review of the achievements of the Katayama Cabinet, the first cabinet to take the reins of government after the Constitution of Japan came into effect. The review focuses on the challenges of democratization and economic reconstruction and reform.

Chapter 4 highlights the transition that occurred in U.S. Occupation policies in response to the Cold War, and scrutinizes how various political forces in Tokyo, Washington (GHQ and the U.S. government), and domestically within Japan coped with the challenges of economic reconstruction and recovery.

Chapter 5 examines various issues and developments leading to the peace treaty. The Japanese plan for returning to the international community is presented together with an outline of the conflicts that emerged between Japan, the United States, and the Allied Powers.

Defeat in the war pressured Japan to accept its "second opening" that followed the Meiji Restoration as the nation's "first opening." What did the Occupation signify as Japan's first step into the postwar era? What did Japan and the Japanese people gain from the Occupation, and what did they lose? What national character and identity did Japan adopt in trying to reconnect with the international community? Japan has now lived in the "postwar" for seventy years, notwithstanding the constant calls and demands for finally bringing the postwar to an end. Mindful of these voices, this book re-examines a "postwar" that has managed to survive the passage of these seven decades.

CHAPTER 1

Defeat and Occupation:
Toward Demilitarization and Democratization

1. From Japan's Surrender to the Establishment of GHQ

U.S. Military Advance and the Occupation of Okinawa

Summer of 1944: The Pearl Harbor Conference in Hawaii

Following the fall of Saipan, the cabinet of Tōjō Hideki collapsed on July 18, 1944, and was replaced by the cabinet of Koiso Kuniaki on July 22. On the battlefield, a fight to the death continued even as the Japanese military steadily retreated. At home, production had collapsed and material resources had become extremely strained. Against this backdrop, all that was heard were calls for the "full implementation of the holy war (*Seisen kansui*)." Japan had lost command of the air and its supply lines had been severed. The country would soon be hurtling toward becoming a totally denuded and unprotected archipelago.

On July 26, President Franklin Roosevelt gathered his Pacific commanders at the Honolulu Headquarters facing Pearl Harbor to discuss strategy. The principal participants were General Douglas MacArthur and Admiral Chester Nimitz. During the spring of 1944, the idea had begun to gel in Washington for transferring the forces under MacArthur's command to the Pacific Command under Nimitz, and to bypass the Philippines to advance directly on Taiwan.

This strategy was unacceptable to MacArthur, primarily because it would rob him of the opportunity to fulfill the promise he made—"I shall return"— three years earlier when forced to abandon the Philippines.

MacArthur had already made up his mind arriving at the meeting with a counter proposal. He argued that retaking the Philippines would sever all of Japan's supply lines, both sea and air, which would paralyze Japanese industries and lead to an early surrender. He further argued that, as a part of U.S. territories, there was a moral obligation to take back the Philippines and to liberate the several thousand American prisoners of war that were being held there.

MacArthur took three hours to complete his long-winded presentation. It is reported that after the meeting, Roosevelt went to his accompanying doctor to ask for aspirin. "Give me an aspirin for before I go to bed. In fact, give me another aspirin to take in the morning. In all my life, nobody has ever talked to me the way MacArthur did."[1]

I Shall Return

MacArthur's proposal was adopted and on October 3, orders were issued to MacArthur and Nimitz for the advance on Luzon Island in the Philippines, Iwo Jima (in the Ogasawara Islands), and Okinawa. On the Japanese side, the Imperial Headquarters had assumed the U.S. advance would proceed along the line of defense that connected the Philippines to Taiwan and had consequently transferred part of its defensive forces from Okinawa to Taiwan.

Prior to the advance on the Philippines, Nimitz attacked Japanese outposts scattered between the Nansei Shotō and Formosa on October 10. Launched at 6:00 a.m., the attack on the Nansei Shotō targeted airfields on the main island of Okinawa, including the Kita Airfield (located in Yomitan Village) and the Oroku Airfield, and extended to Miyako Island and other outlying islands. The defensive forces on the Japanese side were ill-prepared for the attack and were no match for the American forces. As a result, anchored battleships and aircraft in transit were destroyed without putting up any effective resistance. The fierce aerial attacks also hit civilian targets, resulting in the destruction of ninety percent of the city of Naha. Precious stockpiles of foodstuffs were also lost in the attack.

On October 11, the American fleet turned to attack Japanese airbases in Taiwan. With Japanese forces fighting back, the so-called Formosa Air Battle unfolded on October 12.

On October 20, MacArthur landed on Leyte Island in the southern Philippines to fulfill his pledge that he would return. Following the victory in Leyte, MacArthur started his advance toward the capital city of Manila. On February 6, 1945, MacArthur proclaimed, "Manila has been regained."

---

1   Manchester, William, *American Caesar: Douglas MacArthur 1880–1964*, Dell, 1978, p. 431.

However, MacArthur would need several more months to establish control over the whole country. Nimitz landed on Iwo Jima on February 19, but was made to pay a far greater price than had been expected due to the stiff resistance of the island's defenders.

Also during February, President Roosevelt, Prime Minister Churchill, and Premier Stalin gathered in Yalta on the Soviet Union's Crimean Peninsula to discuss the postwar reorganization of Europe. It was at this time that Roosevelt and Stalin entered into a secret agreement on the war against Japan. The Soviet Union pledged to join the war against Japan within three months of Germany's surrender. In return, the United States agreed to the reversion of southern Sakhalin and the cession of the Kurile Islands to the Soviet Union.

Even as the Allies were meeting in Yalta, the Shōwa Emperor ordered seven senior statesmen to present their prognosis of the war situation and possible countermeasures. Among these statesmen were Konoe Fumimaro, Hirota Kōki and Tōjō Hideki. Responding to the Emperor's order, Konoe submitted a document that has been called the Konoe Memorial to the Throne, in which he argued that prolonging the war would incite domestic unrest and ultimately result in a communist revolution. Konoe recommended an early end to the war on the grounds that the United States was amenable to allowing the continuance of the Imperial Household. It is reported that at this juncture, Konoe was the only one among the seven to unambiguously recommend ending the war. The Emperor is said to have responded saying, "This will be difficult to realize without achieving one more military gain."[2] The Emperor sided with the strategy of "suing for peace after dealing one additional blow."

Battle of Okinawa and Birth of the Suzuki Kantarō Cabinet

As Japanese forces continued to retreat on all fronts in the Philippines, the aerial bombing of the Japanese mainland was rapidly accelerating. The low-lying areas of Tokyo were reduced to ash in the Great Tokyo Air Raid carried out between

---

2 Fujita Hisanori, *Jijū-chō no kaisō* [Memoirs of a Grand Chamberlain], Chūō Kōronsha, 1987, p. 66.

the evening of March 9 and the early hours of March 10. Thereafter, incendiary bombing attacks rapidly spread to Osaka, Kobe, Nagoya, and other major cities.

Iwo Jima fell on March 17, and on March 26, the American forces landed on the Kerama Islands located a mere 30 kilometers west of Okinawa. On the same day, Nimitz released U.S. Navy Military Government Proclamation No. 1 addressed "to the People of the Islands of Nansei and Adjacent Waters Occupied by United States Forces." Known as the Nimitz Proclamation, it announced the suspension of the powers and authority of the Japanese government in the Nansei Shotō and established a military government consisting of troops in the field. This effectively started the military occupation of Okinawa, which differed importantly from the occupation of the Japanese mainland. Because Okinawa was occupied "in the course of hostilities," its occupation did not come under the provisions on the Potsdam Declaration. What applied to the occupation of Okinawa were the provisions of international law in times of war as stipulated in the Hague Laws of Land Warfare Respecting the Laws and Customs of War on Land (Annex, Section III).

On April 1, American forces began to land on Okinawa with the first landings targeting the western coastline of the middle of the island. Thereafter, American forces advanced southward along the coast of Yomitan and Chatan as they headed toward the Imperial Army Headquarters located in Shuri City (present-day Naha City). This movement of troops divided Okinawa into two sectors: the middle and southern parts of the island that became the scene of intense fighting, and the northern parts of the island where fighting was relatively light. Residents of the former sector became the victims of ferocious naval bombardment that they referred to as the "Storm of Steel" and the "Storm of Blood." Not long after the bombardment, they would be thrown into the abyss of starvation.

On April 5, the Koiso Cabinet resigned en masse after peace initiatives with Chiang Kai-shek fell through. On the same day, the Soviet Union announced that it would not extend the Japan-Soviet Neutrality Pact. Following these developments, Admiral Suzuki Kantarō, the 77-year-old President of the Privy Council, was appointed to form a new cabinet. Suzuki had earned the trust of the Emperor after serving as grand chamberlain during the 1930s. Having sensed that the real intent of the Shōwa Emperor was to end the war, Suzuki quietly waited for an appropriate opportunity and hoped to sue for peace after rendering a blow to the American forces in the Battle of Okinawa.

But the fighting in Okinawa never took a favorable turn for Japan. The Imperial Army was forced into one retreat after another until it finally prepared to make a last stand at Mabuni (present-day Itoman City) at the southern tip of the island on May 30. By this time, the 32nd Army, which at this point was in charge of the defense of Okinawa, had already lost 80 percent of its men. By May 31, the American forces had succeeded in occupying Shuri.

On June 6, Commander Ōta Minoru of the Imperial Navy forces in Okinawa sent his final communication to the Vice Minister of the Navy in a telegram that ended with this plea. "As the people of Okinawa Prefecture have fought so valiantly, I implore that they be accorded special consideration in future generations." Shortly thereafter, Ōta took his own life on June 13 in an underground bunker of the Imperial Navy Headquarters at Tomigusuku. Next, on June 23, Commander Ushijima Mitsuru of the Okinawa Defense Force and his chief of staff Lieutenant Colonel Chō Isamu took their own lives at the Imperial Army Headquarters at Mabuni. This effectively ended the Battle of Okinawa.

On the Japanese side, approximately 90,000 soldiers were killed in the Battle of Okinawa, including volunteers from the local population. Non-combatant deaths are estimated to have been around 100,000. On the American side, casualties are estimated to have reached 49,000.

Non-Combatant Camps in Okinawa

The American forces created a number of internment camps in non-combat zones located in the mid-northern section of Okinawa to accommodate civilians who were found hiding in the mountains or bunkers to avoid the fighting. Their immediate purpose was to establish military bases throughout Okinawa and maintain order in preparation for a future landing on the Japanese mainland.

Twelve internment camps were established throughout the island including camps in such locations as Chinen, Koza, and Maehara. Japanese soldiers and military porters who were conscripted from Korea were held in separate camps. The total number of internees, excluding soldiers and civilian military employees came to over 222,000 as of June 23, 1945. This was equivalent to an astounding 85 percent of the total population of Okinawa and its neighboring islands.

The camps were simple facilities surrounded by barbwire fences and the internees were required to put up tents and build primitive shacks to avoid the elements. Food and sanitary conditions were extremely poor, and residents would have starved to death without outside help. U.S. forces assisted the residents without payment, but this assistance did not go beyond minimal amounts of food, clothing, tents, medicine, and other necessities. People were enlisted to work in "military projects" that included the construction of internment camps, provision of miscellaneous services in U.S. military installations, and the post-hostility cleanup of Okinawa. Participants were paid for their services with food and other necessities in a simple barter system that provided them with just enough to stay alive.

Life in the internment camps was subject to a variety of rules and restrictions. Internees were not allowed to move between camps, were not allowed to go out after dark, and were not even allowed to seek information on the safety of family members. These were the conditions that prevailed as Okinawa launched into the postwar era.

Defeat and Acceptance of the Potsdam Declaration

Plans for Advancing into the Japanese Mainland

On April 8, 1945, the Joint Chiefs of Staff gave approval to Operation Downfall, the military plan for dealing a final blow to the Japanese mainland. Operation Downfall comprised three distinct stages. In the first stage, bases located in Okinawa, the Marianas, and the Philippines would be used to execute aerial and naval bombardments and blockade both Kyushu and Honshu. These operations were designed to set the stage for the advance on Kyushu, referred to as Operation Olympic, which would be carried out in stage two. After landing on Kyushu, the bombardment and blockade of Honshu would be stepped up to the next level. The third and last stage was dubbed Operation Coronet, which consisted of advancing and controlling the Kanto Plain, destroying the core of

Japan's industrial base and putting an end to all organized resistance.

President Roosevelt suddenly died on April 12, and was succeeded by Vice President Harry Truman. On May 7, Germany surrendered unconditionally to the Allies, leaving Japan as the only Axis power left standing.

In June President Truman gave approval to Operation Olympic. Initially, the advance of Kyushu was scheduled for December 1, but following the surrender of Germany, this was moved up by a month to November 1. At the same time, Operation Coronet was set to start on March 1 of the following year. Ultimately, November 15, 1946, was identified as the tentative target date for the ending of hostilities. As far as Washington was concerned, the surrender of Japan was still an event in the distant and uncertain future.

Operation Blacklist: MacArthur's Plan for the Occupation of Japan

On June 14, 1945, the Joint Chiefs of Staff directed General MacArthur in Manila to draw up plans for the occupation of Japan in "preparation for a sudden collapse and surrender of Japan." In response to this directive, work started in Manila on a plan for the peaceful occupation of Japan, which was code-named Operation Blacklist. This was followed by the establishment of the Military Government Section on August 5. Headed by Brigadier General William Crist, the deputy commander of the Okinawa Military Government, the Military Government Section was formed on the assumption that Japan would be subjected to direct military rule.

The third and final version of Operation Blacklist was completed on August 8. While continuing to assume the installation of direct military government, its objectives were defined as follows: (1) cessation of hostilities and speedy disarmament of the Japanese armed forces, (2) transfer of all the powers of the Japanese government to the Allied military command, (3) maintenance of law and order by Japanese government officers and policemen, and (4) seizure of military material and facilities and the demobilization of the Japanese armed forces.

The final version of Operation Blacklist identified the Kanto Plain, Nagasaki, Sasebo, Kobe, Osaka, Kyoto, Aomori (Ōminato), and Seoul as initial landing points from which U.S. forces would advance toward Fukuoka, Nagoya, Sapporo, and Busan, respectively. Other landings would be made in Hiroshima and Okayama from the Seto Inland Sea, as well as in Kochi, Tsuruga, Sendai, and Niigata.

Japanese Initiatives for Ending the War

After the fall of Germany in May, Japan wavered between the two options of uncompromising resistance and suing for peace. In its meeting of May 18, the Supreme War Direction Council came to two decisions. First, it was agreed that as a minimal step, actions would be taken to prevent the Soviet Union's entry into the war. Second, it was agreed that the Soviet Union would be approached to mediate a peace agreement. The secret mission of contacting the Soviet Union was assigned to the senior statesman, Hirota Kōki, who would secretly contact Yakov Malik, the Soviet Ambassador to Japan.

In its meeting of June 8, the Imperial Conference (*Gozen kaigi*) concluded that a landing of U.S. forces on the Japanese mainland was now inevitable. The Conference then adopted the Fundamental Policy for the Conduct of the War, which consisted of a commitment to the preservation of the national polity and full defense of the homeland. It was reported during this meeting that Japan had exhausted its powers to maintain the war effort. It was immediately after this meeting of the Imperial Conference that the Shōwa Emperor explicitly expressed his wish for an end to the war. Speaking to Lord Keeper of the Privy Seal Kido Kōichi, the Emperor explained the need to end the war, whereupon Kido formulated his "Draft Proposal for Settling the Situation," which was later submitted to Prime Minister Suzuki for his consideration.

The Imperial Conference met again on June 22, at which time the Emperor stated that it was reasonable to continue the war in line with the decision of June 8, but that it was also necessary to examine means by which to settle the situation. Responding to the Emperor's statement, Prime Minister Suzuki, Minister of the Navy Yonai Mitsumasa, and Minister of Foreign Affairs Tōgō Shigenori outlined a policy for requesting the Soviet Union to mediate a peace agreement. The Minister of the Army stated that the matter "requires due caution" but did not go so far as to express opposition. With this, the decision was finalized to attempt secret peace negotiations with the Soviet Union as an intermediary. The following day marked the virtual end of the Battle of Okinawa.

No answer was ever received from the Soviets. On July 13, the government of Japan contacted the Soviet Union on a proposed visit to the Soviet Union by Konoe. At approximately the same time, Stalin and Foreign Minister Molotov were preparing to depart for Potsdam, located in the outskirts of Berlin.

The Potsdam Conference and the U.S.-U.S.S.R. Feud

The Potsdam Conference was scheduled to start on July 17, 1945, with the arrival of Truman, Churchill (who on July 28 was replaced by the Labor Party's Clement Attlee following the defeat of the Conservative Party in the general election), and Stalin. Marking his debut on the stage of international politics, Truman was clearly nervous about the prospect of crossing swords with his two veteran counterparts.

A day before the first meeting, Stalin paid a visit to Truman and stated very straightforwardly that the Soviet Union was "prepared to enter into hostilities with Japan in mid-August," faithfully meeting the terms of the secret agreement that had been reached at Yalta. Stalin also reported that the Soviet Union had received a request concerning a visit by Konoe. Stalin then explained the three options that he felt were available to him: to ignore the request, reject the request, or leave some room for Japan to entertain some hope. Stalin then concluded that he intended to take the third option. Stalin was still looking for an excuse to abrogate the Soviet-Japan Neutrality Pact, which would have to be done before the declaration of war.

Japan was not the main subject of the Potsdam meetings, which had been given the codename "Terminal." The participants clashed over the Polish issue and other matters related to the postwar reorganization of Europe in disputes that already pointed to the start of U.S.-U.S.S.R. conflicts over their different visions for the postwar order.

It was not until the eighth meeting held on July 24 that advances were made on the question of Japan. It was on this day that Truman for the first time showed his counterparts his draft of the demand for Japan's unconditional surrender (later to be called the Potsdam Declaration). It was also at this time that Truman conveyed to Stalin that the United States had successfully developed a new weapon of unprecedented destructive force, though this reference to the atomic bomb was left vague. It is reported that Stalin maintained an expressionless look when replying that he hoped the new weapon would be used "effectively" against the Japanese people.

Potsdam Declaration

On July 26, the Potsdam Declaration was issued in the name of the United States, Great Britain, and China. Truman carefully excluded the Soviet Union from the declaration on the grounds that the Soviet Union had yet to enter into war with Japan. The declaration comprised thirteen articles and stated, "The full application of our military power backed by our resolve will mean the inevitable and complete destruction of the Japanese armed forces and just as inevitably the utter devastation of the Japanese homeland." The declaration also stated "Japan shall be given an opportunity to end this war" by accepting certain conditions.

These conditions can be summarized as follows: elimination of militarism; restriction of the territory of Japan to Honshu, Hokkaido, Kyushu, Shikoku, and the small islands in their vicinities; disarmament of Japanese armed forces; revival and strengthening of democratic tendencies among the Japanese people; and establishment of freedom of speech, religion and thought, and respect for the fundamental human rights.

A particularly noteworthy element of the Potsdam Declaration is contained in Article 10 that explicitly states, "The Japanese Government shall remove all obstacles to the revival and strengthening of democratic tendencies among the Japanese people." This statement points to an important shift in basic policy for the occupation of Japan. Whereas direct military government and control were assumed for occupation in the course of hostilities, the Potsdam Declaration clearly committed to a framework of indirect rule by the occupying forces effected through the Emperor and Japanese government.

It is notable that the subject of the sentence in the original draft was "the Japanese people," which was amended to read "the Japanese Government" as suggested by the British.[3]

While Truman welcomed Stalin's promise to join the war against Japan, in the course of the meetings, he began to doubt whether the United States and the Soviet Union could really get along. By the time he departed Potsdam, Truman had come to a certain conclusion.

Anxious as we were to have Russia in the war against Japan, the experience at Potsdam now made me determined that I would not allow the Russians any part in the control of Japan. Our experience with them in Germany and in Bulgaria, Romania, Hungary, and Poland was such that I decided to take no chances in a joint setup with Russians. As I reflected on the situation during my trip home, I made up my mind that General MacArthur would be given complete command and control after victory in Japan.[4]

This decision would critically undermine the framework for postwar U.S.-U.S.S.R. cooperation, and can be identified as the start of the clash of the two postwar superpowers.

Shōwa Emperor and the "Imperial Decision"

The July 27 meeting of the Supreme Council for the Direction of the War was split on how to respond to the Potsdam Declaration. Foreign Minister Tōgō emphasized that no response should be given so that Japan could retain the chance to end the war. In contrast, the military demanded that the prime minister sternly reject the Potsdam Declaration, arguing that failure to do so would deal a devastating blow to morale.

Reports on the content of the Potsdam Declaration appeared in the Japanese newspapers on July 28 under such headlines as "Tripartite Conspiracy" and

---

3 Amakawa Akira, *Senryōka no Nihon: Kokusai kankyō to kokunai taisei* [Japan under the Occupation], Gendai Shiryō Shuppan, 2014, p. 145.
4 Geselbracht, Raymond H., *The Memoirs of Harry S. Truman: A Reader's Edition*, 2019, p. 223.

"Laughable and Cunning Conspiracy." Next to these articles, the newspapers carried Prime Minister Suzuki's statement, "We shall simply disregard [*moku-satsu*] the declaration."[5] Faced with the military's unyielding position, Suzuki had no confidence that an agreement could be reached on peace. However, the Allied Powers interpreted the prime minister's use of the word *mokusatsu* to mean, "reject" the declaration. This would ultimately lead to the decision to drop the atomic bomb on Hiroshima on August 6.

On August 8, the Soviet Union declared war on Japan ahead of its initial schedule. On the following day, the Soviet Army began to advance southward through Manchuria as an unstoppable force, leaving Japan with two options. Would it now accept the Potsdam Declaration and sue for peace, or would it continue to fight at all costs?

Japan's Supreme War Direction Council met on August 9. During this meeting, Foreign Minister Tōgō and Naval Minister Yonai argued in favor of Japan's surrender on the condition of the preservation of the national polity. Army Minister Anami Korechika, Chief of the Army General Staff Umezu Yoshijirō, and Chief of the Navy General Staff Toyoda Soemu countered that other conditions needed to be added to the terms of surrender. Specifically, they called for the inclusion of conditions pertaining to war crimes, disarmament, and the scope of occupation. The two sides could not come to an agreement and the meeting was deadlocked. As the two sides argued, news arrived concerning the atomic bombing of Nagasaki. The meeting was reconvened in the evening in the presence of the Emperor, and it was in this meeting that the Emperor rendered his "imperial decision" in favor of peace. However, the military continued to insist on the attachment of one condition, which was the preservation of national polity. It was finally decided that the United States would be contacted on the possibility of the preservation of national polity, which denoted the preservation of the authority and rule of the Emperor.

The telegraphed response received on August 12 contained no concessions from the Americans. "The authority of the Emperor and the Japanese government to rule the state shall be subject to the Supreme Commander of the

---

5 *Asahi Shinbun*, July 28, 1945.

Allied Powers. The ultimate form of government of Japan shall, in accordance with the Potsdam Declaration, be established by the freely expressed will of the Japanese people." On the following day, August 13, the Supreme Council for the Direction of the War met in a joint session of the cabinet. Again, no consensus could be reached on the condition of the preservation of national polity. On August 14, the Emperor took the unusual step of acting himself to convene a meeting of the Imperial Conference. The "imperial decision" for peace was re-affirmed in this meeting and a final decision was made on Japan's surrender. On the same day, Lord Keeper of the Privy Seal Kido called on Prince Higashikuni Naruhiko to form a new government. This message was conveyed to Prince Higashikuni by Matsudaira Yasumasa, Chief Secretary of the Lord Keeper.

Japan's Defeat and the People of Japan

From early morning on August 15, radio broadcasts repeatedly announced that an important announcement was to be made at noon. Even as the summer day grew hotter, people began to gather at homes and elsewhere to listen to the broadcast that would convey the announcement. All were holding their breath as they heard the voice of the Emperor for the first time. "Having been able to safeguard and maintain the structure of the Imperial State, I am always with you, our good and loyal subjects, relying upon your sincerity and integrity." With this message, the Emperor announced that Japan was defeated and would accept the terms of the Potsdam Declaration.

The Home Ministry immediately began to receive reports from throughout the country on the people's reactions to the broadcast. "Both military personnel and the people were stunned by the sudden announcement" (Ōita Prefecture). "Roughly 70 percent of the public expected the Emperor's broadcast to be a call for a final thrust in the war effort. Thus, people seemed to be stunned, disappointed, and resentful of the announcement of peace and the end to the war" (Osaka Prefecture). "The general response of the people can be summarized in these words. 'This is regrettable but we are greatly relieved.' This sense of relief was particularly strong among the women" (Gunma Prefecture).[6]

For the people of Japan, the end of the war came as a bolt out of the blue. Therefore, it is not surprising that the public was stunned by the unexpected turn of events. On the other hand, finding that the long years of war had finally come to an end, it was quite natural for the public to be overcome by a sense of relief and liberation. But it did not take long for the people to be drawn back to the grim reality of daily life: a life of starvation and deprivation that had continued through the long war years.

On August 15, the cabinet of Prime Minister Suzuki Kantarō resigned en masse. On the following day, August 16, an imperial order was delivered to Prince Higashikuni Naruhiko instructing him to form a new government. At the same time, three members of the imperial family were hastily dispatched overseas to ensure the surrender of Japan's overseas forces. Prince Asaka was sent to China, Prince Takeda to Korea, and Prince Kan'in to the southern front.

Japan's Leadership on August 15: Defeat Is Not Necessarily Bad

It is interesting to consider how Japan's postwar political leaders—particularly those who would rise to the post of prime minister in later years—interpreted the events of August 15.

As a prewar foreign minister, Shidehara Kijūrō had promoted a policy of harmonizing with the United States and Britain. Due to his positions, Shidehara was hounded by the military during the war years and was reduced to living a highly restricted life. It is reported that Shidehara wept when he learned the war had ended, but it did not take long for him to compose and re-orient himself. "Having arrived at this juncture, it does not behoove the people to spend their days sorrowfully counting the age of children that were lost to them. Nay, the most important thing is to concentrate all our energies on reconstructing the nation, a task we must undertake with courage, patience, and hope."[7] Beginning

---

6 Awaya Kentarō, ed., *Shiryō Nihon gendaishi, 2: Haisen chokugo no seiji to shakai* [Modern Japanese History in Sources, vol. 2: Politics and Society after the Defeat], Ōtsuki Shoten, 1980, pp. 151–154 and 162.
7 Shidehara Peace Foundation, ed., *Shidehara Kijūrō* [Shidehara Kijūrō], Shidehara Peace Foundation, 1955, pp. 546–547.

on this day, Shidehara reclused himself and remained silent as an expression of penitence.

Yoshida Shigeru heard the Emperor's broadcast on his sickbed in Ōiso. The malnutrition he had experienced while confined by the military police had taken its toll. But he was in good spirits and exuded a strange sense of exuberance and confidence.

So far the decisiveness and completeness of our acceptance of defeat stands unparalleled in the annals of world history. This is where the momentum for reconstructing the nation will emerge. The cancer of militarist policies must be excised, the world of politics shall be clear and transparent, public morals must be promoted, and foreign relations must be completely recast. In addition, the world of business will be resurrected through the promotion of science and the injection of American capital. Ultimately, if the true essence of the nation will be manifested to a higher degree than ever before, this defeat is not necessarily bad.[8]

Ashida Hitoshi was at the Kōjunsha Club in Ginza when the Emperor's message was broadcast on the radio. "We stood at attention and wept in stunned silence. It was a dignified and solemn scene."[9]

Hatoyama Ichirō was in Karuizawa when he learned of the end of the war. "The country folk were all sobbing loudly. I too was among those who wept that day. Those emotions prevailed at that moment, but were soon replaced by a growing awareness that the reconstruction of Japan had to be achieved under the aegis of democracy and through the agency of parliamentary politics of the highest order." [10]

Ishibashi Tanzan noted the events of August 15 in his diary in the blandest of terms. "The Emperor's broadcast at noon announced the end of hostilities." By

---

8   Yoshida Shigeru to Kurusu Saburō, (August 27, 1945), Yoshida Shigeru Kinen Zaidan, ed., *Yoshida Shigeru shokan* [Letters of Yoshida Shigeru], Chūō Kōronsha, 1994, pp. 553-554.
9   Shindō Eiichi and Shimokōbe Motoharu, eds., *Ashida Hitoshi nikki, dai 1-kan* [Ashida Hitoshi Diary, vol. 1], Iwanami Shoten, 1986, p. 47.
10 Hatoyama Ichirō, *Hatoyama Ichirō kaikoroku* [Memoirs of Hatoyama Ichirō], Bungei Shunjū Shinsha, 1957, p. 23.

contrast, his entry three days later was unusually emotional. "In a certain sense, I had joined forces with the United States, Britain, and others to battle Japan's internal unreasonableness and evil. It is for this reason that Japan's defeat in the war has brought no sorrow to me."[11]

How about those politicians who would soon congregate under the banner of the Social Democratic Party (also known as the Socialist Party) of Japan? How did they react to the end of the war? Katayama Tetsu was at his home in Katase (present-day Fujisawa City) in Kanagawa Prefecture on that fateful day. Katayama writes that he was awaiting the "inevitable arrival of the age of peace with high hopes." With the war ended, Katayama would join forces with his comrades of old to establish a socialist political party.

Nishio Suehiro was in Osaka at the end of the war and wrote about "weeping with sorrow" and at the same time "shedding tears of relief and joy." Even while caught between these two emotions, Nishio wasted no time in turning his attention toward rebuilding Japan's labor unions and socialist political parties. On the day the war ended, Nishio travelled to Kyoto to confer with Mizutani Chōzaburō, and on August 17, he travelled to Tokyo to consult with Matsuoka Komakichi, both of whom were among his prewar comrades.

At the end of the war, Suzuki Mosaburō was appealing his conviction in the Popular Front Incident of 1937 that involved the establishment of an anti-fascist popular front. Of the events of August 15, Suzuki wrote, "I went to the streets and cried uncontrollably." He explained that there was no way of immediately knowing what policies the occupation would espouse and what conditions would emerge under those policies.

Those who would join the ranks of Japan's postwar political leaders had been forced into silence as members of the wartime resistance. Thus, for them, wartime Japan was to be refuted and Japan's defeat spelled a long-awaited liberation. These leaders were already rushing to build a new Japan without knowing what direction the occupation would take.

---

11 Ishibashi Tan'ichi and Itō Takashi, eds., *Ishibashi Tanzan nikki* [Diary of Ishibashi Tanzan], Misuzu Shobō, 2010, (August 15 and 18, 1945).

Establishment of the Higashikuni Cabinet

Prince Higashikuni Naruhiko accepted the call to form a new government. Writing about his commitment to overcoming the postwar crisis as the nation's first prime minister from the imperial family, he wrote, "If only I can succeed in overcoming the extreme confusion of the immediate postwar and setting the general course for the future of the nation, I am sure leaders will arise from among the politicians to take my place."[12]

Prince Higashikuni ranked among the Emperor's closest family members. He himself was married to the ninth daughter of the Meiji Emperor, while his son, Prince Morihiro, was married to Princess Shigeko, the oldest daughter of the Shōwa Emperor. Prince Higashikuni liked to refer to himself as the "mischievous prince" and had spent seven years studying in France after the First World War. During those years spent in France, he had interacted widely with liberals as well as socialists such as Georges Clemenceau, and was fully acquainted with pacifist and democratic thought.

The Emperor had appended the following instructions to his imperial order to Prince Higashikuni to form a new government. "In particular, respect the Constitution and be guided by the Imperial Rescript in your endeavors to control the military, maintain order, and overcome the current situation."

With the cooperation of Konoe Fumimaro and Ogata Taketora, Prince Higashikuni finished appointing his cabinet on August 17. However, those who were finally appointed hardly matched the image of the young and energetic leadership that Prince Higashikuni had himself hoped for. The ministers were safe choices drawn from the ranks of older, veteran conservatives. On August 19, Deputy Chief of the Army General Staff Kawabe Torashirō was dispatched to Manila to negotiate the arrival of the Occupation Forces. Kawabe returned on August 21 with the news that the advance party would be arriving in Japan on August 23 and that General MacArthur himself would be landing in Atsugi before the end of August.

---

12 Higashikuni Naruhiko, *Ichi kōzoku no sensō nikki* [Wartime Diary of an Imperial Prince], Nihon Shūhōsha, 1957, (August 16, 1945).

**Prince Higashikuni Naruhiko
(1887–1990)**
After graduating from the Army War College, he lived and studied in France from 1920 to 1926 and was considered a candidate for prime minister in prewar Japan due to his liberal ideas. During the war, he served as General Defense Commander-in-Chief. It was hoped he would navigate the nation through the immediate postwar turmoil, but he resigned his post as prime minister on October 9, following the issuance of the so-called Civil Liberties Directive.

The arrival of the Occupation Forces was delayed due to a typhoon, and the advance party finally arrived on August 28. On the same day, Prince Higashikuni held a press conference to express his commitment to transitioning from the wartime order to a new order. What he advocated was the "collective repentance of the hundred million (*Ichioku sōzange*)," a phrase which echoed the wartime mottos of "one hundred million hearts beating as one (*Ichioku isshin*)" and "the hundred million as a flaming jewel (*Ichioku hinotama*)." He went on to state that he intended to dissolve parliament shortly and to hold a general election. In preparation for the election, he instructed all cabinet ministers with jurisdiction to immediately implement a number of steps that would satisfy the preconditions for holding elections. These included the re-examination of the election system, the liberation of political prisoners, and upholding the freedoms of speech, assembly, and association. However, the General Headquarters (GHQ) of the Supreme Commander for the Allied Powers (SCAP) stepped in before these reforms could be implemented.

MacArthur Arrives in Japan: Structure of the Occupation

MacArthur's Two "Hats"

In the evening of August 14, 1945, President Truman proclaimed victory in the war against Japan and announced that he had appointed MacArthur as the Supreme Commander of the Allied Powers in Japan. The pronouncement made at the White House followed Japan's formal acceptance of the Potsdam Declaration. At the same time, Truman responded to two proposals that had been made by Stalin. First, Stalin had proposed that the commander of the Soviet forces in the Far East be given a position on par with MacArthur as Supreme Commander of the Allied Powers in Japan. Second, Stalin had indicated that the Soviet Union was prepared to occupy half of the island of Hokkaido. In light of the overwhelmingly important role that the United States had played in the war with Japan, Truman rejected both.

MacArthur welcomed his appointment as Supreme Commander for the Allied Forces, writing that this was "Mar's last gift to an old warrior."[13] In addition to his title of Supreme Commander of the United States Army in the Pacific (reorganized as the United States Forces in the Far East in January 1947), the appointment gave MacArthur a second "hat" as the Supreme Commander of the Allied Powers. MacArthur would thereafter use his two supreme-commander "hats" interchangeably to battle the forces in Washington, D.C.

MacArthur was born in 1880 at the U.S. Army's Little Rock Barracks located in Little Rock, Arkansas, and graduated first in his West Point class with a 98 percent average. He became a general in the army at age 50 and was appointed Army Chief of Staff in 1930, becoming the youngest appointee to this post. Clearly MacArthur was an outstanding professional soldier.

MacArthur had developed a keen interest in Asia since he toured the region in 1905 and 1906. By the time he arrived in Japan, he had already spent sixteen years in the Philippines and other parts of Asia. At the end of the war, MacArthur did not return to Washington to be briefed on his new appointment. Instead he headed straight for Japan.

On the August 29 flight from Manila to Japan, MacArthur puffed on his iconic corn cob pipe while excitedly outlining his plans for reforming Japan.

First destroy the military power. Punish war criminals. Build the structure of representative government. Modernize the constitution. Hold free elections. Enfranchise the women. Release the political prisoners. Liberate the farmers. Establish a free labor movement. Encourage a free economy. Abolish police oppression. Develop a free and responsible

---

13 Manchester, *American Caesar*, p. 466.

Douglas MacArthur (1880–1964)

Born in Little Rock, Arkansas, MacArthur graduated first in his West Point class in 1903. Under the influence of his father, Arthur MacArthur, who was U.S. Commander in the Philippines, MacArthur developed a keen interest in Asia. In 1905, he was appointed aide-de-camp to his father who was serving as military attaché to the U.S. Embassy in Japan. During the First World War, MacArthur fought and was injured on the Western Front. In 1930, he was appointed Army Chief of Staff at the youngest age in history. He was involved in the expulsion of the Bonus Army protesters in 1932, an action taken to reinforce his image as a fierce anti-communist to counter rumors that he was backed by communists.

In 1935, he resigned his post as Army Chief of Staff and moved to the Philippines to work as military adviser to the government of the Philippines. In 1937, he officially retired from the Army but returned to active duty in July 1941 at the behest of the president to serve as Commander of the U.S. Army Forces in the Far East. After Pearl Harbor and the Japanese invasion of the Philippines, MacArthur was forced into a series of retreats until his escape to Australia in March 1942. It was at this time that he uttered the famous words, "I shall return." In April, he became Commander of the Allied Powers in the Southwest Pacific with command over U.S., British, Australian, and Dutch forces. Following Japan's acceptance of the Potsdam Declaration, MacArthur was appointed Supreme Commander of the Allied Powers (SCAP) on August 14, 1945, and continued to wield enormous power over Japan until his removal from command in April 1951.

press. Liberalize education. Decentralize the political power. Separate church from state.[14]

It was on this day that MacArthur received a copy of SWNCC-150/4/A, "United States Initial Post-Surrender Policy for Japan" (hereinafter, Initial Post-Surrender Policy). SWNCC stood for "State, War & Navy Coordinating Committee," a three-party coordinating committee formed for administering occupied areas. Although the reforms that MacArthur had outlined during his flight to Japan were all contained in the Initial Post-Surrender Policy, he did not mention that point.

---

14 MacArthur, Douglas, *Reminiscences*, MacGraw-Hill, 1964, pp. 282–283.

"The Blue-Eyed Tycoon"

On August 30, MacArthur landed at Atsugi Airfield. Walking down the steps of his personal C-54 transport, the *Bataan*, MacArthur shook hands with Lieutenant General Robert Eichelberger, who had come to greet him, and calmly said, "Bob, from Melbourne to Tokyo is a long way, but this seems to be the end of the road."

MacArthur was referred to as the "blue-eyed tycoon" during the Occupation. Of his position, George Kennan wrote that he "played the role of a virtual king of old." MacArthur himself was amused by the status that had been given to him.

"I held virtually unlimited authority over the Japanese people. No colonial governor, conqueror or commander in history could equal the power that I had over the Japanese people. My authority was supreme."[15]

Until he was relieved of his command in April 1951, MacArthur almost never left Tokyo, let alone Japan. Every day he followed the same route between his residence at the U.S. Embassy and the Dai-Ichi Seimei Building that housed GHQ. Furthermore, he almost never appeared before the public and never directly spoke to the Japanese people.

MacArthur demanded absolute loyalty from his subordinates. He preferred not to interfere in problems related to the Japanese themselves and subscribed to the policy of allowing the Japanese to resolve their own problems. On the other hand, he was always critical of decisions made by his superiors back in Washington. At times, he ignored the decisions that had been made by the President or the Joint Chiefs of Staff, which frequently placed him on a collision course with Washington.

A strong and highly opinionated commander had been assigned to direct the Occupation of Japan. Consequently, the Occupation of Japan quickly devolved into "MacArthur's occupation." MacArthur was known for his right-leaning Republican positions, but the face that emerged in Japan was not only that of a victor but also that of a reformer. MacArthur himself described his role in the following words.

"Power is one thing. The problem of how to administer it is another. My

---

15 MacArthur, Douglas, *Makkāsā taisen kaikoroku* [Reminiscences], Tsushima Kazuo, trans., Chūō Kōron Shinsha, 2014, p. 407.

professional military knowledge was no longer a major factor. I had to be an economist, a political scientist, an engineer, a manufacturing executive, a teacher, even a theologian of sorts."[16]

Signing of the Instrument of Surrender

The signing of the Instrument of Surrender took place aboard the USS *Missouri* in Tokyo Bay on September 2. The Japanese signatories were Foreign Minister Shigemitsu Mamoru, who signed on behalf of the Japanese government, and Chief of Army General Staff Umezu Yoshijirō, who signed on behalf of the military.

MacArthur was accompanied by Lieutenant General Jonathan Wainwright and Lieutenant General Arthur Percival, both of whom had been prisoners of war in the Philippines and Singapore. The choice of companions was intended to erase the dishonor that the two lieutenant generals had been forced to experience, but was also designed to maximize the stark contrast between the victors and the defeated. The scene of the surrender was further choreographed with the display of the American flag that had been hoisted nearly a hundred years earlier on Commodore Perry's flagship, the USS *Mississippi*, as he pressured Japan to open its doors to the world. The message was clear: MacArthur had come to pressure Japan into a second "opening."

MacArthur addressed the participants in the signing ceremony with the following words. "We are gathered here, representatives of the major warring powers, to conclude a solemn agreement whereby peace may be restored. The issues involving divergent ideals and ideologies have been determined on the battlefields of the world, and hence are not for our discussion or debate. Nor is it for us here to meet, representing as we do a majority of the peoples of the earth, in a spirit of distrust, malice, or hatred." Rather than blame the vanquished, he called for the realization of world peace built on the foundations of "freedom, tolerance, and justice."

His speech had taken its inspiration from the second inaugural address of President Lincoln delivered shortly before the end of the Civil War.

---

16 MacArthur, *Reminiscences*, pp. 281–282.

Signing of the Instrument of Surrender aboard the USS *Missouri* on September 2, 1945
MacArthur followed the Japanese plenipotentiaries in signing the document. Behind him stood
Lieutenant General Jonathan Wainwright and Lieutenant General Arthur Percival who had been
prisoners of war in the Philippines and Singapore, respectively.

Threat of "Direct Military Government": Retracting the Three Proclamations

Just a few hours after MacArthur delivered his speech filled with high ideals, the
Japanese government was pulled back into the cold reality of the Occupation.

At 4:00 in the afternoon of the signing ceremony, Deputy Chief of Staff of
SCAP Richard Marshall summoned to his office Suzuki Tadakatsu. As director
of the Yokohama Liaison Office, Suzuki was in charge of negotiations with the
Occupation Forces in Yokohama. During the meeting, Suzuki was handed the
so-called "three proclamations." In addition to the proclamation on occupation
through direct military control, these included directives on the use of English
as the official language and the use of military currency. Suzuki immediately
called for the retraction of the three proclamations on the grounds that they
contravened the terms of the Potsdam Declaration, which indicated that Japan
would be "ruled through the Emperor and the Japanese government." Marshall

rejected Suzuki's argument.

Given that the directives bore MacArthur's signature, the Japanese side could not ignore them as a nightmare in the late summer. Late that night, the director of the Central Liaison Office, Okazaki Katsuo, went to see Marshall. Responsible for all negotiations with the Occupation Forces, Okazaki presented his desperate pleas and finally convinced Marshall to suspend the promulgation of the proclamations. But the ultimate decision belonged to MacArthur and there was no way to predict what that might be.

Early the next morning, September 3, Foreign Minister Shigemitsu went to Yokohama to talk directly with MacArthur and succeeded in prevailing upon him. MacArthur's response is recorded as follows. "We have no intention on destroying Japan and enslaving its people. Quite the contrary, we hope to find a way to save Japan in its current crisis. If the Japanese government shows sufficient good faith, the problem is easy to solve."[17] Thanks to the negotiations that continued late into the night, the nature of the Occupation was pushed back from direct military control to indirect rule.

The question remains why MacArthur backed down from an extremely important decision that had already been conveyed to the Japanese side. Why did he accede so easily to the Japanese request?

The original assumption of the U.S. government was that Japan would be occupied in the course of hostilities and placed under direct military government. This assumption was fully affirmed in Operation Blacklist formulated on August 8, while MacArthur was still in Manila. However, the Potsdam Declaration called for indirect rule that would be implemented through the Japanese government. Consequently, on August 11, SWNCC began to hurriedly work on a revision to expunge direct military government and replace it with indirect rule. These revisions were finally adopted on August 31 (and approved by President Truman on September 6).

As previously noted, a copy of the Initial Post-Surrender Policy had reached MacArthur on August 29, which meant that MacArthur did not have enough

---

17 "Shigemitsu gaimu-daijin Makkāsā kaiken" [Meeting of Foreign Minister Shigemitsu with MacArthur], Etō Jun, ed., in *Senryō shiroku, 1* [Historical Records of the Occupation, vol. 1], Kōdansha, 1989, pp. 270–276.

time to amend the standing plans for military government. It appears that the "three proclamations" were issued because of the considerable confusion that existed within the Occupation Forces.

Hosokawa Morisada, a son-in-law and aide to Konoe, left the following notes. "Several incidents of assault and rape by U.S. soldiers have been reported, but these are no more than a drop in the bucket compared to what our soldiers did in China."[18] Foreign Minister Shigemitsu wrote, "Generally, soldiers are under strict control and there have been very few cases that would inflame the antipathy of residents. There is a world of difference with the behavior of Japanese troops that had been stationed in China and the southern front."[19] These two similar journal entries should be borne in mind as examples of comparison of the respective occupations by Japan and by the U.S.

Establishment of the General Headquarters of Supreme Commander for the Allied Powers

Accompanied by his staff, MacArthur left Hotel New Grand in Yokohama on September 8, 1945, and arrived an hour later at the U.S. Embassy in Tokyo. On September 17, the General Headquarters of the Army Forces in the Pacific (GHQ–AFPAC) also moved out of Yokohama and relocated in the Dai-Ichi Seimei Building facing the Imperial Palace.

On this day, MacArthur announced that it would be possible to reduce the U.S. forces in Japan from an estimated 500,000, as of August, to around 200,000 within six months. Made without any prior consultation with Washington, this announcement created considerable consternation among the Joint Chiefs of Staff, the State Department, and the White House. Two days later, Under Secretary of State Dean Acheson fired a word of warning to MacArthur. "The Occupation Forces are a policy instrument and are not policy makers." Acheson followed this up on September 22 with a directive dated September 6, which

---

18 Hosokawa Morisada, *Hosokawa nikki, ge* [Hosokawa Diary, vol. 2], Chūō Kōronsha, 1979, p. 437.
19 Itō Takashi and Watanabe Ikuo, eds., *Shigemitsu Mamoru shuki* [Memoirs of Shigemitsu Mamoru], Chūō Kōronsha, 1986, p. 293.

delineated the authority delegated to MacArthur (Message to General of the Army Douglas MacArthur concerning the Authority of the Supreme Commander for the Allied Powers). The Initial Post-Surrender Policy released at the same time explicitly stated that the "policy is to use the existing form of Government in Japan, not to support it."

At around the same time as MacArthur's September 8 move to Tokyo, U.S. forces began to move into various parts of Japan to start their occupation. Led by Lieutenant General Eichelberger, the Eighth Army moved to occupy eastern Japan, while the Sixth Army led by Lieutenant General Walter Krueger occupied western Japan. Shikoku and Kyushu were occupied by British Commonwealth Forces. By early December, a total of 430,000 Occupation Forces were in place throughout Japan. It should be noted that the Sixth Army left Japan in 1946, and the Occupation thereafter was placed under the unified command of the Eighth Army.

Even as the discord with Washington continued, MacArthur began to take steps for transitioning from military to civilian rule and ordered his chief of staff, Richard Sutherland, to formulate a new organizational plan for civilian rule.

The Economic and Scientific Section (ESS) was launched on September 15, and the Civil Information and Education Section (CIE) was formed on September 22. Finally, on September 26, Chief of Staff Sutherland announced the disbandment of the Military Government Section. With the establishment of the Government Section (GS) and eight other special staff sections on October 2, the General Headquarters (GHQ) was ready to go into operation with full force (Table 1-1). MacArthur manned these general staff sections and special staff sections with trusted aides that had been at his side since the Philippines.

At this time, the structures of the Occupation of Japan by the Allied Powers were still unsettled, and the task of formulating concrete policies for Japan's demilitarization and democratization was left to the GHQ and its special staff sections.

Table 1-1 Organization Chart of the General Headquarters (October 2, 1945)

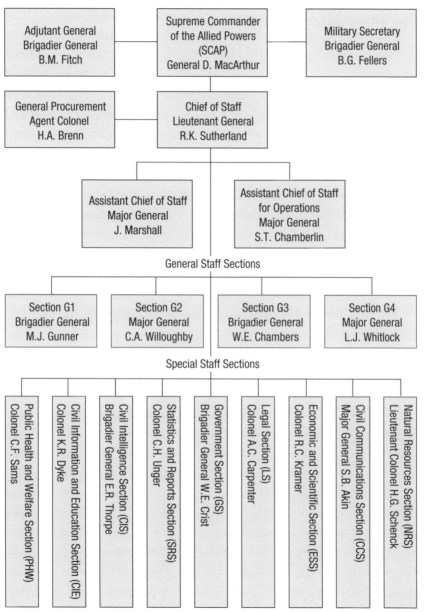

Compiled by the author from GHQ/SCAP, *History of Non-Military Activities of the Occupation of Japan, 1945–1951, vol. 2, Appendix*

U.S. Policies for the Occupation of Japan: Initial Post-Surrender Policies and Basic Initial Post-Surrender Directives

As can be seen from the preceding sections, MacArthur did not embark on governing the Occupation of Japan with a clean slate. Led by the State Department, the U.S. government been preparing plans for post-surrender Japan since the start of hostilities. Policies for Japan were hotly debated between two opposing camps. The "soft peace guys" represented by Joseph Grew, the former U.S. ambassador to Japan, argued in favor of appeasement, while the "hard peace guys" called for the implementation of stern policies.

Ultimately, however, the surrender of Japan had come earlier than expected, leaving no alternative but to launch the Allied Occupation of Japan in line with the principle of indirect government as expressed in the Potsdam Declaration. The Occupation Forces themselves were subject to considerable confusion as witnessed by the incident of the "three proclamations." It was already September 6 when the Initial Policy for Post-Surrender Japan was formally approved by the president, and the basic principles were not confirmed until September 22 when Secretary of State Acheson released the policy. It is notable that the Initial Post-Surrender Policy was finally submitted to and approved by the Far Eastern Commission (FEC) in June 1947.

On November 3, the U.S. government issued to MacArthur instructions entitled Basic Directive for Post-Surrender Military Government in Japan Proper (JCS1380/15) (hereinafter, Basic Initial Directive). This directive was not released to the public, but constituted formal instructions to MacArthur on the Occupation of Japan.

The Initial Post-Surrender Policy and the Basic Initial Directive identified the principal objectives of the occupation of Japan. Both documents placed emphasis on demilitarization and democratization to prevent Japan from ever again threatening the peace and safety of the United States and of the world. In the political sphere, these central objectives were to be achieved through dismantlement of the military, punishment of war criminals, and the promotion of democracy. In the economic sphere, they were to be achieved through demilitarization consisting of the prohibition of the production of materials that were at the foundation of military power and the disposition of related facilities, along with the promotion of the development of democratic organizations in labor, industry, and agriculture.

Basically, MacArthur's Occupation of Japan would henceforth be guided by the Potsdam Declaration and the two documents that had been formulated by the United States government. According to Theodore Cohen who served as the head of GHQ's Labor Division, the Initial Post-Surrender Policy was not seen by the military as constituting an order, while that the Basic Initial Directive was viewed as a foundation for formulating occupation policies.[20]

While the Basic Initial Directive called for the thorough demilitarization and democratization of Japan, it also contained harsh provisions for the purging of business leaders from public positions and the dissolution of large industrial and banking conglomerates (zaibatsu). It also stipulated that the Supreme Commander would not himself assume responsibility for the management of the Japanese economy. Thus, it took the position that Japan itself was to blame for the country's pitiable current state and that the Japanese themselves would have to take responsibility for rehabilitating their economy. However, from the perspective of GHQ, the emergence of economic paralysis and social turmoil was not at all desirable. Like it or not, before long, GHQ would find itself deeply involved in the management of the Japanese economy.

Be that as it may, saddled with a shortage of personnel and unsure of the road ahead, GHQ had no choice but to feel its way in the dark as it commenced its operations. As the first step, the contents of the Basic Initial Directive were finely categorized and assigned to departments, divisions, and offices charged with realizing the objectives set forth in the document. It was decided that all formal orders issued by GHQ to the Japanese government would henceforth take the form of a memorandum. Notwithstanding this decision, MacArthur at times conveyed his orders directly through letters written to the prime minister and informal memos sent to responsible government officers, as well through oral exchanges.

---

20 Cohen, Theodore, *Remaking Japan: The American Occupation as New Deal*, Free Press, 1987, p. 3.

Allied Powers Clash over Managing the Occupation

Just as MacArthur was working on building the organizational structure of GHQ, conflicts began to emerge among the Allied Powers on how to manage the Occupation.

As previously mentioned, Truman was firmly committed to excluding the Soviet Union from the Occupation of Japan. Against this backdrop, on August 21, 1945, the U.S. government proposed the establishment of the Far Eastern Advisory Commission for consulting on matters related to occupation policies. According to the proposal, the Commission would be placed in Washington, D.C., and membership would include Great Britain, China, and the Soviet Union. Moreover, the Commission was to be a consultative or advisory body with no authority to restrict the actions of the Supreme Commander in any matter.

While China and the Soviet Union accepted the U.S. proposal, Great Britain countered with a proposal for creating the Allied Control Council for Japan consisting of five member nations that included Australia. The council would have decision-making powers and would exist alongside the Far Eastern Advisory Commission to deliberate on the management of the Occupation of Japan. The British proposal was made in response to pressure from Australia, which had been excluded from the deliberations of the major powers notwithstanding the large sacrifices that it had made in the war with Japan. While Great Britain withdrew its proposal at the meeting of foreign ministers held in London at the end of September, the Soviet Union simultaneously began making strong demands for the establishment of the Allied Control Council that resembled the earlier British proposal.

The first meeting of the Far Eastern Advisory Commission was held in London on October 30 with ten countries in attendance. The Soviet Union absented itself while continuing to demand the adoption of its proposed Allied Control Council for Japan. The first meeting of the Far Eastern Advisory Commission adjourned after selecting an interim chairman.

The issue of whether or not to create the Allied Control Council for the Occupation of Japan soon became a pawn in the U.S.-Soviet power game. The United States and Great Britain had excluded the Soviet Union from the occupation of Italy. In turn, the Soviet Union had excluded the United States and Great Britain from the occupation of three Eastern European countries (Romania, Bulgaria, and Hungary). The establishment of a deliberative council for the Occupation of Japan would have created room for Soviet intervention as had already happened in Germany. In any case, it was realized that the Occupation of Japan could not proceed without some form of Allied authority. To break the impasse, the United States, Great Britain, and the Soviet Union began moving toward a compromise solution.

On December 16, the foreign ministers of the three countries gathered in Moscow to hammer out a compromise. While the dominant position of the United States was generally acknowledged and maintained, two adjustments were made. First, the decision was made to abolish the Far Eastern Advisory Commission and replace it with the Far Eastern Commission to be based in Washington. Second, an Allied Council for Japan would be created and based in Tokyo as a consultative and advisory body to GHQ.

During this period, no information was provided to MacArthur on the deliberations of the foreign ministers' meeting in Moscow. The fact is that he did not even know that Japan was being discussed in Moscow. MacArthur would later express his dissatisfaction with Washington's concessions on the creation of the Far Eastern Commission and the Allied Council. "They… were, I suppose, to oversee my supervision of the occupation."[21]

The Far Eastern Commission and the Allied Council for Japan

The Far Eastern Commission was established in Washington, D.C., as the supreme decision-making body on occupation policies. Membership consisted of a total of eleven countries. Four countries—the United States, Great Britain, China, and the Soviet Union—had veto power on all matters, while the remaining seven countries did not. The latter group consisted of France, the Netherlands, Canada, Australia, New Zealand, the Philippines, and India. (Pakistan and Burma [Myanmar] were added to the Commission in November 1949.) The Commission

---

21 MacArthur, *Reminiscences*, p. 291.

was assigned two central functions. First, it was tasked with formulating policies, principles, and standards by which Japan would satisfy its surrender obligations as stipulated under the Potsdam Declaration, with the exception of matters related to the military provisions and territorial issues mentioned in the Declaration. Second, it was tasked with reviewing SCAP's implementation of occupation policies. It should be noted that the Commission's authority did not extend to constitutional revision and other fundamental changes in the form of government. This would later lead to a clash between MacArthur and the Far Eastern Commission on the question of revising the Constitution of Japan.

All policy decisions made by the Far Eastern Commission were to be conveyed to GHQ through the U.S. State Department and Joint Chiefs of Staff. At the same time, the United States retained the right to independently issue interim directives to GHQ. This arrangement ensured that the United States would be able to safeguard its interests.

Membership in the Allied Council for Japan comprised the four countries of the United States, Great Britain, China, and the Soviet Union. Based in Tokyo, it was intended to function as a local agency of the Far Eastern Commission, and was assigned a limited function of consulting and advising GHQ. In practice, however, it became a platform for U.S. and U.S.S.R. propaganda battles (Table 1-2).

Due in part to the delaying tactics of the U.S. government, the first meeting of the Far Eastern Commission was not held until February 26, 1946. The first meeting of the Allied Council for Japan was further delayed, so it did not convene until April 5. MacArthur attended the first meeting of the Council to give a long-winded speech emphasizing that the Council was restricted to an advisory function. He never again attended a meeting of the Council.

As the Supreme Commander of the Allied Powers, MacArthur was placed under the authority of the Far Eastern Commission. However, the Commission was never able to effectively execute its powers as MacArthur adopted the strategy of racking up a long series of faits accomplis while ignoring both the Far Eastern Commission and the Allied Council for Japan.

Thus while Japan was to be occupied by the Allied Powers, the Occupation in reality was a singularly American Occupation that was carried out by MacArthur.

Table 1-2 Structure of Indirect Government in the Occupation of Japan

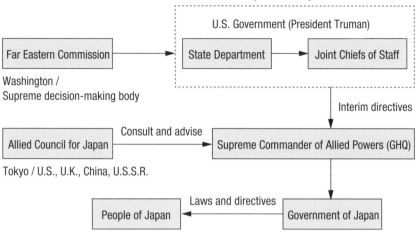

Birth of the Government Section: The Engine for Reform

Organaization of the Government Section and the Assignment

Formally established on October 2, GHQ's Government Section was assigned the following four specific functions: (1) the demilitarization of the Imperial Japanese Government and all subordinate governmental agencies and subdivisions, (2) the decentralization of the Imperial Japanese Government and the encouragement of local responsibility, (3) the elimination of the feudal and totalitarian practices which tend to prevent government by the people, and (4) the elimination of those relationships between government and business which tend to continue Japanese war potential and to hamper the achievement of the objectives of the occupation. The Government Section was immediately tasked with drawing up its recommendations on these four points (GHQ/SCAP General Directive No. 8).

In this way, the Government Section was assigned responsibility for the demilitarization, democratization, and decentralization of the Japanese government. The adoption of indirect government instead of direct government by the Allied Powers meant that all matters pertaining to occupation policies would be conveyed to the Japanese people through the agency of laws and ordinances. On the other hand, this arrangement implied that legislation and other acts of parliament were subject to the approval of the Government Section under whose jurisdiction the parliament had been placed. Thus, the Government Section had been granted immense authority to intervene in all areas of Japan's political system.

The Government Section was initially divided into two departments, consisting of an administrative department in charge of Japanese affairs and a department for Korean affairs, the later of which was disbanded in February 1946. The remaining administrative department was headed by Colonel Charles Kades, who had been a lawyer as a civilian. The department was further divided into an Operations Group and a Planning Group. The Operations Group, comprising an External Affairs Team, a Legal Team, and an Internal Affairs Team, was charged with formulating policies.[22]

While the Government Section would later prove its worth and shrewdness in implementing democratic reforms, including the revision of the constitution, at the start, it was utterly weak and ineffective. First of all, the Government Section was one of the special staff sections placed under the general staff sections. This meant that the Government Section reported to SCAP through the four general staff sections and the Chief of Staff, allowing the military officers serving as aides to MacArthur to control and interfere in its operations. Consequently, the Government Section was frequently unable to implement the policies that it had devised. Secondly, Brigadier General Crist, who initially headed the Government Section, was unable to carve out a position of any strength in an organization dominated by the so-called "Bataan boys" who had been with MacArthur for the length of his campaign.

Whitney Appointed to Head the Government Section: Energizing the Government Section

Successfully implementing the policies of the Government Section depended significantly on personal proximity to MacArthur. But Crist had clearly failed in this respect and his subordinates had become increasingly frustrated as time

---

22 Amakawa Akira and Fukunaga Fumio, eds., *GHQ Minsei-kyoku shiryō: Senryō kaikaku, bekkan* [GHQ Government Section Materials: Reforms of the Occupation, Appendix], Maruzen, 2002.

went by. It was against this backdrop that Major General Courtney Whitney was brought in to head the Government Section on December 15. Whitney was widely known to be very close to MacArthur, to the point of being considered an alter ego of the Supreme Commander.

Whitney was born in Maryland in 1897. After receiving his law degree from George Washington University Law School, he enlisted in the U.S. Army Air Corps but left the army in 1927 to open a law practice in Manila, which he maintained until 1939. In the following year, Whitney returned to active duty and joined the MacArthur command in 1943 as a lieutenant colonel of the Army Air Corps. In this assignment, Whitney was placed in charge of organizing and leading the guerilla war against Japanese forces. Through these services, he had succeeded in winning MacArthur's deep trust and confidence.

Courtney Whitney (1897–1969) Chief of GHQ's Government Section. After receiving his law degree, Whitney opened a law office in Manila. As one of MacArthur's favorite officers, Whitney was appointed to head the Government Section in December 1945 and is said to have been the only person permitted to enter MacArthur's office without knocking. As "commander of Japan's democratization," Whitney played a leading role in formulating the policies of the Occupation.

It was said that Whitney was the only person in GHQ who could meet MacArthur without an appointment. According to Kades, the two were in the habit of meeting every day at 5 a.m. to spend an hour in conversation.[23] Whitney also had a very special talent for accurately reading MacArthur's very complicated and convoluted thoughts and was able to accurately express MacArthur's thinking on the most complex of issues. It is reported that even his handwriting resembled MacArthur's.

Backed by the implicit trust that MacArthur placed in him, Whitney began to create an environment that would allow the Government Section to lead the process of democratization. Reacting to these initiatives, the G3 (the three

---

23 Kades, Charles, interview by Fukunaga Fumio, August 25, 1989.

general staff sections of GHQ) acted on January 22, 1946, to formally propose a plan for re-assigning authority. The gist of the plan was that the G3 and other staff sections would "assume responsibility for policy coordination" whenever a policy proposal was submitted by a special staff section. For example, the process would work as follows with regard to "strengthening of democratic tendencies and processes," an objective stipulated in the Basic Initial Directive with direct bearing on constitutional revision. In this case, the Government Section would have primary jurisdiction for initiating action, while the Economic and Scientific Section and the Civil Information and Education Section would act as auxiliary sections. Finally, G3 would be responsible for overall policy coordination.

Whitney quickly responded to these efforts to strengthen the authority of staff sections under G3 with a counter-argument presented on January 25. The thrust of his argument was that non-military activities for which the Supreme Commander was ultimately responsible should be assigned to civil servants with training in human relations and the social sciences rather than to the military personnel in the staff sections who had been trained in military matters. Whitney went on to argue that priority should therefore be given to decisions made by the special staff sections that comprised officers with civilian backgrounds.[24]

Whitney thereafter succeeded in energizing the Government Section by moving forward on the pending issues of revising the Election Law and purging designated people from engaging in public service. But Whitney's success did not resolve the friction between the general staff sections and the special staff sections. Conflict would re-emerge from time to time between the two groups. The nexus of the conflict was between the Government Section and Section G2 headed by Major General Willoughby, whom MacArthur had called "my little fascist." While the Government Section sought to promote democratization, Willoughby placed far greater emphasis on maintaining law and order as a critical element in ongoing anti-Soviet strategies. But this was not the only area of conflict. Friction also existed between the special staff sections, such as between the Government Section and the Economic and Scientific Section. All in all, GHQ was far from being a completely united, monolithic organization.

---

24 Amakawa, *Senryōka no Nihon*, pp. 118–119.

2. The Beginning of Postwar Politics

The Civil Liberties Directive and the Liberation of Political Prisoners

First Postwar Session of the Imperial Diet and Arrest of War Criminals

Just two days after the signing of the surrender instrument aboard the USS *Missouri*, the 88th extraordinary session of the Imperial Diet was convened on September 4, 1945, making this its first postwar session. In his policy speech to the Diet, Prime Minister Higashikuni presented a candid outline of the events leading to the surrender of Japan and followed this with a solemn call to the nation. "We have received the Imperial command, and I call upon the whole nation to orderly and scrupulously obey the august command and march forward toward the realization of a new and prosperous era." Here again, Higashikuni enunciated his theory of the "collective repentance of the hundred million" saying, "We should reflect calmly upon our own conduct, each and every one of us, whether at the front or at home, whether in or out of the Government. A general repentance is demanded of the whole nation. We should start anew with fresh and chastened spirit, keeping in mind the lessons of the past."

The Great Japan Political Association, the successor to the Imperial Rule Assistance Association and the majority party in the Imperial Diet, refrained from following up on the prime minister's speech with demands for more detailed explanations of the causes and responsibility for the war.

The House of Representatives was adjourned after only two days and the adoption of two resolutions: "Resolution on Expression of Gratitude and Condolence to Officers and Soldiers of the Imperial Army and National Volunteer Corps," and "Resolution on Obedience to the Imperial Command." The session had been punctuated by angry cries from independent politicians who comprised the opposition. "The Great Japan Political Association must take responsibility for the war," they yelled. "The Great Japan Political Association must be disbanded!"

On September 11, the Occupation Powers issued warrants for the arrest of 39 suspected war criminals. The list included Tōjō Hideki and other cabinet ministers who had held office at the inception of the war. This action was in line with Article 10 of the Potsdam Declaration that stated, "stern justice shall be meted out to all war criminals." The Japanese side proposed that it should be allowed to "dispose of" war criminals as it saw fit, but this was rejected. The suspected war criminals were thereupon arrested and placed in Sugamo Prison. The arrest of Tōjō and others shocked the Japanese government leaders and engendered a deep sense of anxiety. How would this affect the preservation of national polity? In other words, how would the Emperor and the imperial institutions be treated?

On September 19, GHQ issued the so-called Press Code, followed by the Radio Code on September 22. While promoting the freedom of the press, these two directives prohibited criticism of the Allied Powers.

On September 20, Foreign Minister Yoshida Shigeru met with MacArthur to sound him out on the possibility of arranging a meeting with the Emperor. During his meeting with Yoshida, MacArthur emphasized the virtues of democracy. To this, Yoshida responded that after the First World War, both democracy and party politics had made great advances in Japan, to the point of being "excessive." However, Yoshida argued, these developments were displaced by militarism that rose up due to the Great Depression. "For the time being, the most important thing is to feed the people, provide them with jobs and endeavor to bring stability to their lives."[25]

The Emperor Visits MacArthur

On September 27, the Shōwa Emperor went to the U.S. Embassy in Tokyo's Toranomon district to meet MacArthur. In his *Reminiscences* published in 1964, MacArthur recounts the meeting in these words.

---

25 "Yoshida Makkāsā kaidan" [Yoshida MacArthur Meetings], Etō, ed., in *Senryō shiroku, 1,* pp. 290–292.

I had an uneasy feeling he might plead his own cause against indictment as a war criminal.... But my fears were groundless. What he said was this: 'I come to you, General MacArthur, to offer myself to the judgment of the powers you represent as the one to bear sole responsibility for every political and military decision made and action taken by my people in the conduct of the war.' A tremendous impression swept me. This courageous assumption of a responsibility implicit with death, a responsibility clearly belied by facts of which I was fully aware, moved me to the marrow of my bones. He was an Emperor by inherent birth, but in that instant I knew I faced the First Gentleman of Japan in his own right.

Even after the publication of MacArthur's *Reminiscences*, various theories continued to abound on whether the Emperor had actually said in this meeting that he would "bear sole responsibility." In 2002, the Ministry of Foreign Affairs and the Imperial Household Agency released a number of documents pertaining to this meeting, none of which contained any mention of the conversation between the Emperor and MacArthur. As such, the truth of what transpired in that meeting remains uncertain. On the other hand, circumstantial evidence indicates that the statement attributed to the Emperor was generally accurate. One such instance can be found in a cable sent to Washington by George Atcheson Jr., a State Department adviser to the Diplomatic Section: one month after MacArthur's meeting with the Emperor, Atcheson wrote that the Emperor wished to "take responsibility as the leader of the Japanese people."[26]

In any case, Foreign Minister Yoshida was relieved to find that the meeting between MacArthur and the Emperor had gone smoothly. Yoshida's concern can be traced to the strong negative feelings toward the Emperor that prevailed among the Allied Powers and particularly the Australians. Neither was U.S. public opinion particularly favorable to the Emperor at this point.

---

26 Yamagiwa Akira and Nakamura Masanori, eds., *Shiryō Nihon senryō 1: Tennō-sei* [Documents on the Occupation of Japan 1: Emperor System], Ōtsuki Shoten, 1999, p. 520.

Civil Liberties Directive Issued without Prior Notice

On September 29, a photograph of the Emperor standing next to MacArthur appeared in the three leading Japanese newspapers–*Asahi Shinbun*, *Mainichi Shinbun*, and *Yomiuri Shinbun*. The government immediately acted to prohibit the distribution of the newspapers on the grounds that the photograph "profaned the august." Another troubling incident followed on October 3 when Minister of Justice Iwata Chūzō and Minister of Home Affairs Yamazaki Iwao met with members of the foreign press. During this meeting, the two ministers rejected the possibility of abolishing the Peace Preservation Law and the Special Higher Police.

GHQ immediately responded to these actions of the Japanese government by issuing the so-called Civil Liberties Directive on October 4, a directive formally entitled "Removal of Restrictions on Political, Civil, and Religious Liberties" (SCAPIN-93). The Civil Liberties Directive established freedom of speech, including criticism of the imperial institutions, and ordered the liberation of political prisoners. Following the issuance of this directive, the Japanese government abolished a total of fifteen laws and related ordinances, including the Maintenance of Public Order Law. The government also ordered the disbandment of the Special Higher Police. Furthermore, approximately 5,000 civil servants were fired or removed from their posts. These included Home Affairs Minister Yamazaki, the Director of the Police Affairs Bureau of the Home Affairs Ministry, the Chief of the Metropolitan Police and all top police officers, and all officers of the Special Higher Police sections of Prefectural Police Departments.

Foreign Minister Yoshida was shocked by the Civil Liberties Directive. What is more, the government had not been given any prior notice of its issuance. For Yoshida, this incident proved that the framework of "indirect government" did not preclude "acts of direct military government." Noting that the Occupation policies were implemented "as if to encourage a red revolution," Yoshida was made to realize that Japan was governed "as if it were under the rule of the U.S. military."[27]

---

27 "Yoshida gaimu-daijin Sazarando sanbōchō kaidanroku" [Notes of Meetings of Foreign Minister Yoshida and Chief of Staff Sutherland], Etō, ed., in *Senryō shiroku*, *1*, pp. 356–357.

Taking MacArthur's dismissal of Home Affairs Minister Yamazaki to be a vote of no confidence, the Higashikuni Cabinet resigned en masse on October 5. However, it can be said that Prime Minister Higashikuni had already completed his principal function by this time, which was to make a peaceful transition to the postwar and accept the Occupation Forces into Japan without serious incident or confusion.

Shidehara Kijūrō (1872–1951) Going from prewar diplomat to postwar politician, Shidehara served as Minister of Foreign Affairs in four prewar cabinets. "Shidehara diplomacy" was valued for its successes in international cooperation but criticized by the military for being "weak-kneed." At the end of the war, he initially refused to head up a new government but relented on the urging of the Shōwa Emperor and came out of retirement to serve as prime minister.

On October 10, a total of 439 political prisoners were released from prison, including Tokuda Kyūichi, Shiga Yoshio, and other leaders of the Japanese Communist Party. Released from Fuchū Prison after 18 years of imprisonment, Tokuda and his comrades quickly issued a statement entitled "An Appeal to the People." Most notably, the statement contained demands for the abolition of the emperor system and imperial institutions, and announced that action would immediately get underway to rebuild the Japanese Communist Party. While the reference to the Occupation Forces as a "liberation army" would later become a point of contention within the party, there was no question that Tokuda and the other political prisoners had in fact been liberated by the Occupation Forces. The communists were further encouraged by the fact that the Soviet Union stood among the Allied Powers.

A call went out for a "people's meeting" to be held on the same afternoon at the Hibiya Public Hall (the venue was changed to the Hikō Kaikan due to bad weather). Some 2,000 people attended the meeting. Later, the participants marched through the streets and congregated in front of General Headquarters in Hibiya, where they cheered, "Long live the Occupation Forces!" After that, they dispersed peacefully and went home.

Launching the Shidehara Cabinet: Last Service to the Country

After the resignation of the Higashikuni Cabinet, Lord Keeper of the Privy Seal Kido, and Hiranuma Kiichirō, President of the Privy Council, commenced a search for a replacement with three principal criteria in mind. First, the new prime minister would have to be someone the Americans would find acceptable. Second, the candidate would have to be free of any suspicion of having committed war crimes. Third, the candidate should be seasoned in diplomacy. They quickly narrowed the field to two candidates, both of who had previously served as diplomats. The top candidate was Shidehara Kijūrō and the second was Yoshida Shigeru.

On October 6, an imperial order was delivered to Shidehara directing him to form a new cabinet. He initially refused, citing his advanced age and lack of interest in domestic affairs. But he ultimately accepted the appointment on the strong urging of the Emperor. He is reported to have said, "This will be my last service to the country," when accepting the appointment. These words accurately conveyed his true feelings.

Shidehara had continued to absent himself from the center stage of politics even after the war ended. But in October, he had entrusted Yoshida with a document that he had titled "Measures for the Postwar." In it, he had written the following: "In their relations, the great powers of the world do not have friendships that have lasted a century, nor do they have such long-lasting enmities. Note that among the Allied Powers, there are many important matters on which their interests clash. We can turn yesterday's foe into tomorrow's friend. This is not necessarily a difficult task to accomplish." Shidehara proceeded to draw the following conclusions from his observation: The people must be informed of the gravity of the situation that has resulted from Japan's defeat, and no opportunity must be lost in global affairs in creating a new situation that is advantageous to Japan. It is extremely important for the government to investigate the causes of Japan's defeat and publish its findings.[28]

While it is unclear to what extent Shidehara was aware of the rivalry

---

28 Shidehara Peace Foundation, *Shidehara Kijūrō*, pp. 548–550.

between the U.S. and U.S.S.R., he was suggesting that Japan should throw itself into the arms of MacArthur in order to gain an advantageous position for the nation. Shidehara was already 73 years old at this time, but the keen sense for international affairs that he had nurtured as a diplomat had certainly not lost any of its sharpness.

Shidehara was born in Osaka in 1872 (Meiji 5) and had joined the Ministry of Foreign Affairs after graduation from the Faculty of Law of Tokyo Imperial University. In 1915, he was appointed Vice Minister for Foreign Affairs and had taken on the post of Ambassador to the United States in 1919. He had attended the Washington Naval Conference as one of Japan's plenipotentiaries and had assisted Japan's Minister of the Navy, Katō Tomosaburō. During the early years of the Shōwa era, he served as Minister of Foreign Affairs for a period of five years in cabinets of the Constitutional Democratic Party (Minsei-tō) and was instrumental in promoting cooperative relations with the United States and Great Britain. "Shidehara diplomacy" was frequently attacked by the military for being "weak-kneed diplomacy." In 1932, Shidehara became a member of the House of Peers but had remained silent throughout the war years.

It seems MacArthur was concerned about the appointment of Shidehara as prime minister and is reported to have asked Yoshida, "This is an old man. Does he speak any English?" Clearly MacArthur was not apprised of Shidehara's brilliant career as a professional diplomat.

The Shidehara Cabinet was launched on October 9. Shidehara had turned to an old friend, Tsugita Daizaburō, for help in appointing his cabinet, which included Japan's last two Ministers of the Army and the Navy. Tsugita was close to the Constitutional Democratic Party and was a former Vice Minister for Home Affairs. Yoshida Shigeru stayed on as Foreign Minister, and Matsumura Kenzō moved from his former post of Minister of Welfare to Minister of Agriculture. Ashida Hitoshi was brought in from the Liberal Party to fill the post of Minister of Welfare vacated by Matsumura.

GHQ cast a cold and suspicious eye on the newly formed Shidehara Cabinet. The Office of the Political Adviser, which had been in charge of political analysis, sent a memo to MacArthur stating that the members of the Shidehara Cabinet were for the most part "centrist" or "center-right." The memo went on to conclude that the Shidehara Cabinet was no more than a "makeshift govern-ment" that could be expected to accomplish little more than to continue the tasks stipulated in the Potsdam Declaration's terms of surrender. The analysis viewed the Shidehara Cabinet as a caretaker cabinet that would prepare the way for the next cabinet, which would emerge from the forthcoming general election and include the representatives of "political parties."[29]

On October 15, the General Staff Office of the Imperial Army and the General Staff Office of the Imperial Navy—two organizations that stood at the core of the Japanese military—were formally disbanded. The following day, October 16, MacArthur released a statement. "Today the Japanese Armed Forces throughout Japan completed their demobilization and ceased to exist as such…. Approximately seven million armed men have laid down their weapons in the accomplishment of the extremely difficult and dangerous surrender in Japan, unique in the annals of history, not a shot was necessary, not a drop of Allied blood was shed."[30]

MacArthur envisaged the progress of the occupation of Japan in three distinct stages: military, political, and economic. The completion of demobili-zation marked the end of the military stage and cleared the way for the political stage of the occupation. It was at this point that MacArthur declared to the world he would commence on the "democratization of Japan."

Political Parties and Associations Resurrected: Formation of Socialist, Liberal, and Progressive Parties

Toward the Formation of New Political Parties: Prewar and Wartime Memories

The political parties that were to play a central role in Japan's postwar politics began to be resurrected at around this time.

The composition of the Imperial Diet in August 1945 immediately after the

---

29 "Memorandum for Records (G. Atcheson Jr.), The Supreme Commander and Chief of Staff," (October 9, 1945), Fukunaga Fumio, ed., in *GHQ Minsei-kyoku shiryō, 3*, p. 148.
30 *Asahi Shinbun*, October 17, 1945.

surrender was as follows. The vast majority belonged to the Great Japan Political Association, which held 377 seats. Next, 21 seats were held by the Imperial Rule Assistance Youth Corps Diet Members Society, a splinter group of the Greater Japan Political Association that was centered on the former members of the Imperial Rule Assistance Young Men's Corps. In addition, there were 25 independents and a total of 43 vacancies. Almost all of the sitting members of the Imperial Diet had been elected under the "imperial assistance system" put in place by the Tōjō Cabinet for the lower house election of 1942. In other words, almost all members had been nominated to run in the election by the government's Imperial Rule Assistance Council.

New developments soon began to percolate in the Imperial Diet that paralleled the conditions that prevailed after the defeat. The first to take action was the group of Diet members led by Hatoyama Ichirō (Dōkō-kai Group) who had won their seats without the nomination of the Imperial Rule Assistance Association.

On August 11, just a few days before the end of the war, Ashida Hitoshi had visited Hatoyama Ichirō in Karuizawa to urge him to form a new political party. Hatoyama hesitated at the time saying, "I don't like the idea of rushing to action as if we were waiting for the end of the war." But on the day the war ended, a group of politicians from the Dōkō-kai Group gathered at the Kōjunsha Club in Ginza to discuss the formation of a new political party. Participants in this meeting included Ashida, Andō Masazumi, and Uehara Etsujirō. Ashida had planned to meet some others on this day, including Katayama Tetsu, who also belonged to the Dōkō-kai Group.[31] Hatoyama and his group were hoping to create a party that would unite all politicians who had steadfastly opposed the military and the Imperial Rule Assistance Association. It was agreed that this framework would include people who had belonged to the former Constitutional Democratic Party, such as Saitō Takao and Kawasaki Katsu.

Those who would later form the Socialist Party were also beginning to stir. While the movement was initially centered on various prewar proletarian parties

---

31 Akiyama Hisashi, *Hara Hyō nikki* [Hara Hyō Diaries], *Economist*, vol. 71, no. 43, October 12, 1993, pp. 80–85.

and factions, these pre-existing organizations would soon become splintered along ideological lines and human networks. These fissures would quickly give way to intense debate and conflict between the right wing of the movement (Social Democratic Party), the center (Japan Labor-Farmer Party), and the left wing (Japan Proletarian Party).

Katayama Tetsu, who belonged to the Social Democratic Party, met with such allies as Hara Hyō and Nishio Suehiro on August 24 to discuss the formation of a new political party. Leaders of the Social Democratic Party, including Matsuoka and Yonekubo Mitsusuke, joined Katayama's group on August 31 to discuss the "unification of the proletarian camp." At around the same time, the other wings of the socialist movement were also taking the first steps toward the formation of new political parties. Suzuki Mosaburō, Katō Kanjū, and others who would later coalesce in the Japan Proletarian Party were working to convince Marquis Tokugawa Yoshichika, a descendant of the Owari Tokugawa Clan, to head a new party. Similarly, Kawakami Jōtarō and Miyake Shōichi of the Japan Labor-Farmer Party were hoping to make Count Arima Yoriyasu, who had shown a strong interest in social movements since the prewar years, a candidate for heading a new party.

On August 23, Hatoyama and his allies, who would later form the Liberal Party, crossed paths with Nishio and others who leaned toward the Social Democratic Party. Hatoyama proposed to Nishio the formation of a single party that would build on their long-standing "anti-Tōjō" alliance to create a united front for Japan's progressive political elements. Hatoyama reasoned that while they obviously subscribed to divergent ideologies, these differences should be put aside so that the two camps could come together to take the first critically significant steps in the postwar era. The proposal ultimately failed due to differences in their respective support groups, and the two sides parted "leaving faint political reverberations."[32] It is reported that Suzuki Mosaburō, the future leader of the left wing of the Socialist Party, was also considering an alliance with the Liberal Party at this time.

---

32 Hatoyama, *Hatoyama Ichirō kaikoroku*, pp. 24–25, and Nishio Suehiro, *Nishio Suehiro no seiji oboegaki* [Political Recollection of Nishio Suehiro], Mainichi Shinbunsha, 1968, pp. 38–40.

The members of the Imperial Diet had each spent the war years in his own way and in line with his own convictions. For this reason, the question of war responsibility cast a dark shadow on the formation of postwar political parties. The chasm created by wartime memories and trauma was too great to be bridged even among conservative politicians. This set off an internal political dynamic that essentially differed from the conflict that would later emerge between Japan's conservative and progressive parties.

On September 14, the Greater Japan Political Association was dissolved, a development that added momentum to the push to form new parties. This was followed by the September 30 dissolution of the Great Japan Patriotic Industrial Association, a wartime umbrella association of labor organizations.

The Socialist Party: Unification of Proletarian Parties

The first postwar party to be formed was the Socialist Party of Japan. The party was established under the leadership of Nishio Suehiro, Mizutani Chōzaburō, and Hirano Rikizō, all of whom were from the right wing of the socialist movement. Mindful of the repeated schisms that had torn the prewar proletarian parties apart, Nishio was committed to creating a single and unified socialist party, claiming that anything less would fail to attract the people. Guided by this vision, Nishio lobbied for the participation of left wingers such as Suzuki Mosaburō, Katō Kanjū, and others associated with the Japan Proletarian Party, arguing to his own right-leaning base that Katō and his group did not pose a threat, as they would be no more than a small minority in the new party.

The initially proposed name for the newly formed party was Shakai Minshu-tō (Social Democratic Party), but this was rejected for being too similar to the name of another party *Shakai Minshū-tō*. The founders finally settled on the name the Japan Socialist Party (Nihon Shakai-tō), while retaining "Social Democratic Party" as the party's formal English appellation.

On September 13, a convocation letter went out under the names of Abe Isoo, Kagawa Toyohiko, and Takano Iwasaburō. These were elders with long track records of participation in social movements and were considered to be sympathetic to the movement. Following a preparatory meeting held on

September 22, the Japan Socialist Party was launched in a founding convention held on November 2.

The decision was made in the party convention to leave the seat of party chairman vacant and to instead assign Katayama Tetsu to the post of secretary-general. At its inception, the party counted among its members a total of 17 standing members of the Imperial Diet. The decision not to elect a chairman followed on a failure to reach a consensus as Miyake Shōichi and others attempted to recruit people from outside the fold to fill the post, such as Arima Yoriyasu. As the Occupation Forces' position on socialism was unknown, the decision was made to keep the party platform as simple as possible to avoid persecution. Thus, what emerged from the convention was the following bare-bones statement.

1. As a unified body of the working class, we shall seek to secure the political freedom of the people and thereby establish democratic systems.
2. We reject capitalism and shall act resolutely for socialism and thereby stabilize and improve the lives of the people.
3. We oppose all forms of militarist thought and actions and shall pursue cooperation among the nations of the world to realize permanent peace.

In addition to the above, a general policy statement was drawn up comprising a total of 71 articles. In a sense, these articles were no more than a restatement of the various policies that had been advocated by prewar proletarian parties. On the other hand, it is notable that many of the articles paralleled the democratization policies of the Occupation Forces. Principal among these were the democratization of the constitution based on a broadly based national consensus, democratization of local government, official recognition of labor unions, farmland reform, nationalization of core industries, and the guarantee of equal rights to men and women.

However, the party offered no clear statement on how these objectives were to be achieved, and it soon appeared that the Socialist Party was "having difficulty keeping up with the series of directives for democratization that MacArthur was issuing. To be honest, it was as though New Year's and the midsummer Bon Festival had arrived together. That is how busy these times were."[33]

The Liberal Party: Anti-Imperial Rule Assistance Association and Anti-Tōjō

The Liberal Party was formed on November 9 by Hatoyama Ichirō and others, just one week after the formation of the Socialist Party. Hatoyama was elected to the post of party president, and the post of secretary-general went to Kōno Ichirō. The new party included a total of 46 current members of the Imperial Diet. While the party was formed around Hatoyama and members of the Diet who formerly belonged to the Constitutional Association of Political Friendship (Seiyūkai) who shared Hatoyama's political philosophy, the Liberal Party made a conscious effort to create a new political party by recruiting members from other circles, including government bureaucrats, scholars, and journalists. Among those who joined the party were Minobe Tatsukichi, the constitutional scholar known for his theory of the Emperor as an organ of State, the popular writer Kikuchi Kan, and the journalist Ishibashi Tanzan.

The party commissioned scholars and academics to provide advice for formulating and enunciating their policies. Thus, constitutional issues were referred to Minobe and Miyazawa Toshiyoshi, and economic and business issues were referred to Ōuchi Hyōe and Arisawa Hiromi. The party platform was summarized in the following five articles.

1. We shall voluntarily implement the Potsdam Declaration and eradicate militarist elements in order to build a new Japan that conforms to the accepted values of the world.
2. We shall uphold the national polity, establish a democratic and responsible political system, and institute freedom in academia, the arts, education, and matters of belief to promote progress and achievement in thought, speech, and action.

---

33 Yamazaki Hiroshi, *Nihon shakaitō jūnenshi* [Ten-year History of the Socialist Party of Japan], Taibunkan, 1956, p. 21.

3. We shall strengthen government finances, promote free economic activities, and rebuild agriculture, industry and commerce in order to improve the national economy.
4. We shall promote ethical politics and social morality to bring brightness and cheer to the lives of the people.
5. We shall respect human rights, raise the status of women, and actively pursue social policies to achieve stability and happiness in the lives of the people.

The Liberal Party went on to list the following among its basic policies: to adopt a revised constitution "that will preserve national polity and establish a responsible political system," enfranchise women, institute public election of prefectural governors, respect human rights, and guarantee freedom. These policies projected a fresh image for a party committed to moving forward in the postwar era. The reference to the promotion of free economic activities was meant to stand as an antithesis to the controlled economy of the war years. As previously noted, the members of the Liberal Party felt a stronger affinity with the Socialist Party than with the progressive parties that remained in the orbit of the former Great Japan Political Association.

The Progressive Party: Difficult Birth of a New Party

The Socialist Party and Liberal Party were relatively free of the dark shadows of war responsibility and were thus able to launch into establishing new parties with little delay. The story was significantly different for members of the Great Japan Political Association who held an absolute majority in the wartime Imperial Diet. This group was held back from establishing a new party due to the unpredictability of GHQ policies on war responsibility.

Another troublesome problem was the conflict between the two leading prewar political parties—Seiyūkai and the Constitutional Democratic Party— that continued to vie for leadership in postwar Japan. Ultimately, it took the external pressures of the formation of the Socialist Party and the Liberal Party combined with the fast-approaching general election to move this camp to meet on November 16 to form the Progressive Party (Shinpotō). The seat of party president remained unfilled (until Machida Chūji, the former president of the defunct Constitutional Democratic Party assumed the post in December), while Tsurumi Yūsuke was elected to serve as secretary-general. The newly formed party, which included 273 current members of the Imperial Diet, put together the following platform.

1. We shall uphold the national polity, pursue the thorough institution of democracy, and establish responsible government centered on the Diet.
2. We shall respect personal freedoms, foster character based on cooperative self-government, and shall strive resolutely to build world peace and enhance the welfare of humankind.
3. We shall commit to procuring work for all without duress, enhance economic production and achieve fair distribution through industrial adjustment, and build a new economic system to ensure the survival of all the people.

Contrary to its name, the Progressive Party was the most conservative party in the immediate postwar setting.

Other political parties were also readying to make their postwar debut. The Japan Communist Party began to stir after Tokuda Kyūichi was freed from prison under the Civil Liberties Directive of October 4, and a three-day conference was called into session (the Fourth Japan Communist Party Convention) on December 1 to rebuild the party. The party platform that emerged from the conference called for the abolition of the imperial system and its institutions and the establishment of a republican form of government based on the will of the people. Both prescriptions were rooted in the "1932 Thesis" (*Nihon ni okeru jōsei to Nihon kyōsantō no ninmu ni kansuru tēze* [Thesis on the Situation in Japan and the Mission of the Japan Communist Party]) that had been formulated by the Comintern in 1932.

From a very early stage, the Japan Communist Party approached the Socialist Party to propose the formation of a united front. At the same time, however, the Communist Party criticized the Socialist Party as "social fascists" in the pages of *Akahata*, its official party newspaper. Commentaries appearing in the *Akahata* unambiguously stated, "We cannot immediately enter into a united front with such an entity." These attacks would breed a deep distrust of the Communist Party within the ranks of the Socialist Party whose members quickly concluded that the Communist Party was "holding out its right hand for a handshake while forming a fist with its left."

The Japan Cooperative Party was formed on December 18 under the leadership of Sengoku Kōtarō, an industrial cooperatives leader and the Higashikuni Cabinet's Minister of Agriculture. Sengoku was joined by Funada Naka, Kurosawa Torizō and others in bringing together Diet members with strong ties to rural communities to form the new party. The membership of the Japan Cooperative Party included members of the National Defence Society, otherwise known as the "New Kishi Party," which had been formed immediately before the surrender around Kishi Nobusuke, a former Minister of Commerce and Industry. The Japan Cooperative Party was committed to "preserving the imperial system and establishing a democratic form of government based on the principle of all the people under the Emperor (Ikkun banmin)." The party distinguished itself by advocating the principles of cooperation "based on diligence, autonomy, and reciprocal affection."

GHQ's Assessment of Political Parties

The Socialist Party, Liberal Party, and Progressive Party were intricately intertwined in their formative processes and personal networks, and shared a strong awareness of the uninterrupted continuum that spanned Japan's prewar and wartime years. What they held in common was a desire to restore Japan's prewar "democratic" tradition: the system of government based on party politics that had thrived until the Manchurian Incident. There was no significant fissure between the three parties on matters of policy. For instance, on the question of the structure of the national polity and the fate of the Emperor and the imperial system, the Liberal and Progressive Parties both advocated "preserving the national polity," while the Socialist Party chose the wording "retaining the imperial system." However, this unawareness and insensitivity to the political changes that would soon take place as a result of Japan's defeat and occupation were soon put to the test by the drastic and surgical intervention of GHQ in the form of the purge of designated persons from public positions.

GHQ was closely observing Japan's newly formed political parties. At this point in time, systematic analysis of the political parties was being conducted by the Office of the Political Adviser, an overseas agency of the State Department that had been created to keep an eye on MacArthur. Between October 1945 and April 1946, the Office of the Political Adviser was putting together monthly reports on political parties.

For example, a passage from these monthly reports reads as follows. "Hatoyama's party is named the Liberal Party, but it would be far more appropriate to call it the Conservative Party. Hatoyama does not represent any new or revolutionary thinking." The report then concludes, "There is no doubt that the party is sympathetic to conservative positions. What they mean by liberalism is limited to the realm of thought and has little to do with real action. We believe that Hatoyama's Liberal Party will play a moderately conservative role in the early stages of the regeneration of Japanese politics."

The analysis of the Progressive Party states as follows. "This party is directly descended from the Imperial Rule Assistance Association, Japan's wartime totalitarian party." The report goes on to dismiss the party in these terms. "This party cannot in any way be expected to play an effective leadership role in the new Japan." Regarding the Japan Cooperative Party, the reports state as follows. "It would be unfair to label this party as reactionary or non-democratic. Nevertheless, the fact is that this party represents the right wing of political thought in Japan."

The reports of the Office of the Political Adviser on Japan's political parties were frequently critical and contained many sharp remarks. However, the reports generally looked to the Socialist Party with positive expectation. Thus, while remarking that the party lacked unity, the reports conclude, "From the perspective of its membership and platform, the Socialist Party holds out the greatest hope today for the political and economic reform of Japan."

Revival of Associations and Movements

Parallel to the resurrection of political parties, a revival of various social movements began to emerge at this time.

Among the first social movements to be revived in postwar Japan was the women's movement. Already by August 25, the Women's Committee on Postwar Policies had been formed by such prewar activists as Ichikawa Fusae and Akamatsu Tsuneko. Among its first acts, the committee petitioned the Higashikuni Cabinet for the enfranchisement of women.

The labor movement was also quickly revived by such prewar activists as Matsuoka Komakichi who worked energetically to establish labor unions throughout the country. The movement held its first conference on October 10, which coincided with the liberation of political prisoners. Leaders of the wartime Japan Trade Union Congress, such as Kōno Mitsu and Miwa Jusō of the Great Japan Patriotic Industrial Association, were excluded from the conference as the movement coalesced around the former members of the Japanese Federation of Trade Union. More than 100 labor leaders came together at the conference, most of who were from the ranks of prewar moderates and the legal left, such as Takano Minoru. The conference installed a Central Preparatory Committee with 31 members, which included Matsuoka. The conference also affirmed the goal of unifying prewar labor activists and working to establish and strengthen national and local labor organizations.

Two factors accelerated the revival of the labor movement. First was the positive and encouraging attitude of the Occupation Forces toward labor unions. The second was the enactment of the Trade Union Law in December 1945.

The move to create labor unions spread rapidly between the end of 1945 and the spring of 1946. The total number of labor union members stood at 380,000 at of the end of December, already equaling the prewar level. By June 1946, this number had mushroomed to 3,750,000 members. While this expansion certainly drew its force from the severity of the postwar crisis that directly threatened the lives of the people, in many instances this expansion simply reflected the reconstitution of prewar Great Japan Patriotic Industrial Association into postwar labor unions. This reconstitution involved the creation of independent labor unions in each enterprise that included both factory workers and staff members in its fold. This became the foundation for enterprise unions, one of the most important features of Japan's postwar labor unions.

Agrarian movements also experienced a revival as such prewar activists as Hirano Rikizō, Sunaga Kō, Nomizo Masaru, and Kuroda Hisao prepared to reactivate farmers' unions. On November 3, 1945, a national panel was formed to prepare for the launch of the Japan Farmers' Union (Nichinō), and a conference for re-establishing this organization was held on February 9, 1946.

Toward the International Military Tribunal for the Far East

On November 18, 1945, GHQ issued a directive freezing the assets of the imperial family.

On November 20, the Nuremberg trials got underway bringing Nazi Germany's war criminals to justice. The Nuremberg trials would serve as a model for the International Military Tribunal for the Far East (Tokyo Tribunal), and they prompted the convocation of similar trials in Tokyo. On November 29, MacArthur received a top-secret directive from the Joint Chiefs of Staff instructing him to immediately gather evidence supporting the Emperor's war responsibility.

On December 2, GHQ identified a total of 59 persons suspected of war crimes. This included individuals such as Nakajima Chikuhei and Ōta Masataka, who ranked among the leaders of the Progressive Party. The government was particularly shocked by the fact that this list of suspects included a member of the imperial family, Prince Nashimoto Morimasa. On December 6, Lord Keeper of the Privy Seal Kido Kōichi and Prince Konoe Fumimaro were summoned to present themselves to GHQ. On the same day, Joseph Keenan arrived in Japan to take his post as chief prosecutor of the Tokyo Tribunal. In this role, Keenan would earn the moniker of the "fiendish prosecutor."

On December 15, GHQ issued a directive ordering the separation of Shinto from the government, which added to the agitation of those who surrounded the Emperor.

Democratic Reforms Initiated by the Japanese Government: Labor and Farmland Reform, and Zaibatsu Dissolution

Post-Defeat Bureaucrats: An Alternate Vision for the Postwar Era

A political vacuum followed the defeat of the nation. The military had collapsed, the Privy Council and the House of Peers had ceased to function, and political parties were still in a state of infancy. It was the bureaucrats who stepped in to fill this void.

One of the organs of the bureaucracy that stood up with particular vigor immediately after the end of the war was the Special Investigative Bureau of the Ministry of Foreign Affairs. The Committee had been formed by the end of August and thereafter met regularly and frequently. The Committee's membership combined a "professors' group" from the Laborers and Farmers Faction (Rōnōha) that included Ōuchi Hyōe, Arisawa Hiromi, and Wakimura Yoshitarō, with a "group of economists" that included Tsuru Shigeto and Nakayama Ichirō. Beginning in September, the Bureau issued a series of reports that would serve as a blueprint for Japan's postwar economy. Among these reports was *Nihon keizai saiken no kihon mondai* [Basic Issues in the Reconstruction of the Japanese Economy]. Ōkita Saburō served as the de facto secretariat of the Bureau and played a leading role in drafting these reports. Ōkita was concurrently serving in two critically important agencies of the Cabinet: the coal committee and Economic Stabilization Board.

Members of the professors' group had been arrested in 1938 in connection with the Popular Front Incident. They were charged for violating the Peace Preservation Law but were later acquitted. After their acquittal, in recognition of their outstanding investigative and analytical skills, these scholars and researchers had been assigned to work in various government agencies during the war years. After the war, Ōuchi and his colleagues provided their services in economic analysis to both the left and right and played an important role in economic policymaking. For instance, they cooperated with the Yoshida and Katayama Cabinets on the right, and on the left, they consulted with the Institute for Socialist Political and Economic Research that had been created by the Socialist Party with Suzuki Mosaburō as its director.

At about this time, the Ministry of Commerce and Industry brought together a group of experts and academics to discuss ideas and plans for postwar Japan, many of whom were serving concurrently on the Investigative Committee of the Ministry of Foreign Affairs.

The following statement, reported to have been made sometime during October 1945, is attributed to Yamamoto Takayuki, the chief of the Postwar Coordinating Department of the Ministry of Commerce and Industry. "Society will now begin to change, and the Socialist Party may well take the reins of government. It is imperative for us to study what is unfolding before us." The members of the Postwar Coordinating Department were keenly interested in the policies and experiences of President Roosevelt's New Deal, and were particularly focused on the nationalization and government management of basic industries and labor participation in corporate management through the creation of joint management councils.[34] Yamamoto would later join the Headquarters for Economic Stabilization Board under the Katayama Cabinet.

Revision of the Election Law

A move to revise prewar election laws and systems got underway shortly after the establishment of the Shidehara Cabinet in October 1945. As the Initial Policy for Post-Surrender Japan delivered to MacArthur called for actively encouraging the formation of democratic and representative bodies, it is reported that Chief Secretary Tsugita (corresponding to today's Chief Cabinet Secretary) issued instructions saying, "Hurry up and get these bodies functioning before GHQ starts breathing down our necks."

Two individuals seized the initiative in proposing revisions to the Election Law. These were Home Affairs Minister Horikiri Zenjirō and Vice Minister Saka Chiaki, who had expert knowledge regarding Japan's election systems. On October 11, Horikiri submitted his proposed revisions to a special meeting of the Cabinet. The Horikiri plan that was approved in principle contained the

34 Kōno Yasuko, *Nihon no rekishi 24: Sengo to kōdo seichō no shūen* [History of Japan 24: The Postwar Period and the End of Rapid Economic Growth], Kōdansha, 2002, pp. 37–38.

following main features: the enfranchisement of women, lowering of the voting age and the age of eligibility, and the adoption of a large-constituency system. Horikiri hoped that women voters would not lean disproportionately toward either the left or the right and expected them to be "neutral and moderate." On October 23, the Cabinet formally adopted a series of revisions. Women were fully enfranchised, the voting age was lowered to 20, the eligible age was lowered to 25, and large prefecture-wide electoral districts were adopted. This was followed on October 26 with a decision to adopt a proposal made by Vice Minister Saka for eliminating the single voting method and replacing it with a restricted plural voting method (two votes per ballot in districts with six to ten representatives, and three in districts with eleven to fourteen representatives).

Bills for the revision of the Election Law were submitted to the 89th session of the Imperial Diet on December 1. None of the political parties opposed the adoption of large electoral districts. This was primarily due to a shared awareness that maintaining the existing medium-sized constituency system was not feasible because of the massive movement of people that had occurred during the war. While many members of the Diet voiced their support for the enfranchisement of women, there were those who expressed reservations and argued that it was too soon to grant suffrage to women. Their concerns centered on the fear that women's suffrage was inconsistent with the values of the traditional family system, and that the level of political awareness remained unacceptably low among women.

Parliamentary debate centered on the proposed restricted plural voting method, which faced strong opposition for a number of reasons. First, opponents argued that the system was generally unfair and allowed a voter simultaneously to vote for candidates from two or more different political parties. It was also argued that the system could be used by weak candidates to garner votes by teaming up with stronger candidates. Given their status as minority parties in the Diet, both the Liberal Party and the Socialist Party had proposed the adoption of a proportional representation method. Now, the two parties submitted amendments calling for a single voting system that they reasoned would make it easier for minority parties to win seats. Ultimately, the House of Representatives voted in favor of a restricted plural voting method (one vote per ballot in districts with five or fewer representatives, two in districts with six to ten representatives, and three in districts with more than eleven representatives). The House of Representatives also adopted a series of amendments submitted by the Progressive Party for strengthening election regulations.

The revised Election Law was promulgated on December 17. As per the government's original bill, a restricted plural voting method was adopted for the election of the House of Peers. Specifically, single voting was eliminated and replaced by two votes per ballot in districts with ten or fewer seats and three votes per ballot in districts with eleven or more seats. Following the enactment of the law, the Shidehara Cabinet immediately dissolved the Diet and scheduled an election of the House of Representatives to be held in January. However, GHQ stopped the announcement of the election on the grounds that it needed to examine whether the revised Election Law was sufficiently democratic in spirit and content. More importantly, it needed time to prepare for the purge of public officials that would include some standing members of the Diet.

A thorny problem emerged in preparing for the election, which was that the extent of the territory of Japan had to be determined. The Potsdam Declaration had limited the territory of Japan to the four main islands and had not fully clarified the status of outlying islands. Initially, the Japanese government intended to include the islands of Habomai, Amami, and the Izu Islands in the scope of the election, while excluding various islands where travel by sea had been suspended. The latter group comprised Okinawa, Kunashiri and Etorofu Islands, and the Kurile Islands. Ultimately, the following decision was rendered by the head of GHQ's Government Section, Major General Courtney Whitney. All islands south of 30 degrees north latitude were excluded from the scope of the elections on the grounds that the Japanese government itself had excluded Okinawa. Additionally, the Habomai Islands were excluded on the grounds that they were effectively occupied by the Soviet Union and were not under the jurisdiction of Supreme Commander of the Allied Powers. Following this order, a memorandum was presented to the Japanese government on June 1, 1946, separating all territories south of 30 degrees north latitude from the mainland of Japan. This was subsequently adopted as "Government and Administrative Separation of Certain Outlying Areas from Japan" (SCAPIN-677).

Labor Reform: Enactment of the Labor Union Law

As in the case of the revision of the Election Law, the Japanese side took the initiative in enacting the Labor Union Law and pursuing farmland reform. Related bills were duly submitted on December 6 to the 89th session of the Imperial Diet.

The discussion of labor union laws began in 1919 during the Paris Peace Conference that followed the end of the First World War. The first concrete steps were taken when the Ministry of Agriculture and Commerce and the Ministry of Home Affairs formulated draft bills on labor unions in quick succession. In 1920, a bill authored by political parties was submitted to the Diet. Although it was adopted by the House of Representatives in 1931, the bill was subsequently shelved in the House of Peers and ultimately discarded.

Prince Higashikuni, Japan's first postwar prime minister, had lived in Europe and had a general appreciation for labor problems and issues. He had written, "In addition to a Ministry of Welfare, steps shall be taken to newly create a Ministry of Labor that will be in charge of future developments and activities related to labor problems and labor union legislation." In a meeting held on October 1, 1945, the Cabinet approved "Plans for deliberations related to labor union legislation," a document that was based on a draft proposal drawn up by the Ministry of Welfare. A Council on Labor Laws was subsequently empaneled. This preceded, by ten days, MacArthur's famous Five Major Reforms directive for the democratization of Japan, which will be discussed below. Those playing important roles in drafting the related bills included Suehiro Izutarō, an expert on civil and labor laws, and several labor movement activists that included Matsuoka Komakichi and Nishio Suehiro.

The draft bills on labor union legislation were passed on to Welfare Minister Ashida of the Shidehara Cabinet which followed the Higashikuni Cabinet, and submitted to the House of Representatives in December. The bills were passed and promulgated on December 22. The newly enacted laws were epoch-making as they contained provisions for the right to organize and the right to collective bargaining. Furthermore, with the exception of the police, firefighters, and prison wardens and officers, all civil servants were granted the right to strike.

Farmland Reform: Persistent Opposition and Half-Hearted Reform

Farmland reform had moved forward during the prewar years under the initiative of bureaucrats of the Ministry of Agriculture and Forestry. While farmers accounted for 50 percent of Japan's prewar population, tenanted-land covered a total area of about 2.36 million *chōbu* (approximately 2.35 million hectares), which was equivalent to approximately half of the nation's farmland. Adding the area held by small-hold farmers, 67 percent of the nation's farmland was essentially tilled by tenant farmers. The creation of owner farmers was a goal to which the bureaucrats of the Ministry of Agriculture and Forestry had been committed since the prewar and war years. In light of the grave postwar food crisis, now there was a pressing need to liberate and transfer farmland to tenant farmers as a means of incentivizing production and increasing food output.

It is notable that reform of land ownership and the tenant farming system were nowhere mentioned in the Potsdam Declaration or in the Initial Policy for Post-Surrender Japan. However, the upheavals of the defeat and occupation presented an excellent opportunity for realizing these changes. The Agriculture Bureau of the Ministry of Agriculture and Forestry grabbed this opportunity and finalized its draft reforms on October 13.

As a long-time proponent of owner farming, Agriculture Minister Matsumura initially formulated a plan for liberating all tenanted farmland holdings in excess of one *chō* five *tan* (approximately 1.48 hectares) to their tenants. But the ministry's bureaucrats advised against this plan, arguing that it was too radical. Acting on this advice, the final government proposal featured the liberation of all land held by absentee landlords, and the liberation of all tenanted farmland holdings in excess of three *chōbu* (approximately three hectares) that was owned by village-dwelling landowners. An additional feature of the proposal was to change the system of tenancy rent from payment in kind to payment in cash.

The proposal that had been hammered together by the Ministry of Agriculture and Forestry met with strong opposition in the Cabinet and was further revised to raise the level of maximum ownership by village-dwelling landowners to five *chōbu* (approximately five hectares). However, under this concession to landed interests, only 900,000 *chōbu* out of a national total of 2.36

million *chōbu* under tenancy would be liberated, a mere 38 percent of the total. It is noteworthy that even this half-hearted reform proposal came under vicious attack and resistance from the two conservative parties in the Diet, the Liberal and Progressive Parties.

In the midst of this heated debate GHQ's Natural Resources Section (NRS) suddenly presented the Japanese government with its "Memorandum of Rural Land Reform" (SCAPIN-411), a document demanding that measures be taken to "destroy the economic bondage which has enslaved the Japanese farmer to centuries of feudal oppression." However, GHQ had not formulated a concrete plan or program, and the Memorandum had been written without any prior consultation or interaction with the Japanese government. What had prompted the writing of the memorandum was GHQ's strong dissatisfaction with the Japanese proposals that were being debated in the Diet. The Memorandum contained an order instructing the Japanese government to submit its proposals for farmland reform by March 15, 1946.

The Memorandum had a tremendous impact in accelerating the debate on the proposed bills and led to the adoption of the revised Farmland Adjustment Law in the House of Representatives and House of Peers on December 27 and its promulgation two days later on December 29. The newly enacted law implemented the so-called "first farmland reform" featuring the following provisions: all land owned by absentee landowners was liberated, village-dwelling landowners were permitted to own no more than five *chōbu*, and tenancy rent on any remaining farmland was to be paid in cash rather than in kind. However, as noted above, this provided for the liberation of only 38 percent of the tenanted farmland. The reform was also incomplete in other ways. For example, the transfer of land from landowners to tenants was to take the form of outright sale. In light of these shortcomings, GHQ ordered the implementation of a further round of reforms in June 1946.

Zaibatsu Dissolution: Demilitarizing and Democratizing the Economy

In contrast to the active measures taken in labor and farmland reform, the business community's efforts to take the initiative in economic reform were blocked by the Occupation Forces.

During the war years, the business community fielded a total of four powerful associations: the Japan Economic Federation, the Council for the Control of the Key Industries, the National Federation of Chambers of Commerce and Industry, and the National Federation of Commerce and Industry Cooperatives. These organizations, which were used to corral businesses and industries in supporting the war effort, faced a pressing need to reconstitute themselves to meet peacetime exigencies. When Commerce and Industry Minister Nakajima Chikuhei requested the business community to come up with its recommendations for the Japanese economy, the four organizations came together in October 1945 to form the Committee of the Japan Business Federation (Keidanren), which thereafter would serve as the liaison between the business community and GHQ.

Business leaders accepted Japan's defeat with positive expectation and even with some modest hope. For example, Edo Hideo of the Mitsui zaibatsu wrote of the oppression he had been subjected to after the Manchurian Incident of 1931. "We were constantly criticized for being pacifists, libertarians, and sympathetic to the United States, and the military and rightists looked upon us with disdain and suspicion." Edo expected that the end of the war would open the way to peacetime industries that Mitsui was particularly adept at developing and managing, and believed that the Americans and the British would not be particularly antagonistic toward the Mitsui businesses.[35]

Contrary to these expectations, the Initial Post-Surrender Policy that was released on September 22 referred to the "large industrial and banking conglomerates which have exercised control of a great part of Japan's trade and industry," indicating that the business community would soon be subjected to serious trials and tribulations. GHQ was particularly antagonistic toward the zaibatsu that controlled large business groups through their holding companies, and identified these enterprises as belligerent organizations on par with military and bureaucratic cliques.

---

35 Andō Yoshio, ed., *Shōwa seiji keizai-shi e no shōgen, ge* [Testimonies on Showa Political and Economic History, vol. 2], Mainichi Shinbunsha, 1966, pp. 140–151.

At the end of September, Colonel Raymond Kramer, who headed GHQ's Economic and Scientific Section, issued the so-called directive on zaibatsu dissolution to the representatives of Japan's four leading zaibatsu: Mitsui, Mitsubishi, Sumitomo, and Yasuda. The directive spelled out the policy of dissolving the zaibatsu holding companies that controlled vast arrays of subsidiary and affiliated enterprises. Even while the zaibatsu attempted to resist the policy, on November 6, the Economic and Scientific Section presented the Japanese government with its plans for dissolving the holding companies of the four major zaibatsu.

Next, GHQ proceeded to pressure the Japan Economic Federation into dissolution. With a membership that encompassed the industrial, commercial, and financial sectors of the Japanese economy, GHQ reasoned that the Japan Economic Federation was a powerful organization that was closely tied to zaibatsu interests. It should be noted that Keidanren, which would stand at the apex of Japan's postwar business organizations, evolved out of the Committee of Keidanren that was formed as a conduit to the Occupation Forces. When formally established in August 1946, Keidanren was forced to accept a number of conditions that were laid out by GHQ. These included a pledge not to protect or preserve zaibatsu influence and a pledge that its officers would be elected through democratic processes.

In November 1945, the U.S. Reparations Mission to Japan arrived in Tokyo. The mission was headed by Edwin Wendell Pauley, an oil industry executive known to be a tough negotiator. In December, the mission released the Pauley Interim Report formally known as the "Plan for Immediate Implementation of Reparations by Japan."

The interim report argued that Japan should be completely demilitarized by eliminating all military capacity, and recommended that all surplus heavy industrial equipment and overseas assets be used in the payment of reparations primarily to Asian countries that had suffered harm and damage at the hands of Japan. Regarding living standards, the report recommended that the living standards of the Japanese people "should be kept within limits so as not to exceed the living standards of other Asian countries." The interim report also contained references to zaibatsu dissolution, farmland reform, and the purging of business leaders.

Faced with these harsh recommendations, the business community became paralyzed with fear and uncertainty that its facilities and equipment could be dismantled and removed at any time. In January 1946, MacArthur expressed doubt as to whether heavy industrial equipment would be of any use to countries receiving them as reparations. Consequently, the Pauley recommendation was referred to the Far Eastern Commission for consideration under its Interim Reparation Plan. However, the referral did not move forward smoothly because of the conflicts of interest that had emerged among the Allied Powers.

In January 1946, a second investigative mission arrived in Japan headed by Professor Corwin Edwards of Northwestern University, an expert on international cartels. This marked the start of full-fledged progress toward zaibatsu dissolution and the institution of anti-trust policies. In May 1947, the Edwards Report was submitted to the Far Eastern Commission by SWNCC under the title of "Policy on Excessive Concentration of Economic Power in Japan" (FEC-230).

The Separation of Okinawa: Nansei Shotō after August 15

Japan's Defeat and Okinawa: Establishment of the Okinawa Advisory Council

At 8:00 a.m. on August 15, 1945, just four hours before the broadcast of the Emperor's declaration of the end of the war, a total of 124 internees were brought to Ishikawa in Misato Village (present-day Misato City) from sixteen camps spread throughout the main island of Okinawa.

Colonel Murray, the Deputy Commander for Military Government in Okinawa, conveyed to the perplexed and bewildered group that had been assembled that morning that the war was ending with the surrender of Japan. He then went on to state, "The U.S. Military Government will continue to provide leadership and material support. However, responsibility and administration must be gradually transferred to the people of Okinawa."[36] Murray's message to the group

---

36 Okinawa Prefecture Okinawa Historical Materials Section, ed., *Okinawa-ken shiryō: Sengo 1 Okinawa shijun-kai kiroku* [Okinawa Prefecture Historical Documents: Postwar 1 Records of the Okinawa Advisory Council], Okinawa Prefecture Board of Education, 1986, pp. 12–13.

implied that the burden of administration would be borne as much as possible by the people of Okinawa. The problem was that the prefectural government office and other government agencies had been completely destroyed. At the same time, the military government was grappling with its own problems since the fall of Okinawa, such as the shortage of civilian officers and translators. The reconstruction of the administrative bodies that were needed for executing the work of the military government literally had to start from scratch on both the American and Okinawan sides.

The Okinawa Advisory Council was formed on August 20 in Ishikawa with fifteen members headed by Shikiya Kōshin as chairman. The Council was designed to function as an advisory panel to the military government while also acting as a conduit between the military and local residents. The expectation was that the Council would convey the decisions of the military government to the municipalities and in turn channel their needs and requests back to the military government. A number of specialized departments were subsequently formed under the Council to tend to such routine functions as policing, education, food distribution, medical and sanitary services, and personnel matters.

On September 13, the military government issued its Guidelines on Emergency Measures on Local Administration in an effort to promote the formation of local administrative bodies. Subsequent to this order, "municipalities" were formed to coincide with the location of clusters of internment camps. On September 20, "municipal assembly" elections were held in twelve internment camp districts, followed by "mayoral elections" held on September 25. It is noteworthy that the Guidelines stipulated that "all residents above the age of 25 have the right to vote and are eligible for election." This effectively enfranchised women seven months before the enfranchisement of women on the Japanese mainland.

These newly formed municipalities were placed under corresponding military districts where they were governed by military administrative officers. The military administrative officers wielded total authority and their orders were absolute. As such, the elected mayors were mayors in name only. In reality, "This was a coarse and humble post, often no more than a liaison between the military and local residents, and at times a mere procurer of Okinawan labor to meet the needs of the military."[37]

Separation and Isolation from the Japanese Mainland

It was not until the end of October 1945 that the Okinawan people were released from internment camps and allowed to return home or to neighboring areas. What they found were the ruins of their homes and villages juxtaposed to the shiny brand new U.S. military bases and camps that were springing up everywhere. Although the people were allowed to return home, they were still prohibited from moving about freely.

The U.S. military did not fully liberate the central and southern sections of Okinawa where U.S. military installations were concentrated. As of September 1947, the total land area requisitioned by the U.S. military came to about 43,000 acres (approximately 174,000 hectares), equivalent to fourteen percent of the total area of the mainland of Okinawa. To begin with, most of the population of Okinawa lived in the central and southern parts of the island, and most of the arable land was concentrated in this area. To further complicate the situation, the military government paid no regard to existing land ownership in allotting residential and farmland to residents, but acted on its own. This allotment system was implemented under the authority of the respective commanders of the military districts or the heads of municipalities. However, it should be noted that Okinawa's land registries had been destroyed in the war and there was no easy way to determine ownership in the first place. Moreover, citing the provisions of the Hague Convention respecting the Laws and Customs of War on Land and arguing that Okinawa would remain under war conditions until the independence of Japan, the U.S. military did not pay rent on the land that it was using.

Surrounded by the U.S. military bases, the people of Okinawa eked out a living by working for the military and tilling the farmland that had been allotted to them. To survive, they supplemented their income with the meager rations that were handed out to them.

---

37 Taira Tatsuo, *Taira Tatsuo kaisōroku* [Memoirs of Taira Tatsuo], Nanpōsha, 1963, pp. 2–3.

In January 1946, the GHQ directive establishing the area of The Ryukyu Islands south of 30 degrees north latitude as a separate administrative district[38] was delivered to Okinawa. What this directive did was to maintain the current status of Okinawa as a territory "under U.S. Occupation." Consequently, Okinawa would never be reconstituted as a territory "under the Occupation of the Allied Powers."

Thus forced into "separation and isolation" from the Japanese mainland, Okinawa would embark on its own unique postwar path.

Washington's Okinawa Policies: The Conflict between the State Department and the Military

The U.S. military stationed in Okinawa faced two difficult issues.

First, the surrender of Japan had robbed the occupation of Okinawa of its original intent and rendered the purpose of the occupation increasingly ambiguous. This loss of purpose was reflected in Washington's inability to come to a decision on how to treat Okinawa. Second, the organizational status and position of the military government in Okinawa remained unsettled.

At the end of October 1945, the Department of the Army identified Okinawa as a critically important strategic position for U.S. national security, a status that Okinawa shared at this point with the Aleutian Islands, Panama, Hawaii, the Mariana Islands, and the Philippines. In light of its importance, the Department of the Army argued that Okinawa should be placed under the exclusive strategic control of the United States, or at the very least under United Nations trusteeship.

The State Department took a very different approach. First of all, it identified Okinawa to be among the "small islands" of the former territories of Japan that had to be returned after "demilitarization." From this perspective, the State Department argued that the occupation of Okinawa was in violation of the principle of non-aggrandizement of territory as spelled out in the Atlantic Charter. Secondly, it took the position that the occupation of Okinawa placed

---

38 SCAPIN-677: Governmental and Administrative Separation of Certain Outlying Areas from Japan.

an undue financial burden on the United States and jeopardized relations with the Soviet Union.

In September 1945, the military government of Okinawa was integrated into the U.S. Navy as a subordinate organization. In doing so, the military government had been assigned a low status in the military hierarchy and would soon begin to experience a dramatic weakening of its capabilities due to postwar cuts in the defense budget and the return of personnel to the United States.

The conflict between the State Department and the military over Okinawa resulted in a decision rendered in November 1946 "not to do anything" for the time being. The shelving of the Okinawa debate meant the U.S. forces would continue their occupation and control of Okinawa with no clear policy guidance from Washington and no definite budgetary outlay. For this reason, a systematic approach to policymaking was totally lacking, and whatever policies were developed locally were ad hoc and spur-of-the-moment in the extreme.

Separation of the Nansei Shotō: Island-by-Island Government

As in the case of Okinawa, the Amami Islands, Miyako Islands, and Yaeyama Islands were also separated from the mainland of Japan on January 1946. Developments on these island chains deserve some attention.

The Amami Islands were an integral part of Kagoshima Prefecture, and the Amami branch of the Kagoshima Prefecture Office was quick to resume operation after the end of the war. Six months after the defeat, U.S. military government had not yet arrived on the Amami Islands. The GHQ directive separating it from the mainland was conveyed to the Amami Islands in February 1946, followed by the arrival of U.S. military forces and the establishment of the Northern Ryukyu Islands Military Government in March, marking the start of military government. In October, the Provisional Government of Northern Ryukyu Islands was established and its head became the governor of the Provisional Government of Northern Ryukyu Islands, which was placed under the control of the Northern Ryukyu Islands Military Government.

The Miyako and Yaeyama Islands were part of Okinawa Prefecture, but started on a different postwar path than the Okinawa mainland that had been ravaged by war. These islands experienced a period of lawlessness when all contact with the Okinawa mainland was severed. The U.S. military arrived in the islands in December 1945, followed by the establishment of the Southern Ryukyu Islands Military Government in March 21, 1946. Finally, civilian governments were formed separately for Miyako and Yaeyama and placed under the authority of the military government.

The Northern and Southern Ryukyu Islands Military Governments functioned as auxiliary agencies of the military government and held jurisdiction over the sub-prefectures and civilian government organizations that were formed in these islands. However, they were not directly connected to the military government in Okinawa. As such, the U.S. military governed and controlled the Nansei Shotō—extending from Amami in the east to Yonaguni in the west—by effectively separating and isolating them from both Okinawa and the Japanese mainland.

CHAPTER 2

Reform under the Occupation and Fresh Start for Political Parties

1. Birth of the Constitution of Japan

At the Beginning: Konoe Fumimaro, Shidehara Kijūrō, and MacArthur

The Potsdam Declaration and Constitutional Reform

The Potsdam Declaration contained no demand for or even mention of constitutional reform. However, the Constitution of the Empire of Japan (hereinafter, the Meiji Constitution) did not provide guarantees for democracy; freedoms of speech, thought, and religion; or respect for fundamental human rights, as mentioned in the Potsdam Declaration. It was easy to see that the Meiji Constitution would have to be revised to meet these requirements. But at the beginning of the Occupation, GHQ did not issue specific instructions to the Japanese government on this matter. Thus, there was no way to predict the scope of the revision that would be required.

Notwithstanding the absence of any substantive guidance, there was some movement at the sub-ministerial levels of the Japanese government to examine constitutional revision. For instance, the Cabinet Legislation Bureau had already started looking at the constitution by mid-September 1945. The initiative was launched by Irie Toshio, chief of the Bureau's First Department, and featured the start of an informal administrative review. On September 18, Irie submitted a memorandum to the Director of the Bureau entitled "End of the War and the Constitution."

The Irie memorandum pointed out that certain technical revisions were needed to reflect the dismantlement of Japan's military system. Thus, it proposed changing "civil and military officers" to "government officers." It also proposed the deletion of provisions pertaining to the supreme command of State, the law of siege, and the elimination of military conscription. The memorandum also touched on matters requiring consideration as a consequence of Japan's acceptance of the Potsdam

Declaration. These included the disposal of matters that came under the supreme power of State in the Meiji Constitution, reconstituting the House of Peers, abolishing the Privy Council, and establishing procedures for constitutional revision.[1]

Parallel to this, the Ministry of Foreign Affairs was considering its own approach to constitutional revision. "On the matter of revising the Constitution and establishing a consultation system that conforms to the spirit of democracy, as a general rule, action should be taken as the occasion may demand."[2] However, due to the government's passive stance, these early developments did not lead to any concrete action.

The Konoe Initiative

Konoe Fumimaro was the first person on the Japanese side to take real action toward constitutional revision. Konoe at this time was a member of the Higashikuni Cabinet, which he served as a minister without portfolio with deputy prime minister status.

On October 4, Konoe visited MacArthur for the second time. During his discussions with the Supreme Commander of the Allied Powers, Konoe argued that it was the "Marxists" who had made the emergence of militarist elements possible and advocated that the "forces of feudalism centered on the Imperial Household" had actually worked to restrain the militarists. Konoe then turned to MacArthur with a question. "If you have any thoughts or instructions on the organization of government and the composition of the parliament, I would very much like to be informed of them." It is reported that MacArthur responded to this question in a resolute tone.

First, the Constitution must be revised to sufficiently include elements of liberalism. Second, the Imperial Diet is reactionary. If the Diet is dissolved

---

1 Satō Tatsuo, *Nihonkoku kenpō tanjōki* [Record of Establishment of the Constitution of Japan], Chūō Kōron Shinsha, 1999, pp. 18–19.
2 "Jishuteki sokketsuteki shisaku no kinkyū juritsu ni kansuru ken" [On the Emergency Adoption of Measures Requiring Autonomous and Immediate Decisions], (October 9, 1945), Etō Jun, ed., in *Senryō shiroku, 3* [Historical Records of the Occupation, vol. 3], Kōdansha, 1989, pp. 57-62.

and an election held on the current Election Law, there will be no change in the type of people elected. To avoid this, the right to vote must be expanded, women must be enfranchised, and the rights of workers must be safeguarded.[3]

Then he continued to encourage Konoe, "You come from the forces of feudalism, but at the same time, you are a cosmopolitan well aware of global affairs. Moreover, you are still young. Stand resolutely at the head of leadership. If you were to gather liberalist elements and present the nation with a proposal for revising the constitution, the Diet would follow your lead."

George Atcheson Jr. of the Office of the United States Political Adviser for Japan was present at this meeting and cabled the Secretary of State to inform him that constitutional revision had been brought up. In this cable sent on the same day as the meeting, Atcheson warned that it was necessary for the U.S. government to immediately define its position on Japan's constitutional reform.

On the following day, October 5, the Higashikuni Cabinet resigned en masse. Having lost his position in the Cabinet, Konoe hurriedly met with the Lord Keeper of the Privy Seal Kido Kōichi to discuss his options. It was decided that Konoe would continue to work on constitutional revision as an imperial appointee in the Office of the Privy Seal.

On October 8, Konoe visited Atcheson to seek his advice on revising the constitution. Atcheson responded by outlining some key points, which he said were no more than his personal and informal comments. The revisions suggested by Atcheson included strengthening the powers of the Diet, clarifying the accountability of government to the Diet in line with the British model, restraining the powers of the House of Peers and Privy Council, and explicitly guaranteeing the fundamental rights of the people. It is notable that Atcheson did not touch on the status of the Emperor at this point, but advocated the appointment of civilians to the ministerial posts related to the military. This can be interpreted as meaning that Atcheson believed that the Japanese military would continue to exist during the Occupation. In any case, Atcheson reported

---

3 "Konoe Kokumushō Makkāsā gensui kaidan yōroku" [Record of Meeting of Ministry of State Konoe and General MacArthur], Etō, ed., *Senryō shiroku*, *3*, pp. 97–103.

the informal comments that he had made to Konoe to the Secretary of State.

The State Department responded to Atcheson's report on October 16 stating that the purpose of constitutional revision was to establish parliamentary government. On the question of the Emperor and the imperial system, the document separately listed conditions that would apply if the imperial system were to be retained or abolished. The document stipulated that the following condition would apply if the imperial system were to be retained. "Any ministers for armed forces which may be permitted in future should be civilians and all special privileges of direct access to throne by military should be eliminated."[4] The State Department generally concurred with Atcheson's recommendations and instructed him to continue his discussions with Konoe and to keep the State Department informed. Furthermore, Atcheson was informed that a full report of the State Department's views would be sent to him in the near future. However, MacArthur would soon push Atcheson out of the process of constitutional revision.

Shidehara–MacArthur Discussions: Two Visions of Democracy

In the afternoon of October 11, Shidehara visited MacArthur to report on his assumption of the prime minister's post. During this meeting, MacArthur urged the liberalization of the Constitution and issued his directive on the Five Major Reforms.

These five reforms consisted of enfranchising women, encouraging labor unions, democratizing education, democratizing economic institutions, and abolishing secret and oppressive organizations. On the question of the enfranchisement of women, Shidehara informed MacArthur that the decision to enfranchise women had already been finalized in the Cabinet meeting held the same morning. MacArthur welcomed this and said, "Let's keep up this pace." Shidehara then presented his own thinking on democracy and democratic government.

---

4 Telegram Received From: Secretary of State, October 17, 1945, Records of Japan, Tokyo Embassy, Records of Japan, Tokyo Consulate General and Records of Office of the U. S. Political Advisor for Japan, Tokyo - Office of the U.S. Political Advisor for Japan, Tokyo, Classified General Correspondence, 1945-52 - Box No. 3 "1945 vol. 6: 800-873," Sheet No. FSP03457, National Diet Library, Originals in U.S. National Archives & Records Administration, RG84.

I understand that your intent is to democratize and liberalize Japan's systems and organizations in general. When I was a member of the Cabinet twelve or thirteen years ago, a tide of liberal democracy was sweeping over Japan. But this tide receded after the Manchurian Incident and reactionary elements came to the fore and gained power. As a result, the development of democracy was halted. However, as a consequence of the recent and rapid changes that have occurred, all the sources and causes of obstruction have been completely swept away. Therefore, I expect that it will not be difficult for Japan to once again begin to advance in the direction of the flowering that was seen in Japan over a decade ago.[5]

Shidehara continued to expound on his position, saying it would take a long time for Japan to establish democracy on the American model, and that the time needed to achieve this could not be easily estimated. But he explained that the establishment of a "Japanese model of democracy" was not a "matter for the distant future." Regarding the Japanese model of democracy, Shidehara offered the following definition: "A principle that the will of the masses is respected and reflected in politics." Shidehara's thinking was heavily influenced by the political developments of the early years of the Shōwa Era and his own experiences as Foreign Minister in the political party-based cabinets of this period. As earlier noted, Yoshida shared Shidehara's belief on this point.

Japanese Conceptions of Constitutional Revision: Konoe Draft, Matsumoto Draft, and Political Parties Draft

Establishment of Constitutional Problems Investigation Committee

Shidehara was confident that democracy could be fully realized under the Meiji Constitution, and that everything depended on how the provisions of the constitution were applied. As such, Shidehara took a very passive and skeptical

---

5 "Shidehara Makkāsā kaidan" [Conference between Prime Minister Shidehara and General MacAthur], Etō, ed., in *Senryō shiroku, 3*, pp. 105–113.

stance toward MacArthur's demands for constitutional revision. Similarly, the Shidehara Cabinet was uncomfortable with the constitutional research that Konoe was carrying out independently as an imperial appointee in the Office of the Privy Seal.

Constitutional revision came up for discussion in the Cabinet meeting of October 13. State Minister Matsumoto Jōji strongly advocated the Cabinet's direct involvement in constitutional research and revision. Matsumoto stated that preparation for constitutional revision came under "affairs of state" and argued, "If the government continues to do nothing, this may very well affect the fate of the Cabinet. The government must take some action."[6] Welfare Minister Ashida voiced his opinion as follows. "The current constitution is not compatible with Article 10 of the Potsdam Declaration. Moreover, the idea of a constitution granted by the Emperor is incompatible with what the Americans understand to be democracy."[7]

Following this discussion, the Constitutional Problems Investigation Committee (hereinafter, Matsumoto Committee) was established within the Cabinet on October 25 with Matsumoto Jōji as its chairman. The word "revision" or "reform" was consciously excluded from the title of the committee and emphasis was placed on the concept of "investigation." What this implied was that the Matsumoto Committee would begin its work by investigating whether or not constitutional revision was needed in the first place. This appellation accurately reflected the passive stance that prevailed in the government at this time.

Thus, Japan and the United States would embark on the process of rebuilding the nation without ironing out the inconsistencies and differences in commitment to democracy and democratization that existed on the respective sides.

---

6 Ōta Kenichi et al., *Tsugita Daizaburō nikki* [Diary of Tsugita Daizaburō], Sanyō Shinbunsha, 1991, p. 87.
7 Shindō Eiichi and Shimokōbe Motoharu, eds., *Ashida Hitoshi nikki* [Ashida Hitoshi Diary], Iwanami Shoten, 1986, p. 52.

The Phantom Konoe Draft and the "Four Matsumoto Principles"

During this period, criticism of Konoe was steadily growing, both in Japan and abroad. At home, some questioned whether it was advisable for someone in the Imperial Household Ministry to be working on constitutional revision. Abroad, the *New York Times* opined that Konoe was not suited for drafting revisions to the constitution and stated that no one would be surprised if Konoe were treated as a war criminal.

On November 1, GHQ suddenly announced that the "General Headquarters had nothing to do with the constitutional investigation conducted by Konoe." With this abrupt announcement, GHQ broke its relations with Konoe. On December 6, a warrant for the arrest of Konoe on charges of war crimes was issued. On December 16, the day on which he was to surrender himself, Konoe took his own life.

What kind of constitutional revision was Konoe hoping to institute? Entitled "Outline of Revision of the Constitution of the Empire of Japan," Konoe advocated in his draft that the construction of the new Japan could not be achieved by merely reinterpreting the Meiji Constitution or changing the manner of its application. He argued that constitutional revision was necessary for the nation to move forward. The Konoe draft subjected the Imperial prerogative to convene and dissolve the Diet, declare war and peace, enter into treaties and other functions to the "consent" of the Diet. In other changes, supreme power over the military was reconstituted as an "affair of state," the scope of the freedoms of citizens was expanded, cabinet ministers were rendered accountable to the Diet, the Privy Council was abolished, and the right of the Diet to deliberate on the budget was affirmed. The Konoe draft was assessed to be "far more progressive"[8] than the Matsumoto draft discussed below. It is believed that the progressive elements of the draft reflected Konoe's adoption of the various comments that he had received from Atcheson.

After GHQ announced that it was severing its ties with Konoe, the

---

8 Jiji Tsūshinsha, ed., *Kenpō kaisei: Kaisetsu to shiryō* [Constitutional Revision: Commentary and Documents], Jiji Tsūshinsha, 1946.

Matsumoto Committee took the lead in constitutional revision. On December 8, Matsumoto for the first time outlined the so-called "four Matsumoto principles" that would serve as guidelines in determining the direction of constitutional revision. Matsumoto's explanation of the four principles was given in response to a question directed to him in the deliberations of the Budget Committee of the House of Representatives.

The four principles can be outlined as follows. (1) No change shall be made in the fundamental principle concerning the sovereignty of the Emperor. (2) Certain limitations shall be placed on matters subject to the Emperor's prerogative, and the scope of matters requiring the resolution of the Diet shall be expanded. (3) Ministers of state shall be held accountable to the Diet in all affairs of the state. (4) Protection afforded to the rights and liberties of the people shall be strengthened, and means shall be adopted for providing adequate relief and restitution when such rights have been violated.

The Matsumoto draft went very little beyond preserving the status quo. However, from the perspective of the theory of the Emperor as an organ of State—the prevailing constitutional theory that marked the heyday of Taishō Democracy—the Matsumoto draft was probably as progressive as it could be.

Drafts for Constitutional Revision Proposed by Political Parties and the Public

During this period, political parties were also busy preparing their own proposals for constitutional revision. The first to act was the Communist Party, which announced "Essentials of the New Constitution" in November 1945. The Communist Party draft affirmed the sovereignty of the people; fully enfranchised all men and women above the age of 18; upheld the political, economic, and social freedoms of the people; asserted the freedom to monitor and criticize the government; and called for the protection of the right to life, the right to work, and the right of education. It should be noted that the Communist Party was at this time organizing activities under the banner of "Food before Constitution." Consequently, its final draft entitled the Constitution of the People's Republic of Japan was not published until July 8, 1946.

A number of competing drafts for constitutional revision were successively released after the start of 1946. These drafts, which reflected the vision that each party had for postwar Japan are outlined in Table 2-1.

The Communist Party was the only party to advocate the sovereignty of the people. Sovereignty was assigned to the Emperor in the drafts proposed by the government and the Progressive Party and to the State in the drafts proposed by the Liberal and Socialist Parties. The Liberal Party advocated that sovereignty lies in the State, based on Minobe Tatsukichi's theory of the Emperor as an organ of State. On announcing the draft adopted by his party, Hatoyama stated, "The combined rights of sovereignty must rest with the Emperor as the scion of an unbroken line of sovereigns and the head of state."

In its draft constitution, the Socialist Party assigned sovereignty to the national community, which included the Emperor. As for the right to exercise sovereignty, the draft read, "These shall be divided, the principal parts of which shall be assigned to the Diet, while the Emperor shall be retained with a smaller part of sovereign authority." The idea was to restrict the scope of the Emperor's powers and to sequester those powers within non-political areas.

Nevertheless, significant differences remained within the Socialist Party on the question of the imperial system. An interesting counterpoint is found in the proposal of Morito Tatsuo, a member of the Socialist Party's constitutional revision drafting committee who had been expelled from Tokyo Imperial University in 1920 following criticism of articles he had published. Morito advocated the separation of the Emperor's political and religious functions and argued, "The people's rights must be protected, and the Emperor must be no more than a moral symbol. The position of the Emperor should be close to that of British and Scandinavian kings."[9] Finally, it should be noted that the Progressive, Liberal, and Socialist Parties all subscribed to the position of retaining the Emperor and imperial system.

The Progressive, Liberal, and Socialist Parties were in agreement on

---

9 "Office of the United State Political Adviser (G. Atcheson Jr.), Views of Japanese Labor Economist (Tatsuo MORITO) on Constitutional Reform and other Current Japanese Problems," (November 13, 1945), Fukunaga Fumio, ed., *GHQ Minsei-kyoku shiryō: Senryō kaikaku, 3* [GHQ Government Section Materials: Reforms of the Occupation, vol. 3], Maruzen, 1999, pp. 152–155.

strengthening the powers of the Diet and limiting or abolishing the sovereignty of the Emperor. The government and Progressive Party (Shinpotō) drafts advocated limiting the supreme power of the Emperor, and abolishing the Emperor's power of supreme command, prerogative to organize the Army and Navy, power in case of an emergency, and the right of issuance of ordinances by his own order. On the other hand, the Liberal and Socialist Parties advocated the complete abolition of the Emperor's sovereignty. Setting aside the question of supreme command, the draft constitutions of neither party made any direct reference to the question of the military.

Furthermore, the three parties were in basic agreement on expanding the powers of the Diet and maintaining a bicameral structure. The Progressive Party defined the role of the Diet to be that of an advisory system. What was interesting was the proposed method for electing the prime minister. The Progressive Party's draft provided for "appointment by the Emperor on advice of the Speaker of the House of Representatives." The Socialist Party called for "appointment by the Emperor as nominated by the speakers of both houses of the Diet." In either case, the parties did not go so far as to stipulate that the prime minister was to be elected by resolution of the Diet.

On the subject of human rights, the Progressive Party referred to these as the "rights of subjects." The Liberal Party took it a step further to state, "The freedoms of thought, expression, belief, and academic and artist freedoms shall not be limited by law without due cause." After listing the freedoms of expression, assembly, association, publication, belief, and communication, the Social Party's draft made explicit mention of the right to life in the following passages. "The people have the right to life, and shall receive the protection of the State in old age." "The people have the obligation to work, and the labor force shall be afforded special protection." These provisions reflect the influence of the Weimar Constitution.

With the exception of the Communist Party, none of the political parties touched on the question of making changes in the matter of sovereignty. However, all of the drafts did contain provisions for reducing or abolishing the powers of the Emperor and strengthening those of the Diet. Thus in all instances, some efforts had been made to distance the new constitution from the prewar

Table 2-1 Draft Constitutions of Political Parties

	GHQ Draft	Matsumoto Committee	Progressive Party	Liberal Party	Socialist Party	Communist Party (Outline for a New Constitution)	Constitution Investigation Association
Sovereignty	People	Emperor	Emperor	State (Emperor as organ of State)	State (National community including the Emperor)	People	People
Emperor System	Retain (Emperor as symbol)	Retain	Retain (Preserve national polity)	Retain (Preserve national polity)	Retain	Abolish	Retain
Supreme Power of Emperor		Reduce supreme power, strengthen cabinet powers	Eliminate supreme command, power to organize Army and Navy, and power in an emergency	Abolish grant command authority to cabinet	Abolish		Limited to ceremonies of State
Diet	Supreme organ of government and only legislative body; Unicameral structure	Bicameral structure	Strengthen powers of the Diet, act as counsel to cabinet; Bicameral structure	Strengthen powers of the Diet; Bicameral structure	Strengthen powers of the Diet; Bicameral structure		Bicameral structure
Cabinet				Cabinet responsible to Diet	Cabinet responsible to Diet		
Prime Minister	By resolution of Diet		Appointed by Emperor on advice of Speaker of the House of Representatives		Appointed by Emperor as nominated by speakers of both houses of Diet		Nominated by speakers of both houses of Diet
Human Rights	Fundamental human rights	Rights and responsibilities of subjects	Rights and responsibilities of subjects	Freedom of thought, expression, belief, and academic and artistic freedom	Freedom of expression, assembly, association, publication, belief, and communication	Political, economic, and social freedom	Fundamental human rights
Miscellaneous					Right to life	Rights to life and education	Right to life, equality of men and women

Source: Compiled by the author from Jiji Tsūshinsha, ed., *Kenpō kaisei: Kaisetsu to shiryō* [Constitutional Revision: Commentary and Documents], Jiji Tsūshinsha, 1946.

political structure.

Among all the draft constitutions, one that particularly stood out was the draft formulated by the Constitution Investigation Association, a group of private citizens put together by Professor Takano Iwasaburō formerly of Tokyo Imperial University. Other members of the group included Suzuki Yasuzō, a constitutional historian who held no office at the time; Murofuse Kōshin, a political critic; and the previously mentioned Morito Tatsuo, a member of the Socialist Party's constitutional revision drafting committee. The Constitution Investigation Association's draft constitution clearly stipulated that sovereignty resided in the people by stating that sovereignty "derives from the Japanese people" and "the Emperor shall rule over the ceremonies of the State." The draft also upheld fundamental human rights and respect for social rights. Particularly noteworthy was its explicit reference to the equality of men and women. "In all matters both public and private, men and women are fully endowed with equal rights." The Constitution Investigation Association released its final draft on December 27. In January 1946, Milo Rowell, the Government Section officer in charge of constitutional investigation, forwarded the draft to Brigadier General Whitney, head of the Government Section, with the comment that it included "outstanding liberal" provision. It is reported that GHQ used this draft as a model for its own.[10]

MacArthur's Three Basic Points: The Government Section's Nine Days of Secrecy

The Emperor's Declaration Denying His Divinity

January 1, 1946, witnessed the release of the Imperial Rescript on the Construction of a New Japan, better known as the Emperor's "Declaration of Humanity."

In this document, the Emperor first referred to the Five Clauses of the Charter Oath that had been proclaimed at the time of the Meiji Restoration. This

---

10 Memorandum for Chief of Staff (M. Rowell), Comments on Constitutional Revision proposed by Private Group, January 11, 1946, and Takayanagi Kenzō et al., *Nihonkoku kenpō seitei no katei, 1* [Formation Process of the Constitution of Japan, vol. 1], Yūhikaku Publishing, 1972, pp. 26–27.

was followed by the Emperor's renunciation of his divinity. "The ties between Us and Our people have always stood upon mutual trust and affection. They do not depend upon mere legends and myths. They are not predicated on the false conception that the Emperor is divine, and that the Japanese people are superior to other races and fated to rule the world."

More than thirty years after this declaration, the Emperor touched on this declaration in a press conference held in August 1977 and stated that his reference to the Five Clauses of the Charter Oath was intended to convey the following thought. "The Meiji Constitution was formed on the basis of the Five Clauses of the Charter Oath, and democracy is by no means a foreign import."

Immediately after the Emperor's Declaration of Humanity, MacArthur responded with a statement welcoming the declaration. "By it he undertakes a leading part in the democratization of his people. He squarely takes his stand for the future along liberal lines."[11]

Washington and the Allied Powers: SWNCC-228

On January 11, 1946, SWNCC-228 titled "Reform of the Japanese Governmental System" reached Tokyo from Washington. The document had been drafted by Hugh Borton, the head of the State Department's Office of Far Eastern Asian Affairs. SWNCC-228 contained all of the salient elements of constitutional reform including (1) sovereignty of the people, (2) respect for fundamental human rights, and (3) guarantee of the freedoms of speech, religion, and thought.

On the subject of the imperial system, the document stated that retention of the Emperor Institution in its present form was not consistent with the general objectives of the Occupation and argued, "The Emperor Institution should be reformed along more democratic lines." However, the document stipulated that the retention or abolition of the Emperor Institution would follow the "freely expressed will of the Japanese people." In other words, it did not contain any definitive instruction on whether the institution should be retained or abolished.

---

11 "Press Release: Gen. MacArthur Sees Liberalism in Imperial Rescript," (January 1, 1946), *Asahi Shinbun*, January 3, 1946.

Charles L. Kades (1906–1996)
A lawyer with a law degree from Harvard University, Kades joined the military after a stint with the State Department. As the key figure in drafting the Constitution of Japan, Kades was promoted to deputy chief of the Government Section and was known for his support of centrist forces in promoting the democratization of Japan. Kades left Japan in December 1948.

In other sections, SWNCC-228 placed special emphasis on the following two points. First, the ministers of State (including ministers of military services) must, in all cases, be civilians. Second, as outlined in the following passage, the Japanese side must be made to take the initiative.

Only as a last resort should the Supreme Commander order the Japanese Government to effect the above listed reforms, as the knowledge that they have been imposed by the Allies would materially reduce the possibility of their acceptance and support by the Japanese people for the future.[12]

On January 17, the Government Section met with a group of visiting representatives of the Far Eastern Advisory Commission. During this meeting, Tomas Confesor, the representative of the Philippines, asked point-blank, "Is GHQ preparing a draft of the constitution?" Charles Kades, Chief of the Public Administration Division, responded to this question with a "No." It was at this time that Kades provided the explanation that, "Revision of the constitution comes under the jurisdiction of the Far Eastern Advisory Commission."[13]

MacArthur met with the Far Eastern Advisory Commission on January 29, at which time he stated that the question of constitutional reform had been taken out of his hands by the Moscow Agreement [December agreement reached by U.S., U.K., and U.S.S.R. foreign ministers on the establishment of the Far Eastern

---

12 "Reform of the Japanese Government System (SWNCC 228)," GHQ/SCAP Records of Various Sections, Administrative Division: Box No. CHS-1.
13 Report of Government Section to Far Eastern Commission [Government Section Meeting with Far Eastern Commission], January 17, 1946, Records of the Far Eastern Commission, 1945–1952 Box No.94, GS; Report of Government Section to FEC, Sheet No. FEC(B)0485-0487, National Diet Library, Originals in U.S. National Archives & Records Administration, RG43.

Commission]. Previously, he had made certain suggestions and a committee was formed to revise the constitution. But insofar as his part in this work is concerned, he had ceased to take any action whatever. Thus, while admitting that he had made certain suggestions, MacArthur unambiguously denied that he had issued any order or directives on the matter of the constitution.[14]

It is notable that on January 25, the U.S. government delivered SWNCC-228 to the Far Eastern Advisory Commission while its representatives were still in Japan. It was based on this document that the Far Eastern Commission finalized its July 2, 1946, "Basic Principles for a New Japanese Constitution," which is discussed below.

Proposal on "Renunciation of War"

Through these two meetings with the Far Eastern Advisory Commission, GHQ was made aware of the keen interest that the Far Eastern Advisory Commission had in constitutional revision. As discussed below, Brigadier General Whitney, who headed the GHQ Government Section, had by this time completed the revision of election laws and the purge of designated government officials, and was ready to start work on rewriting the constitution. On January 24, Whitney issued a critical order to Kades who headed the Public Administration Division of the Government Section. Kades was tasked with investigating whether MacArthur as the Supreme Commander of the Allied Powers had the authority to undertake constitutional reform.

On the same day, Shidehara paid a visit to MacArthur to thank him for the penicillin that had been delivered to him to help with a severe illness. This meeting marked the first discussion on the subject of "renunciation of war," which later became widely known through the publication of MacArthur's *Reminiscences*. In his memoirs, MacArthur reveals what Shidehara had to say on this subject.

---

14 Memorandum by the Secretary General of the Far Eastern Advisory Commission (Johnson), January 30, 1946, *FRUS*, The Far East, vol. 8, Document 132, Tokyo.

He [Shidehara] then proposed that when the new constitution became final that it should include the so-called no-war clause. He also wanted it to prohibit any military establishment for Japan—any military establishment whatsoever. Two things would thus be accomplished. The old military party would be deprived of any instrument through which they could someday seize power, and the rest of the world would know that Japan never intended to wage war again.[15]

MacArthur notes that Shidehara added that Japan was a poor country and could not really afford to pour money into armaments anyway. Whatever resources the nation had left should go to bolstering the economy. This passage indicates that Shidehara was the first to propose the inclusion of the clause on the "renunciation of war" in the constitution. It should be noted, however, that much doubt has been cast on the accuracy or veracity of this passage.

It appears to be true that Shidehara was interested in the idea of renunciation of war at this time. Support for this can be found in the so-called Ōdaira Memo—notes taken by the daughter of Ōdaira Komatsuchi, an advisor to the Privy Council and close friend to Shidehara. As previously noted, Shidehara was fighting a serious illness at this time. According to the Ōdaira Memo, Shidehara had said that he could not die before ensuring the Emperor would be retained, and was very anxious to settle this matter before all else. Shidehara had then argued, "The only way to abolish war from the surface of the earth is to renounce war."[16] But no evidence can be found in the Ōdaira Memo or anywhere else that would support MacArthur's contention contained in his *Reminiscences* that Shidehara was the first to propose the inclusion of renunciation of war in the constitution.

Three days later, Whitney and Kades met with Shidehara to confer on the purge of government officials. It is reported that during this meeting held on January 28, Whitney suggested that Japan could improve its international image if the Emperor were to issue a rescript on the renunciation of war as he had done

---

15 MacArthur, Douglas, *Reminiscences*, McGraw-Hill, 1964, p. 303.
16 Ōtake Hideo, ed., *Sengo Nihon bōei mondai shiryōshū, dai 1-kan* [Documents of Japan's Postwar Defense Issues, vol. 1], Sanichi Shobō, 1991, pp. 66-67.

with his Declaration of Humanity.[17] In the present author's own discussions with him, Kades responded that it was probably Whitney who had proposed the wording of Article 9.[18]

William Macmahon Ball, the Australian political scientist and British Commonwealth representative to the Allied Council, later outlined the exchange between MacArthur and Shidehara in a cable sent to the Foreign Minister of Australia as follows.

"On the subject of renunciation of war, Shidehara asked MacArthur, 'What kind of military would we be allowed to maintain?' MacArthur replied, 'Japan will not be permitted to maintain any form of military.' Shidehara then asked, 'Would this be the renunciation of war?' to which MacArthur replied, 'Yes. I believe it would be to your advantage to proclaim the abandonment of war.'"[19]

While various theories have been posited, no definitive evidence has been found that would identify the original proposer of Article 9. However, the bulk of available historical documents and testimonies points to MacArthur and Shidehara reaching a consensus on adopting the renunciation of war as a means of defusing international criticism and a condition for maintaining the Emperor system.

Protecting the Emperor and the Mainichi Shinbun Scoop

On January 25, the day after his meeting with Shidehara, MacArthur sent a fateful cable to Washington on the status of the Emperor. "No specific and tangible evidence has been uncovered with regard to his exact activities which might connect him in varying degree with the political decisions of the Japanese Empire during the last decade." On the basis of this assessment, and from the perspective of facilitating the Occupation and guarding against communist influence, MacArthur concluded that the Emperor should not be tried as a war criminal. To this statement, MacArthur appended a veiled threat stating that if

17 Amakawa Akira, *Senryō-ka no Nihon* [Japan under the Occupation], Gendai Shiryō Shuppan, 2014, p. 126.
18 Kades, Charles, interview by Fukunaga Fumio, August 27, 1994.
19 Rix, Alan, ed., *Nihon senryō no hibi: Makumahon Bōru nikki* [Intermittent Diplomat: The Japan and Batavia Diaries of W. Macmahon Ball], Takemae Eiji and Kikuchi Osamu, trans., Iwanami Shoten, 1992, pp. 65–67.

the Emperor were to be tried, "It is quite possible that a minimum of a million troops would be required." MacArthur had come to believe that the Emperor had to be retained in the interest of maintaining a smooth and peaceful occupation, and had decided to come out clearly in favor of protecting and preserving the Emperor. From that moment on, GHQ was tasked with achieving the twin goals of promoting democratization while preserving the imperial system.

On February 1, *Mainichi Shinbun* shocked the country by printing one of the draft constitutions that had been drawn up by the Matsumoto Committee. The draft in question had been formulated by Tokyo Imperial University Professor Miyazawa Toshiyoshi, a member of the Matsumoto Committee.

The Matsumoto draft was formulated in line with the above-mentioned "four Matsumoto principles." As such, it recognized the sovereignty of the Emperor and had almost nothing to say about the Emperor's supreme powers. The rights of "subjects" had been reworded to be the rights of "the people." However, many of these rights came with the caveat, "necessary restrictions may apply for the preservation of public order."

Because it left the status of the Emperor substantially unchanged, GHQ concluded that the Matsumoto draft was "extremely conservative in character."[20] Brigadier General Whitney, the Chief of the Government Section, commented, "the reactionary group carrying the ball on constitutional reform were way off the beam that you [MacArthur] could agree to."

On the same day, Whitney advised MacArthur on the question of whether the authority of the Supreme Commander of the Allied Powers extended to constitutional revision. Drawing on the report that had been submitted by Kades, Whitney concluded that the Supreme Commander did have authority "in the absence of any policy decision by the Far Eastern Commission on the subject."[21] On February 2, the day after the Mainichi scoop, Whitney submitted a memorandum recommending that "guidelines be given to them" before the submission of the government draft.

---

20 Memorandum for the Supreme Commander, Subject: Constitutional Reform (Matsumoto Draft), February 2, 1946, Alfred Hussey Papers; Constitution File No.1, Doc. No.2, National Diet Library.
21 Memorandum for the Supreme Commander, Subject: Constitutional Reform, February 1, 1946, Alfred Hussey Papers; National Diet Library.

Nine Days Given to Government Section

On February 3, MacArthur and Whitney put together the so-called "MacArthur Notes" consisting of three basic points on constitutional revision (MacArthur's Three Basic Points). These were (1) The Emperor is the head of state, (2) Japan renounces war even for preserving its own security, and (3) the feudal system of Japan will cease.[22]

On the following day, February 4, Whitney called a meeting with Kades and all the other members of the Government Section and announced that the Government Section would "sit as a Constitutional Convention." The deadline for the project was set at February 12. On the day following the deadline, Whitney was scheduled to meet with Foreign Minister Yoshida and other members of the Japanese government to discuss the constitutional draft produced by the Japanese side.

Whitney addressed the members of the Government Section. The Japanese government draft was, he said, "expected to be strongly rightist in tone. I intend to convince the Foreign Minister and his group, however, that the only possibility of retaining the Emperor and the remnants of their own power is by their acceptance and approval of a Constitution that will force a decisive swing to the left."[23] Noting that Japan had shifted dramatically toward the "right" during the war, the idea was to push Japan toward the "left."

The Government Section was given only nine days to complete its task. The members did not even have time to wonder why this task was being assigned to them in the first place. With Kades standing at the center of the project, seven sub-committees were immediately formed. The work went on with very little rest or sleep. Following exhaustive discussions and debates, the final draft was completed in the late hours of February 12 (Table 2-2).

Even as the Government Section was toiling over its draft, other initiatives were also moving forward. Having obtained the approval of the Emperor, the

---

22 Three Basic Points Stated by Supreme Commander to be "Must" in Constitutional Revision, About February 4, 1946, Alfred Hussey Papers; Constitution File No.1, Document No.5, National Diet Library.
23 Takayanagi et al., *Nihonkoku kenpō seitei no katei, 1*, pp. 100–107.

Matsumoto Committee formally submitted its draft constitution to GHQ on February 8. The draft was entitled "Gist of the Revision of the Constitution" (hereinafter, Matsumoto Draft) and was based on Matsumoto's own four principles. Appended to this submission was a document entitled "General Explanation of the Constitutional Revision" that Matsumoto himself had penned.

February 13, 1946: GHQ versus the Government of Japan

On February 13, 1946, Whitney, Kades, and other representatives of GHQ met for discussions with State Minister Matsumoto, Foreign Minister Yoshida, and others from the Japanese side.

Whitney started the meeting by commenting on the draft constitution submitted by the Japanese government on February 8. "The draft of constitutional revision which you submitted to us the other day is wholly unacceptable to the Supreme Commander as a document of freedom and democracy." Whitney then presented a copy of the draft constitution that had been prepared by the Government Section (hereinafter, GHQ Draft). According to GHQ records, "At this statement of General Whitney, the Japanese officials were obviously stunned—Mr. Yoshida's face particularly manifesting shock and concern." Whitney then continued.

As you may or may not know, the Supreme Commander has been unyielding in his defense of your Emperor against increasing pressure from the outside to render him subject to war criminal investigations. He has thus defended the Emperor because he considered that that was the cause of right and justice, and will continue along that course to the extent of his ability. But, gentlemen, the Supreme Commander is not omnipotent. He feels, however, that acceptance of the provisions of this new Constitution would render the Emperor practically unassailable. He feels that it would bring much closer the day of your freedom from control by the Allied Powers, and that it would provide your people with the essential freedom which the Allied Powers demand in their behalf.

The Supreme Commander has directed me to offer this Constitution to

Table 2–2 Government Section Organization Chart for Drafting the Constitution of Japan

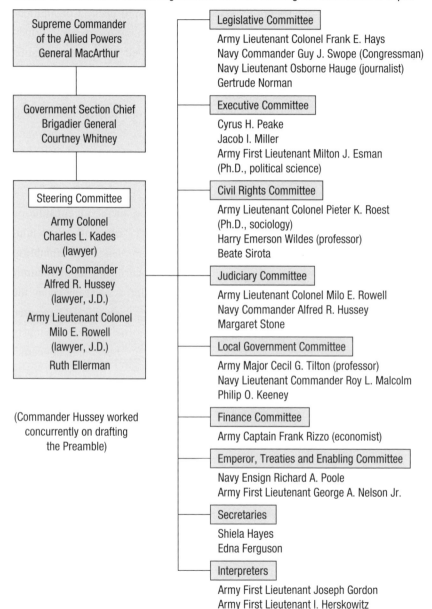

Supreme Commander of the Allied Powers General MacArthur	**Legislative Committee**
	Army Lieutenant Colonel Frank E. Hays
	Navy Commander Guy J. Swope (Congressman)
	Navy Lieutenant Osborne Hauge (journalist)
	Gertrude Norman
Government Section Chief Brigadier General Courtney Whitney	**Executive Committee**
	Cyrus H. Peake
	Jacob I. Miller
	Army First Lieutenant Milton J. Esman (Ph.D., political science)
Steering Committee	**Civil Rights Committee**
Army Colonel Charles L. Kades (lawyer)	Army Lieutenant Colonel Pieter K. Roest (Ph.D., sociology)
	Harry Emerson Wildes (professor)
	Beate Sirota
Navy Commander Alfred R. Hussey (lawyer, J.D.)	**Judiciary Committee**
	Army Lieutenant Colonel Milo E. Rowell
Army Lieutenant Colonel Milo E. Rowell (lawyer, J.D.)	Navy Commander Alfred R. Hussey Margaret Stone
Ruth Ellerman	**Local Government Committee**
	Army Major Cecil G. Tilton (professor)
	Navy Lieutenant Commander Roy L. Malcolm
	Philip O. Keeney
(Commander Hussey worked concurrently on drafting the Preamble)	**Finance Committee**
	Army Captain Frank Rizzo (economist)
	Emperor, Treaties and Enabling Committee
	Navy Ensign Richard A. Poole
	Army First Lieutenant George A. Nelson Jr.
	Secretaries
	Shiela Hayes
	Edna Ferguson
	Interpreters
	Army First Lieutenant Joseph Gordon
	Army First Lieutenant I. Herskowitz

Compiled by the author from Suzuki Akinori, *Nihonkoku kenpō o unda misshitsu no kokonokakan* [Nine Days behind Closed Doors that Gave Birth to the Constitution of Japan], Sōgensha, 1995.

your government and party for your adoption and your presentation to the people with his full backing if you care to do so, yet he does not require this of you.[24]

MacArthur was in a hurry. While it is true that he was dissatisfied with the Matsumoto Draft, that alone would not explain his uncompromising demand for speed. Having already decided to retain the Emperor, MacArthur wanted to make sure the Far Eastern Commission would not have a chance to intervene and upset his plans. By nature, MacArthur disliked the interference of others. Having made up his mind to maintain the Emperor system, MacArthur could easily foresee that the Far Eastern Commission would stand in his way if given a chance. As the supreme policy making organization of the Occupation of Japan, the Far Eastern Commission included the Soviet Union and Australia in its membership, countries which had radically different ideas on retaining the Emperor. In addition to these considerations, MacArthur had a second reason to be in a hurry. With the general election for the House of Representatives scheduled for April, MacArthur wanted to have his draft constitution ready for presentation to the people of Japan in the election.

Japanese Government Resists, Then Accepts

The GHQ Draft contained provisions that the Japanese side had not even imagined would be included. Among these were the Emperor as symbol of the state and the renunciation of war. Yoshida and Matsumoto, who had directly received the GHQ Draft, turned ashen with shock. But the shock was no less severe for Prime Minister Shidehara, who learned of the GHQ Draft through the reports of others. For a period of six days, the GHQ Draft was locked away in a safe in the Prime Minister's residence and its contents were not shared with the Cabinet.

In the estimation of Matsumoto, known as a great legal scholar, the GHQ Draft was a poorly concocted document that had been put together by a group of ignorant foreigners. For example, the GHQ Draft had opted for a unicameral

---

24 Takayanagi et al., *Nihonkoku kenpō seitei no katei*, *1*, pp. 327–329.

parliament. Asked for an explanation, Whitney had replied that Japan did not need a bicameral structure because, unlike the United States, Japan was not composed of states. Stunned by this response, Matsumoto would later comment that Whitney did not understand the parliamentary system. But the proposal for a unicameral parliament seems to have been a conscious ploy. Predicting that the Japanese side would demand a bicameral structure, the Government Section was ready to cede this point in order to "stand firm on more important matters."

Matsumoto approached Whitney requesting that he be given another chance to explain the Matsumoto Draft. The argument he made was that the Matsumoto and GHQ drafts appeared to be diametrically opposed but in their underlying principles the two did not stand as widely apart as seemed at first sight.

Whitney rejected this plea and increased the pressure on the Japanese side. On February 18, Whitney said, "Unless this issue is met forthrightly by the Japanese Government, …it is quite possible that a constitution might be forced on Japan by the Allied Powers which would render the term 'drastic'…far too moderate." Whitney continued to up the ante. "Unless I hear from the Cabinet within 48 hours, …the Supreme Commander will take the constitution to the people directly."[25]

The Cabinet met on the following day, February 19. The session started with a dire pronouncement made by a pale and shaken Matsumoto. "A matter of extreme gravity has occurred." Prime Minister Shidehara, Home Minister Mitsuchi Chūzō and Justice Minister Iwata Chūzō were shocked to learn of the turn of events and declared, "We cannot accept this."[26] The Cabinet was unable to arrive at a consensus.

On February 21, Shidehara visited MacArthur and was told, "The American draft endeavors to retain the Emperor." The Cabinet met again on February 23 and concluded that there was no choice but to accept the GHQ Draft. At the end of the cabinet meeting, Shidehara, Yoshida, and Chief Cabinet Secretary Narahashi Wataru left to report the matter to the Emperor. It is reported that the Emperor responded in the following manner. "If that is what they are insisting,

---

25 Ibid., pp. 366–369.
26 Shindō and Shimokōbe, *Ashida Hitoshi nikki*, (February 19, 1946).

approving the draft should be acceptable. It should be acceptable to alter Article 1 to symbolic Emperor to mirror the British case. The voice of the people is the voice of the gods. This has been the spirit of our ancestors."[27]

Having obtained the Emperor's approval, the government finally began to work seriously on the GHQ Draft. A group was formed around Matsumoto to formulate the text of the constitution based on the GHQ Draft. Under unrelenting pressure from the Government Section to speed up the process, a revised draft was compiled within the government and hand-carried by Matsumoto to GHQ on March 4. This draft then underwent a series of revisions that were completed on March 5 following extensive discussion and debate between the American and Japanese sides, which at times became very heated.

The Emperor had stated that accepting the GHQ Draft "could not be helped."[28] But in reality, the Emperor was greatly relieved to see that the imperial system would be retained and that succession to the throne would not require the approval of the Diet.

At around this time, the question of the Emperor's abdication had been broached in an article appearing in *Yomiuri Hōchi Shinbun* that purported to record an "interview with an unnamed high official (Higashikuni) of the Imperial Household Ministry." Distressed by the article, Deputy Grand Chamberlain Kinoshita Michio wrote in his diary that it threatened to bring to naught all that MacArthur had done. For this reason, MacArthur headquarters was working frantically to achieve as soon as possible a proclamation of a democratic constitution established by the will of the people so as to push back the global tide against the Emperor. Thus, they were pressuring and demanding the release of such a constitution at the earliest possible date.[29]

---

27 Matsumura Kenzō, *Sandai kaikoroku* [Memoirs of Three Generations], Tōyō Keizai Shinpōsha, 1964, p. 290.
28 Shindō and Shimokōbe, *Ashida Hitoshi nikki*, (February 19, 1946).
29 Kinoshita Michio, *Sokkin nisshi* [Journal of an Attendant], Chūō Kōron Shinsha, 2017, (March 5, 1946).

Release as Government Draft

On March 6, the draft that had been jointly written by the Government Section and the Japanese side was released to the public under the title of "Outline of a Draft for a Revised Constitution." This document was attributed to the Japanese government. In the evening of March 6, Commander Hussey hurriedly left Atsugi Airfield to hand-deliver a copy to Washington.

This government draft was totally different from the initial Matsumoto Draft. Having gained a general idea of the Matsumoto Draft as scooped by *Mainichi Shinbun*, the public was surprised and confused by the contents of the new government draft.

Following the release of the draft, the General Affairs Bureau of the Foreign Ministry catalogued the comments and reactions to the draft in a document entitled "International and Domestic Opinions on the Draft of the Constitution Revision." The document summarized its findings in the following words: "Many found it odd that it differed so conspicuously from what the public was previously informed to be the government draft." "The wording gives the impression of being a translation." The review concluded, "The above impressions were strongly reinforced by the inclusion of the peculiar provision on the 'renunciation of war.' Consequently, the draft gives the impression that it is a draft treaty more than a draft constitution." However, regarding the contents of the Draft for a Revised Constitution, the review noted the following positive reactions: "Efforts have been made to harmonize the maintenance of the Emperor system with popular sovereignty." "The contents provide a sense of relief."

The Progressive and Liberal Parties announced that they supported the Draft for a Revised Constitution in principle. For instance, commenting on the fact that the government draft preserved the Emperor system, advocated respect for fundamental human rights and renounced war, the Liberal Party stated that these were in complete agreement with the principles contained in the draft constitution produced by the party.

The Socialist Party also indicated its support and commented that it was an expression of enthusiasm for the faithful implementation of the provisions of the Potsdam Declaration and democratic politics. On the other hand, the Socialist

Party did note certain reservations, commenting that too many matters were left under the supreme authority of the Emperor.

The Communist Party effectively voiced its opposition by proposing the adoption of five provisions, including the abolition of the Emperor and explicit enumeration of the rights of working people. In any case, it can be surmised that with the exception of the Communist Party, the political parties in general welcomed the government draft.

Reorganization of the Government Section

The Government Section was the only GHQ section that worked on drafting the constitution, which earned it the status of "MacArthur's political brain." Thus, it would thereafter function as the "engine of democratization." To properly equip it for its newly gained status, the Government Section henceforth went through a series of reorganizations.

As the first step, the Public Administration Division of the Government Section was reorganized in February 1946. The Public Administration Division, which was in charge of reforms, was sub-divided into six branches: Legislative and Liaison Branch (headed by G. Swope, later replaced by J. Williams), Political Parties Branch (P. Roest), Local Government Branch (C. Tilton), Government Powers Branch (A. Hussey), Review and Reports Branch (O. Hauge), and Opinions Branch (F. Rizzo). In May 1946, the six branches were elevated to the status of divisions.[30]

Kades was elevated from his position as Chief of the Public Administration Division to Deputy Chief of the Government Section. In his new post, Kades developed his relationship of trust with Whitney as he prepared to play a key role vis-à-vis the Japanese government as the person in charge of implementing the early reforms for democratization. All the important position papers and reports generated within the Government Section would henceforth cross the desk of Kades either in the form of internal memos referred to as "memorandum for the record" or memos addressed to the chief of the Government Section

---

30 Amakawa and Fukunaga, eds., *GHQ Minsei-kyoku shiryō, bekkan.*

referred to as "memo for the chief."

The elevation of the six branches to division status was designed to set the stage for promoting various legal reforms in line with the new constitution once it had been promulgated. Swope and Williams would focus on reforming the Diet, Roest on political parties and election laws, and Tilton on reforming local government.

By early 1946, the power structure within GHQ was shifting from the conservative Staff Sections that Yoshida Shigeru had been negotiating with to a Government Section committed to actively pursuing democratic reforms—a shift that would mark the start of a long of line of "pilgrimages to the Government Section" by Japanese leaders. Seeking endorsement in this way to gain authority was reminiscent of the "pilgrimages to *Zagyosō*" by Japanese politicians in the late 1920s and 1930s as they hurried to pay their respects to Saionji Kinmochi, the last of the Meiji founding fathers.

The Allied Powers and the Constitution of Japan: Far Eastern Commission Erupts

State Department's Quandary and Response

The State Department had been given no prior notice or warning of the March 6 release of the draft constitution. What was most galling was that the State Department did not even have a copy of Outline of a Draft for a Revised Constitution. But the State Department was not in a position to directly contact GHQ on this matter, and had to go through the Joint Chiefs of Staff and the Army Chief of Staff.

Hugh Borton, who headed the State Department's Japanese Affairs Division, described the situation in Washington as follows.

If we admitted that General MacArthur's announcement had taken not only the American delegation to the FEC but the Department of State completely by surprise, it would have revealed the lack of communication between SCAP and Washington on this vital issue.... But the controversy concerning the commission's authority in constitutional matters was further complicated by disagreement within the American delegation on the strategy that the United States should follow. The armed services representative maintained that General McCoy should veto any statement proposed by the FEC that was critical of General MacArthur or of his draft constitution. On the other hand, Dr. Blakeslee [U.S. government representative on the FEC Steering Committee] and I, with the full approval of Division Chief Vincent, took the position that some of the criticisms of General MacArthur's actions were justified.[31]

The Office of the Political Adviser, the State Department's agency in Tokyo, had also been left out of the loop.

Max Bishop of the Office of the Political Adviser cabled the following message to Washington on March 8. "There is some danger that in future the Japanese may regard this draft plan as having been prepared for them rather than as having been created by them. Should this eventuality materialize, Japan's attitude towards its new Constitution, if adopted as appears likely, might be radically altered." In a second cable written on March 19, Bishop added the following comments to express his concern. "The majority of the Japanese people believe the draft is an American product, which reduces the possibility that the Constitution will be accepted and supported by the people over the long run."[32]

Setting aside the surprise of not being informed in advance, there was nothing in the draft itself that was surprising to Washington. As reported by Borton, "[It] seems to be consistent with the SWNCC document.... The draft of the proposed constitution goes well beyond the recommendations of SWNCC papers to ensure a peacefully inclined and responsible government in Japan."[33]

31 Borton, Hugh, *Spanning Japan's Modern Century: The Memoirs of Hugh Borton*, Lexington Books, 2002, pp. 169–170.
32 Takemae Eiji and Okabe Fuminobu, *Nihonkoku kenpō kenshō dai 1-kan: Kenpō seiteishi* [Verifying the Constitution of Japan, vol. 1: History of the Drafting of the Constitution of Japan], Shōgakukan, 2000, p. 241.
33 Borton, *Spanning Japan's Modern Century*, p. 170.

Counterattack by the Far Eastern Commission

As the supreme policymaking body for the Occupation of Japan, the Far Eastern Commission was infuriated by the unexpected release of the draft constitution.

MacArthur had clearly said, "The question of constitutional reform has been taken out of my hands." It therefore strained credulity that the Japanese government, which was under MacArthur's control, would on its own accord suddenly release its draft for constitutional revision. With such comments as we have been "circumvented" and "blindfolded," the Far Eastern Commission could hardly contain its ire. A British diplomat filed the following report with London: "This was obviously written in English and later translated. The draft is completely American in tone. A constitution like this will not last long after the Occupation."[34]

On March 20, the Far Eastern Commission submitted two requests to the U.S. government. The first called for a report on deliberations that had taken place in the Diet on the draft constitution, and the second requested that ample opportunity be given to the Japanese people to consider draft constitutions other than the one that had been released. Along with these requests, the Commission proposed the postponement of the election of the House of Representatives scheduled for April. They felt that not enough time had been given for democratic forces to develop and emerge in Japan.

Caught between GHQ and the Far Eastern Commission, the U.S. government found itself in an uncomfortable position. On April 9, General McCoy, the Commission's U.S. representative, conveyed the Commission's three requests to MacArthur. Following this, on April 10, the Commission requested that someone representing MacArthur be dispatched to Washington to explain the situation. But MacArthur avoided responding to these requests and allowed a whole month to go by. This failure to act only deepened the rift between the Commission and MacArthur.

---

34 Takemae and Okabe, *Nihonkoku kenpō kenshō dai 1-kan*, p. 242.

2. From the Purge to the Birth of the New Diet

The First Postwar Election of the House of Representatives: April 1946

First Purge of Public Officials

As previously noted, GHQ had blocked an earlier Japanese proposal for holding a lower house election. The official reason given for the delay was that the revision of election laws remained under consideration. However, of greater importance was the need to prevent the return of authoritarian elements and wartime cooperators to the newly elected Diet. In the estimation of GHQ, the majority of the Japanese public was politically immature. GHQ reasoned that due to this immaturity, it was highly probable that people who had made a name for themselves since the prewar years would be elected to the Diet.[35] To allow a fresh slate of politicians to be seated, there was a pressing need to formulate policies for purging veteran politicians with questionable or undesirable backgrounds from public office.

Concerning the so-called "purge of public officials," the conflict between the Government Section and the G2 Staff Section under Brigadier General Willoughby is well known. Mark Gayn, the *Chicago Sun* correspondent in Tokyo, describes these developments under the December 20, 1945, entry in his book, *Japan Diary*:

> A few days ago, the conflict between the two camps broke into the open. The occasion was a hush-hush conference called on the sixth floor of the Dai-Ichi Building to consider a draft directive purging war criminals from Japanese political life. Representatives of all the sections in Headquarters were present, and a split developed almost at once.

---

35 Fukunaga, ed., *GHQ Minsei-kyoku shiryō, 2*, pp. 53–55.

The opponents of the draft brought forth a variety of arguments:

(a) A sweeping purge would throw Japan into chaos, and even conceivably produce a revolution;

(b) If a purge is necessary, it must be carried out gradually, to give the Japanese a breathing spell after each blow; and

(c) Only the highest leaders should be purged, for discipline calls for obedience to orders, and subordinate officials had no choice but to obey.

The opposition to the purge included a solid phalanx of the four military staff sections, spearheaded by spokesman for Military Intelligence [Willoughby]. Siding with them was one of the State Department's representatives. The main support of the purge came from the Government Section, with scattered backing from other Headquarters branches.... Sharp words were traded during the four-hour debate, and a lot of red herrings were dragged across the table. But in the end, compromises were made, and the original purge directive emerged in a greatly watered-down form.

Two directives were issued by GHQ on January 4, 1946. The first (SCAPIN-548: Abolition of Certain Political Parties, Associations, Societies and other Organizations) ordered the dissolution of ultra-nationalist organizations. The second (SCAPIN-550: Removal and Exclusion of Undesirable Personnel from Public Office) ordered the so-called purge of undesirable persons from public office.

The latter directive covered seven categories of personnel: (A) war criminals; (B) career military and naval personnel, special police and officials of the war ministries; (C) influential members of ultra-nationalistic, terrorist, or secret patriotic societies; (D) persons influential in the activities of the Imperial Rule Assistance Association, Imperial Rule Assistance Parliamentarians, and the Political Association of Great Japan; (E) officers of financial and development organizations involved in Japanese expansions; (F) governors of occupied territories; and (G) additional militarists and ultra-nationalists.

Of special interest is the composition of category G. The Government Section, which had jurisdiction over the purge, was authorized to determine who was a militarist and who was an ultra-nationalist. As a "memorandum case," the Government Section was empowered to make this determination by itself without external consultation. It is notable that the category G provision was later applied in purging Hatoyama Ichirō, Ishibashi Tanzan, and Hirano Rikizō.

Government Section and Revision of Election Laws

Even as the purge from public office was moving forward, Whitney began to work on the revision of election laws. On the last day of 1945, a meeting was held at GHQ to examine a proposal submitted by the government of Japan for the revision of election laws. Present at the meeting were 21 staff members of the Government Section, plus others from the Office of the Political Adviser, the Civil Information and Education Section, G2, and the Civil Intelligence Section. The participants overwhelmingly supported adding further revisions to the Japanese draft.

On January 2, 1946, Whitney convened a second meeting to re-examine the proposal. Participation in this second meeting was restricted to members of the Government Section. The large constituency system was welcomed because it would deliver a blow to old, established interests and to backroom fixers. Other features of the proposal, such as lowering the voting age and enfranchising women, were also welcomed as being "natural and obvious measures." On the other hand, the participants were divided on the questions of the methods of restricted plural voting and actually writing in the candidate's name.[36]

Those who favored restricted plural voting (Pieter Roest and others) argued that it would contribute to the democratization of Japan by improving the chances for new political parties and new candidates. As for write-in ballots that would require voters to write the name of the candidate they were voting for, it was argued that this would be proof of the public's level of education, and that this method was favored by Japanese public opinion.

Those who stood in opposition (Milo Rowell and others) argued that the plural voting method constituted an incomplete exercise of civil rights, and that

---

36 Ibid., pp. 52–87.

it should therefore be replaced by a perfect plural voting. On the issue of write-in ballots, it was argued that this would lead to cheating and other irregularities by election officials and would also have an undesirable impact on both voting behavior and election results. This group therefore argued in favor of printed ballots. At the end of the debate, a show of hands indicated that those who stood in opposition were in the majority with a count of "fifteen to four."

But Whitney simply ignored the vote. Instead of siding with the majority view opposing the two provisions, he gave the nod to those who favored the Japanese proposal. Whitney's decision was based on the judgment that, since the purge from public office was already underway, upholding the Japanese proposal and early implementation of a general election would expedite the process of "democratization."

Whitney's decision greatly encouraged the Government Section. Justin Williams, a staff member of the Legislative Branch of the Government Section, has commented on Whitney's decision. Williams wrote that prior to this point, all the memoranda drafted by the Government Section had fallen into the GHQ's bureaucratic quagmire. However, Whitney's decision had changed everything and everybody "rejoiced at having a boss who could and would throw his weight around."[37] Whitney had resolved the issues of the purge and revision of election laws by excluding the other sections. This accomplishment significantly strengthened the position of the Government Section in GHQ.

In accordance with Whitney's recommendation, MacArthur issued a directive (SCAPIN-584) to the Japanese government on January 12, advising the government that it was authorized to hold a general election of members of House of Representatives at any time after March 15, 1946.

The Shock

The directive on the purge from public office was released with no prior notification given to the Japanese government. In the sense that it surprised and

---

37 Williams, Justin, *Japan's Political Revolution under MacArthur: A Participants Account*, University of Georgia Press, 1979, p. 78.

shocked the Japanese side, the directive stood together with the earlier Civil Liberties Directive. It was immediately assumed that the purge would affect several members of the current cabinet. These were Home Affairs Minister Horikiri, Agriculture and Forestry Minister Matsumura, and Education Minister Maeda Tamon.

Prime Minister Shidehara was ill at this time with severe pneumonia but expressed his dismay from his sickbed. "Mac has done it again with this ridiculous directive."[38] Shidehara even considered en masse resignation of the Cabinet. But he relented and agreed to stay on under the advice of the Emperor and the urging of Matsumura and other Cabinet members. Ultimately, six members of the Cabinet would be purged from public office. In addition to the three previously mentioned ministers, Transportation Minister Tanaka Takeo, State Minister Matsumoto, and Chief Cabinet Secretary Tsugita were purged and removed from office. Shidehara survived through a reorganization of the Cabinet.

Because the purge covered all Diet members who had been nominated by the Imperial Rule Assistance Association Political Framework Council, the purge directive threw the political parties into turmoil. Of the 274 Diet members belonging to the Progressive Party, a total of 260 were purged, including the party's president and secretary-general. A mere fourteen members, including Saitō Takao, were excluded from the purge. In the case of the Liberal Party, 30 members out of a total of 43 were purged. In the Socialist Party, ten members out of a total of 17 were purged, and in the Cooperative Party, 21 members out of a total of 23 were purged.

In directing the purge from public office, GHQ had opted for an extreme surgical procedure that would forcibly detach the political parties from their most prominent members of the prewar and wartime periods. Having lost their old leaders in one fell swoop, the parties were now faced with the existential challenge of filling the vacuum that had been left.

---

38 Matsumura Kenzō, *Sandai kaikoroku* [Memoirs of Three Generations], Tōyō Keizai Shinpōsha, 1964, p. 272.

Choosing between the Popular Front and the Anti-Communist League

The shock of the purge combined with the upwelling of popular movements to promote the establishment of a "democratic front." This broad-based movement brought together a wide range of democratic elements that rallied around the Socialist and Communist Parties.

On January 10, 1946, Yamakawa Hitoshi, widely known as a socialist from the prewar years, called for the "immediate formation of a popular front" and the gathering together of all democratic forces.

On January 12, Nosaka Sanzō returned to Japan for the first time in fifteen years. Nosaka, a leader of the Communist Party of Japan, had defected to the Soviet Union in 1931 and had been engaged in political activities in Yan'an, China since 1940. Nosaka had traveled to Moscow in early October 1945, and he returned to Japan via Mukden (present-day Shenyang), Pyongyang, and Seoul. It is believed that in his meetings with Soviet leaders, Nosaka had obtained the consent of the Soviet leadership on some salient aspects of postwar policy. Concerning the political system, the imperial institutions would be abolished but the Emperor would be retained, and the Shōwa Emperor would be pushed to abdicate.[39]

On January 14, Nosaka and Tokuda Kyūichi released a joint statement in which the two moved away from earlier demands for the immediate removal of the Emperor and the abolition of the emperor system. Instead, this moderate statement took the position that the matter of the Emperor should be determined in accordance with the will of the people at a later date when Japan had been properly democratized. On the same day, the *Asahi* editorialized, "A powerful and truly unified popular front built upon a well-established foundation of popular organizations should be launched as soon as possible." On the following day, January 15, the *Yomiuri* wrote, "The time is now ripe for forming a democratic front."

On January 26, a "welcome home people's conference" was held for Nosaka at the Hibiya Public Hall (Yamakawa Hitoshi headed the organizing committee).

---

39 Wada Haruki, *Rekishi toshite no Nosaka Sanzō* [Nosaka Sanzō as History], Heibonsha, 1995, See chapter 4.

The event served as the virtual launching of the movement. Taking the podium, Nosaka spoke of building a "Communist Party loved by the people" and called for the formation of a "popular front" comprising a wide spectrum of democratic elements. However, caught in the vortex of distrust and extreme wariness that the Socialist Party had for the Communist Party, the movement would collapse even before the election—leaving as its only remnant the Democratic People's Front of Kyoto. The Socialist Party had rejected working with the Communist Party in a joint struggle and had instead resolved to form the "Democratic League for National Salvation" in May following the election.

Hatoyama Ichirō of the Liberal Party felt deeply threatened by such popular front movements and on February 22 called for a gathering of conservative forces unified around the principles of "anti-communism." Hatoyama warned that the destruction of ultra-rightist fascism was now in danger of being immediately replaced by ultra-leftist extremism. To protect and save the nation from this fate, Hatoyama called on the leaders of the conservative parties to put aside minor differences and to unify under a common cause for establishing forces resolutely committed to political stability.[40]

The other conservative parties remained suspicious of Hatoyama, reasoning that his call for unity was nothing more than a ploy for aggrandizing the Liberal Party. On the other hand, GHQ took Hatoyama's anti-communist statement very seriously, a fact that would later play a key role in the decision to purge Hatoyama from public life.

House of Representatives Election of April 1946

Japan's first postwar general election (the 22nd election of the House of Representatives) was held on April 10, 1946. As a result of the enfranchisement of women and the lowering of the voting age, the number of eligible voters had more than doubled from the previous election, increasing from less than 15 million voters to about 37 million. The number of candidates for the 466 lower house seats came to a total of 2,770. Of all the candidates, 2,624 were

---

40 *Asahi Shinbun*, February 22, 1946.

running for the first time, while the number of female candidates came to 79. Meanwhile, the total number of political parties came to 363. Without doubt, the revision of the election laws and the purge had had an immense impact on the Japanese political scene. Anxious to ensure a democratic election, the Occupation forces were mobilized in large numbers to monitor the election with U.S. military personnel posted at voting stations.

The voting rate reached 72.1 percent. Having garnered a total of 140 seats, the Liberal Party emerged as the leading party, followed by the Progressive Party with 94 seats, the Socialist Party with 93 seats, the Cooperative Party with fourteen seats, and the Communist Party with five seats. Finally, minor parties and independents took a total of 118 seats. (A run-off election was held for two seats that did not reach the legally required minimum number of votes.)

The Liberal Party outperformed the Progressive Party that had sprung from the former Great Japan Political Association. This in itself was taken as evidence of a "re-direction of popular sentiment." Also noteworthy was the fact that the Socialist Party had increased its seats five-fold to 93, becoming a leading political force in the Diet. No less noteworthy was the fact that the Communist Party was seated in the Diet for the first time. Among those elected to office, a total of 375 (81 percent of the total) had never before served in the Diet, and a total of 39 were women.

MacArthur expressed his satisfaction with these results.

It was Lincoln who said the people are wiser than their rulers. We have seen that these words also apply to Japan. The Japanese people responded joyfully to the opportunity to express their will freely. They rejected the extreme political philosophies of both the left and the right, and chose a broad, middle road. Thus, democracy has made a healthy advance.[41]

---

41 *Yomiuri Shinbun*, April 25, 1946.

The Shocking Purge of Hatoyama: Formation of First Yoshida Cabinet

Shidehara Cabinet's Efforts to Form a Ruling Coalition

Because the House of Representatives election yielded no single majority party, the political situation remained in flux for some time. It was widely believed that the Shidehara Cabinet would retire after the election to make way for a party-based Cabinet. Contrary to these expectations, however, the day following the election, Chief Cabinet Secretary Narahashi Wataru announced that "the Shidehara Cabinet will not resign en masse." The cabinet's decision to remain in office would soon be referred to as the "stay-put stratagem."

Commenting on this event, Narahashi would later recount, "I was encouraged by the General Headquarters."[42] The first action that Narahashi took was to call on independents and minor parties to come together around the Progressive Party to form a coalition "to the left of the Liberal Party and to the right of the Socialist Party." Soon thereafter, Narahashi extended a hand even to the Socialist Party and attempted to hold talks with Nishio Suehiro and Hirano Rikizō. On April 16, Shidehara affirmed Narahashi's announcement of April 11. "It would be irresponsible for me to throw down the reins of government unless and until the Liberal, Progressive, and Socialist Parties form a coalition that would create a stable political foundation and thereby present a clear outlook for the smooth implementation of constitutional revision."[43] On the following day, April 17, Shidehara formally joined the Progressive Party and pledged that he was prepared to serve as the party's president.

Faced with this "stay-put stratagem," the Socialist Party criticized Shidehara's efforts to form a ruling coalition as being "contrary to the constitution." On April 19, the Socialist Party joined forces with the Liberal, Cooperative, and Communist Parties to form a "Four-Party Joint Committee for Overthrowing the Shidehara Cabinet." This would become the first and the last time the Liberal and Communist Parties would join forces in a common

---

42 Narahashi Wataru, *Gekiryū ni sao sashite* [Riding the Rapid Currents], Tsubasa Shoin, 1968, p. 127.
43 Shidehara Peace Foundation, ed., *Shidehara Kijūrō* [Shidehara Kijūrō], Shidehara Peace Foundation, 1955, p. 700.

cause. As pressure continued to build, Welfare Minister Ashida tendered his resignation on the same day. Ultimately, the Shidehara Cabinet was left with no alternative but to dissolve itself on April 22, leaving a political vacuum that would be remain unfilled for a full month.

Hatoyama Purged

On April 23, 1946, Shidehara turned to Hatoyama urging him to form a cabinet. At around this time, rumors were beginning to spread that Hatoyama would soon be purged. It is true that various complaints and documents had been delivered to GHQ that depicted Hatoyama in an unfavorable light. For instance, these documents showed that as a prewar Chief Cabinet Secretary, Hatoyama had played a key role in the Conference on Eastern Strategies, where decisions had been made on hardline China policies, including policies for aggressive intervention in Manchuria and Mongolia. Other documents outlined the role he had played as Minister of Education in the Takigawa Incident, which involved the firing of Professor Takigawa Yukitoki of Kyoto Imperial University, a noted liberal scholar of jurisprudence.

Hatoyama had already been targeted for criticism. On April 6, a banquet held with foreign correspondents had turned into an eight-hour long inquisition on his various positions, including why he had heaped praise on Hitler and Mussolini in his book *Sekai no kao* [Figures of the World]. Notwithstanding these ominous signs, Hatoyama moved ahead to form a cabinet. His decision to do so could be attributed in part to his natural optimism. But there were also other reasons. Hatoyama prided himself on having refused to join the Imperial Rule Assistance Association and considered himself to have been a resister during the war years. Additionally, the excitement of emerging victorious from the general election made the prospect of taking the reins of government too strong to resist.

Shidehara hoped the Liberal and Progressive Parties would come together to form a ruling coalition. Contrary to his predecessor, however, Hatoyama preferred the Socialist Party as a coalition partner. This was a choice that was grounded in the developments that preceded the formation of the two parties.

But Hatoyama was soon to be jilted. On April 23, the Socialist Party adopted an all-or-nothing platform of "taking the post of prime minister, or otherwise remaining in the opposition." The decision followed a clash that pitted Nishio and the right-wing elements of the party against the left wing and moderate elements. The latter group had ultimately emerged victorious from the fray. Hatoyama then opted to forgo a coalition and chose the path of forming a minority cabinet buttressed only with a promise from the Socialist Party that it would provide external support to the cabinet.

On May 1, May Day was celebrated in Japan for the first time in eleven years. In Tokyo, 500,000 people congregated in front of the Imperial Palace with such slogans as "Down with the reactionary conservative government" and "Establish a popular democratic government headed by the Socialist Party."

On May 3, Prime Minister Shidehara presented himself to the imperial court to nominate Hatoyama as the next head of government. The following day, May 4, Hatoyama patiently awaited the arrival of the Emperor's "imperial command," but what was delivered to him instead was an order purging him from public office pursuant to Section G of GHQ's purge directive. This was indeed a bold or even brazen order, as it meant that the leader of the party that had won a plurality in the election was being purged from public life.

Hatoyama recorded his deep disappointment in his diary. "The reasons cited for the purge were completely unexpected. I have been expelled from a parliamentary career of more than 30 years and have been robbed of the opportunity to form a cabinet without a chance to utter a single word of explanation."[44]

Everything now went back to square one. On May 5, Shidehara met with Chairman Katayama of the Socialist Party and requested him to form a coalition government. Katayama responded by proposing a four-way coalition to be based on the previously mentioned Four-Party Joint Committee that included the Socialist, Liberal, Cooperative, and Communist Parties. In reality, Katayama had no real prospect for successfully forming a coalition that would contain both the Liberal and Communist Parties. Given Hatoyama's earlier failure to

---

44 Itō Takashi and Suetake Yoshiya, eds., *Hatoyama Ichirō to Kaoru nikki, jō* [Diary of Hatoyama Ichirō and Kaoru, vol. 1], Chūō Kōron Shinsha, 1999, p. 440.

form a coalition cabinet, there was no reason to believe the Liberal Party would now agree to join such a coalition. Within the Socialist Party, the right wing was demanding that all ties with the Communist Party be severed, while the left wing vociferously opposed the exclusion of the Communist Party from the coalition. Some suspicion remains as to whether Shidehara was truly prepared to hand the reins of government to the Socialist Party in the first place, but ultimately Shidehara rejected the notion of a single-party cabinet headed by the Socialist Party. The reason he gave was simply that such a cabinet would not have majority support in the Diet.

Food May Day and the Establishment of the Yoshida Cabinet

Following Hatoyama's purge, the Liberal Party began urgently searching for someone to take his place. The first choices rejected the party's calls, citing their advanced age. These included Kojima Kazuo, an elder statesman of the Constitutional Association of Political Friendship (Seiyūkai), and Matsudaira Tsuneo, a former Imperial Household Minister. After these rejections, the name of Foreign Minister Yoshida Shigeru came up as a candidate to replace Hatoyama.

Yoshida informed the Liberal Party that he would replace Hatoyama and accept the post of prime minister on three conditions: he would not engage in fundraising, the Liberal Party would not interfere in his selection of cabinet ministers, and he would be free to quit at anytime he chose. It is reported that the Hatoyama side appended a condition, which was that Yoshida would "vacate the post upon the return of Hatoyama." But Yoshida later denied having accepted this condition. The Liberal Party accepted Yoshida's three conditions and the "imperial command" was duly delivered to Yoshida on May 16. Yoshida was not interested in pursuing a coalition with the Socialist Party, and instead turned to Shidehara's Progressive Party as a coalition partner. The two conservative parties had been launched under the leadership of two party politicians: Hatoyama and Machida. But now they were preparing to receive two former diplomats with pro-American and pro-British leanings as the leaders of their parties. Yoshida would take the mantle of leadership in the Liberal Party, and Shidehara would

stand at the helm of the Progressive Party.

The People's Rally for Obtaining Food ("Food May Day") held on May 19 adopted a petition demanding a solution to the food shortage. The petition, which was to be submitted to the Emperor, featured resolutions opposing reactionary government and calling for the formation of a democratic front led by the Socialist and Communist Parties. The large crowd that had gathered marched through the streets of Tokyo, while Tokuda Kyūichi and others made their way into the Prime Minister's residence where they remained for more than two hours. One of the workers who participated in the march was arrested on charges of lèse-majesté for displaying a placard that read, "Imperial Edict. The national polity has been maintained. I am eating my fill. You people, starve and die. –Imperial sign and seal." This later came to be known as the "placard incident," while the crime of insulting the Emperor would later develop into a point of contention between GHQ and the Japanese government in the process of revising the criminal code.

Yoshida Shigeru (1878–1967)
Yoshida became a politician after a successful career as a diplomat. He left the diplomatic corps in 1939 after serving as Japan's Ambassador to the United Kingdom. Noted for his "anti-Tōjō" activities during the war, he was appointed Foreign Minister after the end of the war. Yoshida became the President of the Liberal Party following the Hatoyama purge and served as Prime Minister on three occasions during the occupation period, pursuing independence through policies of low military spending and emphasis on economic recovery and growth.

The Japanese side simply did not have the power to quell the political and social demonstrations that accompanied the Food May Day, the first political demonstrations of postwar Japan. The demonstrations finally came to an end on the following day with a statement issued by MacArthur that read, "I find it necessary to caution the Japanese people that the growing tendency toward mass violence and physical processes of intimidation, under organized leadership, present a grave menace to the future development of Japan…and to the basic purposes and security of the occupation itself." MacArthur closed with the warning that if such conditions persisted, "I shall be forced to take the necessary steps to control and remedy such a deplorable situation."[45] The statement had the effect of quickly cooling the "revolutionary fervor" that had overtaken Tokyo.

On May 22, a coalition government of the Liberal and Progressive Parties was formed with Yoshida Shigeru as Prime Minister. Ishibashi Tanzan was appointed Finance Minister. As Minister of Agriculture and Forestry, Yoshida chose Wada Hiroo, the Director of the Agricultural Administration Bureau. Soon thereafter, Yoshida negotiated directly with MacArthur and succeeded in extracting promises for food assistance.

Yoshida Shigeru was born in 1878 (Meiji 11) as the fifth son of Takeuchi Tsuna, a civil rights activist from Kochi Prefecture. As a small child, he was adopted into the family of Yoshida Kenzō and in marriage became the son-in-law of Makino Nobuaki (the second son of Ōkubo Toshimichi). After graduating with a law degree from Tokyo Imperial University, Yoshida joined the Foreign Affairs Ministry. During his career as a diplomat, he served as Consul-General in Mukden, followed by a term as Vice Minister of Foreign Affairs and Ambassador to the United Kingdom. Yoshida retired from the diplomatic corps in 1939. During the war, he remained under the close watch of the military for his pro-American and pro-British positions, and was at one time arrested by the military police.

As a diplomat, Yoshida had served the Empire of Japan as an aristocratic conservative. But now he had accepted the role of raising the curtain on Japan's new age.

Constitutional Assembly and the Enactment of Laws

Reorganization of Political Parties

The 90th Extraordinary Session of the Diet was convened on May 16, 1946. The distribution of seats at the start of the session was as follows: Liberal Party

---

45 General MacArthur Today Issued the Following which Warns Demonstrations and Disorders by Mass Mobs, (May 20, 1946), Statements by MacArthur, Box No. 2195, Folder 22, GHQ/SCAP Records, Government Section, National Diet Library, Originals in U.S. National Archives & Records Administration, RG331.

143 seats, Progressive Party 97 seats, Socialist Party 95 seats, Communist Party 6 seats, Japan Democratic Party Preparation Association 38 seats, Cooperative Democratic Club 33 seats, Shinkō Club 29 seats, and Club of Independents 25 seats. One of the noteworthy features of this period was that the minor political parties and independents resisted becoming integrated into the larger previously existing parties. Instead of joining old established parties, their preferred choice was to create new ones.

The Japan Democratic Party Preparation Association was formed by Sasamori Junzō, Okada Seiichi, and independent members of the Diet who would later move to the People's Party and finally to the People's Cooperative Party. Their initial aim in forming the Association was to create a party that stood "to the left of the Liberal Party and to the right of the Socialist Party." The Cooperative Democratic Club was formed around the Japan Cooperative Party and included various minor parties and independents, and was renamed and launched as the Cooperative Democratic Party on May 24. Miki Takeo, who would serve as Prime Minister in the 1970s, first belonged to the Japan Democratic Party Preparation Association before joining this Cooperative Democratic Party.

The Shinkō Club consisted primarily of the Shinsei Dōshikai, the members of which had a professional background in education, and was formed with the addition of the members of the Seisō Parliamentarians Club.

The Club of Independents numbered among its members Ozaki Yukio, who had been called the "god of constitutionalism" in the prewar years. Eight women Diet members, including Tokano Satoko, also belonged to the Club of Independents. In September, several members of the Japan Democratic Party Preparation Association and the Shinkō Club came together to form New Political Association (Shinsei-kai), which served as the foundation for the People's Party that was formed at the end of September.

Yoshida's Position on Constitutional Reform

The newly formed Yoshida Cabinet faced two immediate challenges. The first challenge was the enactment of the Constitution of Japan, and the second was economic recovery and the resolution of the severe food crisis.

Yoshida's first exposure to the GHQ draft constitution came when he was handed a copy by Whitney, the Chief of the Government Section. It is reported that upon reading the draft, Yoshida thought to himself, "What is this awful thing they have brought over!" But Yoshida kept his opinion to himself as he was committed to playing the role of a "good loser" vis-à-vis the Occupation forces. Looking at the broader picture, Yoshida calculated that it would ultimately be to his advantage to respond positively to GHQ demands. Yoshida recounts what was going through his mind. "We did not formulate a revised constitution solely from the perspective of enacting a constitution and the laws to go with it. Full consideration was given to how to ensure the peace and security of the Imperial Household."

Yoshida approached constitutional reform with a "diplomatic sense," and considered the process to be "akin to negotiating a treaty with a foreign country." Finally, he concluded that for the purpose of regaining the independence of Japan, "It is necessary to present the Japanese public and the world with evidence that Japan is a democratic and peaceful nation. This must be done as soon as possible so as to regain their trust." Thus, with his eyes fixed firmly on the eventual signing of a peace treaty, Yoshida was prepared to accept what was being demanded of him.[46]

On May 13, the Far Eastern Commission finalized a document entitled "Criteria for the Adoption of a New Japanese Constitution," which identified the following three principles to be strictly observed in the process of enacting a new constitution: (1) allow adequate time and opportunity for full discussion and consideration of the terms of the new Constitution, (2) assure complete legal continuity from the Constitution of 1889, (3) ensure that the new Constitution is adopted in such a manner as to demonstrate that it affirmatively expresses the free will of the Japanese people.[47]

On June 21, MacArthur released a statement addressed to the Japanese government outlining these requirements without mentioning that this was a directive from the Far Eastern Commission. MacArthur had plainly released this statement for the benefit of the State Department and the Far Eastern Commission.

---

46 Yoshida Shigeru, *Kaisō jūnen, dai 2-kan* [Memoirs of Ten Years, vol. 2], Shinchōsha, 1957, pp. 30–31.
47 FEC 031-7, dated May 16, 1946.

Constitutional Assembly: 90th Extraordinary Session of the Diet

On June 25, the Bill for Revision of the Imperial Constitution was submitted to the plenary session of the House of Representatives. A previous version of this draft had been published on March 6 in the name of the Japanese government. Following the Prime Minister's explanation of the proposal and an exchange of questions and answers in the plenary session, the draft constitution was sent on June 28 to the House of Representatives Special Committee on Constitutional Reform chaired by Ashida Hitoshi.

The questions raised in the plenary session focused on the issue of national polity, and more specifically on whether or not any change would be made in the Emperor's authority to exercise sovereign power. The original GHQ draft stated that the status of the Emperor was based on the "sovereign will of the people." However, Article 1 of the Bill had been amended to read, "The Emperor shall be the symbol of the state and the unity of the people, deriving his position from the sovereign will of the people." The wording of Articles 2 through 7 was identical to the final wording of the Constitution of Japan. The fact of the matter was that the Bill for Revision of the Imperial Constitution did not contain an explicit statement affirming the sovereignty of the people. The government responded to related questions by explaining that this pointed to a change in the "form of government" and that it did not imply a change in the national polity in which the Emperor exercised sovereign power. In his opening questions on behalf of the Liberal Party, Kita Reikichi (the younger brother of Kita Ikki) pursued this matter. "Do you not think that it is necessary and that it is your responsibility to carefully and thoroughly explain to the people that this constitution does not make any change in the national polity?"

The reality of the debate, however, was more accurately represented in the "*yamabuki* (or globeflower) theory of the constitution," a reference to a flower that is multi-blossomed yet bears no fruit, that was presented by the Liberal Party's Kitaura Keitarō. "The Emperor has been given many brilliant colored flowers to hold. There is the power of appointment and the power of attestation, and beyond these the power to convene the Diet. Yes, they are all flowers. Some have seven petals and some even may have eight, and all are in bloom. But the sad fact of this globeflower-like constitution is that it does not bear even a single fruit."[48]

The two conservative parties—the Liberal and Progressive Parties—pressed for two changes to be made in the draft. The first would alter the status of the Emperor from a symbolic one to the head of state. Then, as head of state, the scope of the Emperor's powers would be expanded. Strangely enough, though they comprised the ruling parties, the Liberal and Progressive Parties had chosen to oppose the government proposal.

On July 6, Inukai Takeru, chairman of the Progressive Party's General Council, presented a personal proposal to the General Council on changes to be made in the draft constitution. Inukai proposed that articles pertaining to the sovereignty of the Emperor be left unchanged, and retracted the earlier proposal for recognizing the Emperor as head of state. Other salient features of the proposal included the immediate abolition of the aristocracy, and the protection of the rights and obligations of workers.[49] The Inukai proposal was designed to effect a transformation in the Progressive Party, while at the same time resolving the dilemma that faced the ruling parties. The proposal drew the attention of the Government Section as the "first step toward liberalism."[50]

On the same day, July 6, GHQ received the Far Eastern Commission's "Basic Principles for a New Japanese Constitution," which included provisions for popular sovereignty and the abolition or democratization of the Emperor system.[51]

Surprised by the contents of the document, MacArthur took immediate action. Reasoning that the Japanese government would lose face if the document were to be released to the public, MacArthur acted to stop its release and quickly dispatched Kades, Deputy Chief of the Government Section, to the Prime Minister's official residence.

Meeting with the leaders of the Japanese government, Kades argued that

---

48 History of the Non-Military Activities of the Occupation of Japan, 1945 through December 1951, vol. 7, Constitutional Revision, National Diet Library, Originals in U.S. National Archives and Records Administration, RG331.
49 *Asahi Shinbun*, July 8, 1946.
50 "Memorandum for Chief Government Section (H.E. Wildes), Political Parties" SDDF (B) 0012-0012, (July 1-15, 1946), Fukunaga, ed., in *GHQ Minsei-kyoku shiryō, 3*, pp. 262–267.
51 FEC 031-27, dated July 16, 1946.

the "expression used in the Japanese text is extremely unclear on the question of sovereignty," and demanded a revision be made to "explicitly state that sovereignty rests with the people." The government initially resisted making this change but ultimately relented. The revision containing an explicit reference to popular sovereignty was thereafter submitted to the Diet as a joint proposal made by the Liberal and Progressive Parties.

On the subject of Article 9, the Communist Party's Nosaka Sanzō asked whether this signified a rejection of the right of self-defense. Responding to this query, Yoshida said, "It is a well-known fact that practically every war in recent years has been undertaken in the name of national defense. Therefore, I believe the recognition of the legitimate right of self-defense would provide an incentive to embark on other types of conflict." Other than this exchange, Article 9 was only very briefly debated in the plenary session of the Diet. Even as the Progressive Party's Inukai Takeru had called Article 9 the "masterpiece" of the constitution, the general feeling in the Diet was to affirmatively accept the contents of Article 9.

Nevertheless, several other proposals were submitted on Article 9. The Special Committee on Constitutional Reform argued that the wording of the government draft rejecting the "maintenance of military force" gave the definite impression that the government "had been given no choice" other than to accept the draft constitution. To rectify this impression, the Special Committee proposed the addition of the phrase, "Aspiring sincerely to an international peace based on justice and order" at the head of the article. It was argued that this phrase would be taken to be Japan's message to the international community.[52] Another proposal submitted by the Socialist Party called for the establishment of social rights in Article 25 by inserting the sentence, "All people shall have the right to maintain the minimum standards of wholesome and cultured living."

On October 7, 1946, the Constitution of Japan was adopted in both the House of Representatives and the House of Peers, and was thereafter promulgated on

---

52 Teikoku kenpō kaisei-an iinkai sho-iinkai sokki-roku, dai 90 teikoku gikai shugiin, Fukkoku ban [Stenographic Notes of the Subcommittee of the Committee on Reforming the Imperial Constitution–90th session of the Imperial Diet, House of Representatives, Reprint edition], Gendai Shiryō Shuppan, 2005, pp. 78–91.

November 3. In what constituted a monumental transition, the Emperor was made the symbol of the State, and popular sovereignty, renunciation of war, and respect for fundamental human rights were enshrined in the new Constitution of Japan. Furthermore, it defined the Diet to be the "highest organ of State power" and the "sole law-making organ of the State." The Constitution required that the Prime Minister be a civilian as well as a member of the Diet. A majority of the ministers of state also had to be members of the Diet. These provisions heightened the fundamental role of political parties and significantly enhanced their status compared to the prewar era.

The Second Farmland Reform: Fruits of the Occupation

In addition to deliberating on the draft constitution, the 90th session of the Diet also debated bills related to farmland reform. As previously noted, GHQ was dissatisfied with the first farmland reform program formulated by the Japanese government on the grounds that it did not go far enough.

In March 1946, the Japanese government submitted a revised farmland reform program to GHQ, which had been reformulated in accordance with the GHQ memorandum issued in December 1945. But the revision was once again rejected by GHQ as being incomplete and deceptive, unsuited for eradicating the ailment that afflicted Japan's agrarian land system. GHQ next called on Wolf Ladejinsky, an agriculture specialist and adviser to the Natural Resources Section, to draft a proposal for farmland reform. Concurrently, MacArthur requested the Allied Council for Japan to examine the bills for land reform. E.E. Ward, economic adviser to the British Commonwealth Representative of the Allied Council for Japan, wrote, "MacArthur, although hostile to the Allied Council, was prepared to make use of it when it suited his purposes."[53]

In June, the Allied Council made changes to the Ladejinsky proposal by lowering the limit on landowner holdings from three *chōbu* to one *chōbu* (approximately one acre). The revised draft was then submitted as the British

---

53 Ward, Eric E, *Nōchi kaikaku towa nande attano ka* [Land Reform in Japan 1946–1950], Nōbunkyō, 1990, pp. 132–133.

proposal and was approved by MacArthur.

As in the case of the constitution, GHQ wished to release the farmland reform program in the name of the Japanese government, a role that would be assigned to Agriculture and Forestry Minister Wada and Prime Minister Yoshida. In turn, Yoshida delegated the matter entirely to Wada, saying that he was a conservative and "I don't like the idea of land reform. I don't want to implement it. But if you say that it must be done, I will go along."[54]

On October 11, the revised Farmland Adjustment Law and the Owner-Farmer Establishment Special Measures Law were enacted without amendment and were promulgated on October 21. Implemented on the advice of GHQ, this second farmland reform carried forward the provisions of the first farmland reform concerning the elimination of absentee landlords and rent payment in cash. Additionally, land ownership by village-dwelling landowners was limited to one *chōbu* (four *chōbu* in Hokkaido). All tenanted land exceeding this limit was to be compulsorily purchased by the government and sold to the tenants. This reform drastically reduced the area of tenanted farmland from about 2.36 million *chōbu* (approximately 2.35 million hectares) immediately after the war to about 510,000 *chōbu* (approximately 510,000 hectares). Tenanted land now accounted for only 9.9 percent of all farmland compared to 45.9 percent before the reform. The parasitic system of landownership that had been a major factor in exacerbating income inequality since the Meiji Period had now been eliminated.

MacArthur would later brag that this farmland reform was "one of the most successful in history. The redistribution formed a strong barrier against any introductions of Communism in rural Japan."[55] It is reported that when the farmland reform bills were passed in the Diet, MacArthur gazed at the picture of his father on his desk and said, "Father, this is what you wanted." MacArthur's father, Arthur, had in fact attempted to implement farmland reform in the Philippines forty years earlier but had failed.[56]

---

54 Andō Yoshio, ed., *Shōwa seiji keizai-shi e no shōgen, ge* [Testimonies on Shōwa Political and Economic History, vol. 2], Mainichi Shinbunsha, 1966, p. 44.
55 MacArthur, Douglas, *Makkāsā taisen kaikoroku* [Reminiscences], Tsusima Kazuo, trans, Chūō Kōron Shinsha, 2014, p. 479.
56 Finn, Richard B, *Winners in Peace: MacArthur, Yoshida, and Postwar Japan*, University of California Press, 1992, p. 131.

Temporary Committee for the Investigation of Legal Systems: Aspects of Reform under the Occupation

The GHQ Government Section believed that various laws needed to be developed parallel to constitutional revision. Following the March 6 release of the Bill for Revision of the Imperial Constitution, the Japanese government also concluded that it was necessary to form a commission to deliberate on legislation that would have to be enacted in line with the new constitution. Preparations for the establishment of such a body soon began to move forward.

On July 3, 1946, the government established the Temporary Committee for the Investigation of Legal Systems and a total of four sections that were placed under its jurisdiction. Section One was placed in charge of matters related to the Imperial Household and the Cabinet, Section Two covered matters pertaining to the Diet, Section Three was placed in charge of judiciary matters, and Section Four was assigned matters related to government finances and local government. Each section formed its own subcommittees that liaised with the respective government ministries and agencies. In the third plenary session convened on October 26, a total of 19 recommendations were submitted. These recommendations formed the basis for formulating numerous laws that were enacted in line with the enforcement of the new Constitution of Japan.

When the 92nd session of the Diet was convened at the end of December 1946, the Yoshida Cabinet was ready to submit a long list of important legislation for deliberation and enactment. These included the Diet Law, the Court Law, the Local Autonomy Law, the Basic Law on Education, the School Education Law, and the Labor Standards Law, all of which were passed successfully.

The Government Section immediately began to review the new legislation in light of the provisions of the Constitution of Japan. What this review implied was that the Government Section itself was now bound by the framework of the Constitution in its pursuit of democratization.

Among the various laws that were enacted, it is interesting to note Yoshida's assessment of the Basic Law on Education and the Labor Standards Law, the implementation of both of which came with considerable economic costs and difficulties. Concerning the Basic Law on Education, Yoshida wrote, "Respect for human rights and equal access to education are the essence of this law. This is the common-sense approach to education for any advanced democracy." Concerning the Labor Standards Law, Yoshida commented, "The inclusion of provisions on eight-hour workdays and equal pay for men and women signifies immense progress over the former Factory Law in terms of labor relations legislation. This is an excellent law even when compared to international standards."[57]

GHQ Government Section and Yoshida Shigeru

Yoshida took pride in successfully enacting the long list of laws. "For the most part, the rails have now been laid for the birth of the new Japan,"[58] he gloated. But the challenges of revising the Civil Code and Penal Code remained, and Yoshida continued to resist the abolition of the crime of lèse-majesté against the Emperor and the Imperial Household until the very end.

In December 1946, the Government Section ordered the Justice Minister to immediately abolish the crime of lèse-majesté (Penal Code Articles 73-76). A week later, Yoshida sent a letter to MacArthur arguing in favor of retaining the provision on the grounds that the dignity of the Emperor as symbol had to be protected in the laws of the land. In his response, MacArthur emphasized the importance of equality before the law and called for the abolition of the crime of lèse-majesté. Yoshida claimed that MacArthur's message conveyed a recommendation and not a directive. Arming himself with this argument, Yoshida kept mum. As a result, the revision of the Penal Code was stretched out and postponed.

The Government Section grew increasingly suspicious of Yoshida as he continued to exhibit both open and covert resistance. Alfred Oppler, Chief of the Government Section's Law Division, later described the attitude of the Government Section toward Yoshida. "I, for one, and several of my colleagues in the Government Section, did not completely trust him; we felt instinctively

---

57 Yoshida, *Kaisō jūnen, dai 2-kan*, p. 98 and 232.
58 Ibid., p. 102.

some passive resistance to our reformatory policies."[59]

Yoshida was aware of these sentiments as witnessed in his own writings. "It seems I was not much liked by Brigadier General Whitney and the other members of the Government Section." Yoshida proceeded to analyze the cause of the negative feelings. "I myself am not sure of the reason, but if I had to guess, I would say that it had something to do with the fact that I almost never showed my face at the Government Section on my own accord."[60]

The present author had an opportunity to ask Kades about his relation with Yoshida. Kades chose his words carefully and said with a wry smile, "He [Yoshida] never came."[61]

The Government Section was now preparing to tackle new challenges that had to be overcome within the framework of a parliamentary system. These included restructuring the political system and developing new laws in line with the new Constitution of Japan, and establishing a government that was worthy and suited to the newly installed constitutional system. In the eyes of the Government Section, the two conservative parties—the Liberal and Progressive Parties—represented those forces that were committed to preserving and resurrecting the old order. Consequently, the Government Section pinned its hopes on the Socialist Party, which had adopted a moderate and middle-of-the-road approach. In the estimation of the Government Section, the Socialist Party was "independent from the right wing pollution of the Liberal and Progressive parties and the leftist domination by the aggressive Communist Party."[62]

---

59 Oppler, Alfred Christian, *Legal Reform in Occupied Japan: A Participant Looks Back*, Princeton University Press, p. 176.

60 Yoshida, *Kaisō jūnen, dai 1-kan*, p. 108.

61 Kades, interview by Fukunaga, August 25, 1989.

62 "Memorandum for the Chief Government Section (P. Roest), Visit of Socialist Leaders," (May 27, 1946), Fukunaga, ed., *GHQ Minsei-kyoku shiryō, 3*, pp. 244–247.

Establishment of the Okinawa Civilian Administration: From Wartime to Peacetime

Birth of the Okinawa Civilian Administration

In Okinawa, the return of residents to their previous areas of residence was more or less complete by April 1946. The military government took this opportunity to re-establish the prewar local administrations (city, town, and village-based) and to appoint administrative heads for these various local units.

The return to a peacetime environment meant that the role of the Okinawa Advisory Council was at last coming to an end. After all, this administrative organization was predicated on the internment of large portions of the population in camps located throughout the island. As the first step in the transition, the military government instructed the Okinawa Advisory Council to deliberate on establishing a central executive agency that would stand above the municipalities. Records indicate that the Okinawa Advisory Council engaged in active discussions on a number of fundamental issues. One idea was to formulate a separate and independent constitution for Okinawa that would be modeled after the U.S. Constitution. Another idea was to resurrect the political systems and institutions of the Ryukyu Kingdom. But these discussions and movements were swept away when the U.S. military government announced its new policy in March 1946. "Prewar local administrations are simple and good. The military government shall stand at the top, and a prefectural assembly shall be formed to hear the will of the people."

On April 11, 86 representatives were summoned to Ishikawa City to nominate candidates for the governorship of Okinawa. They were members of Okinawa Advisory Council, elected mayors, and officers selected from ten civil departments including general affairs of local administration and agriculture, forestry and fisheries. Three candidates were nominated and from among these candidates, the military government appointed Shikiya Kōshin, a former educator, as governor. This marked the installation of the first governor of Okinawa who was a native of the island.

On April 24, the Okinawa Central Government (renamed the Okinawa Civilian Administration in December) was launched. Concurrently, the "Okinawa

Assembly" was formed as an advisory body to the governor. Membership of the assembly consisted of individuals who had served on the previous prefectural assembly and a number of supplementary members appointed by the military government. However, the assembly was convened irregularly and with little enthusiasm. It was reported that the assembly was generally neglected or ignored when important decisions were being made on budgetary matters and reforming government administration.

The establishment of the Okinawa Civilian Administration brought an end to the postwar confusion in government administration. However, the military government was quick to make its authority known. "The military government is the cat and the Okinawan government is the mouse. The mouse will play so long as the cat lets it." "Until the signing of a peace treaty, the voice of the people shall not be recognized nor shall it exist." "The authority of the U.S. military government remains absolute until the end of the peace conference."[63]

Restoring the Money Economy

At approximately this time, the military government was endeavoring to return from a barter economy based on U.S. military surplus to normal economic and social structures.

In March 1946, a money economy was restored on the mainland of Okinawa. Under this arrangement, legal tender consisted of military script referred to as the "B-Yen" and the new Japanese yen. Prior to this, with the exception of some isolated islands, the money economy had completely ceased to exist in Okinawa. Following the March 1946 return to a money economy, monetary policies underwent several changes. A cash-based wage system was finally restored in May when residents began to be paid for their labor in cash.

In the following month, the military government announced that the free distribution of military supplies would be terminated. Concurrently, wide-ranging economic controls were introduced covering all aspects of production,

---

63 Okinawa Prefecture, Okinawa Historical Materials Section, ed., *Okinawa-ken shiryō: Sengo 1 Okinawa shijun-kai kiroku* [Okinawa Prefecture Historical Documents: Postwar 1 Records of the Okinawa Advisory Council], Okinawa Prefecture Board of Education, 1986, p. 493.

sales, and consumption. For instance, the free marketing of agricultural products was prohibited, and producers were henceforth required to sell all their marketable products to either village stores or agricultural cooperatives. Such publicly managed local stores were established throughout the islands of Okinawa at the average rate of five stores per village.[64] The income from these stores would be used to finance the activities of municipal governments.

The restoration of a money economy did not imply an immediate return to peacetime economic and social conditions as the military government continued to maintain strict economic controls. As a reaction to these controls, an extensive network of black markets soon emerged.

Governing Okinawa: Transition from the Navy to the Army

The Okinawa Civilian Administration was established on July 1, 1946. Just as the new arrangement was beginning to function, responsibility for the military government was transferred from the U.S. Navy to the Army. The military government was now placed under the direction of the Commander of the U.S. Army Forces, Western Pacific, but no change was made in the fact that the military government of Okinawa had no direct contact with Tokyo.

It was not until January 1947 that all branches of the U.S. armed services in the Far East were placed under the Commander-in-Chief, Far East (CINCFE) headed by Supreme Commander MacArthur. Even then, however, Okinawa was not brought under the direct control of the General Headquarters for the Allied Powers (GHQ) and instead remained under CINCFE. Now under the jurisdiction of the U.S. Army, MacArthur appointed the commanding general of the Philippines-Ryukyus Command (PHILIRYCOM) to head the military government of Okinawa. This decision was primarily based on the need to sort and transfer to Okinawa the huge volume of strategic materials that the U.S. military had stockpiled in the Philippines during the war. Although the Okinawa military government was placed under the General Headquarters of the Far East

---

64 Bank of the Ryūkyūs Research Department, ed., *Sengo Okinawa keizai-shi* [Postwar Economic History of Okinawa], Ryūkyū Ginkō, 1984, p. 154 and 169.

Command through PHILIRYCOM, it continued on its own course and did not receive direct orders from Tokyo.

Although who had jurisdiction in Okinawa remained ambiguous and unsettled, it was fast becoming the terminus for the army's military hardware and the dumpsite for equipment and dropouts from the military command.[65] During the following three years, Okinawa would remain the "forgotten island," which neither Washington nor MacArthur's GHQ showed much interest in.

Intensification of the Labor Movement: Rapid Inflation and the General Strike of February 1

Economic Crisis: From Economic Struggle to Political Struggle

Now that the new Constitution of Japan was in place, attention turned to the economic crisis and the challenge of rebuilding an economy on the verge of collapse.

Defeat in the war had decimated Japan's national wealth, her territories had been radically reduced, and the postwar economy had to be reclaimed from the ashes of the war. The inflation that had taken hold of the nation knew no bounds and output continued to decline, creating an extremely severe economic environment that weighed heavily on people's lives. The central areas of Tokyo and all other major cities had been leveled during the war and the nation was teetering on the brink of starvation. People were quickly reduced to exchanging their clothes for food—a survival tactic that came to be known as the "bamboo shoot strategy" of stripping away layers of belongings one by one. Struggling for survival, workers everywhere rose up to protect their jobs and their lives. At the center of this movement stood Japan's newly invigorated labor unions.

The inaugural rally of the Japanese Federation of Trade Unions (Sōdōmei) was held on June 8, 1946. The new organization represented a total of 1,699 labor

---

65 Okinawa Prefecture, Bunka shinkō-kai kōbunsho kanri-bu shiryō henshū-shitsu, ed., *Okinawa ken-shi shiryō-hen 14: Ryūkyū rettō no gunsei 1945–1950 gendai 2 (Wayaku-hen)* [Okinawa Prefecture Historical Documents 14: Military Government of the Ryukyus 1945–1950 Contemporary 2 (Japanese translations)], Okinawa Prefecture Board of Education, 2002, p. 164.

unions with a combined membership of 860,000 workers. Sōdōmei was then under the right-wing leadership of Matsuoka Komakichi and other labor activists, and closely tied to the Socialist Party. June 1946 also saw the formation of the more progressive Congress of Industrial Unions of Japan (Sanbetsu Kaigi), which was patterned after the Congress of Industrial Organizations (CIO) in the United States. With the support of GHQ, Sanbetsu Kaigi pursued a "bottom-up" approach to organizing labor and succeeded in bringing together twenty-one industrial unions with a combined membership of 1,560,000 workers. Among the twenty-one industrial unions that joined Sanbetsu Kaigi were unions representing press, publishing, coal mining, and postal workers. Politically, Sanbetsu Kaigi was strongly influenced by the Communist Party. The leadership in these two umbrella organizations consisted of white-collar activists who had emerged from workplaces after the war. Thus, Japan's postwar labor movement was split into two groups from the start.

The first sparks of a labor offensive were seen in August and September when the General Federation of National Railways Workers' Unions (Kokutetsu) and the All-Japan Seamens' Unions (Kaiin) rose up to protest the firing of workers. This was followed in October when the Council of Electric Industry Workers Unions (Densan), the Union of Press and Communications Workers, the All-Japan Coal Workers Union (Zentan) and others began to agitate for higher wages. Kokutetsu and Kaiin succeeded in forcing the cancellation of the firings, while Densan succeeded in negotiating a wage agreement that increased wages and promised the payment of living wages. Claiming that a "general strike is the imperative of the political struggle," the Communist Party's Tokuda called for "bringing down the Yoshida Cabinet and establishing a People's republic government." Tokuda would place the Sanbetsu Kaigi at the forefront of this movement. This labor offensive soon spread to government workers who demanded pay scales on par with the private sector. In pursuit of this objective, Kokutetsu (the predecessor to the National Railways Workers' Union [Kokurō]), the All Japan Communication Workers' Union (Zentei) and other public sector unions came together to form the Joint Struggle Committee of All Government and Municipal Workers' Unions (Kyōtō) in November.

Following a proposal made by Katō Kanjū of the Socialist Party's Labor

Affairs Committee, a convention of the National Council of Labor Unions (Zenrōkon) was convened at the end of November. The convention brought together a total of seventeen major labor unions, including Sanbetsu Kaigi and Sōdōmei. With support from Sōdōmei, the Zenrōkon moved quickly to organize national mass meetings for the security of livelihood and the overthrow of the Yoshida Cabinet which were held on December 17. Thus, steady momentum was building for the labor movement to transition from an economic struggle to a political offensive that was focused on removing the Yoshida Cabinet.

On December 24, GHQ released the Far Eastern Commission's "Sixteen Principles Regarding Measures to Promote Labor Unions in Japan." While the principles allowed labor unions to engage in political activities, they prohibited labor movements and activities that would obstruct the purposes of the Occupation. Notwithstanding this potentially restrictive provision, Sanbetsu Kaigi welcomed the sixteen principles and emphasized their importance in guaranteeing the rights of workers in concrete detail. As such, Sanbetsu Kaigi interpreted the document to be evidence of the Allied Powers' support for its own activities.

GHQ Tackles Inflation

In October 1946, Thomas Bisson, an economist assigned to the Government Section, issued a dire warning concerning raging inflation. Analyzing its onerous impact on wage earners, Bisson argued that failure to address inflation constituted the greatest threat to the purposes of the Occupation and went on to show that instead of implementing counter-inflationary policies, the Japanese government had opted for policies that were adding fuel to inflation and actually seemed to welcome the rapid rise in prices. During this period, Bisson had grown increasingly dissatisfied with Finance Minister Ishibashi Tanzan's fiscal policies, which are discussed in a later section.[66]

In January 1947, George Atcheson of the Office of the U.S. Political

---

66 Bisson, Thomas A., *Nihon senryō kaisōki* [Reform Years in Japan, 1945–47: An Occupation Memoir], Sanseidō, 1983, pp. 310–316.

Adviser filed a report addressed to President Truman in which he emphasized the successes achieved in political reform, including the establishment of a new constitution. However, on the subject of the Japanese economy, Atcheson stated that the situation was deplorable and that, "whether we like it or not, Japan has become an economic responsibility of the United States."[67] Atcheson went on to recommend an early resolution of the issue of reparations and the expansion of trade, and concluded with a warning that inflation had emerged as an obstacle to pursuing the democratization of Japan.

Pursuing Coalition Partnership with the Socialist Party

On the same day that the People's Meeting for Removing the Yoshida Cabinet was held, the Socialist Party joined forces with the Cooperative Democratic and the People's Parties to submit a motion for dissolving the Diet. The Socialist Party was initially planning to tender a non-confidence motion but switched to a dissolution motion in a show of solidarity with the other two parties.

Yoshida was now exposed to attack from both inside and outside the Diet. To escape the impasse, Yoshida approached the Socialist Party with a coalition proposal. Yoshida's aim was to form a "national unity government" and internalize the Socialist Party and the labor movement that it led.

Several negotiating sessions involving various intermediary channels were held between the end of 1946 and early 1947. On December 28, Yoshida tabled a partnership agreement that included the offer of a specific cabinet post to the Socialist Party's Secretary-General Nishio. But throughout these negotiations, within the Liberal and Progressive Parties, there remained strong opposition to the coalition that Yoshida was contemplating. On the same day, Cabinet members belonging to the two parties and the secretary-generals of the two parties (Ōno Banboku of the Liberal Party and Tanaka Man'itsu of the Progressive Party) assembled and adopted two positions. First, they committed to opposing the inclusion of the Socialist Party in the coalition, and second, they agreed on the

---

67 The Political Adviser in Japan (Atcheson) to President Truman, January 5, 1947, *FRUS*, The Far East (Tokyo), vol. 6, pp. 159–160.

"removal of all independents from the Cabinet."

While the call for the removal of independent Cabinet members presumably implied a transition to a purely party-based Cabinet, it was obviously aimed at eliminating Agriculture and Forestry Minister Wada of the left wing. Ultimately, the coalition negotiations collapsed in mid-January when Yoshida and the Socialist Party failed to reach a compromise on the question of whether or not Finance Minister Ishibashi should be removed.

Political Realignment for Economic Reconstruction

While coalition negotiations failed, the challenge of economic reconstruction was gradually changing the relations among political parties.

Finance Minister Ishibashi analyzed the status of the Japanese economy as being one of excess capacity, excess labor, and under-employment. Based on this analysis, Ishibashi advocated aggressive investment to achieve full employment, and was using price gap subsidies and Reconstruction Finance Bank loans (*fukkin*) as levers for stimulating and expanding output. The resulting fiscal deficits were financed through bonds and loans, the principal portion of which was absorbed by the Bank of Japan through the issuance of currency. Thus, Ishibashi was pursuing an aggressive policy of fiscal expansion to spark economic growth. The problem, however, was that output was not expanding as hoped due to the shortage of raw materials and other resources. Consequently, the excess liquidity was spilling over into the markets and exacerbating the inflation in a process that would come to be known as the "*fukkin* inflation." GHQ monitored Ishibashi's fiscal policies with growing concern as the inflation rate continued to climb.

Yoshida for his part was pursuing another approach as recommended to him by the Sub-committee on Coal, the Prime Minister's private advisory body that included Arisawa Hiromi and others. Concluding that industrial reconstruction was being obstructed by certain key bottlenecks, Yoshida committed to a policy of "super-prioritizing increased output of coal and steel," which involved concentrated investment of funds and resources in those two sectors. It was hoped that this strategy of a priority production system would lead to subsequent expansion in coal and steel output and trigger expansion in other industrial sectors.

Because Yoshida's "priority production system" pursued the expansion of output and was less concerned with cooling inflationary pressures, it shared basically the same trajectory as Ishibashi's expansionary fiscal policies. However, there was one critical difference in the two approaches. As opposed to Ishibashi's market-oriented approach, Yoshida was moving Japan toward a mixed economy that contained elements of centralized planning and organization. As a principal advocate of the latter approach, Arisawa called for the "coming together of political forces that will support the implementation of our NEP (new economic policy)."

Sōdōmei was also undergoing changes at this time as it transitioned away from labor offensives aimed at raising wages and protesting the firing of workers. In its new direction, Sōdōmei entered into a cooperative relation with the Economic Fraternalists' Association (Dōyūkai) and promoted the establishment of an Economic Rehabilitation Council that would be committed to gradual reform based on "labor-capital cooperation." The Socialist Party quickly fell into step with Sōdōmei and advocated that the Economic Rehabilitation Council play a central role in increasing industrial output through such measures as the democratization of the economy, economic planning, labor participation in management, and labor-capital cooperation. Parallel to these developments, the Progressive Party shifted to the left of the Liberal Party by adopting the philosophy of "modified capitalism" that accepted the separation of ownership and management, and labor participation in management. This effectively reduced the gap that separated the Progressive Party from the Socialist Party and Sōdōmei. Through this process of realignment, a commitment to labor participation in management became established as a widely shared principle in the pursuit of industrial democratization.

Meanwhile, the Communist Party and Sanbetsu Kaigi continued to adhere to the "principle of revolution"—the seizure of the reins of government by political forces representing the working class—as the most effective path to economic reconstruction.

The Political Party Law: Eliminating "Domination by Political Bosses"

As previously noted, the general elections of April 1946 gave birth to numerous new parties and first-time Diet members. However, the crowding of the political scene with a jumble of minor parties had resulted in considerable political instability. On the other hand, labor movements were gaining momentum as politics slipped further into crisis. The deteriorating situation prodded both GHQ and the Japanese side to consider various measures for bringing greater stability to the nation's politics.

In one such step, the Liberal and Progressive Parties of the conservative wing of Japanese politics began to advocate a return to medium-sized electoral districts with single-vote ballots, a measure that would create greater stability of government by blocking the expansion of the Socialist and Communist Parties. The second step involved enacting a Political Party Law, an initiative that was led by Lieutenant Colonel Roest who headed the Political Parties Branch of the GHQ Government Section.

The Political Party Law being considered by Roest would restrict the scope of political parties and introduce simple printed ballots in the belief that this would bring order to the jumble of minor parties and encourage policy-oriented elections based on major parties.[68] The Roest proposals went further to include provisions designed to democratize and liberalize the organization of political parties by bringing greater transparency to the election of party leaders and party finances. The fundamental idea was to create a system of political parties that conformed to the principles enunciated in the Constitution of Japan, and which would prove conducive to the democratic development of political parties. Concurrent to this, first-time Diet members in the conservative parties were attempting to democratize the systems and arrangements within their parties in a move to escape the domination of traditional political bosses.

In December 1946, the Home Affairs Ministry completed its "Outline of the Political Party Bill" and entered into consultation with Roest. However, the bill

---

68 "MCGS (P. Roest), Political Parties," (November 25, 1946), Fukunaga, ed., *GHQ Minsei-kyoku shiryō, 2*, p. 275.

met stiff opposition in the Cabinet from State Minister Saitō Takao and others who claimed that the bill would lead to the control of political parties by the state and bureaucracy. The bill thus became stalled in the Cabinet and was later shelved when MacArthur directed the holding of a general election.

Second Purge from Public Office: From Demilitarization to Democratization

On January 4, 1947, the Government Section released the second arrow of its "democratization reforms" that directed the second purge of undesirables from public office.

In its original iteration, the purge was intended to be one step in the plan for demilitarizing Japan. However, in order to avoid confusion, the first purge was primarily limited to central government officials. The second purge was scheduled to go into effect before the general elections of April 1947 and primarily targeted public officials at the prefectural level with the intent of promoting the democratization of local politics by decommissioning the conservative political machine.

The scope of the purge was further expanded to include business leaders and intellectual figures. The economic purge in particular was intended to sever the existing financial ties between the political parties and the business community.

Thus, the purge transitioned from being a policy measure for "demilitarization" to a step in the direction of the far broader objective of "democratizing" Japan. Through this transition, the purge came to be seen by GHQ as one of the key metrics in the process of "democratization."

A total of 96 Diet members were purged following the issuance of the second purge directive. With 42 members purged, the most seriously affected was the Democratic Party that had evolved out of the Progressive Party. This was followed by the Liberal Party with 30 members, the People's Cooperative Party with eleven members, and the Socialist Party with ten members purged. Under the provisions of the second purge, by May 1948 approximately 220,000 persons were eventually purged.

General Strike of February 1

In his New Year's message of January 1, 1947, Prime Minister Yoshida criticized the labor movement and called its leaders a "band of lawless malcontents." Yoshida's broadside immediately drew a strong reaction from the labor movement. Even Arisawa and the "professors' group" who were advising Yoshida on economic matters began to distance themselves from the Prime Minister.

On January 18, Kyōtō announced a general strike to go into effect at midnight on February 1. When both Sanbetsu Kaigi and Sōdōmei pledged their support, the prospect of a general strike suddenly appeared likely.

GHQ found the increasing radicalization of the labor movement troubling, but was caught in a dilemma. On the one hand, GHQ could not allow the general strike to go forward in light of its governance duty that required it to prevent the social upheaval and confusion that could very well result from the strike. On the other hand, GHQ was anxious to avoid any form of direct intervention. Theodore Cohen, Chief of the Labor Division of the Economic and Scientific Section, wrote as follows: "The sight of Japanese workers fighting against U.S. soldiers would have made the communists happy, but certainly would not have been an edifying scene for the world to see."[69]

On January 22, William Marquat, the Chief of the Economic and Scientific Section, invited labor union representatives to a meeting where he informally advised them to call off the general strike. Acting on this advice, the Socialist Party and Sōdōmei backed down and withdrew their support. The Communist Party, however, ignored the advice and remained committed to the general strike. Kyōtō and Sanbetsu Kaigi dismissed reports of GHQ intervention as a false rumor and continued to prepare for the general strike. But all came to an end when MacArthur directed the cancellation of the strike on January 31.

GHQ found it had no choice but to intervene because the labor movement threatened to exceed the bounds of parliamentary democracy. In announcing the cancellation of the general strike through a radio broadcast on the same night, Ii Yashiro, chairman of Kyōtō, tried to ease the shock by using the

---

69 Cohen, *Remaking Japan*, p. 284.

expression, "one step back, two steps forward." Developments surrounding the failed general strike and the thought that a quasi-revolution was moving forward outside the parliamentary framework would alter the relatively tolerant attitude that the Government Section had so far maintained toward the Communist Party. Tolerance was replaced by a growing sense of caution and suspicion. It should be noted that while the political offensive failed, the labor unions did win significant victories in their economic offensive. Thus, on February 24, labor unions demanding a three-fold increase in wages came away with a two-fold increase in wages and a guarantee of an average monthly salary of 1,200 yen.

Formation of the Anti-Yoshida Front: Government Section Tilts toward the Socialist Party

February 6, 1947, witnessed the formation of the Economic Rehabilitation Council. Centered on Dōyūkai and Sōdōmei and committed to the principle of "labor-capital cooperation," the launch of the new organization signaled the derailment of the "principle of revolution" advocated by the Communist Party and Sanbetsu Kaigi. With the addition of the Socialist Party, the united anti-Yoshida front of "politicians, workers, and capital" was now in place to take on the ruling coalition.

In March, the inspection mission of the World Federation of Trade Unions (WFTU) arrived in Japan, an event that led to the formation of the Federation of All Japan Lobor Union (Zenrōren). Centered primarily on Britain's Trades Union Congress (TUC) and the Soviet Union's All-Union Central Council of Trade Unions, WFTU had been formed in October 1945 as a central organization for the labor unions of 56 countries, including America's Congress of Industrial Organizations (CIO). (The American Federation of Labor [AFL] did not join WFTU.) Zenrōren now emerged as an umbrella organization for 4,460,000 workers who belonged to such organizations as the Sanbetsu Kaigi, Sōdōmei, Kokutetsu, and the Japanese Congress of Industrial Organizations, and can be said to have unified the Japanese labor movement. However, as indicated by its name, Zenrōren was essentially a central liaison body. Furthermore, it was unable to function effectively due to the "unanimity requirement" inserted by

Sōdōmei as a precondition for its participation.

After the failed general strike of February 1, GHQ began to view the Communist Party with growing suspicion. In a conversation that took place between the Government Section's Williams and Nosaka Sanzō in March 1947, Nosaka is recorded to have said, "GHQ's feeling toward the Communist Party has changed for the worse since the spring of 1946."[70] During this period, criticism of the Communist Party's control of the labor movement was beginning to appear within Sanbetsu Kaigi, a development that can be seen as the first signs of the democratization of the labor unions.

The movement to bring down the Yoshida Cabinet, which morphed into the general strike of February 1, increased the distance between the GHQ Government Section and Yoshida and heightened the Government Section's expectations for the Socialist Party. A document of the Government Section describes this process of realignment.

The fundamental cause of all the turmoil is the nation's impoverished economy. The present government cannot be expected to save the situation. Moreover, there is no doubt that the only hope lies in political salvation. The Shidehara and Yoshida Cabinets have clearly failed to act effectively in the face of the nation's deteriorating economic conditions. Although the Liberal and Progressive Parties probably control a majority of the people, it is questionable whether they can implement the most well thought out plan without the support of the Socialist Party. The hope of the workers is clearly focused on the Socialist Party. And even though coalition-building efforts have faded, the Socialist Party unmistakably continues to be supported by the masses. Given their present quandary, the people can be expected to mount new political criticism.[71]

---

70 "Conference -Diet Building-, JW-Nosaka-HL," (March 18, 1948), Fukunaga, ed., *GHQ Minsei-kyoku shiryō, 3*, p. 525 and 528.
71 Ibid., pp. 414–416.

CHAPTER 3

Trajectory of the Middle- of-the-Road Government:
Turning Point in Reforms

1. Birth of the Katayama Cabinet: Formation of the Japan-U.S. "Reformists" Alliance

The Truman Doctrine: East-West Confrontation Intensifies

MacArthur Directive on General Elections

On January 31, 1947, Prime Minister Yoshida was preparing to reshuffle the Cabinet in an attempt to ride out the political storm engendered by the General Strike called for February 1. Meanwhile, on February 6, Yoshida received a letter from MacArthur urging him to hold an election of the House of Representatives as soon as possible.

> Momentous changes in internal structure, in economic outlook, and in the whole fabric and pattern of Japanese life have occurred since the last general election nearly a year ago. It is necessary, in the near future, to obtain another democratic expression of the people's will on the fundamental issues with which Japanese society is now confronted.[1]

MacArthur was unhappy with the Communist Party and the Congress of Industrial Unions of Japan (Sanbetsu Kaigi) for their role in pushing ahead with the general strike. But he had also grown suspicious of Yoshida for failing to squash the strike.

William Macmahon Ball, the British Commonwealth Representative to the Allied Council for Japan, described MacArthur's impatience in a letter dated February 8 addressed to his home government.

---

1 Sodei Rinjirō, ed., and trans., *Correspondence between General MacArthur, Prime Minister Yoshida & Other High Japanese Officials [1945–1951]*, Hōsei Daigaku Shuppankyoku, 2000, p. 50.

MacArthur thinks the Yoshida Cabinet must be removed. He believes the fiscal policies of Ishibashi [Finance Minister Ishibashi Tanzan] are disastrous. MacArthur pressured Yoshida to remove Ishibashi, who is completely incompetent and stubborn. But Yoshida answered that it was necessary to keep Ishibashi as a kind of symbol.

MacArthur stated that he recognizes the need of immediate and direct economic controls over resources, prices and wages in Japan…. MacArthur continued to say it was important to find a political leader that would implement this plan. He knew the Yoshida Cabinet would be unable to do this. But he knew of no one that could replace Yoshida. If he couldn't find a political leader to replace Yoshida, this would lead to the frightening possibility of direct military government.[2]

There is no way of knowing how serious MacArthur was about introducing direct military government. However, what is perfectly clear is that the General Strike on February 1 had triggered an unprecedented level of urgency and anxiety in MacArthur.

The Truman Doctrine

Western Europe was going through its own crisis between 1946 and 1947. In addition to the ruins left behind by the war, the challenges of inflation, economic stagnation, and food shortage were becoming increasingly serious with each passing day. Strikes were frequent, and the Communist Parties that had joined the fight against fascism during the war were gaining momentum in France and Italy. The U.S. government feared that this economic turmoil could metastasize into political turmoil.

Early 1947 witnessed the birth of Communist Party dictatorship regimes in Central and Eastern European countries, which were quickly drawn into the Soviet sphere of influence. While the U.S. and British governments were deeply

---

2   Rix, Alan, ed., *Nihon senryō no hibi: Makumahon Bōru nikki* [Intermittent Diplomat: The Japan and Batavia Diaries of W. Macmahon Ball], Takemae Eiji and Kikuchi Osamu, trans., Iwanami Shoten, 1992, pp. 173–174.

troubled by these developments, no concrete countermeasures were taken and the situation was allowed to continue. In February, the Paris Peace Treaties were signed between the Allies and the Axis powers of Italy, Hungary, Bulgaria, Romania, and Finland. During the same period, the Soviet Union had its eyes on Turkey and Greece in its search for a route to the Mediterranean.

On March 12, U.S. President Truman addressed the joint session of Congress, explaining that the world was divided into two alternative ways of life—totalitarianism and freedom—and that, "At the present moment in world history, nearly every nation must choose between" these alternatives. Truman pledged that the United States would act against "totalitarian regimes imposed on free peoples, by direct or indirect aggression" to prevent the "collapse of free institutions and loss of independence." With this, Truman concluded, "We shall not realize our objectives unless we are willing to help free peoples," and announced that the United States was prepared to provide military assistance to Turkey and Greece.[3] This marked the birth of what would come to be known as the Truman Doctrine.

In June, the United States announced the Marshall Plan featuring the investment of large amounts of funds to assist in Europe's recovery and reconstruction. To formulate the details of the plan, Secretary of State George Marshall turned to the State Department's Policy Planning Staff and to George Kennan, known as a leading "Soviet hand" and the architect of the "containment policy." The Marshall Plan would be designed to rescue the countries of Western Europe from the maelstrom of political and economic turmoil.

The Truman Doctrine signaled to the world that whatever harmony may have existed among the Allied Powers during the war had now crumbled to be replaced by an implacable conflict between the United States and the Soviet Union. Although the Marshall Plan was open to all countries, the Soviet Union and the other countries of the Eastern Bloc rejected the notion of participating in its programs. Instead, at the end of September 1947, the Soviet Union moved to form the Communist Information Bureau (Cominform) as an organization

---

3   Address of the President to Congress, Recommending Assistance to Greece and Turkey, March 12, 1947, The Truman Doctrine, Harry S. Truman Administration, Harry S. Truman Library and Museum.

intended to promote solidarity among the communist parties of various countries. It should be noted that the principal battleground of the Cold War remained squarely in Europe at this time. In Asia, on the other hand, the Soviet Union maintained a cautiously cooperative attitude with the United States.

MacArthur's Call for an "Early Peace Settlement" with Japan

On March 17, 1947, MacArthur expressed his support for an "early peace settlement" with Japan. The statement appeared to pay no attention to the newly minted Truman Doctrine and gave the impression that the Occupation was nearing its end.

The disarmament and demilitarization of Japan had already been completed, the new Constitution of Japan had been promulgated, and the process of democratization was nearing its end. The challenge that remained was the economic reconstruction of the nation. MacArthur emphasized that an early signing of a peace treaty required the opening of private international trade. From the outset, MacArthur had believed that the Occupation faced a time limit of two to three years, and his mind was now turning to the presidential election of November 1948 and his plans for announcing himself as a candidate. To maximize his chances in the election, MacArthur reasoned that he needed to make a triumphal return with the fruits of the Occupation under his belt.

On March 22, MacArthur sent a message to Prime Minister Yoshida instructing him to expand and strengthen the Economic Stabilization Board (ESB) as a necessary step toward putting Japan on track to economic reconstruction. MacArthur wrote, "It is essential that the Japanese Government, through the Economic Stabilization Board which was created for this purpose, take early and vigorous steps to develop and implement the integrated series of economic and financial controls which the current situation demands."[4] Following this directive, control and management of the Japanese economy became a GHQ priority on par with "democratization." MacArthur "set about headlong to

---

4 Sodei, *Correspondence between General MacArthur, Prime Minister Yoshida & Other High Japanese Officials [1945–1951]*, pp. 54–56.

accomplish the directed reforms as soon as possible."[5] It should be noted that the letter of March 22 was originally drafted by Tsuru Shigeto, who at this time was working at the Economic and Scientific Section. Shortly after drafting the letter, Tsuru would be assigned to the ESB.

Back in Washington, the finishing touches were being put on a draft peace treaty in a project led by Hugh Borton, the head of the State Department's Bureau of East Asian Affairs. It was understood that the most important objective of the treaty would be to prevent Japan's return to militarism. To achieve this purpose, the draft treaty contained a number of provisions for the control of the economy and other aspects of Japanese society. Furthermore, to ensure the full implementation of these controls, the draft treaty envisioned monitoring and supervision by a Conference of Ambassadors representing the member nations of the Far Eastern Commission. The period of monitoring and supervision was projected to continue for a period of 25 years from the signing of the peace treaty. In this and other details, the draft treaty was highly restrictive and punitive in nature. As an aside, it is interesting to note that the original draft prepared by Borton explicitly provided for the return of Okinawa to Japan.

In July, Secretary of State Marshall communicated with the ten nations of the Far Eastern Commission proposing that a preliminary peace conference be held on August 19. The Soviet Union rejected the two-thirds supermajority provision contained in the American proposal and instead suggested that decisions should be made in meetings of the foreign ministers of four countries—the United States, Britain, China, and the Soviet Union. China also rejected the Marshall proposal in order to maintain its veto power. Britain replied that it would be difficult for it to participate in the preliminary peace conference because the scheduled date overlapped with the British Commonwealth's Canberra Conference. Ultimately, no consensus could be reached and the proposal did not materialize.

Issues related to Japan were thus thrown into the vortex of international politics and the development of U.S. Occupation policies toward Japan was subsequently given over to the initiative of a group that included Under-Secretary of the Army William Draper and George Kennan.

---

5   Cohen, Theodore, *Remaking Japan: The American Occupation as New Deal*, Free Press, 1987, p. 309.

General Election of April 1947: Socialist Party Rises to the Top

Reviving Medium-Sized Electoral Districts

As the general election of April 1947 approached, conservative forces led by the Liberal and Progressive Parties began to actively lobby for the revival of medium-sized electoral districts with single-entry ballots. One of the leaders of the movement, Home Minister Uehara Etsujirō explained to the Government Section that this arrangement would lead to a more stable two-party political system. But his pleas were rejected by Brigadier General Whitney, the Chief of the Government Section. Whitney countered with the argument that there had only been one general election under the current large electoral district and restricted plural voting system, and no judgment could be made until it had been tried at least once more.

Within the Government Section, heated debate continued on the most desirable size of electoral districts and type of ballot. Many opposed medium-sized electoral districts on the grounds that the system would naturally work to the advantage of conservative political machines in rural and outlying areas. Many were also critical of single-entry ballots on the grounds that they restricted the range of choices for voters. For this reason, they supported continuing the existing system of restricted plural voting.

It is particularly interesting to note the conclusion that the Government Section had reached on a two-party system in the course of these discussions. "Japan is likely to have more than 2 parties for a long time to come, representing at least the differences between conservative, laissez-faire, socialist, co-operative and class-war views of economic life."[6] What the Government Section had in mind for Japan was a moderate, multi-party system.

However, MacArthur and Whitney opted to adopt the position of "non-intervention," because it was highly unpopular among the ranks of the Government

---

6 "Memorandum for the Chief Government Section (P.K. Roest), Conference on House of Representatives' Election Law Revision Bill" (February 4, 1947), Fukunaga Fumio, ed., in *GHQ Minsei-kyoku shiryō: Senryō kaikaku, 2* [GHQ Government Section Materials, 2], Maruzen, 1997, pp. 237–242.

Section. For instance, Alfred Hussey, the special assistant to the chief of the Government Section, commented as follows:

> Generally speaking, the feeling was that many of the losses suffered to date could be made up if, by means of a free and impartial election, a center party such as the Social Democrats could be brought into power. If at this stage a controlled election is held which results in the return of a completely conservative majority, the consequences both to Japan and to the Occupation will unquestionably be most serious.[7]

Reorganization of Political Parties: Formation of the People's Cooperative Party and Democratic Party

MacArthur's instruction to hold a general election accelerated the reorganization of Japan's political parties. On March 8, 1947, the Cooperative Democratic Party and the People's Party merged to form the People's Cooperative Party. The newly formed party counted a total of 78 members of the Diet in its ranks, and Miki Takeo of the Cooperative Democratic Party was chosen to lead the party as secretary-general. The party's platform was summarized in three points.

1. We shall establish national politics centered on the Diet.
2. We shall reconstruct the Japanese economy based on cooperative principles.
3. We shall contribute to world peace and culture based on humanitarian principles.

Changes were also afoot in the Progressive Party, where a long-standing debate had raged between the Shidehara faction and the "youth faction" led by Inukai and others. While the Shidehara faction advocated a merger with the Liberal Party, the "youth faction" consisting of younger members of the Diet opposed the merger.

At the end of December 1946, a meeting of Diet members belonging to

---

7   Ibid., "MCGS (A. Hussey), The General Election" (February 4, 1947), pp. 256–257.

the Progressive Party released a new platform and policies for the pursuit of modified capitalism. In the party conference held on January 31, 1947, a series of new rules and principles were adopted for open and transparent election of party leaders and the disclosure of the party's financial accounts. Following these developments, the Progressive Party was dissolved on March 31, and various elements of other parties were brought in to form the Democratic Party. These included Ashida Hitoshi and others who came over from the Liberal Party, plus a few who left the People's Cooperative Party to join the new entity. The newly formed Democratic Party boasted a total of 145 Diet members, making it at that point the leading party in the Diet. The Democratic Party elevated Shidehara to the post of supreme adviser while real power in the party was claimed by Ashida, Inukai, and several others. The party's platform was summarized in four points.

1. We shall maintain the spirit of the new Constitution, establish a democratic political system, and resolutely implement innovative policies that are urgently needed for the construction of a peace-loving nation.
2. We shall endeavor to bring stability to the lives of people by democratizing industries and pursuing rapid recovery and reconstruction based on a comprehensive economic plan.
3. We shall promote education that aims to develop character and individuality, cultivate religious sentiment, endeavor to raise the standards of culture among the people, and contribute to global advances in the arts.
4. We shall endeavor to regain international trust and cooperate in constructing a peaceful world.

In stating that it would "maintain the spirit of the new Constitution," the Progressive Party was distancing itself from its prewar identity rooted in the Great Japan Political Association and was clearly attempting to make a fresh start as a centrist party that stood to the "left of the Liberal Party and to the right of the Socialist Party." But the Democratic Party would soon suffer a serious setback on account of the second purge that preceded the election of the House of Representatives. The purge effectively robbed the new party of its key members, including Inukai and Narahashi.

Elections of April 1947

April 1947 started and ended with elections. The first election of the month took place on April 5, consisting of the first open election of the governors and mayors. Next, the first election of the House of Councillors was held on April 20. This was followed on April 25 with the election of the House of Representatives. Finally, elections of local assembly members were held on the last day of the month.

In the election of prefectural governors held on April 5, veterans and incumbents who had been nominated by the government under the prewar system dominated the outcome. Out of a total of 46 gubernatorial elections, incumbents and previous office holders won in 29 elections. The total number of incumbents plus newly elected conservatives came to 42, accounting for 90 percent of all governors. Socialist candidates won in only four gubernatorial races—Hokkaido, Nagano, Tokushima, and Fukuoka—in what turned out to be a "national landslide" for conservatives. In mayoral elections held on the same day, Socialist candidates won in the major cities of Yokohama, Nagoya, Kyoto, Osaka, and Kobe.

In the election of the House of Councillors where 250 seats were at stake, independents and minor parties took a total of 122 seats. The Socialist Party with 47 seats emerged as the leading party in the upper house, followed by the Liberal Party with 38 seats and the Democratic Party with 30 seats. These results accurately foretold the outcome of the lower house elections held five days later. In the House of Councillors, many of the newly elected independents came together to form the Green Breeze Society (Ryokufūkai) that committed to judging matters on a case-by-case basis rather than to developing a concrete platform.

The election of the House of Representatives was held on April 25. Here again the Socialist Party emerged as the leading party with a total of 143 seats, followed by the Liberal Party with 131 seats, the Democratic Party with 124 seats, the People's Democratic Party with 31 seats, the Communist Party with 4 seats, and independents and minor parties with 33 seats.

Commenting on the outcome of the lower house elections, *Asahi Shinbun* wrote that the results "reflect the tide of the times" and explained that the outcome "reflects the defeat in the war and the suffering that the people face. At the same time, in an election conducted under the watchful eyes of the international community, the people have shown that they are endowed with a full measure of political and democratic awareness."[8] On April 27, MacArthur released a statement on the election to the following effect.

With the recently held series of elections, the last preparatory step necessary for the inauguration of the new Japanese constitution has been accomplished.... The Japanese people have firmly and decisively rejected its [comunist] leadership and overwhelmingly have chosen a moderate course, sufficiently centered from either extreme to insure the preservation of freedom and the enhancement of individual dignity.[9]

Working to Form a Coalition Government: Liberal Party Breaks Away

Because the election failed to produce a majority party, the same process of coalition building that followed the previous election ensued. Upon hearing that the Socialist Party had won the largest number of seats, the party's Secretary-General Nishio Suehiro is reported to have famously said, "This spells trouble." On the other hand, the party's Chairman Katayama Tetsu responded to the news of victory with determination. "The forthcoming administration must be one that is centered on the Socialist Party as the leading party."

While the Socialist Party had emerged as the leading party, the difference between the number of seats it won and the number won by the Liberal Party and the Democratic Party was marginal. In the three-cornered contest that ensued, there was no guarantee that the Socialist Party would take the premiership. As the Liberal and Democratic Parties in combination held a majority of the seats, a possibility existed for a conservative coalition. But Yoshida Shigeru, President of the Liberal Party, had other things in mind. "As things have turned out, it is

---

8   *Asahi Shinbun*, April 28, 1947.
9   Statement on Elections of April 1947, April 27, 1947, Statements by MacArthur, Box No. 2195, Folder 22, GHQ/SCAP Records, Government Section, National Diet Library, Originals in U.S. National Archives & Records Administration, RG331.

important for us to remain calm and to be good losers," he advocated. "We should facilitate the emergence of a government of the Socialist Party."[10] Yoshida believed that his party should remain faithful to the normal course of constitutional government, in which losers should retreat into opposition. Of course, it is not difficult to imagine that Yoshida wanted to give the Socialists a chance so that they could prove their ineptitude.

It was Nishio who took the initiative in forming a coalition. A native of Kagawa Prefecture, Nishio was born in 1891 (Meiji 24) and had emerged as a leader of the labor movement after rising to the post of Director of the Osaka Federation of the Friendship Society (Yūaikai) in 1920. He had served two terms in the prewar Diet after winning a seat as a member of the Social Democratic Party (Shakai Minshū-tō) in the first universal male suffrage election held in 1928.

While carefully avoiding any explicit reference to a Socialist-led government, Nishio

Nishio Suehiro (1891–1981) From labor leader to politician, Nishio served fifteen terms in the Diet after winning a seat in the first universal male suffrage election of 1928. Even during the war years, he continued to maintain a seat without nomination by the Imperial Rule Assistance Association. In the postwar years, he led the Socialist Party with his skilled negotiating and executive abilities. Nishio served as the Chief Cabinet Secretary of the Katayama Cabinet and as Vice Premier in the Ashida Cabinet. Nishio was arrested in connection to the Shōden Scandal but was later acquitted.

mapped out a plan for an "all-Japan coalition cabinet" comprising four political parties: the Socialist Party, the Liberal Party, the Democratic Party, and the People's Cooperative Party. In a meeting of the representatives of the four parties held on May 9, an agreement was reached on forming a "four-party coalition cabinet." This was followed by a series of discussions designed to hammer together a unified policy agreement for the four parties. Nishio prepared a draft agreement that reflected the contents of the March 22 letter of MacArthur to

---

10 Yoshida Shigeru to Makino Nubuaki, (May 3, 1947), Yoshida Kinen Zaidan, ed., *Yoshida Shigeru shokan* [Letters of Yoshida Shigeru], Chūō Kōronsha, 1994, p. 675.

Katayama Tetsu (1887–1978)
Formerly a lawyer and social activist, Katayama served a total of twelve terms in the House of Representatives starting in the prewar years. After the war, he rose to the chairmanship of the Socialist Party, which emerged as the leading party in the first postwar general election, and assumed the post of Prime Minister in May 1947. Katayama promoted democratization with the support of the Government Section, but his administration collapsed under the strains placed on it by the conflicting right and left wings of the Socialist Party.

Yoshida. By drawing on MacArthur's authority, Nishio succeeded in finalizing a four-party policy agreement on May 16.

But Nishio would soon be tested by the two conservative parties in the coalition. The Democratic Party was split into two camps. On one side, the Shidehara faction advocated entering into a coalition with the Liberal Party, and on the other, the Ashida faction supported the coalition proposed by the Socialist Party. On May 18, Ashida acceded to the presidency of the Democratic Party and immediately moved to join the Socialist coalition. On the following day, Yoshida demanded that the coalition exclude the left wing of the Socialist Party that was advocating cooperation with the Communist Party. When Yoshida's demand was rejected, the Liberal Party broke away from the coalition and opted for limiting itself to external support from outside the Cabinet.

United Government by Japan-U.S. "Reformists"

When the Constitution of Japan came into force on May 3, 1947, the Socialist Party's Katayama exclaimed, "I am overcome with joy at the birth of the new Constitution, and it is for this reason that I laud its establishment from the bottom of my heart." Katayama was particularly fond of the Preamble and its references to democracy and pacifism, and commenting, "It is from a completely new perspective that the Constitution extols global awareness and international political morality, and it is with unalloyed courage and a forward-looking spirit that the Constitution employs progressive expressions."[11] On another occasion,

---

11 Katayama Tetsu, *Kaiko to tenbō* [Recollections and Outlook], Fukumura Shuppan, 1967, p. 280.

Katayama said of the Constitution, "While reactionary elements may feel that it was pushed upon them, that certainly is not true in relation to the Japanese people."[12]

On May 23, in a nearly unanimous vote, the House of Representatives and the House of Councillors elected Katayama as the next Prime Minister. On the following day, MacArthur issued a statement welcoming this outcome saying, "Mr. Katayama's selection as the new Prime Minister emphasizes the 'middle of the road course' of Japanese internal politics."[13] MacArthur was particularly pleased that Japan for the first time in its history would be headed by a Christian leader. Charles Kades, Deputy Chief of the Government Section, expressed the hope that the new Cabinet would "remain in power for the full four years permitted by the Constitution or until Japan regained her independence."[14] This marked the start of a united government by Japan-U.S. "reformists." It signified an alliance between the Socialist Party and the Government Section that had taken the lead in promoting Japan's democratization.

Katayama Tetsu was born in Wakayama Prefecture in 1887 (Meiji 20). After graduating from the Third High School, Katayama entered Tokyo Imperial University's College of Law where he majored in German jurisprudence. Finding himself in the heyday of Taishō Democracy, he is said to have studied democracy under Yoshino Sakuzō and socialism under Abe Isoo. After finishing his studies, Katayama became a lawyer and helped Abe form the Social Democratic Party. He won a seat in the House of Representatives in the election of 1930 and served four terms until he was defeated in the election of 1942 when he ran as a non-nominated candidate. Although widely respected for his sincerity and clean and forthright character, Katayama lacked leadership qualities and was frequently called "*guzu Tetsu*" or "indecisive Tetsu," a stinging Japanese pun on his given name.

---

12 Sakamoto Yoshikazu and Robert E. Ward, eds., *Nihon senryō no kenkyū* [Research on the Occupation of Japan], University of Tokyo Press, 1987, p. 456.
13 On Selection of Tetsu Katayama as Prime Minister, May 24, 1947, Statements by MacArthur, Box No. 2195, Folder 22, GHQ/SCAP Records, Government Section, National Diet Library, Originals in U.S. National Archives & Records Administration, RG331.
14 Williams, Justin, *Japan's Political Revolution under MacArthur: A Participants Account*, University of Georgia Press, 1979, p. 49.

It was Nishio Suehiro who covered Katayama's fatal flaws as a political leader. As the Chief Cabinet Secretary in the Katayama Cabinet, Nishio was wont to describe his relationship to the Prime Minister in an analogy. "Mr. Katayama's mission is to bear the cross, and my mission is to follow closely after him wielding an ax."[15]

June 1, 1947, marked the birth of the three-party coalition of the Socialist, Democratic, and the People's Cooperative Parties. The Socialist and Democratic Parties were each given seven Cabinet ministries, while the People's Cooperative Party was given two seats in the Cabinet. The Democratic Party's Ashida Hitoshi took the post of Foreign Minister with the status of Vice Premier. From the Socialist Party, Mizutani Chōzaburō was assigned the Ministry of Commerce and Industry, and Hirano Rikizō became Minister of Agriculture. From the People's Cooperative Party, Miki Takeo became Minister of Communications. The other appointee from this party was Wada Hiroo who had served as Minister of Agriculture in the Yoshida Cabinet. Following on Yoshida's recommendation, Wada was now appointed Director of the Economic Stabilization Board, the body responsible for supporting Japan's wobbly economy.

Pursuing Thorough Democratization: Civil Code, Penal Code, and the Police

Revision of the Civil Code and Penal Code

The Katayama Cabinet faced two primary challenges. One was the development of legal systems and institutions that corresponded to the new Constitution, and the other was the reconstruction of the economy.

Katayama would later write, "I endeavored to place Japan on track toward realizing democratic politics. In this sense, I am satisfied that I played a very important historic role."[16] It is particularly noteworthy that while the Yoshida Cabinet had made the requisite preparations for developing the necessary legal

---

15 Takemae Eiji, *Nihon senryō: GHQ kōkan no shōgen* [The Occupation as Told by Senior GHQ Officials], Chūō Kōronsha, 1988, p. 51.
16 Katayama, *Kaiko to tenbō*, p. 280.

systems and institutions, Yoshida had not been able to bring these efforts to fruition, and it was now left to the Katayama Cabinet to complete the process. In later years, Charles Kades, Deputy Chief of the Government Section would reminisce, "Under Katayama's leadership, we obtained a great opportunity for accelerating the achievement of the goals of the Occupation." "It was an excellent cabinet."[17] A good example of this acceleration can be found in developments related to the revision of the Civil Code.

It was generally assumed that the old Civil Code would have to be revised in line with the new Constitution in order to include explicit provisions for such principles as the dignity of the individual and the equality of the sexes. Matters related to the institution of the family as contained under Part IV (Relatives) and Part V (Inheritance) were identified as particularly thorny and critical areas for revision. The original draft of the revised Civil Code was compiled by the Justice System Investigation Committee that had been established in July 1946 under the aegis of the Ministry of Justice. The draft was submitted for deliberation by the Temporary Committee for the Investigation of Legal Systems and finally to the government in January 1947 under the title of Outline for Civil Code Reform.

The Government Section did not intervene in the drafting and deliberative processes during this entire period. In this regard, Alfred Oppler, Chief of the Courts and Legal Division, commented that equality of the sexes and the principle of individual freedom had to be observed. But other than that, the modernization and revision of issues related to family law were the business of the Japanese people themselves. It was unwise to thrust Western values upon an Eastern nation. Research and preparations for the abolition of the "house system," the "head of household system," and "inheritance by head of household" were led by scholars of civil law (family law) who had been appointed to the drafting committee. These scholars included Wagatsuma Sakae (University of Tokyo), Nakagawa Zennosuke (Tohoku University), and Kawashima Takeyoshi (University of Tokyo). In reality, it was already proving difficult in the prewar years to ensure consistency between the house system and actual practice. The

---

17 Kades, Charles, interview by Fukunaga Fumio, August 25, 1989.

scholars understood their task of the revision to be the reduction of the gap that had come to exist between the law and social reality.

As a prewar lawyer, Katayama had been enthusiastically involved in the movement to revise the house system. As witnessed by the fact that his first book was entitled *Fujin no hōritsu* (Laws Related to Married Women), Katayama was committed to rectifying social conventions and legal systems that had long contributed to the degradation and unhappy plight of women.

Concurrent with the preparation of the government draft on the revision of the Civil Code, a group centered on Katayama completed its own "Draft of the Family Law" in June 1946 with the principal aim of expanding the legal rights of women. Instead of the conventional family system autocratically ruled by the head of household, the Katayama draft envisioned the home and family as a peaceful refuge founded on the principles of trust, love, and respect and mutual assistance among parents and children, family members, and husband and wife. The Katayama draft also contained the following specific measures: (1) abolition of inheritance by the head of household and adoption of a system for equal division of inheritance that recognized the right of inheritance of spouse, (2) elimination of discrimination against children born out of wedlock, (3) freedom of marriage, and (4) abolition of inequality of sexes in divorce. In these details, the Katayama draft was quite similar in content to the government's revision proposal.

The draft of the new Civil Code was submitted to the first session of the Diet on July 23, 1946. The bill was adopted in November with only minor changes and went into force in January 1948.

As it turned out, the most contentious issues in the revision of the Penal Code involved the treatment of crimes of lèse-majesté and adultery. Although the two conservative parties of Liberal and Progressive demanded that provisions against these acts be retained, they were ultimately stricken from the new Penal Code that went into effect on November 15, 1947. The revision of the Civil and Penal Codes can be said to represent instances in which the Katayama Cabinet took the initiative to democratize the legal system.

Reforming the Police: Conflict between the Government Section and the G2 Section

The revision of the police system that had effectively controlled the people before and during the war was one of the key features of the proposed dissolution of the Ministry of Home Affairs that is discussed in a later section. Efforts to revise the police system became intertwined in the conflict between the Government Section and G2 Section (Public Safety Division).

The conflict was rooted in the turf battles that raged within GHQ. While the revision of the police system came under the purview of G2, the Ministry of Home Affairs, which controlled the entire police system, had been placed under the jurisdiction of the Government Section. To further complicate matters, MacArthur had identified two main objectives in police reform: maintaining law and order on a national level, and preventing the resurrection of a "police state." No consensus had been reached within GHQ on which aspect of police reform to prioritize.

For instance, from the perspective of maintaining law and order, G2 advocated the creation of a national rural police force. Additionally, G2 called for retaining the Bureau of Police and Public Security and renaming it the Public Security Agency, and placing the entire police system under centralized control. On the other hand, the Government Section was committed to thorough decentralization and placing the police under local government entities. Another area of contention was the treatment of autonomous police forces. While the Government Section argued that any local government entity with a population of more than 5,000 should be allowed to maintain an autonomous police force, G2 demanded that the cut-off point be placed at municipalities with populations exceeding 50,000 people.

The Japanese government finalized its proposals for revising the police system on July 29, 1947. In several key areas, the proposal was close to the position of the Government Section. The proposal contained no reference to a Public Security Agency, advocated immediate decentralization in six major cities and on the prefectural level, and supported a major reduction in scale of the old national police organization. Upon seeing the government proposal, G2 mounted a furious counter-offensive to push back on the initiatives that were consistent with the position of the Government Section. What resulted was a second government proposal that was released on August 29 through the Minister of Home Affairs, Kimura Kozaemon, and Saitō Takao, Minister of State without Portfolio. The revised proposal called for maintaining the national rural police and placed a police force of 30,000 officers under the jurisdiction of the Public Security Agency. In essence, it paralleled the positions taken by G2.

Caught between the two camps, Katayama wrote to MacArthur requesting his mediation in resolving the problem. In his letter, Katayama first outlined the two proposals that were before him: the "progressive" proposal featuring decentralization and autonomous police forces, and a "conservative" proposal for maintaining the national rural police force. From there, Katayama added that he wanted to adopt a "middle-of-the-road approach that lay somewhere between the two extremes." This meant a mixed structure that combined national rural police and autonomous police forces.[18]

MacArthur's response was delivered to Katayama on September 18. MacArthur had opted for allowing local government entities with a population of more than 5,000 to maintain their own autonomous police forces. In effect, what MacArthur was supporting concurred with "about 80 percent of the Government Section's Whitney-Kades line."[19] Based on this guidance from MacArthur, the Police Law was enacted in December 1947. What emerged was a new structure consisting of a national rural police force with 30,000 personnel and autonomous police forces with 95,000 personnel.

Reforming Boss and Henchmen Systems

GHQ documents contain a file titled "*Oyabun-Kobun* Systems (Boss and Henchmen)."[20] According to Justin Williams, Chief of the Government Section's

---

18 Sodei, *Correspondence between General MacArthur, Prime Minister Yoshida & Other High Japanese Officials [1945–1951]*, pp. 75–78.
19 Local Government Research and Data Center, ed., *Sengo jichi-shi, 9* [Postwar History of Local Government, vol. 9], Bunsei Shuppan, 1977, pp. 111–123.
20 Fukunaga, ed., *GHQ Minsei-kyoku shiryō, 10*.

Parliamentary and Political Division, the Government Section's Deputy Chief Kades personally took the initiative to eliminate what he considered to be the two evils of postwar Japanese society. The first of these evils was the political corruption associated with the illegal disposal of the Imperial Army's wartime stockpiles of goods and materials, and the second referred to the inroads that criminal underworld organizations had made into broad sections of Japanese society, including the police, labor organizations, the business world, and politics.[21]

Following the Shinbashi Incident (armed clashes between the Kantō Matsuda-gumi and rival Taiwanese in Japan in June 1946 over control of the Shinbashi market), the Civil Intelligence Section of the Public Safety Division (CIS/PSD) turned its attention to boss and henchmen systems from the perspective of maintaining law and order. With this, CIS/PSD became engaged in problems related to yakuza organizations and *tekiya* (street vendors active in black markets, considered to be predecessors of yakuza). In the summer of 1947, the Civil Information and Education Section presented its plan to the Government Section for eliminating boss and henchmen systems. After September, interest in related issues began to build throughout GHQ.

On September 11, the newly formed Subcommittee on Boss and Henchmen Systems held its first meeting with representatives from the Government Section, the Economic and Scientific Section, G2, the Natural Resources Section, the Civil Information and Education Section, the Eighth Army, and the General Procurement Agent. Each participating arm of GHQ seemed to have its own specific area of interest.

For instance, the Economic and Scientific Section's Antitrust and Cartels Division was focused on the activities of labor procurement organizations in the construction industry and street-stall associations. The same section's Industrial Division was interested in relations between the police and gangs in coal mining regions, the Finance Division was primarily concerned with the extensive presence of bosses in tax-collecting operations, and the Labor Division was focused on slave labor and sweatshops (*tako beya*). Furthermore, the Civil Transportation

---

21 Williams, *Japan's Political Revolution under MacArthur*, pp. 45–47.

Section was interested in looking at the condition of stevedores and related port-side labor, and the Public Safety Division was concerned with the inroads that gambling Oyabuns (*Kashimoto*), tekiya, and gangsters (*guren-tai*) had made into all areas of Japan's politics, economy, and society.[22]

The Subcommittee met for the second time on September 18, marking the start of the implementation of the plan for the elimination of boss and henchmen systems. At around this time, English language newspapers were reporting at length on the boss and henchmen system. An article written by Darrell Berrigan in the *New York Post* titled "Tokyo's Own Al Capone" drew particular attention.

On September 19, Kades released a statement he called "The Constitution and the Dark Curtain." In it, Kades attacked the close ties between politics and the criminal underworld and called for the "eradication of the enemy of the people."[23] The Government Section was prepared to cut into the ugly underbelly of Japanese society to eradicate any practice or vestige of feudalism or totalitarianism that stood in the way of democratic politics. It is reported that the Kades statement was intended to be a call to local government heads, Diet members, and the electorate to stand in unison to eliminate the evil forces that sought to obstruct the democratic development of Japanese society under the new Constitution of Japan.

In October, the Government Section began to work on new legislation related to boss and henchmen systems. In its third meeting held on October 3, the Subcommittee made two decisions. First, it was decided that *Asahi Shinbun* would, with the cooperation of the Civil Information and Education Section, conduct an opinion poll on boss and henchmen systems. Second, the Subcommittee agreed to petition the Supreme Commander to issue a statement on the subject.

However, the campaign to eliminate the yakuza that was supported by Kades' crusader zeal made no further progress, and very little was ever proposed beyond the GHQ propaganda program that was designed to expose a hidden *kuromaku* (black curtain) government operating in Japan, *tekiya*, and *guren-tai*

---

22 "Memorandum for the Control Coordinating Committee, ESS, 'Report of Oyabun-Kobun Sub-Committee,'" (September 25, 1947), Fukunaga, ed., in *GHQ Minsei-kyoku shiryō, 10*, pp. 45–51.
23 Ibid., "The Constitution of the Dark Curtain," (September 19, 1947), pp. 35–39.

associations who were influencing the government. Thus, the campaign gradually petered out and disappeared within two months of the press conference that Kades had called to make his statement. While MacArthur did not get in the way of the Kades campaign, he could see that boss and henchmen systems were deeply ingrained in Japanese culture. MacArthur had concluded that arrests could be made but there was no guarantee that these traditional ties and institutions could be successfully eradicated.

Political Parties in Okinawa: Moving toward Democracy

Slow Progress in Okinawa

It was not until July 3, 1947, that the people of Okinawa regained the freedom of movement during daylight hours. Prior to this date, people could not even visit a neighboring village without a police permit. It should be noted that freedom of movement after dark was not restored until March 1948.

Progress remained slow in Okinawan society. Land taken by the U.S. military was not being returned on any significant scale and people remained dependent on rations. To further complicate matters, the return of demobilized soldiers and civilians from the southern islands and the Japanese mainland that began in the summer of 1946 led to a rapid increase of the population. By the end of 1947, the total number of returnees came to nearly 174,000 people, and the population of Okinawa grew from about 330,000 at the end of the war to 560,000 by 1948.

Starting in July 1946, food and materials financed by the U.S. Government Appropriation for Relief in Occupied Areas Fund (GARIOA Fund) began to arrive in Okinawa. While this eased the general shortage of food and other materials, it was not sufficient to satisfy everyone's hunger. On the other hand, yen currency brought to Okinawa by returnees increased the supply of money, which in turn triggered hyperinflation and economic turmoil.[24]

---

24 Bank of the Ryūkyūs Research Department, ed., *Sengo Okinawa keizai-shi* [Postwar Economic History of Okinawa], Ryūkyū Ginkō, 1984, p. 85.

In order to increase agricultural production, Governor Shikiya Kōshin wanted to introduce a "system similar to the Farmland Adjustment Law," which in effect would be an Okinawan version of the Farmland Reform enacted in Japan.[25] In the case of Okinawa, however, there were hardly any landowners whose holdings exceeded 1 *chōbu*. For the most part, farmland holdings in Okinawa had always been fragmented and were low in productivity. Thus, the proposed system was primarily aimed at resolving the land disputes that had arisen between cultivators and landowners as a result of the land "allotment system" carried out by previous landowners, the Occupation Forces and local governments.

In the fall of 1947, MacArthur's GHQ sent the following report to Secretary of the Army Kenneth Royall. "Based on what has been accomplished so far and future needs to be met, we expect that in the next five years Okinawa will be able to achieve an unprecedented level of self-sufficiency in the range of 90–100 percent." Considering the prevailing conditions, this projection was unrealistic.[26]

Enactment of Local Elections Law: "Democratization" from Above

In a letter addressed to the governor and dated May 9, 1947, the military government instructed the governor to report on the views of the Okinawa Civilian Administration on the enactment of laws concerning the election of heads of local government and members of the prefectural assembly. At the same time, Cecil Tilton was summoned to Okinawa from Tokyo. As the chief of the Local Government Division of the Government Section, Tilton had been in charge of GHQ's local government reform.

Upon arriving in Okinawa, Tilton explained to the Civilian Administration that GHQ's primary concern was to conduct free elections, and that this required

---

25 Kayō Yasuharu, *Okinawa minsei-fu* [Okinawa Civilian Administration], Kume Shobō, 1986, p. 132–134.
26 Okinawa Prefecture, Bunka shinkō-kai kōbunsho kanri-bu shiryō henshū-shitsu, ed., *Okinawa ken-shi shiryō-hen 14: Ryūkyū rettō no gunsei 1945–1950 gendai 2 (Wayaku-hen)* [Okinawa Prefecture Historical Documents 14: Military Government of the Ryukyus 1945–1950 Contemporary 2 (Japanese translations)], Okinawa Prefecture Board of Education, 2002, p. 194.

the enactment of new laws. Moreover, he explained that such laws did not necessarily have to be written by the military government and that the Civilian Administration was being asked to draft its own laws while using the proposals of the military government as guidelines.[27]

The Civilian Administration responded by forming an Election Laws Drafting Committee. Having gained the approval of the military government, the Law for the Election of Local Government Heads was promulgated in December 1947 as "Military Government Proclamation No. 22." One of the drafters of the law was Kayō Yasuharu, who had worked in the secretariat of the House of Peers until November 1947. In this post, Kayō had gained detailed knowledge and first-hand experience in the formation of the Constitution of Japan. Kayō viewed the enactment of Okinawa's local elections laws in tandem with the enactment and enforcement of Japan's Local Autonomy Law and assessed Okinawa's new laws as "worthy of being recorded in political history as the first step toward local autonomy and the most important development" achieved in line with "Japan's postwar reformation."[28]

In the process of drafting the law, views were expressed favoring the purge of former militarists from public office in Okinawa as had been done on the Japanese mainland. This was considered to be a necessary "aspect of the postwar democratization policy." The matter was put to the military government, and a response was received to the effect that the military government could not decide on its own. Consequently, the military government referred the matter to GHQ. The question was finally settled when GHQ decided that the purge would not apply to Okinawa.

---

27 Okinawa Prefectural Library, Historical Materials Department, ed., *Okinawa-ken shiryō: Sengo 2 Okinawa minsei-fu kiroku 1–2* [Okinawa Prefecture Historical Documents–Postwar 2: Records of the Civil Administration of the Ryukyu Islands 1–2], Okinawa Prefecture Board of Education, 1988–1990, p. 332.

28 Kayō, *Okinawa minsei-fu*, p. 141.

Toward Local Autonomy and Democratization: Formation of Political Parties

Parallel to these developments, the people of Okinawa raised their voices for local autonomy and democratization. These movements were led by prewar activists and returnees who had observed and experienced the unfolding of postwar reforms in Japan.

In May 1947, the Council for the Construction of Okinawa was established as part of a democratic enlightenment movement that had been initiated primarily by returnees from the Japanese mainland. In the following month, the first postwar political party to be established on the mainland of Okinawa came into being under the name of the Okinawa Democratic Alliance. In the declaration of its establishment, the party advocated the "liberation of Okinawa by the people of Okinawa" and called for the "establishment of democratic politics" founded on the principles of parliamentary government and separation of powers.

July saw the establishment of the Okinawa People's Party, an amalgam of prewar labor activists and persons with prior experience in socialist movements. The party chose "Establish an autonomous government of the people" as its slogan. It announced that it would "Fight all conservative and reactionary forces in compliance with the intent of the Potsdam Declaration; establish democracy in all areas of politics, economy, society, and culture; and pursue the liberation of all the peoples of Okinawa."

In September, the Okinawa Social Party was established in Misato Village (present-day Okinawa City). In October, the party merged with the Ryukyu Social Party that had been established in Shuri City to form the Social Party. Concerning the future of Okinawa, the newly formed party was unique in that it supported the assignment of the island to the United States, advocated the adoption of stronger anti-communist policies, and welcomed foreign investment.

All of the parties supported the establishment of a democratic government. Because the administration of Okinawa had been separated from Japan, the parties were not influenced by the political parties of the Japanese mainland and developed along their own lines. Moreover, as Okinawa was under military government, the parties directed their criticism against the Civilian Administration and avoided entanglement with the military government. Another aspect the parties shared was that membership was essentially based on personal ties and geographic identities. As such, considerable time would have to pass before the parties were ready to play substantive roles on the political stage.

During this period, political parties were also being formed in the three island chains of Amami, Miyako, and Yaeyama. In addition to democratization, these political parties called for the realization of the following local objectives: (1) public election of the heads of prefectural branch offices, governors and assembly members, (2) establishment of separate decision-making bodies for each island chain, (3) enactment of democratic laws and legal systems, and (4) amalgamation of the former administrative bodies of Okinawa's three island chains and establishment of a unified government for the whole of the Ryukyu Islands.

Sebald Report

On October 24, 1947, the General Headquarters of the Far East Command ordered the Philippines-Ryukyus Command to establish a Military Government Section. The reason given was that coordinated action had to be taken to address the political, social, and economic problems facing the Ryukyu Islands.[29] At around this time, in Washington, the State Department and the military had come to agree that the "United States shall govern the southern Ryukyu Islands." The consensus reflected the ongoing escalation of the Cold War.

Two years after the end of the war, it was clear that the control and governance of Okinawa was not proceeding smoothly or successfully. Visiting Okinawa in November 1947, William Sebald, Chief of the Diplomatic Section of GHQ, reported on conditions as follows:

[Okinawa] is a small country, occupied by military authorities whose policies are shortsighted and paternalistic, and who lack all appreciation of a long-term policy of democratization leading to the ends of an autonomous

---

29 Bank of the Ryūkyūs Research Department, ed., *Sengo Okinawa keizai-shi*, p. 127.

and peaceful democratic society…. The Military Government officers have little conception or appreciation of United States policies in so far as the Ryukyu Islands in general, and Okinawa in particular, are concerned.

Sebald reported that the military government was run on a "day-to-day basis" and that 500,000 Okinawans were "caught in a net of abject poverty, hopelessness, and inability to aid themselves by their own efforts or limited indigenous resources."[30]

The Treatment of Okinawa: American and Japanese Expectations

Okinawa in the Context of an Early Peace Settlement

Following MacArthur's statement of March 17, 1947, which pointed to an early peace settlement, the Japanese side began to take preparatory steps toward the signing of a peace treaty. The process would be led by Ashida Hitoshi, the Katayama Cabinet's Foreign Minister.

On June 5, 1947, Ashida made a statement at a press conference for foreign journalists to the effect that the Japanese people had doubts regarding the application of the Potsdam Declaration to Okinawa and some of the Kurile Islands. Okinawa was not particularly important to the Japanese economy, but the Japanese wanted the islands returned for sentimental reasons.[31] The Ashida statement created a stir on the question of the reversion of the Okinawa and Amami Islands. But the response of the Allied Powers was cold and critical. It was their position that Japan had absolutely no right to comment or make demands on the content of a future peace treaty.

The matter came up for debate in the Diet, where the Socialist Party's Katō Kanjū criticized the Ashida statement on the Ryūkyū and Kurile Islands. "I believe this clearly violates Article 8 of the Potsdam Declaration [Japanese

---

30 Eldridge, Robert D., *The Origins of the Bilateral Okinawa Problem*, Routledge, 2013, p. 140.
31 *Asahi Shinbun*, June 7, 1947.

sovereignty shall be limited to the islands of Honshu, Hokkaido, Kyushu, Shikoku, and such minor islands as we determine]. What say you?" Ashida responded that he was aware that it violated the Potsdam Declaration to ask for the reversion of Okinawa on the grounds that it comprised an inherent territory of Japan. He added that historically, Okinawa and the Kurile Islands were part of Japan's political and economic sphere and were inhabited by a common people. In conclusion, he explained that the intent of his statement was that Japan should request special consideration of the Allied Powers on this point in drawing up a peace treaty.

On July 22, Ashida was summoned by the Shōwa Emperor to present a private report on diplomatic matters. During this session, the Emperor expressed concern for the future direction of U.S.-U.S.S.R. relations and said, "In the final analysis, Japan should walk in step with the United States as cooperation with the Soviet Union would be difficult." Ashida responded, "I am of exactly the same opinion."[32]

"Okinawans are not Japanese"

In his March 1947 statement on an early peace settlement, MacArthur suggested that the United Nations should be responsible for protecting the national security of Japan's disarmed neutrality. MacArthur explained that this would be predicated on maintaining the overwhelming dominance of the United States in the Pacific area and on placing Okinawa under the strategic trusteeship of the United States.

Appearing before a group of American journalists on July 27, MacArthur made the following two points. (1) Given that the Soviet Union has satisfied its demands on Japan through the military occupation of the Kurile Islands, it is unlikely that it would strongly oppose the drafting of a peace treaty. (2) The Ryūkyū Islands are a natural border. The Okinawans are not Japanese, and there does not seem to be any opposition among the people of Okinawa to America's

---

32 Shindō Eichi and Shimokōbe Motoharu, eds., *Ashida Hitoshi nikki* [Ashida Hitoshi Diary], Iwanami Shoten, 1986, (July 22, 1947).

occupation of Okinawa.

MacArthur's view of Okinawa reflected the views contained in *Ryukyu*, a civilian handbook compiled during the war in the United States.

At around this time, Ashida completed his draft of the so-called "First Ashida Memo" outlining Japanese government requests for a peace treaty and hand-delivered it to George Atcheson Jr., Chief of the Diplomatic Section (Atcheson was killed in an airplane accident and was succeeded by Sebald on September 2), and Whitney, the Chief of the Government Section. Ashida's primary request was for the peace treaty to be based on the Atlantic Charter and the Potsdam Declaration. On the question of "minor islands," the status of which was to be determined by the Allied Powers as stated in the Potsdam Declaration, Ashida requested that, "full consideration be given to the historical, ethnic, economic, cultural, and other ties that exist between the mainland and these islands." The First Ashida Memo was ultimately returned to the Japanese government on the grounds that it was "arrogant" of the Japanese side to present such a document on current international conditions.

In a confidential message written to Secretary of State George Marshall in September, MacArthur emphasized that it was absolutely essential for the United States to retain control over the Ryukyu Islands and wrote, "Failure to secure it for control by the United States might prove militarily disastrous."[33]

The Emperor's Message on Okinawa

On September 19, Terasaki Hidenari, a personal adviser to the Emperor, met with Sebald, the newly appointed chief of the Diplomatic Section. The purpose of the meeting was to convey the Emperor's thoughts on the future of Okinawa, the gist of which can be summarized in the following three points.

1. It is desirable for the United States to continue to militarily occupy the Ryukyu Islands as this will be beneficial to the United States and contribute

---

33 General of the Army Douglas MacArthur to the Secretary of State, September 1, 1947, *FRUS*, 1947, The Far East (Tokyo), vol. 6, Document 413.

to the defense of Japan.

2. America's military occupation of Okinawa should be based on a fiction that takes the form of a long-term lease—from twenty-five to fifty years or more—in which Japan retains sovereignty over Okinawa.

3. This type of method of occupation will convince the Japanese people that the United States has no permanent designs on the Ryūkyū Islands. It will also prevent others, in particular the Soviet Union and China, from making similar claims of rights.

According to the Emperor's way of thinking, Japan would retain sovereignty while offering military base rights in Okinawa to the United States. On the same day, Ashida visited the Emperor to deliver his second private report on diplomatic affairs. Ashida reported that the Emperor expressed very strong interest in preparations for a peace treaty and the future of Japan's national security. Be that as it may, upon receiving the Emperor's response, the U.S. State Department began to use the Emperor's message as justification for changing its policies on Okinawa.

Also during September, Ashida arranged for the so-called "Second Ashida Memo" to be hand-delivered to Lieutenant General Eichelberger, commander of the Eighth Army. The task of delivering the document fell to Suzuki Tadakatsu, Chief of the Yokohama Liaison Office.

Ashida started his second memo with a proposal for Japan to rely on the United Nations to preserve its national security. In the event this proved impossible due to international circumstances, Ashida suggested that Japan's national security would be preserved by providing the United States with military bases. The memo also contained the well-known passage, "at all events...the United States will maintain sufficient military strength on certain strategic points in areas outside of but adjacent to Japan."[34] Although not explicitly mentioned, the memo was proposing full-time stationing of American forces in Okinawa and the Ogasawara Islands combined with the use of bases in Japan restricted to such emergencies as "if and when Japan's independence and security is threatened."

---

34 Eldridge, *The Origins of the Bilateral Okinawa Problem*, pp. 111–112.

2. Middle-of-the-Road Government in Turmoil: The Pursuit of Economic Stability

National Management of Coal Mines and Problems Surrounding Agriculture Minister Hirano

The Katayama Cabinet and the Economic Stabilization Board

While pursuing the "construction of a new Japan," the Katayama Cabinet continued to accelerate the process of democratization and took pains to ensure the process would not stall. On the other hand, it was clear to all that the commitment to democracy could not fill the people's empty bellies and that support for the Cabinet would depend essentially on the degree of success in economic reconstruction. After forming his Cabinet, Katayama addressed the nation in a radio broadcast that aired on June 2, 1947. Entitled "An Appeal to the People of Japan," Katayama called on citizens to brace themselves for breaking through the crisis that had seized the nation. Katayama urged the people to "make sacrifices commensurate with your personal circumstances," and pleaded for "overcoming the scourge of inflation" and "continuing to bear the burden of austerity in order to restore the nation's productive capacity."[35]

With the Economic Stabilization Board (ESB) in the lead, the Katayama Cabinet worked closely with the Economic Rehabilitation Council to do battle with the economic crisis. Under the directorship of Wada Hiroo, ESB recruited its members from various quarters. The principal experts and brains of the endeavor included Tsuru Shigeto, who was working for the Economic and Scientific Section of GHQ and would later serve as president of Hitotsubashi

---

35 Nihon Shakaitō Kettō Yonjushūnen Kinen Shuppan Kankō Kinen Iinkai ed., *Shiryō Shakaitō yonjū nenshi* [Document: Forty-Year History of the Socialist Party], Shakaitō Chūō Honbu, 1986, pp. 222–223.

University; Yamamoto Takayuki, who would later serve as vice-minister of the Ministry of International Trade and Industry; and the economist Inaba Hidezō, who together with Wada had been arrested in the Cabinet Planning Board Incident of 1941. From the business world, ESB recruited such members as Nagano Shigeo, managing director of Japan Iron & Steel Company, and Ōhara Sōichirō, President of Kurashiki Silk Textiles Company. Finally, the ESB roster included such bureaucrats as Tōhata Shirō and Shimomura Osamu. It is also reported that the "professors' group" led by Arisawa Hiromi gave valuable support to ESB.

On June 11, ESB announced its "Outline of Emergency Measures for Overcoming the Economic Crisis." This was followed on July 1 with the announcement of a new price structure that set the average salary at 1,800 yen (civil service salary basis).

The Economic and Scientific Section supported ESB policies, commenting that this represented the government's "first comprehensive plan" for achieving economic stability. However, prices had increased by 60 to 65 times compared to prewar levels, while a salary of 1,800 yen represented no more than an increase of 27 to 28 times. Thus, according to Nishio Suehiro, this marked a difficult start for a "Socialist cabinet widely expected to be the most sympathetic to protecting the livelihood of workers." Nishio lamented that a Socialist cabinet had now been made to "stand in the firing line of criticism leveled against it by the labor movement."[36]

Meanwhile, ESB published its Economic White Paper (July 1947). Written by Tsuru Shigeto, the document was made famous because of the passage, "Households are in the red, companies are in the red, and government finances are in the red." The Paper set out in very blunt terms the dire situation of the economy and called on the people to unite behind the effort to overcome the crisis.

Basically, the Katayama Cabinet continued the "priority production (*Keisha seisan*)" approach espoused by the first Yoshida Cabinet and promoted the recovery of core industries through price-support subsidies and reconstruction

---

36 Nishio Suehiro, *Nishio Suehiro no seiji oboegaki* [Political Memorandums by Nishio Suehiro], Mainichi Shinbunsha, 196, pp. 165–167.

financing. All in all, the Katayama Cabinet achieved a good record in terms of rehabilitating the economy. Coal output reached the goal of 30 million tons, and overall production began to show early signs of recovery. In the following year of 1948, mining and manufacturing output increased by 50 to 60 percent and rose to about 60 percent of the prewar level (1934–1936). Moreover, a look at industrial production for March 1949 shows that output at this point amounted to 77.5 percent of the prewar levels.

In August 1947, MacArthur announced that he had a "present" for the Katayama Cabinet and permitted the establishment of an international trade fund amounting to nearly 140 million dollars. Trade was essential to the economic reconstruction program, and MacArthur's "present" effectively liberalized certain parts of Japan's international trade that had been placed under the control of GHQ. During the election, Katayama had pledged to "promote exports." With this pledge in mind, the government reoriented the previous policy of prioritizing the import of food and began to pay greater attention to restraining domestic consumption in order to export whatever could be exported. The foreign exchange that was earned in this manner would then be used to import essential materials for production.

For the first three months of its existence, everything was smooth sailing for the Katayama Cabinet. However, combining an inflationary monetary policy with price and wage controls proved increasingly difficult. By the middle of 1948, wholesale prices were rising at the rate of 300 percent a year, and inflationary forces had easily rendered meaningless the basic salary standard of 1,800 yen. In July and August, as the nation awaited the autumn rice harvest, the food rationing system that had remained in place since the prewar years began to show signs of extreme duress and rice rations fell behind schedule by 20 days in Tokyo and by as much as 90 days in Hokkaido.

Labor unions rose up in protest as the new price structure began to crumble, resulting in a steady erosion of support for the Katayama Cabinet. Between the fall of 1947 and the beginning of the following year, Zentei engaged in extensive workplace walkouts. The walkouts continued until the Central Labor Relations Commission (Chūrōi) appointed an Ad Hoc Committee on Wages that established a new salary framework that went into effect in January 1948.

The impasse was finally settled through mediation. The settlement featured the payment of a special livelihood supplement equivalent to 2.8 months of the 1,800-yen monthly base. Out of the total livelihood supplement, an amount equal to two months of the monthly base was paid out before the end of the year. However, the Katayama Cabinet faced a crisis when a consensus could not be reached on how to finance the payments for the remaining 0.8 months.

Bill for State Control of Coal Mines

The Katayama Cabinet came under further pressure as the issue of the state management of coal mines developed into a thorny political problem. As the linchpin in the Cabinet and its Chief Cabinet Secretary, Nishio was not a particularly enthusiastic supporter of state control. Nevertheless, he continued to promote it as the "only socialist policy" of the Cabinet.

In June 1947, the Socialist Party finalized its draft bill featuring the state control of all coal mines and the separation of corporate head-office functions from mining operations. Specifically, the bill would allow the government to directly control mining operations without going through the company that owned the mine. Furthermore, each mine would have its own "management council" that would be responsible for locally managing the operations of the mine. Finally, the bill provided for the creation of a "coal mining public corporation" that would be wholly financed and owned by the government.

The Democratic Party responded with its own draft bill that significantly differed from the Socialist bill. First, state management would be limited to coal mines that were in economic trouble. Second, the government would exercise its control indirectly through owner companies. Third, mining operations would be locally managed by persons selected by the company. Finally, the Democratic Party argued that there was no need to create a public corporation. Given that it was supported by coal mine operators and other related interests, the Democratic Party continued to strongly oppose any form of divestiture or the transfer of management rights.

Seeking a resolution to the problem, Katayama wrote to MacArthur appealing for his support. However, in a letter dated September 18, MacArthur indicated that he would remain neutral in this matter, which meant that MacArthur had tossed the problem back to the Japanese government for resolution through the political process.

In light of its commitment to a free market economy, the Liberal Party gradually stepped up its criticism of the Socialist bill. This culminated in a proclamation made on August 19 in which the Liberal Party claimed that state control contravened the "four-party agreement" and announced that it was exiting the coalition completely.

The Government Section was troubled by these developments. In a report compiled at the end of September, the Government Section wrote, "The power struggle for control of Japan's political and economic destiny crosses party lines," prompting "division between the conservative party and socialist party blocs." The report concluded that the "situation is coming to the stage of an urgent crisis."[37]

During the summer months of 1947, Yoshida began to work on uniting the conservative forces in the Diet. In November, the Liberal Party put together its "New Policy Guidelines," a document that outlined a platform for a new party. In it, the Liberal Party stated, "Existing controls shall be abolished and only the minimum necessary level of controls shall be retained. Concrete measures shall be taken to clearly establish that any remaining controls constitute no more than transitional means to the achievement of a liberalized system." The Liberal Party stepped up its criticism of the government, advocating building a trade-oriented economy and in the meantime depending on foreign investments. As the ruling and opposition parties continued to clash with increasing intensity over state control of coal mines, members of the Shidehara faction announced that they were leaving the Democratic Party. Acting on this decision, a group of 22 members came together to form the Dōshi Club on November 28.

---

37 "MCGS (C.P. Marcum), Impending Political Crisis," (September 19, 1947), Fukunaga, ed., in *GHQ Minsei-kyoku shiryō, 3*, pp. 466–468.

Removal of Agriculture Minister Hirano

In the midst of the crisis over state control of coal mines, the Katayama Cabinet was beset by yet another problem, this one involving Hirano Rikizō, the Minister of Agriculture and Forestry. Hirano had often come to loggerheads with Director Wada of ESB on such issues as the price of rice. With the backing of GHQ, Wada and his ESB had taken the lead in formulating the economic policies of the Katayama Cabinet. Hirano, on the other hand, found himself in an increasingly tenuous position. Whenever Hirano and Wada clashed, Chief Cabinet Secretary Nishio took the side of Wada, which eventually created discord and estrangement between the two.

Hirano also managed to earn the displeasure of GHQ. On October 11, 1947, a statement made by Hirano was picked up by the press and was reported to be an expression of Hirano's intent to form a new political party. On October 21, Yoshida announced that he was considering forming a new conservative party and stated, "Agriculture Minister Hirano stands quite close to our line." This was enough to prompt the Government Section to take action. Given his prewar affiliation with the Imperial Way Society (Kōdōkai), Hirano's background had always made him suspect within the Government Section. Katayama and Nishio had repeatedly petitioned GHQ to permit the appointment of Hirano to the Cabinet, and GHQ had consented to the appointment on the condition that Hirano cooperated with the Cabinet. But once appointed, Hirano developed very close ties with G2, the archrival of the Government Section. With his cheerful and open personality, Hirano had no qualms about advertising his relations with G2, which made him even more unpopular with the Government Section.

On October 25, Deputy Chief Kades of the Government Section visited Katayama to convey an order from Brigadier General Whitney, Chief of the Government Section. The order demanded that Hirano be removed from the Cabinet.[38] The Government Section had calculated that the dismissal of Hirano would drive a wedge into the movement to create a new political party. Thus, the

---

38 "Memorandum for the Record (C. Kades), Conference with Prime Minister," (October 24, 1947), Masuda Hiroshi, ed., in *GHQ Minsei-kyoku shiryō, 4*, pp. 620–621.

move was essentially intended to reinforce support for the Katayama Cabinet. On November 4, in accordance with the provisions of Article 68 of the Constitution, Katayama removed Hirano on grounds of non-cooperation with the Cabinet. However, the removal of Hirano backfired as it prompted Hirano's right-wing allies with ties to agricultural interests (the farming lobby) to follow him out of the ruling party. The outcome was to render the left wing of the Socialist Party more powerful than before.

But the Hirano problem did not end there and the situation became even more strained as Katayama struggled to pick a new Minister of Agriculture. The appointment process created conflict among the coalition parties and culminated in the revolt of the left wing of the Socialist Party. On December 13, Katayama chose a moderate, Hatano Kanae, as his new Minister of Agriculture, defying the left wing of the party that was pushing for the appointment of Nomizo Masaru. The following day, the left wing announced that it was assuming the position of opposition within the party. "A minister from our party has wittingly veered from the principles that he should uphold as leader of the party... and has fallen to leading a coalition of three factions centered on the Democratic Party and the People's Cooperative Party." With this announcement, the left wing finalized its confrontational stance toward Katayama, Nishio, and the party leadership.

It was against this background that Yoshida wrote to his father-in-law, Makino Nobuaki, to outline his future plans. Written at the end of 1947, Yoshida summarized his plans for 1948 in the following passage.

In early January, I shall begin to prepare for the establishment of a new conservative party and hope to be able to launch the party when the Diet comes back into session. In addition to the Shidehara faction, I expect others to join, including the right wing of the Socialist Party and various small parties and factions.... If we take the majority, that would naturally lead to a change in government and a general election.[39]

---

39 Yoshida Shigeru to Makino Nobuaki, (December 31, 1947), Yoshida Shigeru Kinen Zaidan, ed., *Yoshida Shigeru shokan* [Letters of Yoshida Shigeru], Chūō Kōronsha, 1994, pp. 676–677.

At around this time, Yoshida was beginning to feel confident that he could hammer together a majority position in the Diet in order to take the reins of government. It is not clear, however, whom he was referring to as the "right wing of the Socialist Party." While it is likely that this pointed to Hirano Rikizō and his group, details are not known.

Dissolution of the Ministry of Home Affairs: Completion of Democratization

Memorandum on Decentralizing the Ministry of Home Affairs

While the Katayama Cabinet was busy pursuing the implementation of its policies, the Government Section had fixed its sights on the Ministry of Home Affairs and was moving quickly to target the ministry in the final stage of its democratization program. For instance, in a meeting with the Ministry of Home Affairs held in May 1947, Deputy Chief Kades of the Government Section is recorded to have made the following comments. "I am battling against time. We are not going to be staying in Japan forever." In a June meeting, Kades said that even after the Constitution came into effect, they could not leave Japan with a centralized government that could become the tool of anti-democratic forces.[40]

In the prewar era, the Ministry of Home Affairs had jurisdiction over a broad range of domestic affairs, such as local government administration, the police, civil engineering, and sanitation, and was widely referred to as the "first among all government ministries."

On April 30, Courtney Whitney, Chief of the Government Section, issued a "Memorandum on Decentralizing the Ministry of Home Affairs." Addressed to the chief of the Liaison Office of the Japanese government, the memorandum stated that the Ministry of Home Affairs stood at the "core of the centralized control" of the people. In preparation for the enforcement of the Constitution of Japan and the Local Autonomy Law, Whitney instructed the Ministry of Home Affairs to be reorganized as a ministry with jurisdiction over local government

---

40 Local Government Research and Data Center, ed., *Sengo jichi-shi 8: Naimushō no kaitai*, p. 47.

administration based on new principles. Whitney set June 1 as the deadline for submission of a response.

On May 1, Kades listed the main points for decentralization and specifically mentioned the elimination of the Bureau of Local Administration, the transfer of fiscal matters to the Ministry of Finance, and the transfer of the civil engineering matters to other appropriate government ministries.

From Decentralization to Dissolution

The Ministry of Home Affairs interpreted Whitney's memorandum as an instruction to decentralize. To stay ahead of Whitney, the ministry immediately embarked on preparing its own proposals for reform, which were submitted to the Cabinet on June 20. The reform plan approved by the Cabinet primarily constituted an internal reorganization of the ministry, which would be renamed the Ministry of Public Administration. Under the plan, the new ministry would have five internal bureaus including a General Affairs Bureau, a Civil Engineering Bureau, and an Investigation Bureau. The Public Security Agency would be reconstituted as a subsidiary and external agency of the ministry. To the greatest possible extent, other administrative functions would be transferred to local government organizations, and the ministry's supervisory powers over local government would be dramatically curtailed.[41]

The Government Section became infuriated when the plan was published in several newspapers. Kades immediately summoned Chief Cabinet Secretary Nishio and the top officers of the Ministry of Home Affairs. The contents of the plan were bad enough, but much of Kades' anger was caused by the fact that a plan had been formulated and published without any consultation with the Government Section. "This ignores all the consultations that we have had," Kades fumed. The meeting ended with an order to formulate a second plan for submission to the Government Section by June 26. It was in this way that the Government Section became directly involved in preparing a reform plan.

---

41 Taikakai Henshū Iinkai, ed., *Naimushō shi, dai 3-kan* [History of the Ministry of Home Affairs, vol. 3], Taikakai, 1970, pp. 1006–1007.

The second plan was ultimately approved by the Cabinet on June 27. The ministry would be dissolved, the Bureau of Local Administration would be reconstituted as the Local Autonomy Commission, and the National Land Bureau would be reorganized as the Construction Board. The Bureau of Police and Public Safety would be reorganized as the Public Security Agency and placed under the Prime Minister's Agency as an external agency. This clearly indicated that the Government Section had transitioned from "decentralization" to "dissolution" in its treatment of the Ministry of Home Affairs.

The move to dissolve the Ministry of Home Affairs gained speed after October when the previously described internal GHQ conflict involving police reform was resolved. On October 9, Kades summoned Sone Eki, Vice Director-General of the Cabinet Secretariat, and others and strongly demanded that related bills be submitted by October 13. In the final iteration of the plan, the Bureau of Local Administration was further divided into a Local Public Finance Committee to be formed as a tentative organization, the Domestic Affairs Bureau and the Committee for National Election Administration. Finally, the Ministry of Home Affairs was dissolved at the end of December 1947.

Enactment of the National Public Service Law: Battle over the Three Primary Rights of Labor

In the eyes of the Government Section, the bureaucracy constituted a "bureaucratic clique" (kanbatsu) that stood on par with the "military clique" (gunbatsu) and the "business clique" (zaibatsu) as the "bastions of Japan's feudalistic totalitarianism." As such, the Government Section believed that the bureaucracy had to be thoroughly democratized. It was against this background that the Economic and Scientific Section received a request for advice from the Japanese government. The question at hand was how to reform the pay structure of civil servants. The Government Section, however, managed to have the referral transferred to itself on the grounds that it was in a better position to cooperate with the Japanese government's self-directed efforts for reform. In this way, the Government Section succeeded in inserting itself into the reform of the civil service system. In pursuit of its objectives, in November 1946, the Government

Section invited a study mission headed by Blaine Hoover, President of the Civil Service Assembly of the United States and Canada.

Upon arriving in Japan, Hoover and his group set out to formulate reforms in consultation with the Research Department on Government Administration created under the aegis of the Cabinet. The plan was submitted to the Katayama Cabinet in June 1947. The Hoover plan, patterned after the U.S. Civil Service Act, featured the establishment of a powerful central personnel agency (National Personnel Authority) and espoused such principles as merit-based appointment and promotion, pay scales based on job classification and responsibilities, the restriction of political activities, and the prohibition of acts of labor dispute.

Hoover requested that his plan be enacted within a few weeks without any revision. However, government ministries and agencies strongly opposed a personnel management system that would operate under the direction of a centralized National Personnel Authority. What confused and upset the government even more was that the Hoover plan did not recognize the right of civil servants to engage in acts of labor dispute. Thus, the three primary rights of labor had not been guaranteed.

Chief Cabinet Secretary Nishio called on Kades to explain the Cabinet's conundrum. The Socialist Party Cabinet was founded on the support of workers, and civil servants accounted for 40 percent of Japan's organized labor. How, Nishio inquired, could such a cabinet turn against its base by accepting the Hoover plan? Nishio pleaded that if the plan were to be adopted in its current form, it could very likely seal the fate of the Katayama Cabinet. Criticism of the Hoover plan had also been voiced by James Killen, the Chief of the Labor Division of the Economic and Scientific Section. Killen's complaint was that the workers' rights had been restricted out of hand.

Personally, Kades stood somewhere between Hoover and the opponents of his plan, Nishio and Killen. When Hoover returned to the United States to recruit staff members for the Civil Service Division to be newly created, Kades took advantage of his absence to obtain the approval of Whitney and MacArthur to revise the Hoover plan. Although the National Civil Service Law promulgated in October 1947 was essentially based on the Hoover plan, several significant revisions had been made. First, the proposed National Personnel Authority was revised to take the form of a Personnel Commission. Second, prohibitions on the right to organize and the right to strike were deleted.

Returning to Japan in December to assume the office of chief of the Civil Service Division and unhappy to see that major revisions had been made in his absence, Hoover immediately went on a counter-offensive. The conflict between Hoover and Killen would later resurface in connection with Order No. 201, which sought to restrict the right of civil servants to engage in labor disputes.

Toward Revision of Occupation Policies: Draper and Kennan

Changes in Washington and the Kauffman Report

By early 1947, a review of Occupation policies was already underway in the United States. What triggered the review was the outcome of the mid-term elections of November 1946. The election saw the defeat of New Dealers at the hands of a coalition of the Republicans and the Southern Democratic Party. Many of the newly elected members of Congress had come to politics from a background in business. Henceforth, as the atmosphere in Washington grew increasingly conservative, GHQ would come under attack for its continued pursuit of New Deal-like policies.[42]

The attack was spearheaded by Harry Kern, a founding member of the Japan Lobby, in articles he wrote for *Newsweek* magazine. Commenting on the purge of business leaders in a January 1947 issue of *Newsweek*, Kern wrote that some 25,000 to 30,000 Japanese business executives who were the "brains of the entire Japanese economic structure" were being purged by the United States, which was the center of capitalism. Kern then opined that the ousted business executives were now considering whether to become "black marketeers or communists." The article contained an appeal to Congress to organize an investigative mission to find out what was actually happening in Japan. Kern's sensationalism aside, the number of companies that actually existed in Japan at this time (including small and medium-sized enterprises) came to

---

42 Cohen, *Remaking Japan*, pp. 425–427.

only 100,000 entities. Moreover, only 1,100 major corporations were named in GHQ's restricted list, and the actual number of purged business executives came to only about 900 individuals.[43] MacArthur immediately issued a rebuttal, but that was not enough to stop *Newsweek*'s anti-GHQ campaign, which continued throughout 1947.

The mood in Washington would soon be affected by the Kauffman Report. Its author, James Kauffman, was a long-time corporate lawyer for such leading U.S. companies as General Electric and Standard Oil. Kauffman arrived in Japan in August 1947 as a member of the second Strike Mission and was engaged in assessing the viability of the Japanese economy as an investment target.

Kauffman's "Report on Conditions in Japan" contained scathing criticism of GHQ economic policies. In it, Kauffman argued that the demilitarization of Japan contained elements of ideological reform and that while he would not go as far as to say that GHQ economic policies were communist-inspired, they very closely approached a "socialist ideal." Kauffman stated in his report that GHQ economic policies had failed and labeled them as being "un-American." Finally, Kauffman argued that Japan, a country that had not been pro-communist, might now move toward communism and grow closer to the Soviet Union. He then concluded that if the United States wanted Japan to act as a buffer against the Soviet Union, it would be absolutely essential for it to overhaul its current Occupation policies. While Kauffman roundly criticized the programs for farmland reform, labor reform, and the purge of public officials, his special ire was reserved for FEC-230, the document outlining the policies of the Far Eastern Commission for undoing the concentration of economic power.

After his return to the United States, Kauffman's report was informally circulated among policymakers in the Truman Administration. Having drawn the attention of high officials in the Department of War, the report succeeded in turning the eyes of Washington to Occupation policies in Japan. Kern, who was continuing his anti-GHQ campaign in the pages of *Newsweek*, took this as his cue to form the American Council on Japan in June 1948. In this effort, Kern recruited Kauffman and Eugene Dooman, a secretary of the former American

---

43 Ibid., p. 166 and 169.

Ambassador to Japan Joseph Grew. Grew himself was brought in as an adviser. The American Council on Japan thus emerged as a type of "Japan lobby" around which criticism of MacArthur's Occupation policies would coalesce.

Draper Arrives in Japan: The Taxpayer's Perspective

William Draper, newly appointed Under-Secretary of the Army, arrived in Japan on September 18, 1947. In the prewar years, Draper had established himself on Wall Street as a major figure in the financial world and had held the post of Vice President of Dillon, Read & Company. After the war, he had served as the senior economic adviser to Lucius Clay, the deputy military governor of the American zone of the Occupation of Germany.

As an investment banker, Draper had been critical of some aspects of Occupation policies for Germany, including decartelization and the purge of business executives from the Nazi period. Additionally, at the newly established Advisory Committee on Fiscal and Monetary Problems, Draper was directly exposed to pressure from the Department of Treasury to reduce the burden of economic assistance to Japan. The huge cost of implementing the Marshall Plan in Europe had created an urgent need to avoid further increases in the cost of the Occupation of Japan.

After a series of meetings with MacArthur, Prime Minister Katayama, and various members of the Cabinet, Draper stated on September 27 that a principal objective in the Occupation of Japan should henceforth be to "reduce the burden on American taxpayers." As the person controlling the purse strings of economic aid to Japan, Draper was announcing that Japan could no longer depend on U.S. assistance to feed and support itself. It is worth noting that Theodore Cohen, adviser to the Economic and Scientific Section, paints a very different picture of the cost of U.S. economic aid to Japan. For instance, Cohen calculates that even at its height, the cost of supporting Japan never exceeded one percent of the annual federal budget and came to no more than $3.40 per American citizen. Moreover, Cohen points out that most of the aid was given in the form of surplus wheat that the U.S. government was purchasing to prop up the domestic prices of agricultural products.

William Draper (1894–1974)
Military officer and investment banker, Draper served as economic adviser to the postwar Occupation of Germany and was critical of denazification for sapping the strength of the German economy. After being appointed Under-Secretary of the Army in 1947, Draper visited Japan and compiled a report on Occupation policies urging primary emphasis on the economic revival and reconstruction of Japan. Draper was later instrumental in dispatching Joseph Dodge to Japan.

Upon returning home, Draper proclaimed that the processes of denazification, demilitarization and the purging of military cliques had been completed in both Japan and Germany, and argued that the two nations should now be allowed to rebuild themselves so that they can become "self-respecting and self-supporting members of the international community." "The objective of our military occupations shall henceforth be the economic recovery of Germany and Japan."[44] Draper was convinced that economic reform programs represented by such policies as zaibatsu dissolution and reparation policies had to be immediately and fundamentally changed.

On October 3, 1947, Draper submitted to SWNCC a document entitled "Economic Recovery of Japan (SWNCC-384)," which outlined his proposals for shifting to Occupation policies centered on achieving an "early revival of the Japanese economy." Draper would thereafter come to play a key role as an advocate for promoting the revival and reconstruction of the Japanese economy.

Draper's pro-business views and activities drew criticism from within GHQ. One such critic was Alfred Hussey, Chief of the Governmental Powers Division of the Government Section. Hussey complained that Draper, along with Secretary of the Navy James Forrestal and Under-Secretary of State Robert Lovett, were being manipulated by certain business interests plotting to return to Japan to gain dominant positions in the Japanese market. The three were Wall Street magnates in their own right, and Draper and Forrestal had both served as executives at Dillon, Read and Company. Theodore Cohen of the Economic and

---

44 Ibid., p. 402.

Scientific Section would later complain that the three were uninterested in the democratization of Japan and that Draper effectively changed the character of the Occupation by looking at the situation from a business perspective.[45]

Draper also played a role in the compilation of the supplementary budget in October 1947, which had become bogged down due to the conflict between the ESB and the Ministry of Finance. Draper threw himself into the fray and emerged in favor of the Finance Division by pressing the Economic and Scientific Section to demand that the Japanese government hew to fiscal conservatism.

George Kennan Arrives in Tokyo: The "Cold War" Perspective

Within the State Department, Draper had the strong backing of George Kennan—the architect of Cold War policies for Soviet "containment" and a frequent collaborator of Secretary of State George Marshall. In the late summer of 1947, Kennan had just finished working on formulating the Marshall Plan when his Policy Planning Study (PPS) took on the task of examining policies related to the Occupation of Japan. This would place Kennan in line to play a key role in changing and reversing policies for the Occupation of Japan.

Kennan surmised that American Occupation policies had weakened Japanese society to the point where it could no longer resist the political pressures of communism. In his estimation, the Occupation program in Japan presented a perfect model of policies formulated for the purpose of opening the door to a communist power grab.

Kennan was also critical of the draft peace treaty that had been prepared by Borton and others at the State Department's Office of Far Eastern Affairs on the grounds that it presupposed the continuation of a cooperative relationship between the United States and the Soviet Union. Kennan was convinced that demilitarization and democratization were no longer critical conditions for signing peace treaties and believed that the revival and reconstruction of Japan and Germany were essential to restoring stability in Europe and East Asia. What Kennan assigned the greatest importance to was the question of how to prevent

---

45 Ibid., p. 405.

"invasions" by internal forces instigated by the Soviet Union as it took advantage of social unrest in target countries.

With this mindset, Kennan set out to redesign Occupation policies for Japan from the perspective of Cold War logic. In order to move forward on the project, he needed to have accurate information on the status of the Occupation and the policies that had been implemented. That meant gathering detailed data on what MacArthur and his GHQ had done so far and what they intended to do going forward. But a major obstacle confronted Kennan. The personal relationship between Secretary of State Marshall and MacArthur was strained, and MacArthur was not about to allow the State Department to interfere in the administration of the Occupation.[46] In March 1948, Kennan left for Japan aiming to ease the mutual animosity and suspicion that marred the relations between Washington and Tokyo.

Disharmony between Washington and Tokyo: Democratization or Recovery

The Antitrust and Cartels Division Charges Ahead

Both GHQ and the U.S. government were now beginning to shift the focus of Occupation policies toward economic recovery and reconstruction. But this shift would engender new friction between Washington and Tokyo on how to balance the demands of democratization and economic recovery.

Japan's Antimonopoly Law was promulgated in April 1947. By July, the dissolution of Mitsui & Company and Mitsubishi Corporation had been ordered by Edward Welsh, Chief of the Antitrust and Cartels Division of the Economics and Scientific Section. Next, as a finishing touch to economic democratization, Welsh and his division set out to implement the policies contained in the Far Eastern Commission's FEC-230, a document outlining measures for eliminating the concentration of economic power. The action plan involved the dissolution of giant corporations and the encouragement of free competition. Motivated

---

46 Kennan, George F, *Memoirs, 1925–1950*, Atlantic Monthly (Little, Brown), 1967, pp. 347–354.

by his conviction that "large and dominating companies are in themselves anti-democratic," Welsh relentlessly pressured the Japanese government to enact necessary laws.

According to Tsuru Shigeto, Welsh adopted a threatening attitude toward Prime Minister Katayama. Waving a copy of FEC-230 in his face, Welsh would say, "The decision has been made in the Far Eastern Commission to eliminate economic concentration in Japan. Bad things will happen if the Japanese side does not accept this. Any effort to resist will be useless." MacArthur supported the enactment of the new legislation, arguing that this would foster the development of "free and competitive businesses."

Caught in a quandary, Katayama sent a letter to MacArthur on September 4, appealing to him to reconsider the enactment of the proposed legislation. Katayama argued that if enacted, the law would further weaken a Japanese economy that was already on its knees and would rob Japan of any hope for becoming a self-supporting and competitive member of the international economy. MacArthur's response was negative. He ominously warned that if the Japanese government were to propose a major revision in the program for eliminating economic concentration, this would create suspicion among other countries and result in the adoption of even stricter policies.[47]

Left with no choice, the government convened an extraordinary meeting of the Cabinet on September 29 to approve the final draft of the proposed legislation aimed at eliminating the oligopolistic powers of large corporations. The bill for the Elimination of Concentration of Economic Power was subsequently submitted to the Diet on October 6.

Enactment of the Law for the Elimination of "Excessive" Concentration of Economic Power

Meanwhile, Under-Secretary of the Army William Draper was stepping up his criticism of the Law for the Elimination of Concentration of Economic Power.

---

47 Sodei, *Correspondence between General MacArthur, Prime Minister Yoshida & Other High Japanese Officials [1945–1951]*, pp. 78–80.

In early October, Draper issued a formal complaint through the Department of the Army petitioning the postponement of the legislation. MacArthur responded on October 24 with a ten-page cable that stridently dismissed the criticism. Any delay in deliberating the bill, MacArthur argued, would only benefit the left wingers and zaibatsu that were advocates of "private socialism."

The military was bewildered by MacArthur's strong opposition. On November 1, Navy Secretary Forrestal wrote to Army Secretary Kenneth Royall saying that the ongoing program for eliminating the concentration of economic power indicated that Japan was being "socialized," and called for the formulation of new comprehensive policies for rebuilding the Japanese economy. Forrestal also warned in his letter that there was a direct relationship between Japan's economic problems and the future national security of the United States.[48]

During this period, Draper was busy campaigning against GHQ and FEC-230 through the pages of *Newsweek*. Ultimately, these developments back in Washington only served to harden MacArthur in his positions. In MacArthur's eyes, the articles that continued to appear in *Newsweek* were inextricably linked to the Kauffman Report, which he saw as part of a "libelous campaign" designed to obstruct his nomination as a presidential candidate. Convinced of the purpose of the anti-GHQ campaign, MacArthur pressed on with plans to speed the enactment of Law for the Elimination of Concentration of Economic Power.

However, resistance to the legislation remained strong on the Japanese side. The general feeling was that breaking up Japan's major companies into a series of small and medium-sized enterprises would undermine the nation's economic strength and render economic reconstruction even more difficult. A simple solution was devised, involving the addition of the term "excessive" to the title of the law. Renamed the Law for the Elimination of Excessive Concentration of Economic Power, the law was enacted in December 1947. Shortly after the law came into force, Japan Iron & Steel was split into Yawata Iron & Steel and Fuji Iron & Steel, while Dai Nippon Breweries was split into Asahi Beer and Nippon Breweries. Although a total of 325 companies had been targeted for divestiture,

---

48 Ministry of International Trade and Industry, ed., *Tsūsan sangyō seisaku-shi fukkoku ban, dai 2-kan* [History of Trade and Industry Policies Reprint edition, vol. 2], Gendai Shiryō Shuppan, 2005, p. 123.

only eleven companies were actually forced to divide their operations.

Purge of Government Officials Ends: Washington and Tokyo

Enactment of the Law for the Elimination of Excessive Concentration of Economic Power heightened distrust in Washington of MacArthur and his GHQ and reinforced Washington's attacks against Occupation policies. The focus of these attacks would soon be trained on ending the purge of government officials. On July 12, 1947, MacArthur wrote to Draper reporting that the investigation of government officials in various fields was nearing completion, and that with the exception of certain ultra-nationalistic and secret patriotic organizations, the dimensions and the criteria of the purge were not expected to be expanded any further. With this report, MacArthur was signaling that the purge programs were coming to an end.

At the end of January 1948, Kades informed the Japanese government that the Government Section had decided to "end all purge investigations by mid-March." Personally, however, Kades believed that it was too early to bring the purge to a close. Because the second purge of government officials had significantly expanded the dimensions of the purge, it was taking more time than expected to complete the necessary investigations. Completion of the screening process was further delayed by the blatantly obstructionist stance taken by G2 and the Civil Intelligence Section.

At the end of May, the Government Section released a statement asserting that purge policies were fully consistent with the objective of democratizing the Japanese government and people, and that purges stood among the explicit and compulsory requirements of the Potsdam Declaration. The statement went on to affirm that the Allied Powers would continue to be fully responsible to the Japanese government in implementing purge polices.

Kades and the Government Section had gone out of their way to assert that the purge had not been completed. Following this statement, MacArthur and the Government Section took pains to avoid direct confrontation with Washington and instead exploited their onsite advantage to block efforts to ease the purge program.

CHAPTER 4

Changing Course in Occupation Policies:
From Democratization to Economic Revival

1. The Limits of Middle-of-the-Road Government: From the Katayama Cabinet to the Ashida Cabinet

Kades' "Central Party" Concept

MacArthur's New Year's Message: 1948

In his New Year's statement on January 1, 1948, MacArthur stated that the "design of a remodeled and reconstructed Japan is nearing completion. The pattern has been etched, the path has been laid. The development now lies largely in your own hands."[1] MacArthur then proceeded to review the achievements of 1947 as follows.

In the economic sphere, the system that allowed the exercise of feudalistic control by a handful of families had been dissolved and the path had been cleared for an economy that contributes to the welfare of all people. In the political field, encouraging reforms had been implemented under the new Constitution. In the social area, systems related to the police, judiciary, and public service had been reformed and "laws have been enacted to temper inordinate bureaucratic power."

After celebrating the fruits of reform, MacArthur stated that in order to ameliorate the continuing destitute condition of the national economy, it would be necessary to abolish economic regulations and eliminate the sanctions that currently impacted international trade. By doing this, the Japanese economy would recover and the country would become more self-reliant.

In a speech delivered in San Francisco on January 6, Army Secretary Kenneth Royall stated, "We hold to an equally definite purpose of building in Japan a self-sufficient democracy, strong enough and stable enough to support

---

1 General MacArthur's New Year's Message, January 1, 1948, Statements by MacArthur, Box No. 2195, Folder 22, GHQ/SCAP Records, Government Section, National Diet Library, Originals in U.S. National Archives & Records Administration, RG331.

itself and at the same time to serve as a deterrent against any other totalitarian war threats which might hereafter arise in the Far East."[2] The key point that Royall was making was that past policies of reparations, the purge of business executives, and decentralization needed to be re-examined from the perspective of achieving a self-sufficient Japan. This was followed by a statement released by Frank McCoy, the U.S. representative to the Far Eastern Commission, on January 21. McCoy explained that the fundamental objectives of the Occupation had already been achieved and the mission of the Far Eastern Commission had effectively been completed. He then indicated that from that point forward, the United States would be taking unilateral action to achieve Japan's economic self-sufficiency.

MacArthur and the U.S. government had come to agree on the need to rehabilitate the Japanese economy. Washington would soon begin dispatching a series of officials to Tokyo, including Kennan, Draper, and Young. Notwithstanding the basic agreement that had been reached, the two sides would henceforth clash on the path to be taken in reviving the Japanese economy. MacArthur held that the pursuit of economic stabilization should not be allowed to obstruct the continued reinforcement of democratization. Washington took the opposite position, demanding that democratization not be allowed to obstruct the pursuit of economic stabilization. This view gradually began to influence GHQ, which until then had effectively functioned as an independent state under MacArthur's force of personality.

From the Government Section to the Economic and Scientific Section

Following MacArthur's proclamation regarding the completion of the reforms, the Government Section began to undergo reorganization that would reduce its size and the scope of its responsibilities. Already on December 15, 1947, the Government Section's Deputy Chief Kades had released a memorandum regarding the ending of the Government Section legislative program. Written at

---

2 Hunter-Chester, David, *Creating Japan's Ground Self-Defense Force, 1945–2015: A Sword Well Made*, Lexington Books, 2016.

a time when Kades was feeling reasonably confident that the dissolution of the Ministry of Home Affairs would be completed successfully, the document indicated that the Government Section would not undertake any further legislative revisions beyond the Penal Code and ten other laws that were currently before the Diet. "It does mean, however, the completion of this Section's legislative program to achieve the objective of the Occupation."[3]

The downsizing of the Government Section began in February 1948 and the first to go was the Political Affairs Division. In March, the Legislative Division was renamed the Parliamentary and Political Division (PPD). Following the Cabinet decision to submit the bill for the National Government Organization Law to the Diet, the National Government Division and then the Courts and Law Division were transferred to the Legal Section. At the end of June, the Local Government Division was transferred to the Eighth Army. As a result, the Government Section was left with only five divisions: the Administrative Division, the Parliamentary and Political Division, the Civil Service Division, the Public Administration Division, and the Public Affairs Division. (This structure was maintained until January 1951.) Parallel to this reorganization, Government Section officers who had been primarily responsible for implementing reforms and whose missions had now been completed began to return home. These included Guy Swope, Carlos Marcum, Alfred Hussey, and Frank Hays.

On the other hand, the Economic and Scientific Section was expanded and reinforced with two new divisions added to its existing nine. Assigned the mission of promoting the economic revival and reconstruction of the economy, the Economic and Scientific Section henceforth wielded an increasingly strong influence over Japanese politics. Justin Williams, Chief of the Parliamentary and Political Division of the Government Section, has described this period as follows.

PPD fueled Government Section's relentless and partially successful campaign to minimize GHQ interference with the Japanese legislative process. The main offender was the oversized and unmanageable ESS

3　"Memorandum for Division Chief (C.L. Kades), End of Government Section Legislative Program," (December 15, 1947), Fukunaga Fumio, ed., in *GHQ Minsei-kyoku shiryō: Senryo kaikaku, 2* [GHQ Government Section Materials: Reforms of the Occupation, 2], Maruzen, 1999, pp. 395–396.

[Economic and Scientific Section]. By withholding clearance of legislative bills for reasons other than noncompliance with occupation objectives, ESS—and occasionally other staff sections—preempted the National Diet's role under the new constitution.[4]

The "Central Party" Concept and the Formation of a "Third Force"

The Katayama Cabinet was marred by internal divisions and turmoil after problems related to national control of coal mines and the dismissal of Agriculture Minister Hirano surfaced. In early 1948, the Socialist Party was stunned by the departure of Hirano Rikizō and fifteen other members of parliament who supported the National Farmers Union. Having quit the Socialist Party, this group moved to form the "New Political Council" in collaboration with various minor groups. However, the initiative was cut short when Hirano was purged on January 13. (The National Farmers Union supporters went on to form the Social Innovation Party in March.)

The third Socialist Party convention was held on January 16 and remained in session for four days. Following the opening remarks delivered by party chairman Katayama, Nishio took the podium to make a frank confession. "The Katayama Cabinet has not necessarily achieved great feats, and the public's criticism is understandable." Yet, he went on to list seven achievements of the Cabinet. According to Nishio, these included overcoming the food crisis, eliminating the labor unrest, establishing the Ministry of Labor and implementing related labor policies, and pushing democratization forward. "Inadequate as the Cabinet may have been, these were accomplished only because it was the Katayama Cabinet that held the reins of government," he reported. Jeers and the angry roar of attendees drowned out his report. Thereafter, the party's left wing rammed through the dissolution of the "four-party policy agreement" and passed a resolution calling for the cessation of interest payments on all military bonds.

In the conference of Liberal Party Diet members held on January 20,

---

4 Williams, Justin, *Japan's Political Revolution under MacArthur: A Participant's Account*, University of Georgia Press, 1979, p. 200.

Yoshida Shigeru rattled the Democratic Party and the People's Cooperative Party by calling for the formation of a "non-socialist coalition" that would also include the Farmers Party and the Dai-Ichi Club of Diet Members.

On January 29, Miki Takeo, chairman of the People's Cooperative Party, came out with a new proposal and called on Ashida Hitoshi of the Democratic Party to join him in forming a "third force." Ashida responded with his own idea, which he called the "progressive central party." Following this exchange of feelers, the middle-of-the-road forces began to coalesce around Ashida to form a new party.[5]

However, the People's Cooperative Party remained lukewarm toward the Ashida initiative because Ashida envisioned absorbing the People's Cooperative Party into the Democratic Party. After all, Miki's primary objective in proposing the formation of a "central party" was to create a stable political force through the union of the Democratic Party, the People's Cooperative Party, and the right wing of the Socialist Party on an equal footing.

The "0.8 Month Supplementary Budget"

While the conflict between the left-wing and right-wing forces intensified within the Socialist Party, the conservative end of the political spectrum was also grappling with the question of how to reorganize itself. It was against this background that the Katayama Cabinet began to move toward its demise. The "0.8 month supplementary budget" (i.e., supplementary budget for paying the remaining special livelihood supplement worth 0.8 months' salary) discussed in Chapter 3 would prove to be its final undoing.

At around this time, the government was compiling a supplementary budget as well as the main budget for the fiscal year 1948. Under its original plan, the government intended to submit a third supplementary budget that would cover a payment of 0.8 months supplementary salary, as well as costs related to the six-plus-three-year education system and police operations. The basic idea was to finance these additional expenses by raising postal rates and railway transport

---

5 *Asahi Shinbun*, January 31, 1948.

rates, plus revenue collected through the anticipated increase in income tax receipts. Because of the pressing need to pay out the supplementary salary, it was decided to handle this element of the supplementary budget separately. This seemingly innocuous decision would bring about a head-on clash between the Ministry of Finance and the Economic Stabilization Board (ESB). This inter-ministerial conflict quickly spilled over into the relations that bound the ruling coalition together and finally came to fuel the internecine battles that were being fought within GHQ, by which time it had developed into a full-blown political issue.

In the interest of maintaining sound government finances, the Ministry of Finance argued that the payment of the supplementary salary should be financed by raising rates on railway transport and communications. ESB, on the other hand, was intent on maintaining the price structure and countered that the government should instead look to the natural increase in income tax receipts that would result from the payment of the supplementary salary to finance the outlay. Under the rules of the Occupation, the government budget required prior approval by GHQ. However, once the matter was referred to the Economic and Scientific Section, the situation became even more complicated due to the differences in opinion that existed within the section.

According to Tsuru Shigeto, who represented ESB in its negotiations with the Economic and Scientific Section, ESB initially appeared to have the upper hand in the debate. However, the Ministry of Finance turned the tables at the last minute and managed to have its proposal approved by the Economic and Scientific Section. This meant that railway transport and communication rates would be raised to directly finance the 0.8 month supplementary salary.

The left wing of the Socialist Party vehemently opposed this outcome and angrily argued that the rate increases were nothing less than a means of taxing the masses and would only accelerate inflation. But what was really inconvenient for the left wing was the fact that the higher rates would go to paying the salaries of government employees.

Suzuki Mosaburō, the left winger who chaired the Budget Committee of the House of Representatives, went to the government and GHQ to plead the case for tabling the rate increases and finding alternative sources of financing. As the conflict between the left wing and right wing of the party intensified, a compromise solution was proposed by Asanuma Inejirō, the moderate Secretary-General of the Socialist Party. The Asanuma compromise as presented to the party's Central Executive Committee combined the acceptance of higher railway transport rates with an adjustment in the allotment of financial sources. Asanuma planned to put the matter to a vote and settle the thorny issue. However, the left wing stood in his way, announcing that they reserved the right to take any future action they saw fit and that they would vote against the budget proposal in committee.

Many of the members of the Lower House Budget Committee were left wingers. Moreover, committee members who belonged to the Liberal Party, Communist Party, and other opposition parties were also committed to voting against the budget proposal. It made no difference that the Socialist Party's Central Executive Committee supported the Asanuma compromise when it was becoming increasingly likely that the budget proposal would be rejected in committee. The Katayama Cabinet found itself in a difficult predicament.

The Government Section and the Cabinet Crisis

Within GHQ, the Government Section did not have jurisdiction over the government budget. However, now that the budget had developed into a critical issue threatening the Cabinet, the Government Section could no longer ignore the matter.

Hoping to break the impasse, Chief Whitney of the Government Section directed Justin Williams, who headed the Parliamentary and Political Division, to mediate a solution. Standing between Finance Minister Kurusu Takeo and Suzuki Mosaburō, Williams attempted to solve the problem by ensuring that the increase in railway transport and communication rates would not directly correspond to the financing amount needed. Williams also consulted with members of the Economic and Scientific Section in search of a way to undo the knot.

On February 5, Williams met with members of the Economic and Scientific Section and pressed them to choose one of two available options: to either accept the proposal formulated by Kurusu and Suzuki, or to come up with an alternative proposal that would be acceptable to both the government and the House of Representatives. In the course of the discussions, Williams emphasized the position that Whitney had advanced, which was that the Cabinet and Diet should be allowed the freedom to manage domestic issues under the new constitution.[6] As such, Williams sought to preempt intervention by the Economic and Scientific Section in Japan's political affairs and to ensure that the budget problem would be resolved by the Japanese themselves. But he was already running out of time, and his efforts would prove futile.

At 7 p.m. on the same day, Suzuki Mosaburō convened the Budget Committee and put the budget proposal to a vote in the absence of ruling party members. The "0.8 month supplementary budget" was soundly rejected, leading to the resignation of the Katayama Cabinet on February 10.

Kades' "Central Party" Concept

While it was Chief Cabinet Secretary Nishio Suehiro who was the de facto leader in the Katayama Cabinet, the role that he played in the "0.8 month supplementary budget" problem is not well known. Records show that at 2 p.m. on February 5, Nishio paid a secret visit to Kades, the Deputy Chief of the Government Section.

Nishio referred to Katayama when he said, "He has already lost control of his own house [the Socialist Party]. Ever since, he has been unable to govern the nation with any sense of stability." Nishio outlined two choices that remained available to the Katayama Cabinet caught in crisis. The first was to dissolve the Diet and call a general election, and the second was to resign en masse.

Nishio continued with his analysis. Dissolving the Diet and calling a general election was the more acceptable path from the perspective of a "party politician." And indeed, this was the path that was supported by the leaders of the Democratic Party and the People's Cooperative Party. However, this was not a wise path from a "patriotic" perspective. The left wing would leave the Socialist Party and form

---

6 "Memorandum for the Chief Government Section (J. Williams), Cabinet Crisis," (February 7, 1948), Fukunaga, ed., in *GHQ Minsei-kyoku shiryō, 3*, pp. 501–502.

a new party. While they might not overtly join forces with the Communist Party, they would be sure to take a more radical position than now. Those remaining in the Socialist Party, including members of the Katayama-Nishio faction, would lose the support of the more left-leaning labor unions and the party would sink to become a "second-rate party as it was during the late 1920s and early 1930s." Ultimately, this would encourage the expansion of the extreme right and extreme left. This outcome could very well undermine the possibility of receiving material assistance from the United States, lead to a dangerous path of class warfare, and run counter to the prevailing public opinion in the Allied countries.

On the other hand, resignation of the Katayama Cabinet would likely result in the election of Yoshida Shigeru as the next prime minister. If Yoshida were to take the reins of government, coal output would suffer, the labor crisis would worsen, and inflationary forces would bear down more heavily on the people. More importantly, the country would descend into even deeper throes of economic and social instability. In closing his analysis, Nishio mentioned the name of Ashida as an alternative to Yoshida.

Kades responded that he was not in a position to give advice because that was the sole prerogative of the Supreme Commander. Having thus qualified his remarks, Kades proceeded to offer his proposal for the formation of a "central party." Kades first divided Japan's political forces into three categories: (1) the Communist Party and the extreme left, (2) the ultra-conservatives [Liberal Party], and (3) progressive democratic forces. Kades defined the third category to consist of an amalgam of the right wing of the Socialist Party, the Ashida faction of the Democratic Party and the People's Cooperative Party. Kades proposed that these three groups should merge to form a "centrist party." Kades had drawn his inspiration from Roosevelt's Democratic Party, which he had previously served. Nishio, however, was not convinced. He replied that the time was not right for forming a centrist party and that the possibility of success was slim. Notwithstanding the reservations voiced by Nishio, Kades' idea was ultimately realized in the birth of the Ashida Cabinet, albeit with some changes to the original design.[7]

---

7   Ibid., "MCGS, Political Trend," (February 6, 1947), pp. 490–498.

Launch of the Ashida Cabinet and Messengers from Washington

Government Section Backs Ashida

With the resignation of the Katayama Cabinet, the Democratic Party moved to nominate Ashida as the next premier. Yoshida and his Liberal Party followed suit, arguing that the next premier should come from the leading opposition party as dictated by the standard rule of constitutional government. The Government Section threw itself into the fray as the conflict between Democratic Party and Liberal Party intensified. The Government Section shunned Yoshida's Liberal Party as being "reactionary" and instead backed Ashida as the next head of government.

On February 6, 1948, Guy Swope, Chief of the National Government Division, gave a newspaper interview that was intended to promote the establishment of an Ashida Cabinet. "From a purely theoretical perspective, both methods [dissolution and general election versus Cabinet resignation] can be said to be democratic.... If the Cabinet resigns en masse, the members of the Diet can consult and form a majority. If a Cabinet can be formed in this way, I believe that would be the most democratic method. Coming from the current situation of a three-party coalition, this would be particularly democratic."[8]

The election of the next premier took place on February 21. The distribution of seats in the House of Representatives favored the Socialist Party with 123 seats, followed by the Liberal Party with 119 seats. The Democratic Party with 106 seats ranked third. But Ashida was able to garner some votes from the Socialist Party and came out on top with 216 votes, compared to 180 votes for Yoshida and Katayama with eight. The voting in the House of Councillors went to a runoff that ended with 104 votes for Yoshida and 102 for Ashida. However, in accordance with the provisions of Article 67 of the Constitution, the designation of the House of Representatives was given precedence and Ashida emerged as the new Prime Minister.

On February 25, Ashida visited Yoshida. In the course of their conversations,

---

8 *Asahi Shinbun,* February 7, 1948, and Fukunaga, ed., *GHQ Minsei-kyoku shiryō, 3,* p. 510.

Yoshida is recorded to have said, "[The difference between the Liberal Party and the Democratic Party] lies in whether cooperation with the Socialist Party is possible or not." Yoshida then confessed, "The truth is that you saved me. The Liberal Party doesn't stand a chance in the current environment."[9]

Ashida Hitoshi was born in 1887 (Meiji 20) in Kyoto Prefecture and joined the Foreign Ministry after graduating from Tokyo Imperial University's College of Law. His first diplomatic assignment placed him in the Russian capital city of Saint Petersburg where he witnessed the Russian Revolution first hand, an experience that deeply affected his view of Russia (and later of the Soviet Union). He later served in Japan's diplomatic missions in such countries as Belgium and Turkey but quit the Foreign Ministry following the Manchurian Incident. In 1932, he successfully ran for the House of Representatives as a candidate of the Constitutional Association of Political Friendship (Seiyūkai). As described in an earlier chapter, Ashida took a leadership role in launching the Liberal Party immediately after the end of the war. In March 1947, he participated in forming the Democratic Party and was elected the president of the newly formed party in May. Ashida had already established himself as an intellectual politician and an academic researcher with an impressive body of publications in the field of diplomatic history.

Ashida Hitoshi (1887–1956) Transitioning from diplomat to politician, Ashida remained a liberal before and during the war. As a prewar politician, Ashida won a seat in the Diet without the nomination of the Imperial Rule Assistance Association. After the war, he played a key role in forming the Liberal Party and was elected president of the Democratic Party in 1947. He served as Foreign Minister in the coalition government headed by the Socialist Party before assuming the office of Prime Minister in 1948.

---

9 Shindō Eiichi and Shimokōbe Motoharu, eds., *Ashida Hitoshi nikki* [Ashida Hitoshi Diary], Iwanami Shoten, 1986, (February 25, 1948).

Birth of the Ashida Cabinet and Formation of the Democratic Liberal Party

The Ashida Cabinet was launched on March 10, 1948. Cabinet members from the Socialist Party included Nishio Suehiro who was appointed State Minister without Portfolio with the status of Vice Premier. Katō Kanjū (Labor Minister) and Nomizo Masaru (State Minister without Portfolio) were also inducted into the new cabinet from the left wing of the Socialist Party. A key question facing Ashida was who to choose as Director of the ESB. Ashida rejected Katayama's recommendation to retain Wada Hiroo in this post and instead gave the nod to Kurusu Takeo, the Finance Minister in the Katayama Cabinet who had openly clashed with ESB. The appointment of Kurusu spelled the end of ESB's role as the control tower in economic affairs. Shortly after the appointment of Kurusu, the experts who had been toiling in ESB began to exit the organization. These included such stellar figures as Tsuru Shigeto, Nagano Shigeo, and Yamamoto Takayuki.

The Ashida Cabinet had come into being with the support of the Government Section, but that did not change that fact that its foundations were weak and unstable. Criticized for being "a monopolizing clique of political power," the Ashida Cabinet was unsteady from the start.

March 15 saw the establishment of the Democratic Liberal Party through the amalgamation of the Liberal Party with the 36 members of the "Democratic Club." The latter itself was the offspring of a merger between Shidehara Kijūrō's Dōshi Club and a group of Diet members led by Saitō Takao who had previously left the Democratic Party. The new entity claimed a total of 152 seats in the House of Representatives, instantly elevating it to the status of the plurality party. The members pledged themselves to faithfully implementing the provisions of the Potsdam Declaration, building a new Japan based on the principles of international justice, establishing responsible politics in accordance with the new constitution, and reconstituting all aspects of government based on the tenets of social justice.

Like the Democratic Party and the People's Cooperative Party, the Democratic Liberal Party made a concerted effort to identity itself as a true postwar party and a viable and responsible actor on the political stage under the new constitution. To emphasize its transformation, the party said it would fully respect the cause of labor while promoting the self-sufficiency of businesses and contributing to the recovery of the industrial economy. The party advocated such basic policies as administrative reform and consolidation, export promotion, and improving the environment for accepting investment from abroad. To return to a market economy, the party stated that it would formulate a long-term plan for industrial reconstruction featuring a gradual transition from the prioritized industries of coal, electric power, steel, and fertilizers to the promotion of such industries as textiles, food products, chemicals, precision machinery, and craft products.

Messengers from Washington: The Arrival of Kennan and Draper

George Kennan arrived in Japan on March 1, 1948, just a few days before the Ashida Cabinet came into being. MacArthur gave a cold reception to the senior officer of the State Department. MacArthur reportedly remarked, "I'll have him briefed until it comes out his ears."[10] True to his pledge, MacArthur spoke for two hours without break in their first meeting, leaving Kennan to listen in bored silence.

On March 2, the report of the second Strike Mission was released, recommending the easing of the onerous reparation requirements placed on Japan in the Pauley Interim Report in an effort to make the Japanese economy self-reliant by 1950. The Strike Report recommended dramatically narrowing the scope of facilities to be used in making reparations. The transition in U.S. government policy toward Japan could be clearly seen in the recommendations. The easing of reparations was to be used to leverage faster recovery and self-sufficiency of the Japanese economy.

Kennan prepared for his second meeting with MacArthur by drawing up a number of questions that addressed three issues: (1) U.S. national security

---

10 Miscamble, Wilson D., *George F. Kennan and the Making of American Foreign Policy, 1947–1950*, Princeton University Press, 1993, p. 261.

policy for East Asia, (2) an intensive program of economic recovery, and (3) relaxation of Occupation control.

MacArthur responded to the three questions as follows. Regarding (1), MacArthur remarked that the strategic boundaries of the United States lay along the islands on the eastern shores of the Asiatic continent. Okinawa was the most advanced and vital point on this strategic boundary, and it was absolutely necessary to retain unilateral and complete control of Okinawa. As for the Japanese islands, he did not believe that it would be feasible for the U.S. to retain bases anywhere in Japan after the conclusion of a treaty of peace. For the U.S. to do so would be to admit the equally legitimate claim of others to do likewise. Regarding (2), MacArthur agreed that economic recovery should be made a primary objective of occupational policy, and commented on the importance of the development of foreign trade and the easing of reparations. Regarding (3), MacArthur offered a rebuttal stating that the Japanese government had been given considerable autonomy, and that reform measures, such the elimination of the concentration of economic power and the economic purge that he had implemented had not been conducted nearly as drastically as suggested by directives from Washington.[11]

Next to arrive was Under-Secretary of the Army Draper. On March 20, Draper landed in Japan as a member of the Draper-Johnston Mission tasked with investigating current economic conditions in Japan. Kennan met with Draper and discussed in detail a full range of issues, including easing of the purge, re-examining policies for eliminating the concentration of economic power, and Japan's national security. The two concluded with an agreement to press for a shift in Occupation policies.

The third meeting between Kennan and MacArthur took place on March 23. This time, Kennan was accompanied by Draper. In the course of their conversations, Draper commented on the need for "early establishment of a small defensive force in Japan, to be ready at such time as U.S. Occupation

---

11 Conversation between General of the Army MacArthur and Mr. George F. Kennan, March 5, 1948, *FRUS*, 1948, vol. 6, The Far East and Australasia (Washington).

forces leave the country."[12] MacArthur rejected the suggestion for two reasons. First, rearmament contravened the fundamental principles that had guided the Occupation. Second, the Japanese had sincerely and unconditionally renounced war and were no longer willing to support an armed force. MacArthur stated that he agreed with promoting Japan's economic recovery, but strongly opposed rearmament.

After returning home, Kennan set out to formulate a new set of policies for Japan (PPS/28: Recommendations with Respect to U.S. Policy Toward Japan), with a clear focus on economic recovery and political stability. The leadership role in Japanese affairs that the State Department's Bureau of East Asian Affairs had been playing was hereafter transferred to the Policy Planning Staff headed by Kennan. Meanwhile, work on a peace treaty was placed on hold.

George Kennan (1904–2005) Diplomat, subsequently historian of diplomacy. Becoming Chief of the U.S. State Department's Policy Planning Staff in 1947, he advocated the doctrine of containment of Soviet influence. He visited Japan twice, first in 1948, stressing a switch in Occupation policy in Japan from demilitarization and democratization to economic reconstruction, and established the path toward the peace treaty.

Debating Economic Rehabilitation: Shock Approach versus Gradualism

Ashida Cabinet and the Foreign Capital Issue

On assuming the office of Prime Minister in March 1948, Ashida proclaimed that the goal of his Cabinet was to work under the new constitution to "build a world ruled by peace, freedom, and justice." To realize this goal, Ashida indicated that his would be a middle-of-the-road Cabinet. Ashida identified economic

---

12 Conversation between General of the Army MacArthur, Under-Secretary of the Army Draper, and Mr. George F. Kennan, March 21, 1948 (Amended March 23, 1948), *FRUS*, 1948, vol. 6, The Far East and Australasia (Washington).

recovery and regaining international trust as critical missions of the Cabinet, and stated that this would be achieved by increasing production, curbing inflation, rationalizing corporate management and introducing foreign capital. Finally, Ashida appealed to the working masses for their cooperation, saying that he sincerely hoped for the sound development of labor unions.

The debate on economic recovery boiled down to two options. The first, referred to as the "shock approach," focused on curbing inflation and sought to extinguish inflationary forces in one bold stroke. The second, referred to as "gradualism," advocated continued emphasis on increasing production combined with a step-by-step approach to extinguishing inflation.

Fearing that the shock approach to extinguishing inflation would lead to a sudden spike in unemployment and business failures, the Ashida Cabinet opted for gradualism. Based on this decision, the Cabinet put together a five-year plan to be launched in fiscal 1949 with the following two principal objectives. First, living standards would be raised within five years to levels approaching the prewar level of 1930–1934. Second, to realize economic self-sufficiency, exports would be promoted to pay for the necessary importation of food and industrial raw materials. The Economic and Scientific Section gave its tacit approval to the plan.

On the issue of foreign capital, the three-party policy agreement signed by the Democratic Party, the Socialist Party, and the People's Cooperative Party stated in the preamble, "We look forward to the introduction of foreign capital, and shall pursue recovery in production and the stabilization of the people's lives." The left wing of the Socialist Party stated that "as part of measures designed to overcome the current crisis," it was in favor of "receiving positive assistance from foreign capital and pursuing a fundamental solution to inflation and a return of production to prewar levels." The opposition Democratic Liberal Party also supported the introduction of foreign capital.

Business associations were particularly excited about the prospects of foreign capital entering Japan. At the end of March, the Economic Fraternalists' Association (Dōyūkai) released its "Opinion on Promoting the Introduction of Foreign Private Capital" and submitted its recommendations to the Ashida Cabinet. The Japan Business Federation (Keidanren) also came out in favor of the introduction of foreign capital as a necessary step in economic recovery. It did, however, mention the concern that the introduction of foreign private capital "may lead to the control of majority interest" by foreign entities.

Among labor unions, the Japanese Federation of Trade Unions (Sōdōmei) noted the need for self-reliant recovery, but admitted that there were limits to this approach and approved the introduction of foreign capital as a means of "priming the pump" for expanding industrial output. In contrast, the Communist Party and the Congress of Industrial Unions of Japan (Sanbetsu Kaigi) strongly opposed the policy. They argued that the measure would benefit foreign capital and Japan's monopoly capitalists, and would place Japanese assets under the control of foreign capital. Furthermore, they predicted that the administrative reforms and business restructuring that would accompany the entry of foreign capital would result in massive layoffs.[13]

While anticipation mounted for the imminent introduction of foreign capital (comprising government loans including GARIOA, EROA, and revolving funds, plus private-sector investment), the process did not move forward smoothly. Before foreign funds could be allowed to flow in, there was a pressing need to put an end to the scourge of extreme inflation.

The March Offensive and the Marquat Memorandum

Just days after coming to power, the Ashida Cabinet was confronted with the "March offensive," a labor offensive mounted by the public employees' unions. On March 11, the government requested the various public employees' unions to formally accept the "2,920 yen base salary" package adopted by the previous Cabinet. The Japan National Railways Workers' Union (Kokurō), which was controlled by anti-communist elements, settled for a ten percent wage increase. But the All Japan Communication Workers' Union (Zentei) and other labor unions under the aegis of Sanbetsu Kaigi refused to settle.

On March 15, Zentei responded to the government with a "labor offensive

---

13 Nakakita Kōji, *Keizai fukkō to sengo seiji* [Economic Recovery and Postwar Politics], University of Tokyo Press, 1998, pp. 153–166.

declaration" and a "statement" predicting the launch of a "labor offensive of historic proportions." On March 18, the union instructed its local chapters to go on all-day strikes beginning on March 23 and followed this up with a "strike declaration" on March 19. Local chapters began to strike beginning on March 25, and preparations were made for a general strike scheduled for March 31.

The Ashida Cabinet proved itself incapable of coping with the growing crisis. Consequently, on March 29, William Marquat, Chief of the Economic and Scientific Section, hand-delivered a memorandum stating that the postal workers' strike came under the provisions of General MacArthur's statement issued at the time of the February 1 general strike. As had happened in the previous year, the looming general strike was squashed by GHQ.

Addressing the Foreign Affairs Committee of the House of Representatives on April 1, Ashida mentioned the Taft-Hartley Act that had been enacted by the U.S. Congress in June 1947 prohibiting strikes by public workers. Suggesting that similar legislation could be adopted in Japan, Ashida referred to the need to restrict labor activities.

Dissolution of the Economic Rehabilitation Council: Labor Movement Splinters and Capital Goes on Offensive

The Katayama Cabinet was supported by the twin pillars of the ESB and the Economic Rehabilitation Council. But the latter body had effectively ceased to function by early 1948. Sharing the same fate was the labor-capital cooperation line that the Council had advocated. Possibilities for cooperation receded as the labor movement became increasingly splintered and business interests mounted an energized campaign supporting the introduction of foreign capital.

During this period, the simmering conflict between pro-communist and anti-communist elements within Sanbetsu Kaigi was growing in intensity. On January 13, 1948, Sōdōmei had issued a statement advocating the "democratization of labor unions," which was intended as a clear message of support for the anti-communist movement welling up among such neutral labor unions as Kokurō, Zentei, the Japan Broadcasting Labor Union (Hōsō), Express Workers' Union (Nittsū), and the All Japan Electric Power Industry Workers Union

(Densan). In February, Secretary-General Hosoya Matsuta of Sanbetsu Kaigi had led the formation of the "Democratization Leagues (Mindō)," a movement aimed at ridding the unions of the control exercised by the Communist Party. At the end of June, Sōdōmei left the Federation of All Japan Labor Union (Zenrōren) on the grounds that there was "no longer any meaning in remaining in Zenrōren that had stooped to becoming a mere sound box for the Communist Party." This finalized the splintering of the labor movement into three camps: Sanbetsu Kaigi, Sōdōmei, and Mindō.

At the same time, the business community went on the offensive with a campaign to support the introduction of foreign capital. In its "Opinion on Promoting the Introduction of Foreign Private Capital" issued in March, Dōyūkai advocated respect for management in a move that signaled its intent to resist labor union excesses. In April, Keidanren released a statement underlining the urgent need to restructure and rationalize businesses in preparation for the introduction of foreign capital and Japan's re-entry into the international economy. April also witnessed the formation of the Japan Federation of Employers' Associations (Nikkeiren). Adopting "Management should be righteous and strong" as its slogan, the new association identified the implementation of effective labor measures as its primary mission. It was against this backdrop that the already comatose Economic Rehabilitation Council was effectively dissolved at the end of April.

As had been the case with the Katayama Cabinet, the Ashida Cabinet had started out as an "alliance of reformists." However, its commitment to harmonization was steadily diluted as it found itself being pulled apart by the growing tension between labor and capital.

Second Session of the Diet: Ruling Parties Splinter

Having overcome the March labor offensive with the help of GHQ, the Ashida Cabinet would now have to confront the challenges of the Diet in session. Since the launch of the Ashida Cabinet, the opposition Democratic Liberal Party had been hinting that it would call for the dissolution of the Diet, a threat that carried weight as the Democratic Liberal Party enjoyed a clear plurality in the Diet.

Aware of the possibility of a snap election, members of the Diet were uniformly restless. On April 3, Chief Whitney of the Government Section sent a letter to Ashida conveying the following message. "It is becoming a matter of increasing concern that members of the House of Representatives are absenting themselves from its sessions to such an extent that it is difficult at times to secure even the quorum necessary to hold legislative affairs."[14] Whitney was nixing the possibility of dissolution and signaling that the Government Section was prepared to buttress the Cabinet. It is ironic that Ashida, who had criticized the Katayama Cabinet as being a "puppet regime," was now forced to rely on the support and intervention of the Government Section for its continued existence.

The Diet soon became bogged down in debate over the forthcoming budget. From the outset, the left wing of the Socialist Party demanded the "cessation of interest payments on military bonds," a thorny issue that immediately split the ruling coalition. In the process of negotiating a three-party coalition agreement, the left wing of the Socialist Party had demanded the cessation of interest payments, while the Democratic Party had voiced its strong opposition throughout the talks. A coalition agreement had been finally concluded by finessing the language and settling on a very ambiguous expression—military bonds would be treated as "suspended." The conflict between the two sides was rekindled as soon as the question of translating this ambiguous expression into action came up. The matter was finally settled through a compromise measure proposed by Chief Cabinet Secretary Tomabechi Gizō. Interest payments would simply be postponed for one year.

Two new problems bogged down the debate over the budget. One had to do with Nishio Suehiro and contributions received from the construction industry, and the other involved raising railway transport and communication rates. The latter problem was particularly serious, as it had already contributed to the demise of the Katayama Cabinet. The Cabinet had previously approved a government plan for raising rates. Specifically, railway rates for both passenger and cargo transport were to be increased by 3.5 times, and communication rates

---

14 "Relations between Allied Forces and the Population of Japan (Bertrand M. Roehner)," Sodei Rinjirō, ed., and trans., in *Correspondence between General MacArthur, Prime Minister Yoshida & Other High Japanese Officials [1945-1951]*, Hōsei Daigaku Shuppankyoku, 2000, p. 219.

were to be increased by 4 times. The three coalition parties, however, could not agree on the details of the program. The Socialist Party advocated a doubling of railway rates, while the Democratic Party called for an increase of 2.5 times in railway passenger rates and an increase of 3.5 times in cargo rates. Finally, the People's Cooperative Party supported an increase of 2.5 times in passenger and cargo rates, plus an increase of 4 times in communication rates. There was disarray among the opposition parties over these issues.

In a letter dated June 29, MacArthur extended support to Ashida by issuing instructions to speed up Diet deliberations on the draft budget.[15] On the following day, June 30, the leaders of the Democratic, Socialist, and People's Cooperative Parties conferred to settle the matter. It was agreed that the increase in cargo transport rates would remain unchanged at 3.5 times, and passenger transport rates would be amended to an increase of 2.55 times. The revised budget bill was put to a vote in the Budget Committee on July 2, but was rejected by one vote due to the continued opposition of Kuroda Hisao and other Socialist left wingers. However, the bill was adopted in the plenary session and sent to the House of Councillors where it was passed and enacted on July 4.

Thus, it was with MacArthur's support that the second session of the Diet was able to adjourn on July 5. Unhappy with the outcome, Kuroda Hisao and five others quit the Socialist Party (to form the Laborers and Farmers Party at the end of 1948). The Democratic Party was similarly hit by six defections, which further weakened the base of the ruling coalition. Furthermore, immediately after adjournment, Nishio resigned his posts as State Minister without Portfolio and member of the Central Executive Committee of the Socialist Party. Although the trust that Ashida placed in Nishio remained unaffected by his resignations, it was clear that Ashida had lost a critical channel of communication with the Socialist Party.

The People's Cooperative Party convened its party convention on July 5, the same day the second session of the Diet was adjourned. Party Chairman Miki addressed the convention with this policy prescription. "Instead of opting for conservative policies, the People's Cooperative Party should tread the path

---

15 Shindō and Shimokōbe, eds., *Ashida Hitoshi nikki*, (June 29, 1948).

of a planned economy. We stand in opposition to uncontrolled capitalism and the directions that it dictates. Faithful to the spirit that animated the formation of our party, we should take the path that lies between conservative forces and the extreme left wing of the Socialist Party." Miki then called for the "formation of a centrist political federation."[16] On the following day, July 6, Ashida responded to this call at a meeting of the Diet members of the Democratic Party. Ashida announced to the assembled group that he was prepared to consider the proposal for creating a "centrist political party." The idea of a centrist political party had been resurrected.

Discussions in the Socialist Party were taking a different path. Among left-wing members, there was growing support for leaving the coalition and joining the opposition, while the right wing insisted on staying. As a result, the gap between the two wings was becoming increasingly unbridgeable. On July 18, Katayama was touring Sendai when he outlined his thoughts in a campaign speech. "The Socialist Party should not remain in the coalition any longer. Doing so would only bring turmoil to the political situation and will also act to the detriment of the party itself." Katayama then continued with his plans for the upcoming Diet session. "An extraordinary session of the Diet will be convened at the end of August. At that time, I intend to immediately move for dissolution."[17]

These developments served to reinforce Yoshida's growing confidence. Yoshida had suffered one defeat as the leader of the Liberal Party in his quest for the premier's post, but he was now feeling confident enough to encourage his party members. "MacArthur has given his assurance that GHQ does not support any specific party."[18]

---

16 *Asahi Shinbun*, July 6, 1948.
17 *Asahi Shinbun*, July 19, 1947.
18 "Control of Japanese Leader Upon the Current Political Situation, (POLAND, No. 431)," (July 10, 1948), Fukunaga, ed., in *GHQ Minsei-kyoku shiryō, 3*, pp. 544–546.

Kobe Korean School Incident: First Declaration of a State of Emergency under the Occupation

The Kobe Korean School Incident (the Hanshin Education Struggle) occurred in late April 1948, just as the Diet was in the midst of heated debate over budget issues. The incident had its origins in the ordered closure of all Korean ethnic schools and became serious enough to invite armed intervention by Occupation forces.

Shortly after the end of the war, GHQ began encouraging the repatriation of Koreans in Japan. This was in keeping with the Basic Initial Post-Surrender Directive, which categorized Koreans as "liberated peoples." At the same time, however, GHQ took a very ambiguous stance on Korean residents. Though they were not "Japanese," they were considered "subjects of Japan," and therefore were to be treated as an enemy population as deemed necessary. Against the backdrop of growing political insecurity following the division of the Korean peninsula into North and South, approximately 600,000 Koreans had opted against repatriation and had remained in Japan. Reflecting the political developments in their homeland, the Korean residents coalesced into two groups: the League of Koreans Residing in Japan (Chōren), which was affiliated with the Communist Party, and the Korean Residents' Union of Japan (Mindan) with clear nationalistic leanings.

In March 1946, GHQ issued a statement affirming that Korean residents in Japan were subject to the laws of Japan. In October 1947, GHQ stated that ethnic Korean schools in Japan would have to abide by the directives of the Ministry of Education. In April 1948, the Ministry of Education ordered the closure of all ethnic Korean schools and stepped up its pressure on Chōren. Responding to this order, Korean residents mounted an opposition movement on the grounds that the order effectively suppressed ethnic education by preventing their children from learning their mother tongue. One of the centers of this opposition movement was located in Kobe, Hyogo Prefecture.

Responding to the April 10 closure order issued by the governor of Hyogo Prefecture, a crowd of several thousand Koreans marched on the Hyogo Prefectural Office on April 24. Making their way into the prefectural office, leaders of the movement held the governor and others captive as they negotiated for the reversal of the order. Ultimately, the governor agreed to rescind the order to close the three ethnic Korean schools located within the city limits of Kobe. At the same time, 70 Koreans who had been arrested in the demonstrations were released.

This course of events did not sit well with the U.S. Military Government Team stationed in Kobe. Viewing the demonstrations as an open challenge to the Occupation and its policies, a state of emergency was declared in the name of the commander of the Kobe Base of the Allied Powers late in the evening of April 24, making this the one and only such declaration to be issued throughout the entire Occupation. Eighth Army Commander Eichelberger arrived in Kobe the following day and took stern measures to quell the movement. Japanese police were mobilized and 1,732 persons were arrested, of whom 136 were put on military trial. Nine were sentenced to the maximum sentence of fifteen years of hard labor.

Reasoning that the Korean ethnic schools were engaged in communist education and indoctrination, GHQ looked upon ethnic Korean schools with growing concern and vigilance. Furthermore, GHQ came to believe that the Kobe Incident had been incited for the purpose of throwing the upcoming elections in southern Korea into turmoil. The United States and Soviet Union had long maintained that the division of the Korean Peninsula along the 38th parallel following World War II was only temporary as they continued to consult on establishing a unified government. However, these talks had completely broken down by the end of 1947. When the Soviet Union rejected the U.S. proposal for a unified election, the U.N. General Assembly adopted a resolution for conducting an election in the south under U.N. supervision. This election was scheduled to be held in May.

On May 10, 1948, an election was held in South Korea, and Syngman Rhee became the first president of the newly founded Republic of Korea in August. The following month, the Democratic People's Republic of Korea was founded in the north with Kim Il Sung as president, thus finalizing the division between north and south.

Following the Korean school incident, GHQ pushed for the adoption of local public security ordinances restricting mass parades and demonstrations, and used the Public Security Ordinance to suppress the activities of Korean organizations.

Toward Economic Recovery: Revision of Labor Policies

Wage Controls: Draper's Unfinished Business

On March 1948, the Draper-Johnston Mission arrived in Japan to consult with MacArthur on current economic conditions in Japan. During his stay, Johnston posed this question to Kurusu Takeo, Director of the Economic Stabilization Board (ESB): "Is economic recovery possible without price and wage controls?"

Economic policies during this period were essentially based on the formulation of a price structure that was then matched to a wage level that would balance and stabilize the economy. In practice, however, the posting of official prices proved ineffective because price levels were seriously skewed by black market prices. This triggered a round of wage increases aimed at catching up with prices, which in turn fueled a vicious cycle of price and wage increases chasing after each other.

In early April, Harry F. Alber, who headed the Price and Rationing Division of the Economic and Scientific Section, contacted Tsuru Shigeto of ESB to inform him of discussions pertaining to wage controls. "Following consultation with the Draper Mission, the decision was made that, if absolutely necessary, GHQ will use a directive to push policies forward. On this point, the predominant opinion within the Draper Mission was particularly firm with regard to labor policies."[19] This exchange indicates that GHQ had by this time begun to examine wage controls as a possible means for controlling inflation.

On May 1, the relevant instruction went out to the Japanese government from William F. Marquat, Chief of the Economic and Scientific Section. First, Marquat ordered the establishment of a Wage Stabilization Board comprised of representatives of labor, business, and government. Second, the Board was

---

19 "Sengo keizai fukkō to keizai antei honbu" [Postwar Economic Reconstruction and the Economic Stabilization Board], Economic Planning Agency, ed., in *Tsuru Shigeto nisshi* [Diary of Tsuru Shigeto], National Printing Bureau, 1988, (April 7, 1948).

tasked with determining stable wage levels by industry, which would be used as reference points in direct control of wages. In his meeting with Prime Minister Ashida on May 14, MacArthur also emphasized the need for wage controls, to which Ashida is reported to have replied, "I agree with the philosophy, but prices of food and clothing must be taken into account if we are to raise real wages."[20] Led by the Economic and Scientific Section, GHQ thereafter prepared for the introduction of wage controls. Parallel studies were undertaken by the Japanese government during this period.

Two approaches—direct and indirect—were considered as viable options in controlling wages. Direct control would be based on a maximum wage rate determined by the government, while indirect control would work by suppressing corporate loans and subsidies that were being used to pay for wage increases.

The three major business associations—Keidanren, Japan Federation of Industries (Nissankyō), and Nikkeiren—mounted their own initiative by forming the Meeting on Wage Stabilizing Measures, which issued its recommendations on June 22 under the title, "Petition on Wage Stabilizing Measures." While concluding that direct control was desirable, the petition noted that indirect control was more appropriate under current circumstances. As the government and business community moved toward the introduction of wage controls, Sōdōmei repeated its strong opposition to any form of wage control.

The Draper-Johnston Report and the Young Mission

Meanwhile in Washington, work was moving forward on creating the necessary conditions for Japan's economic recovery and self-sufficiency.

First among these conditions was the easing of onerous reparation requirements. The Draper-Johnston Report of May 1948 recommended that reparation amounts be significantly reduced even below the levels indicated in the Strike Report issued in March 1948. Specifically, the Draper-Johnston Report recommended that reparations be reduced to 25 percent of the level that had been proposed in 1946 (Table 4-1). The business community welcomed

20 Shindō and Shimokōbe, eds., *Ashida Hitoshi nikki*, (May 14, 1948).

Table 4-1 Reparation Proposals (Unit: million yen, 1939 prices)

	Industrial Facilities	Military Facilities	Total
Pauley Proposal, Nov. 1946	990	1,476	2,466
Strike Proposal, Mar. 1948	172	1,476	1,648
Johnston Proposal, May 1948	102	560	662

Source: Compiled by the author from Nakamura Takafusa, *Shōwa keizai shi* [Economic History of the Shōwa Era], Iwanami Shoten, 1986.

the recommendation. "The Draper Report posited the self-sufficiency of the Japanese economy as the primary objective, and pursued a speedy resolution of the reparation problem in amounts that would not obstruct the realization of this primary objective."[21]

The second condition pertained to preparations for restarting foreign trade. All foreign trade was nationalized at this time and placed under the control of GHQ. Consequently, Japanese trading companies were unable to directly engage in trade. In the case of exports, products intended for export were purchased by the government from domestic suppliers. The process was reversed for imports, with the government making all overseas purchases and reselling these in Japan. Furthermore, there was no common single exchange rate, and rates were separately set for each transaction on a case-by-case basis.

Two days after the release of the Draper Report in May, the Young Mission arrived in Japan. Headed by Ralph Young of the Board of Governors of the Federal Reserve System, the mission was officially known as the Special Mission on Yen Foreign Exchange Policy. The Young Mission completed its report in June, recommending the adoption of a fixed exchange rate by October 1948 as a countermeasure to inflation. The report also contained a series of recommendations for quickly stabilizing the Japanese economy, including cutbacks in the government budget and stabilization of wages.

MacArthur vehemently opposed the recommendations of the Young Report, in part because he felt that Washington had gone over his head. But more importantly, MacArthur believed that adopting a fixed exchange rate was premature

---

21 Keizai Dantai Rengōkai, ed., *Keidanren no nijū nen* [Keidanren's Twenty Years], Keizai Dantai Rengōkai, 1969, p. 72.

and could trigger serious social unrest if rapidly implemented. MacArthur argued that it should be postponed until trade and production levels had recovered to prewar levels. Another consideration was the crisis that had beset the Cabinet following the contribution scandal that had hit Nishio. MacArthur could not bring himself to sign off on the recommendations of the Young Report, knowing that doing so would further deepen the crisis that had gripped the coalition Cabinet of the Democratic and the Social Democratic Parties.

On July 16 Marquat conveyed his "Ten Principles of Economic Stabilization" to ESB Director Kurusu. Marquat made no mention of a fixed exchange rate—the principal recommendation of the Young Report—and instead focused on such objectives as increasing mining and industrial output, upgrading the rationing system, and increasing agricultural production. Insofar as the Ten Principles simply listed the makeshift measures that the Japanese government had implemented to date, they tacitly approved or merely affirmed the policy of intermediate stabilization. The Economic and Scientific Section explained that the Ten Principles represented the shared consensus of Washington and GHQ. However, no clear explanation was forthcoming when the Japanese side asked for background information and the implications of the Ten Principles.[22]

Cabinet Order No. 201

GHQ and Washington were no longer on the same page in terms of policies for rehabilitating the Japanese economy. Even as this rift was becoming more pronounced, a new labor offensive was gaining momentum and the government would very soon become caught up in a new round of battles with labor unions in what would come to be known as the "three major labor problems." The demand made by the National Council of Government and Public Corporation Workers Unions (Zenkankō) for an after-tax base salary of 3,700 yen had been referred to arbitration. The National Public Service Law was up for revision, and the difficult problem of wage stabilization continued to hang over the

---

22 Ministry of Finance, Fiscal History Section, ed., *Tai senryō-gun kōshō kiroku: Watanabe Takeshi nikki* [Confidential Records of Negotiations with Occupation Forces: Watanabe Takeshi Diary], Tōyō Keizai Shinpōsha, 1983, p. 243.

government. In May, the government proposed the formation of an "arbitration commission" that would include a delegation of neutral members. However, in June, Zenkankō rejected the proposal, dismissing it as no more than a "body for brushing aside disputes" and demanding an after-tax base salary level of 5,200 yen that would put public workers on par with private-sector workers. The full list of its demands included opposition to revising the price structure, eliminating mass taxation, opposition to firings and rationalization in government administration, and opposition to the introduction of maximum wage levels.

Handed the government's proposal for an after-tax base salary of 3,700 yen, Zenkankō responded that given the increase of prices by 2.5 times, the increase in transportation charges by 3.5, and the increase in communication rates by 4 times, the 3,700-yen package translated into a 14 percent decrease in real wages. The Council now raised the banner of "Out with the nation-ruining Ashida Cabinet!" Thus, the negotiations between the two sides that had started on June 23 broke down completely on July 3. Subsequently, the matter was referred to the Central Labor Relations Commission (Chūrōi) for arbitration on July 3 with the actual arbitration process to begin on July 14.

It was against this background that MacArthur wrote to Prime Minister Ashida on July 22 calling for the restriction of labor actions by government employees. It can be said that this letter marked a fundamental change in GHQ labor policies. It should be noted that the MacArthur letter had not suddenly emerged out of nowhere, but in fact represented the comeback that Blaine Hoover, the Chief of the Government Section's Civil Service Division, had been angling for since the previous year. Hoover had been infuriated to see that his proposed restriction on labor actions by civil servants had been deleted—in his absence and without his consent—from the structure of the National Public Service Law.

It was Hoover's position that civil servants were the employees of the people and that it was undemocratic to allow civil servants to pressure the people through collective bargaining and strikes. Hoover believed that under the prevailing conditions, the rights that had been given to civil servants supported and fostered the activities of communist forces. Standing on the opposite side of the argument was James Killen, Chief of the Labor Division of the Economic and Scientific Section, who fiercely opposed removing the right to collective bargaining. With his background in the American Federation of Labor, Killen argued that the basic rights of labor guaranteed under the constitution must be extended to civil servants, as was the case in the United Kingdom. As for strikes that threatened the welfare of the public and the principle of sovereignty of the people, Killen pointed out that such actions were already prohibited under the Labor Relations Adjustment Law.

Hoover and Killen argued their respective cases before MacArthur in a session that lasted seven hours. It was highly unusual for division chiefs to present their arguments directly to the Supreme Commander. Ultimately, MacArthur came out in favor of Hoover.

Although he was opposed to Hoover's prescription for introducing an American-style civil service system, Kades did not involve himself in the debate at this time. Kades would later comment, "I didn't want to get involved in this problem."[23] Given that the Hoover position had been approved by both MacArthur and Whitney, Theodore Cohen, adviser to the Economic and Scientific Section, theorized that Kades was not "foolish enough" to take on an "unwinnable battle" and thereby lose the trust of his superiors.[24]

Placing restrictions on labor actions by civil servants was not only criticized in the Far Eastern Commission by the Soviet Union and British Commonwealth nations, but was also strongly questioned within the State Department. Referring to the MacArthur letter, Cohen wrote, "Indeed, July 22, 1948 marks the start of the loss of the support of Japan's working class for American democracy."[25]

Interpreting the MacArthur letter as constituting a direct order, the Ashida Cabinet promulgated Cabinet Order No. 201 on July 31 as a so-called Potsdam Ordinance based on the provisions of the "Imperial Ordinance on Orders Issued Incidental to Acceptance of the Potsdam Declaration" (promulgated and immediately enforced on September 20, 1945). Cabinet Order No. 201 denied

---

23 Takemae Eiji, *Nihon Senryō: GHQ kōkan no shōgen* [The Occupation as Told by Senior GHQ Officials], Chūō Kōronsha, 1988, p. 79.
24 Cohen, Theodore, *Nihon senryō kakumei: GHQ karano shōgen* [Remaking Japan: The American Occupation as New Deal], Ōmae Masaomi, trans., vol. 2, TBS Britannica, 1983, p. 248.
25 Cohen, Theodore, *Remaking Japan: The American Occupation as New Deal*, Free Press, 1987, p. 396.

civil servants the rights of collective bargaining and labor actions. This decision would later become the source of problems related to the right of civil servants to go on strike.

Change in GHQ Labor Policies

There was no consensus among labor unions on Cabinet Order No. 201. The Communist Party and Sanbetsu Kaigi were absolutely opposed to it, while Sōdōmei retorted that the restrictions were the result of the Communist Party's class warfare tactics. Consequently, no organized resistance could be put together. The same fissures were seen among the key elements of Zenkankō, such as Kokurō and Zentei. Split between pro- and anti-Communist Party factions, it even proved difficult to take a unified stance in opposition to the order.

When coal miners belonging to the Japan Federation of Coal Miners' Unions (Tanrō) and the All-Japan Coal Workers' Union (Zentan) demanded higher wages in November, GHQ responded with the three wage principles. These prohibited financing of deficit enterprises, revision of official prices, and payment of subsidies. The idea was to respond to demands for higher wages by suppressing corporate access to funds, such as loans and subsidies.

Prime Minister Yoshida welcomed the three principles as being "consistent with my thinking." He bemoaned the fact that businesses had previously been allowed to access deficit financing from the Reconstruction Financial Corporation or "to get by through other means, such as the revision of official prices to bolster revenue through higher prices, or in certain instances to use direct subsidies from the national treasury. While these methods were unavoidable under the conditions that prevailed at the time, they did fuel the vicious cycle of wage and price inflation."[26]

---

26 Yoshida Shigeru, *Kaisō jūnen, dai 3-kan* [A Memoir of Ten Years, vol. 3], Shinchōsha, pp. 199–200.

The Economic Recovery of Okinawa: Separation from the Japanese Economy

Municipal Elections of February 1948

The Constitution of Japan did not apply to Okinawa, nor did the spate of new legislation including the Civil Code and labor laws. As such, Okinawa remained under existing laws and the rule of the U.S. military government. On the other hand, some progress was made in the areas of politics and government administration, albeit at a very slow pace. This progress was primarily seen in the election of February 1, 1948, for heads of local units of government and the election of February 28 for local assembly members. These elections were held a year later than corresponding elections in Japan and the terms of office were set to expire at the next election scheduled for 1950. Voter turnout was high, at 88 percent for men and 81 percent for women.

In many instances, these local elections were uncontested. Of the total of 55 local elections, 27 elections for local assembly members and 21 elections for heads of local government units were uncontested. Party candidates won in only six contests for heads of local government (three each from the Okinawa People's Party and the Okinawa Democratic Alliance). Similarly, of the 1,192 local assembly members elected, only four were party candidates. Further, only four women were elected to local assemblies.[27]

The February 6 issue of the newspaper *Uruma Shinpō*, the predecessor of *Ryūkyū Shinpō*, carried the headline, "Municipal election results strongly favor new faces." The newspaper went on to report on election results on the Okinawa mainland. "Of the 43 municipal elections held on the Okinawa mainland, incumbents won in only thirteen races. The remaining 30 seats were claimed by new people." It is notable that newcomers won the election against incumbents in six towns and municipalities, including Naha City. Moreover, in nineteen uncontested elections for village head, newcomers won in ten cases.

---

27 Okinawa Prefecture, Bunka shinkō-kai kōbunsho kanri-bu shiryō henshū-shitsu, ed., *Okinawa ken-shi shiryō-hen 14: Ryūkyū rettō no gunsei 1945–1950 gendai 2 (Wayaku-hen)* [Okinawa Prefecture Historical Documents 14: Military Government of the Ryukyus 1945–1950 Contemporary 2 (Japanese translations)], Okinawa Prefecture Board of Education, 2002, p. 96.

These figures underscored the transition in political leadership. Another notable feature was that professional educators won in a total of twenty elections for local government heads.

These local elections generated greater momentum for holding regional elections for governor and assembly members for the Ryūkyū island groups. On April 12, prominent individuals and heads of local government units assembled to issue a statement on restoring autonomy. The U.S. military government responded to this on May 29 with a document titled "Government Authority on the Ryukyu Islands" that emphasized that as long as the Ryūkyū Islands remained under the military government, neither a permanent democratic government nor complete democracy could be established.

Dealing with Inflation

During 1948, the U.S. military government in Okinawa shifted the primary focus of its economic policies from relief measures aimed at saving the population from starvation and unstable living conditions to recovery and reconstruction. The most important objective of the new policy direction was to overcome the inflationary spiral that had continued from 1947 through 1948.

In May, the Bank of the Ryūkyūs was established with the Philippine National Bank as a model. In certain respects, the Bank of the Ryūkyūs was expected to play the role of a central bank in integrating the economies of the four island chains of Okinawa, Amami, Miyako, and Yaeyama that had been split apart under separate military government structures. The new bank was also expected to regulate money supply and undertake rational lending to businesses. In July, the B-Yen military currency became the single currency for the Ryūkyū Islands. Responsibility for issuing the currency, which had previously been assigned to the government of Japan as its contribution to the cost of the Occupation, was now transferred to the United States.

Notwithstanding these advances, people continued to depend heavily on rations distributed by the U.S. military. However, on August 17, the military government suddenly ordered the closing of all village stores, which in effect signified the end of rations. The measure had been taken by the military government in retaliation for the failure of towns and villages to supply their quota of workers for U.S. military projects. Efforts to force the population to supply labor services by cutting off rations were reminiscent of what the Japanese military had done during the war to mobilize the Okinawan population. The order was rescinded on August 26, but the damage had been done to people's livelihoods and to the trust that they had in the U.S. military government.

In November 1948, economic freedom was restored to private enterprises allowing them to engage in a free enterprise system. While trade between the four island chains of Okinawa, Miyako, Yaeyama, and Amami was opened up, it was placed under the jurisdiction and control of the Ryūkyūan Board of Trade. Moreover, private entities were banned from engaging in any form of foreign trade. While these measures helped create an integrated economic zone covering all of the Ryūkyū Islands, there was very little to trade among the islands because there had been no recovery in industrial production.

Until this point, the economic affairs of the four island chains had been separately managed. But now, the U.S. military government was unifying the economies of the entire Ryūkyū region based on the assumption that the region would be fully detached from Japan.

Establishment of the Ryūkyūs Military Government Section

On August 1, 1948, the General Headquarters, Far East Command ordered the Ryūkyūs Command to be established as an independent entity by separating it from the Philippines-Ryūkyūs Command. As a result, the Ryūkyūs Command was placed under the direct jurisdiction of MacArthur as Supreme Commander of the Far East Command. In September, the Military Government of the Ryūkyū Islands was created by the Commander-in-Chief of American Forces in the Far East and John Weckerling was appointed to head the section.

Upon assuming his post, Weckerling announced that a major change had been made in U.S. policies for the economic management of the Ryūkyū Islands and went on to state that measures would be taken to make the region self-sufficient by 1952. The Ryūkyū Military Government Section also released "Ryukyus Military Government Missions," which in effect served as a guideline for recovery policies. These guidelines contained the following points: (1) Okinawa shall be completely separated from Japan, (2) Okinawa shall be unified under a single constitution, and (3) separate local government organizations for the four island chains shall be placed under this structure. This indicated that the military was moving to govern Okinawa based on—but ahead of the release of—the official decisions of the U.S. government.

On September 1, 1949, the military government announced an increase in the prices of rationed goods and the introduction of income taxes. These measures had two objectives. The first was to absorb cash and combat the inflation that had been triggered by the excessive inflow of Japanese currency. The second was to restructure the finances of local government units that had come to depend on revenues from the sale of goods. However, just as the civilian administration had feared, the price increases of rationed goods triggered a massive jump in commodity prices. For instance, the price of rice rose by 6.3 times, flour by 9.1 times and soybeans by 22.2 times. On average, the price of rationed goods increased by 13 times following this measure. As black market prices skyrocketed, municipal finances and the livelihoods of the people suffered.[28]

---

28 Toriyama Atsushi, *Okinawa kichi shakai no kigen to sōkoku* [Origins and Conflicts in Okinawa's Military Base Society], Keisō Shobō, 2013, pp. 89–93.

2. The Dodge Line: Forming a Japan-U.S. "Conservative" Alliance

Yoshida Shigeru Returns

The Shōwa Denkō Scandal

MacArthur's July 22 letter stripped public employees of the right to strike but served to lengthen the life of the Ashida Cabinet that was on the verge of collapse. Once the letter was issued, the struggle over the 3,700-yen base salary that Zenkankō had been fighting for was settled. At the same time, the firmly held view in political circles and the general public that the Diet either would be dissolved or the Cabinet would be forced to resign also fizzled out. On September 14, the leaders of the three parties—the Socialist Party, the Democratic Party, and the People's Cooperative Party—assembled and decided on convening an extraordinary session of the Diet starting in October and lasting thirty days.

But the Ashida Cabinet did not have long to live. The Shōwa Denkō scandal that had surfaced in June had by this time spread to the political world. Shōwa Denkō manufactured fertilizers that were essential to the postwar recovery of agricultural output and used Reconstruction Finance Bank funds to finance its operations. The company was found to have bribed a long list of high officials in the Ministry of Commerce and Industry, ESB, the Reconstruction Finance Bank, and GHQ in order to manipulate the review of its loan applications. Once the scandal broke, the company tried to cover it up with bribes paid to ruling and opposition party members, and even members of the foreign press.

By early September, the investigation had reached the ranks of politicians and the bureaucracy, and arrests began to be made on September 13. On this day, Fukuda Takeo, Director-General of the Budget Bureau of the Ministry of Finance (and Prime Minister in later years) was arrested. This was followed by the September 18 arrest of Ōno Banboku, Secretary-General of the Liberal Party, and the arrest of Kurusu Takeo, Director-General of the ESB, on September 30.

Faced with the arrest of an incumbent minister, the Ashida Cabinet resigned en masse on October 7. However, the Showa Denkō scandal remained wrapped in mystery. Every politician, with the exception of Kurusu, was acquitted, as was Fukuda and every other bureaucrat.

Nominating Yamazaki for Premier: The Government Section Versus Yoshida Shigeru

Once the collapse of the Ashida Cabinet became inevitable, the Government Section moved to block the return of Yoshida to the premiership. Chief Whitney of the Government Section and Deputy Chief Kades settled on nominating Yamazaki Takeshi, Secretary-General of the Democratic Liberal Party, for the job. Acting on their instructions, Justin Williams, the Chief of the Legislative Division, called Masuda Kaneshichi of the Liberal Party and Suzuki Mosaburō of the Socialist Party to obtain their cooperation in supporting the nomination of Yamazaki.

It was at this point that Yoshida mounted his counterattack by calling on G2, the Diplomatic Section (the successor to the Office of the Political Adviser) and other GHQ sections that were hostile toward the Government Section. With their backing in his pocket, Yoshida moved to meet MacArthur on October 9.

Although Yoshida came out of the meeting saying that he had gained MacArthur's "understanding and encouragement," there is no way to determine the accuracy of this account because no formal records remain of this meeting. It is quite possible that MacArthur had said something like "Keep up the good work" as he was wont to do. In any case, those words were enough for Yoshida to make his case to the public.

MacArthur next met with Miki Takeo of the People's Cooperative Party and encouraged him to declare himself a candidate for the prime minister's post. But Miki rejected the suggestion, saying it was unrealistic to think that the Diet's fourth-ranking party could take the helm of the state.

The Government Section put its full force behind Yamazaki, but these efforts came to naught when Yamazaki gave up his seat in the Diet. With this obstacle gone, the stage was set for the launch of the second Yoshida Cabinet.

Williams left an interesting comment on Yamazaki's resignation.

> Yamazaki's action is strictly in keeping with the tenets of <u>bushido</u>, which require that a <u>samurai</u> commit <u>hara-kiri</u> if he causes his lord and master an embarrassment.... In the political realm this is the severest test of popular government since the beginning of the Occupation. If the various political parties desert Yamazaki at this crucial hour, the world will know that the spirit of the <u>47 ronin</u> is still supreme.[29]

It is said that MacArthur "did not appear to be particularly happy" with Yoshida's return to the premiership.[30]

Two days after the launch of the Yoshida Cabinet, Sōdōmei convened its fourth annual convention on October 21. During the four days of the convention, a left-wing motion to expel Nishio Suehiro from the Central Committee was carried. Although Matsuoka Komakichi became the president, the left wing strengthened its position with the election of Takano Minoru to the post of general secretary. Shortly after this, the fourth annual convention of Sanbetsu Kaigi opened in mid-November to an all-out clash between the Mindō faction that demanded the end of control by Communist Party unions and the communist faction that attacked the Mindō faction as being anti-labor. As the confrontation heated up, the Mindō faction walked out of the convention, finalizing the split in the labor front.

Debating the Right to Dissolve the Diet: Last Battle between Yoshida Shigeru and the Government Section

The second Yoshida Cabinet was a minority government based on the relative majority that the Democratic Liberal Party held in the Diet. To reinforce and stabilize his cabinet, Yoshida planned to quickly dissolve the Diet and call a

---

29 "Memorandum for General Whitney, Designation vs. Resignation of Yamazaki," (October 14, 1948), Fukunaga, ed., in *GHQ Minsei-kyoku shiryō, 3*, p. 570.
30 Finn, Richard B, *Winners in Peace: MacArthur, Yoshida, and Postwar Japan*, University of California Press, 1992, p. 212.

general election. On the other hand, the "three centrist parties," comprising the Democratic, Socialist, and People's Cooperative Parties, were committed to postponing dissolution as long as possible.

However, before dissolving the Diet, Yoshida had to take care of two matters that had been carried over from the Ashida Cabinet. One was to revise the National Public Service Law and the other was to finalize a supplementary budget to cover the payment of higher wages for public employees. Legislative bills for revising the National Public Service Law and enacting a new Remuneration Law were held hostage by the opposition parties to press their cause.

The demand of public employees for a salary increase to 7,300 yen had been referred to the Temporary National Personnel Committee for mediation, and the Committee had returned with a recommendation to the government to adopt a salary base of 6,307 yen. However, the government balked at the recommendation, arguing that the necessary fiscal resources were simply unavailable. Subsequently, the government began to formulate a budget that accommodated a salary base of only 5,300 yen. The opposition parties hit back, arguing that passage of the new Remuneration Law was a precondition for debating the revision of the National Public Service Law. The ploy had been devised to delay the dissolution that Yoshida was eyeing.

Concurrently, a heated debate broke out between the ruling and opposition parties on the question of the "right to dissolve the Diet." The opposition parties took the position that the Diet can only be dissolved upon passage of a non-confidence vote as stipulated under Article 69 of the Constitution. To this, the ruling party responded that the Cabinet had the right to dissolve the Diet under the provisions of Article 7 that defines the Emperor's powers in acts in matters of state. Both sides energetically lobbied GHQ to win its support. Claiming that "this session was called solely to consider the National Public Service Law and related measures and that on their passage the House would be dissolved, had been approved beforehand by the Supreme Commander," Yoshida made use of MacArthur's authority to check the opposition.[31]

---

31 Williams, *Japan's Political Revolution under MacArthur*, p. 219.

Chief Whitney of the Government Section moved to counter Yoshida. Acting as the Supreme Commander's messenger, Whitney informed Yoshida that it was impermissible to dissolve the Diet without revising the wages of government employees, and that dissolution under the provisions of Article 7 was tantamount to using the Emperor for political purposes. But Yoshida was not ready to give up, to which Whitney responded that GHQ would not oppose dissolution if, after the passage of the Remuneration Law, a non-confidence vote were to be passed by the opposition parties in accordance with Article 69.

Justin Williams writes of this period, "Ironically it was at this very time that GHQ intervention in Japanese affairs reached unprecedented heights, due to a combination of various reasons: SCAP seeming to run afoul of Washington's instructions, the minority party government doing battle with the majority opposition parties.... Government Section clashing with ESS [Economic and Scientific Section], and Whitney tilting with Prime Minister Yoshida."[32]

However, the Government Section had already passed the peak of its power and influence. The National Public Service Law and related laws were enacted on November 30, but GHQ was split on how to handle the revision of the Remuneration Law. The Government Section sided with the opposition parties while the Economic and Scientific Section backed the Cabinet. Ultimately, MacArthur ruled in favor of the Economic and Scientific Section and the law was duly enacted. On December 23, the opposition parties submitted a non-confidence vote, resulting in the dissolution of the House of Representatives in accordance with Article 69 of the Constitution.

In early December, the Government Section's Deputy Chief Kades left Japan to return to the United States. Kades later explained the timing of his return, saying that after seven years in military services, he felt it was time for him to return to his profession as a lawyer. As a second reason, Kades explained that he wanted to investigate how the reversal in Occupation policies came about in Washington.

---

32 Ibid., pp. 217–218.

The Change in Occupation Policies: NSC-13/2

"Recommendations" for New Occupation Policies

The fateful document was dated October 7, 1948. Written on the eve of the birth of the second Yoshida Cabinet and entitled, "Recommendations with Respect to United States Policy Toward Japan" (NSC-13/2), the document was approved by the National Security Council (NSC), and was treated as top secret. The positions taken by George Kennan as Director of Policy Planning of the State Department staff were finally realized in this document, which would now replace the Basic Initial Post-Surrender Directive (JCS-1380/15) to define the new direction in Occupation policies.

NSC-13/2 suggested that the peace treaty with Japan should be postponed. The reasoning was clear. "In view of the differences which have developed among the interested countries" and "in view of the serious international situation created by the Soviet Union's policy of aggressive Communist expansion," the document concluded that, "this Government should not press for a treaty of peace at this time."

Furthermore, it argued that the peace treaty to be eventually entered into with Japan should be "as brief, as general, and as non-punitive as possible." Having laid this foundation, NSC-13/2 unambiguously stated that the principal priority in Occupation policy should be shifted from reform to economic recovery. Specific attention was given to the encouragement of private enterprises, and various preconditions for success were identified. These included hard work, minimum work stoppages, austerity measures, and balancing the budget to combat inflation.

Regarding the treatment of Okinawa, the document put the matter on hold noting, "Recommendations on this subject are to be submitted separately." The reasoning for postponement was that conditions were not yet in place for the U.S. military to use funds from the federal budget to undertake the construction of permanent bases in Okinawa and defray the costs of economic reconstruction incurred by the people.

For the first time, the U.S. government had decided to make a formal and long-term commitment to the Japanese economy and national security. However, at this point in time, both Kennan and the State Department remained cautious on the question of whether or not the United States would act alone in preserving Japan's national security after the signing of a peace treaty.

MacArthur was informed of NSC-13/2 through Under-Secretary of the Army William Draper on December 1. Strongly objecting to its contents, MacArthur wrote back to Draper on December 18.

> The purport of your message is not understood. Few of the policy decisions contained in NSC-13/2 and none of those referred to for report are within the field of responsibility of CINCFE [Commander-in-Chief, Far East (U.S. Army)]. As previously noted, the international authority of SCAP is based on the Moscow Agreement [for the establishment of the Far Eastern Commission] The international character of SCAP... renders him subject solely to Allied policy either formulated by the FEC or under specific limited circumstances by the United States, if transmitted as an interim directive. This has been conveyed to me as top secret, and if implemented will almost certainly contradict FEC orders.[33]

Putting aside his position as the Commander-in-Chief, Far East Command, MacArthur was choosing to don his hat as the Supreme Commander of the Allied Powers to resist the instructions of his own government.

Nine Principles for Economic Stabilization: Asia's Marshall Plan

Responding to the resistance from MacArthur, on December 18, 1948, Washington conveyed its "Nine Principles for Economic Stabilization" to MacArthur in the form of an "interim directive" with orders to instruct the Japanese government to implement the program. The Nine Principles stood in stark contrast to the gradualism that was being pursued by the New Deal faction in the Economic and Scientific Section and constituted a program that

---

33 Financial History Section, Ministry of Finance, ed., *Shōwa zaisei-shi, dai 20-kan* [The Financial History of Japan: The Allied Occupation Period 1945–1952, 20 English Documents], Tōyō Keizai Shipōsha, 1982, p. 195.

Washington had "forced on Japan from outside."[34]

The Nine Principles consisted of a list of policies that gave concrete form to those parts of NSC-13/2 that referred to economic recovery. These were: (1) balance the budget by curtailing government spending, (2) reinforce tax collection, (3) restrict credit extension, (4) formulate a wage stabilization plan, (5) reinforce price controls, (6) reinforce control of foreign trade and foreign exchange, (7) improve efficiency of rationing system, (8) increase production of domestic raw materials and products, and (9) improve efficiency of food collection program (Table 4–2).

The Japanese side was not given the option of rejecting the nine principles, nor, unlike in the case of the Constitution, was it given the right to deliberate on its contents. The U.S. government viewed the Nine Principles as a program for economic stability on par with the Marshall Plan. While sweetening the deal with the promise of economic aid, it demanded that Japan implement the same program as all other countries that had accepted the Marshall Plan. The U.S. government's position was that Japan would not be allowed to be an exception. One difference, however, stood out. In Europe, the Marshall Plan had propelled the recovery of the entire region of Western Europe. In the Japanese case, the program was not designed to advance the recovery of the entire Asian region, as Japan was the only industrialized country in Asia. Thus, while the Marshall Plan was successful in realizing the objective of achieving recovery and integration of the whole of Europe with a special focus on Germany, the Asian version of the program did not go beyond a recovery that merely served to strengthen the ties between Japan and the United States.

Washington issued very clear orders to MacArthur on the implementation of the Nine Principles. He was to "direct the Japanese government to carry out a stabilization program and not much more."[35] The Nine Principles had effectively robbed MacArthur of the very critical control of the Japanese economy and had transferred decision-making authority on Occupation policies to Washington. This was indeed a highly significant watershed point where the Occupation of

---

34 Cohen, *Remaking Japan*, p. 409.
35 Ibid., p. 427.

Table 4-2 Salient Points of the Young Mission's Recommendations, Ten Principles of Economic Stabilization, and Nine Principles for Economic Stabilization

Young Report (June 12, 1948)
(1) Quantitative restriction of credit
(2) 20 percent cut in budget expenditures
(3) Reinforce tax collection
(4) Improve raw materials allocation
(5) Stabilize wages
(6) Transfer foreign exchange controls to Bank of Japan
(7) Promote food collection

Ten Principles of Economic Stabilization (July 16, 1948)
(1) Increase mining and manufacturing production
(2) Reinforce allocation and rationing systems
(3) Reinforce food delivery
(4) Maintain official prices
(5) Stabilize wages
(6) Reinforce tax collection
(7) Fair distribution of tax burden
(8) Reduce deficits in special accounts
(9) Establish foreign exchange controls
(10) Reinforce credit control

Nine Principles for Economic Stabilization (December 18, 1948)
(1) Balance the budget by cutting government spending
(2) Reinforce tax collection
(3) Restrict credit extension
(4) Formulate a wage stabilization plan
(5) Reinforce price control
(6) Reinforce control of foreign trade and foreign exchange
(7) Improve efficiency of rationing system
(8) Increase production of domestic raw materials and products
(9) Improve efficiency of food collection program

Japan began to be transformed from MacArthur's Occupation to an American Occupation.

Conclusion of the Tokyo Tribunal

On November 12, 1948, the Tokyo Tribunal handed down its verdicts to 35 Class A war criminals. A total of seven, including Tōjō Hideki and Hirota Kōki, were sentenced to death by hanging. Another sixteen, including Kido Kōichi and Hiranuma Kiichirō, were sentenced to life imprisonment. The two former foreign ministers, Tōgō Shigenori and Shigemitsu Mamoru, were respectively sentenced to twenty and seven years of imprisonment. Matsuoka Yōsuke and Nagano Osami died due to illness during their trials, and Ōkawa Shūmei did not appear in court, having been found insane.

On the following day, November 13, *Asahi Shinbun* wrote that the end of the Tokyo Tribunal provided an opportunity for all Japanese people to re-examine the war. "The trials sought to determine the personal responsibility of 25 defendants. But at the same time, the trials put the same question of responsibility to every individual member of the nation—to those who indirectly, directly or passively supported what they called 'national policy,' as well as those who simply went along." *Yomiuri Shinbun* editorialized as follows. "The reconstruction of a democratic Japan will never be achieved if the general public fails to free itself from the grasp of the old adage 'Winners are heroes and losers take all the blame' and chooses to believe that they are being judged only because Japan lost the war."

On December 23, the same day that Yoshida Shigeru dissolved the House of Representatives, Tōjō and six others were executed by hanging. The day following the hangings, Kishi Nobusuke and the other members of the second contingent of Class A war crime suspects were released, thus putting to rest one of the most difficult issues of the postwar period.

The Third Yoshida Cabinet

General Election of January 1949

In his annual New Year's statement delivered on January 1, 1949, MacArthur announced that "now that the emphasis has shifted from political to economic reconstruction" and emphasized the completion of the process of democratization and the start of the implementation of the "Nine Principles for Economic Stabilization." He went on to underscore the significance of the coming general election as an opportunity to create an administration that would implement the Nine Principles.[36]

---

36 To the People of Japan, January 1, 1949, Statements by MacArthur, Box No. 2195, Folder 22, GHQ/SCAP Records, Government Section, National Diet Library, Originals in U.S. National Archives & Records Administration, RG331.

The 24th general election of the House of Representatives was held on January 23. The election focused on the question of economic recovery and who would be given the task of implementing the Nine Principles. The Democratic Liberal Party advocated "production first" in its platform and called for such policy measures as tax cuts, the abolition of economic controls, increased public works spending, and administrative reform. The Democratic Party called for lower corporate taxes as a preparatory step for the introduction of foreign capital, and voiced its opposition to the socialization of core industries, with the exception of the petroleum industry. The Socialist Party platform featured a commitment to lowering taxes, introducing a minimum wage system, and socializing the core industries.

Voter turnout came to 74 percent. While the Democratic Liberal Party was believed to be in the lead throughout the election campaign, the outcome far exceeded earlier predictions. By winning 264 seats, the Democratic Liberal Party achieved the postwar period's first single-party majority in the House of Representatives. On the other hand, all of the three middle-of-the-road parties lost significant numbers of seats, with the Democratic Party falling from 90 to 67 seats, the Socialist Party from 111 to 48 seats, and the People's Cooperative Party from 29 to fourteen seats. By contrast, the Communist Party garnered an important victory by increasing its representation from four to 35 seats. There were several former Cabinet members among the incumbents who lost their seats, including Katayama Tetsu, Nishio Suehiro, Hitotsumatsu Sadayoshi, and Takeda Giichi. On the way to its impressive victory, Yoshida's Democratic Liberal Party had been helped by such factors as the clumsy political leadership of the Katayama and Ashida Cabinets, repeated political scandals, and general frustration with Japan's poor economic performance.

One of the notable features of the general election of January 1949 was the successful candidacy of a group of senior bureaucrats who ran for the Democratic Liberal Party. These included Satō Eisaku, Ikeda Hayato, Maeo Shigesaburō, and Okazaki Katsuo.

MacArthur expressed his approval of the election results and the victory of the Democratic Liberal Party stating, "at a critical moment in Asiatic history has given so clear and decisive a mandate for the conservative philosophy of government."[37]

The Government Section was deeply discouraged by the election results. As a result of his disappointment, Charles Kades, who was back in the United States on leave, chose not to return to Japan. However, the sizeable gap in the distribution of seats overstated the rightward tilt in popular sentiment. For instance, at the previous general election held in April 1947, the Socialist and Communist Parties received a combined 8.17 million votes. In comparison, the Socialist Party, Socialist Reformist Party, the Party for Workers and Farmers, and Communist Party received a combined total of a little less than 8.11 million votes in the January 1949 election.

Justin Williams, Chief of the Parliamentary and Political Division of the Government Section, was not off the mark when he commented in a memorandum dated January 27, 1949, "While there was a decided swing to the left solely within leftist circles, the shift was more apparent than real."[38] Even after this election, there was no change in the Government Section's support for the Socialist Party.

Polarization of Politics

GHQ worried that the election results portended the polarization of Japanese politics into two opposing camps. William Sebald, Chief of the Diplomatic Section, considered the Democratic Liberal Party to be the "extreme right" and believed that the Japanese political system would be best served by a two-party system consisting of moderate liberal party and a conservative party. Both the extreme left and right would be excluded from these two parties, which would be fully capable of alternating as the ruling party.[39]

The following report was published by the Ministry of Foreign Affairs shortly before the formation of the third Yoshida Cabinet.

---

37 Election Statement, January 24, 1949, Statements by MacArthur, Box No. 2195, Folder 22, GHQ/SCAP Records, Government Section, National Diet Library, Originals in U.S. National Archives & Records Administration, RG331.
38 "MCGS, Communist Election Victory, Justin Williams Papers 115-04," (January 27, 1949), Fukunaga, ed., in *GHQ Minsei-kyoku shiryō, 3*, pp. 595–596.
39 Igarashi Takeshi, *Sengo Nichibei kankei no keisei* [American-Japanese Peace-Making and the Cold War], Kōdansha, 1995, pp. 136–138.

General M [MacArthur] has repeatedly defended centrist politics in his statements.... It appears there has been absolutely no change in General M's belief that 'for democratic politics, there is something sacred in a middle-of-the-road government from which the extremes of both left and right have been removed.

In other words, General M...considers a broad centrist approach to be desirable for Japanese politics. Therefore, he does not necessarily reject the participation of an existing political party that has been labeled rightist reactionary. In this sense, perhaps the middle-of-the-road platform advocated by two or three of Japan's political parties cannot necessarily be said to be consistent with the conception of General M.[40]

Birth of the Third Yoshida Cabinet

Although the Democratic Liberal Party had won a majority in the House of Representatives, Yoshida was not satisfied and worked toward creating a conservative coalition to further stabilize his government. As his choice for a coalition partner, Yoshida wooed the Democratic Party. Ashida had resigned his post as President of the Democratic Party during the Shōwa Denkō scandal and Inukai Takeru had succeeded him. Now, the party was seriously divided between the Inukai faction that favored coalition with the Democratic Liberal Party, and the Ashida faction that stood in opposition. Throughout this period, Ashida maintained a negative stance on cooperating with the Democratic Liberal Party. "The Yoshida Cabinet has won an absolute majority, and that is sufficient for running the government. In any case, they will get bogged down sooner or later. What are we to do then?"[41]

Launched on February 16, 1949, the third Yoshida Cabinet included two ministers from the pro-coalition faction of the Democratic Party (Inagaki Heitarō as Minister of Commerce and Industry and Kimura Kozaemon as State Minister without portfolio). On March 7, the division in the Democratic Party became

---

40 Central Liaison Office, Ministry of Foreign Affairs, *Makkāsā gensui no sho-seimei ni mirareru chūdō seiji* [Centrist Politics as Seen in the Statements of General MacArthur], (February 1, 1949).
41 Shindō and Shimokōbe, eds., *Ashida Hitoshi nikki*, (January 24, 1949).

final with a split forming between 41 members in the pro-coalition faction and 66 in the opposition faction. In choosing his Cabinet, Yoshida made it a point to exclude elder statesmen types and gave preference to former bureaucrats. As his Chief Cabinet Secretary, Yoshida chose Masuda Kaneshichi and filled the post of Finance Minister with Ikeda Hayato, a rookie parliamentarian who had just won his first election. As chairman of the party's Policy Research Council, Yoshida selected Satō Eisaku, another newly elected member of the Diet. Yoshida had taken pains to put together a Cabinet that would be his very own.

Immediately after the Cabinet was formed, Yoshida held a press conference where he affirmed his determination to implement the Nine Principles for Economic Stabilization and added that he would carry through with the reform of related administrative organizations. He promised to strengthen the police force and also mentioned the establishment of a "Committee on Un-Japanese Activities," to be patterned after the Un-American Activities Committee of the U.S. Congress designed to counter communist policies. Yoshida went on to advocate a two-party system modeled after the Conservative and Labor Parties of the British parliament. This, he said, would be accomplished by excluding the left wing of the Socialist Party and the Communist Party to form two parties that were in basic agreement on foreign policies and economic policies.[42]

On April 4, Yoshida acted to revise Imperial Order No. 101, which had ordered the dissolution of militaristic organizations. In its place, Yoshida issued the Organization Control Order that mandated registration of the individual members of designated organizations. The scope of the ordinance was expanded beyond organizations characterized by "extreme nationalism" that were banned under the previous order. Instead, the new ordinance mandated the regulation of "anti-democratic organizations" as well, thereby targeting the Communist Party, which at this point held 35 seats in the Diet. The target of the new ordinance had clearly shifted from the right to the left. The Communist Party did not dispute the ordinance and proceeded to register prominent members of its party. This information would later be used in implementing the Red Purge.

---

42 *Yomiuri Shinbun*, February 17, 1949.

Dodge Arrives in Japan: The Shock Approach to Economic Stabilization

The New Economic Tsar

On February 1, 1949, Joseph Dodge arrived in Japan accompanied by Army Secretary Kenneth Royall. The purpose of his visit was to inspect the implementation of the Nine Principles for Economic Stabilization. Dodge's arrival coincided with the disputes between Yoshida and the Democratic Party that both preceded and followed the establishment of the third Yoshida Cabinet.

Dodge was the President of the Detroit Bank and had earned a name for himself by successfully stabilizing the currency in postwar Germany. In recognition of his achievements, President Truman had given him the personal rank of envoy and had gone over the head of GHQ to dispatch him to Japan. Known to be an advocate of the free market economy, Dodge came to rule over Japan as the new "economic tsar."[43]

On February 5 Miyazawa Kiichi, in the company of Finance Minister Ōya Shinzō, met Dodge for the first time. Miyazawa left a record of what Dodge said on this occasion. "What Japan needs now more than anything else is austerity. What the Japanese government and GHQ need most is the courage to push the people to live a life of austerity. Disencumber yourself of dreams and face reality." Miyazawa came away from the meeting with the impression, "This is going to be a tough person to deal with." At the same time, Miyazawa sensed the subtle change in atmosphere that had occurred in Washington.

Marquat [Chief of the Economic and Scientific Section] was a figurehead, and the New Dealers under him had continued to bully the Japanese authorities responsible for the economy. The latter individuals had been raised to try to limit spending to the greatest degree possible, so their view was that the most important thing to emphasize was limiting financial expenditures rather than stabilizing prices or raising wages. The New Dealers had blocked this approach for several years and a great deal of frustration had built up.

---

43 Cohen, *Remaking Japan,* p. 428.

While not sure who Dodge was, Japanese authorities wanted to borrow the power of this seemingly stubborn, older man. At the least, rather than getting into the boat of the New Dealers, the feeling was that Dodge's boat would be a smoother sail.[44]

Dodge made the following statement in a press conference held on March 7. "The Japanese economy is walking on two bamboo stilts, one of which is U.S. aid and the other one large amounts of subsidies from the Treasury. The stilts have to be removed. If the stilts are very tall, you risk falling down and breaking your neck." He followed his metaphor with three demands: (1) The entire government budget, comprising both the general and special accounts, must be made to balance. (2) All subsidies must be abolished. (3) All new lending from the Reconstruction Finance Bank must cease.

This marked the start of the so-called Dodge Line: the policies for fiscal and monetary tightening introduced by Dodge to achieve Japan's economic independence and stability.

Joseph Dodge (1890–1965)
A banker by profession, Dodge worked to stabilize the postwar German currency as a financial adviser to the Occupation of Germany. Dodge arrived in Japan in February 1949 as an adviser to GHQ on fiscal matters. To overcome Japan's extremely high inflation, he implemented the Nine Principles for Economic Stabilization, which included balancing the government's overall budget, and adopting a single exchange rate. This program came to be known as the "Dodge Line."

The Dodge Line and the Yoshida Cabinet

While the Dodge Line stood on the Nine Principles, by far the most important element of the program was its first prescription for balancing the government budget. Dodge rejected the Outline of the Budget for Fiscal 1949 (approved by

---

44 Miyazawa Kiichi, *Secret Talks between Tokyo and Washington*, Rowman & Littlefield Publishers, 2007, p. 3.

the Cabinet on February 23) that had been compiled by the Yoshida Cabinet. In its place, on March 22, Dodge informally presented to the government his own draft budget that had been drawn up by the Economic and Scientific Section. The Dodge budget brushed aside and completely abrogated the pledges that had been made by the Democratic Liberal Party in its platform. Public works spending was cut in half from the target amount of roughly 100 billion yen, the planned cut in income taxes and the abolition of turnover taxes were cancelled, and railway transport and postal rates were to be increased by 50 to 60 percent.

Finance Minister Ikeda Hayato found himself trapped between Dodge and the vehement protests leveled against the austerity budget by the ruling party. Ikeda at one point was contemplating resigning, but Yoshida urged him to stay on, explaining that as in the case of the Constitution, "This is something we must grit our teeth and bear for the greater good." In a letter dated March 17, Yoshida reached out to Kanō Hisaakira, a Japanese banker and an old friend of Dodge's: "Regarding the views expressed by Dodge, I find myself in agreement with each and every point, and have instructed the authorities to move forward on the prescriptions of this Line."[45]

The opposition parties were not permitted to directly criticize the Dodge Line. Throughout the budget deliberations, they could not go beyond making some noise about the Nine Principles and the ruling party's abandonment of its platform. The fact of the matter was that both the Democratic Party and the Socialist Party were too busy settling internal disputes to go after the Dodge Line with any force.

The draft budget that Dodge had shown the government was submitted to the Diet with basically no revisions and was adopted on April 20 with no amendments. Economic aid from the United States would now be credited to a newly established "Counterpart Funds Special Account." These funds were initially used to retire reconstruction finance bonds and to clean up inflation, and were later used for industrial financing.

Upon passage of the budget bill, GHQ took the next step on April 23 of

---

45 Shibata Shinichi, ed., *Yoshida Shigeru shokan, tsuiho* [Letters of Yoshida Shigeru, appendix], Chūō Kōron Shinsha, 2011, p. 92.

dictating a fixed exchange set at 360 yen to the dollar and allowing Japan to return to the world economy.

Yoshida's Transformation: Domestic Affairs Placed on Hold

On the same day that the budget bill was adopted, April 20, Yoshida Shigeru stood before the Committee on Foreign Affairs, House of Representatives, to answer questions. Responding to a question on "Provisions for the Review of a New Japanese Constitution" that had been approved by the Far Eastern Commission in October 1946, Yoshida averred that he currently had no intention of revising the Constitution. With his sights fixed on the peace treaty that would be eventually concluded, Yoshida believed it was wiser to avoid talk of any type on constitutional revision, as such talk could threaten the success of the peace negotiations. Finally, Yoshida stated that by implementing the Nine Principles for Economic Stabilization, he aimed to achieve economic recovery and Japan's return to the world economy and to thus push on toward a "virtual peace treaty."[46]

In a statement released on Constitution Day, May 3, 1949, MacArthur addressed the Japanese people saying that the breadth of domestic issues that they themselves would deal with would be expanded. In July, the Military Government Sections and Military Government Units were renamed Civil Affairs Sections and were thereafter gradually reduced in size, indicating that GHQ was moving toward conforming with policies coming out of Washington.

After carefully observing Dodge the man and the people who stood behind him in Washington, Yoshida had judged that "it was best to work with Dodge."[47] In turn, Dodge had concluded, "The Yoshida Cabinet is America's unique and incomparable asset in the Far East." Dodge made a conscious effort to act as a bridge between conservative leaders in Japan's political, bureaucratic, and business communities and highly placed officers in the U.S. government. In this way, Dodge significantly increased Yoshida's access to Washington

---

46 *Yomiuri Shinbun*, April 21, 1949.
47 Miyazawa, *Secret Talks between Tokyo and Washington,* p. 9.

information.[48]

In the process of implementing the Dodge Line, a change occurred in the objective of economic policies as the focus shifted from "recovery" to "self-reliance." In June, Yoshida ordered the reformulation of the Five-Year Economic Plan that had been prepared by ESB on the grounds that the plan was geared toward economic self-sufficiency and lacked international awareness. Later, Yoshida formally cancelled the plan before its scheduled release in September. Seizing on the strategy of developing the economy through export promotion, Yoshida reorganized the Ministry of Commerce and Industry to create the Ministry of International Trade and Industry in May 1949. Instead of assigning domestic economic development to the new ministry, Yoshida set the stage to make sure that the ministry would be placed in charge of trade promotion. In this way, the Prime Minister was taking the first steps toward reviving Japan as a trade-oriented economy.

The Socialist Party in Turmoil: The Fourth Party Convention

The Socialist Party held its fourth party convention on April 14, 1949. The two wings of the party clashed furiously on such issues as the party's basic character and platform. A fierce debate broke out between Morito Tatsuo, the right winger who had served as education minister in the Katayama and Ashida Cabinets, and Inamura Junzō from the left wing of the party.

Inamura attacked the Katayama and Ashida Cabinets as having lost sight of the socialist revolution and fallen into the trap of what he called the "pursuit of immediate expediency and extreme opportunism." Morito countered saying that as a government formed by the leading party of the Diet, the two Cabinets had "played a certain positive role in advancing toward self-reliant reconstruction," although they had been constantly exposed to attack from both left and right. As to the basic character of the party, Inamura identified the Socialist Party as the "class-based political party of the working masses," while Morito claimed it was the "party of the people's working masses." The debate expanded to include the

---

48 Cohen, *Remaking Japan*, pp. 441–442.

process by which socialism and its ideals would be realized. Morita claimed that the transition from a capitalist economy to a socialist economy would be "realized through a gradual, phased, constructive, and peaceful process." Inamura responded that while he had no problem with the process being a peaceful one, revolution most importantly implied the transfer of political power to a certain class of society.

Katsumata Seiichi, a centrist in the Socialist Party, stepped in to mediate between the two sides, which led to a compromise on the essential question of the whether the party was a "party of the people or the party of a certain class." Thus, the convention closed by affirming that the Socialist Party was a "class-based party of the masses." This compromise, however, did not extinguish the flames of conflict within the party.

On the issue of personnel, while Katayama remained Chairman of the party, the post of Secretary-General went to the Suzuki Mosaburō of the left wing who beat out Asanuma Inejirō from the right wing in a vote. Changes were also made in the membership of the Central Executive Committee, where ten seats each were allocated to the left wing and the right wing, five went to centrists, and five went to labor union representatives. The new allocation was further indication that the left wing had strengthened its position in the party. The advances made by the left wing reflected the support of workers who had joined the Mindō faction, which was comprised of two groups: the Kokutetsu Mindō and the Sanbetsu Mindō. The latter had been created after the February 1 general strike by elements demanding the democratization of Sanbetsu Kaigi.

The Communist Party and the Dodge Line

On the other hand, the Communist Party, which had won 35 seats in the House of Representatives, continued to function under the illusion of achieving a "peaceful revolution." The party dreamed of establishing a "people's government" that would be supported by the Laborers and Farmers Party, the Socialist Party, and other democratic movements, plus organizations of the masses that included labor unions and farmers unions. Speaking at a May Day 1949 meeting,

Secretary-General Tokuda proclaimed, "We are putting together a massive movement to bring down the Yoshida Cabinet by September."

The Communist Party affirmed the Nine Principles for Economic Stabilization as comprising the fundamental principles for rehabilitating the Japanese economy. The party claimed that the Nine Principles would "sweep away misgovernment by the reactionary forces of conservatism" and that the program would set the "preconditions for stabilizing the life of the people, bringing victory to democracy, and achieving the independence of the nation." In taking these positions, the Communist Party had seriously miscalculated how the Principles would affect its supporters.

The Communist Party reacted to the Dodge Line by opposing corporate restructuring and calling for an organized struggle aimed at protecting industries. Sanbetsu Kaigi promoted this struggle too, but individual unions one after another fell back in defeat. The opposition movement thereafter became increasingly radicalized. Thus, at the end of May, members of the Federation of Tokyo Metropolitan Government Workers' Unions clashed with police as they opposed the enactment of the Metropolitan Public Security Ordinance. Furthermore, at the end of June, a mob of 500 workers and Korean residents organized by the Communist Party temporarily occupied the municipal police headquarters of Taira City (present-day Iwaki City), Fukushima Prefecture, in what came to be known as the Taira Incident.

Large numbers of Communist Party members were dismissed from their jobs in the labor rationalization programs that followed the Dodge Line. This significantly weakened Sanbetsu Kaigi as its membership dropped from 1.25 million in November 1948 to 770,000 in November 1949.

Corporate and Administrative Restructuring: The Dark Summer of 1949

Inflationary pressures began to subside and prices became more stable with the implementation of the Dodge Line (Figure 4-3). However, the side effects of the Dodge Line threw the Japanese economy and society into confusion. Tight monetary policies combined with corporate and administrative restructuring churned up a storm of sagging output, sharp increases in dead stock,

Figure 4-3 Wholesale Price Index and Tokyo Retail Price Index

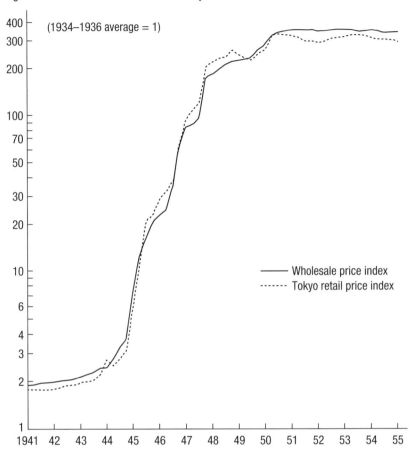

Source: Compiled by the author from Statistics Department, Bank of Japan, *Meiji 20-nen: Shōwa 37-nen oroshiuri bukka shisū* [Wholesale Price Index: 1887–1962], *Taishō 11-nen: Shōwa 42-nen Tōkyō kouri bukka shisū* [Taishō 11 (1922)–Shōwa 42 (1967) Tokyo Consumer Price Index].

bankruptcies of small and medium-sized enterprises, growing unemployment, wage cuts, unpaid wages, and delayed deliveries.

Between February and December 1949, a total of 8,814 businesses underwent restructuring, resulting in the dismissal of about 435,000 employees. Among large corporations, machinery industries were particularly hard hit. For instance, Oki Electric Company reduced its workforce by 2,800 jobs,

Kawasaki Rolling Stock Manufacturing Company by 1,300 jobs, and Mitsubishi Electric Corporationby 1,800 jobs. Under the Law for Elimination of Excessive Concentration of Economic Power, Toshiba, Japan's largest electric machinery manufacturer, was ordered to dispose of 28 of its 44 plants and offices. In July, the company announced that it was curtailing its workforce by 4,600 jobs. In the process of shedding excess labor, companies chose to target the firings with a clear focus on employees who were Communist Party members or Sanbetsu Kaigi activists.[49]

During the same period, a total of 270,000 government jobs were cut under the Law for the Total Number of Civil Servants that was enacted in May. On July 1, Japanese National Railways notified its labor unions that it was dismissing a total of 95,000 workers. On July 4, workers started receiving their dismissal notices with 37,000 workers fired in the first phase of rationalization. In the midst of these developments, Japanese Railways President Shimoyama Sadanori went missing on July 5 and his body was found on a railway track the following day, run over by a train. Known as the Shimoyama Incident, this became one of the representative violent incidents of postwar Japan. All of the major newspapers, with the exception of *Mainichi Shinbun*, reported the incident as a murder and hinted that the crime had been perpetrated by the Communist Party or labor union members. Chief Cabinet Secretary Masuda Kaneshichi released the following statement: "With regard to acts disrupting public order, the government shall act resolutely to fulfill the mandate given to it by the people."

Phase two of the firings at Japanese National Railways started on July 12 with 63,000 workers receiving their dismissal notices. Shortly after these notices went out, on July 15, an unmanned train ran through Mitaka Station on the Chuo Line and slammed into a row of houses. A total of 26 people were killed or injured in this derailment that came to be known as the Mitaka Incident. The authorities arrested nine Communist Party members of Kokurō. The government shortly thereafter released a statement saying that the incident had been instigated by communists whose purpose was to create social unrest.

---

49 Ōkōchi Kazuo and Matsuo Hiroshi, *Nihon rōdō kumiai monogatari sengo-hen, jō* [Tale of Japan's Labor Unions: The Postwar Period, vol. 1], Chikuma Shobō, 1973, pp. 315–325.

On August 17, three were killed in a train derailment near the Matsukawa Station on the Tohoku Main Line. This Matsukawa Incident led to the arrest of twenty Communist Party members of the Toshiba and Japanese National Railways labor unions.

Media reports on the three mysterious incidents—Shimoyama, Mitaka, and Matsukawa—that followed in close succession implied that the Communist Party and labor union members were responsible for the gruesome deaths and destruction. These reports had a major negative impact on labor movements. As a result, there were no further acts of sabotage against the Japanese National Railways, and the rationalization and dismissal of postal workers that started in August went forward without any notable resistance. The total number of labor union members declined significantly after the three incidents, dropping from 6.65 million workers in June 1949 to 5.77 million. The unionization rate also dipped by nearly ten percentage points to reach 45.9 percent.

The Shoup Recommendations

September 1949 saw the release of the so-called Shoup Report produced by a mission investigating the Japanese tax system headed by Carl Shoup, a professor of public finance at Columbia University. The report contained policy recommendations on tax reform, an element that was missing in the Dodge economic policies that had been formulated as part of the U.S. plan for rehabilitating the Japanese economy.

The Shoup Report contained the following three basic recommendations. First, stabilize tax revenues by adopting a tax system centered on direct taxation with a primary focus on income taxation. Second, ensure fairness in tax burdens by adopting progressive income taxation. Third, reinforce the fiscal resources of local government by redistributing prefectural taxes and municipal taxes, first of all, and adopting an equalization grant system to replace the existing local allocation tax for fiscal adjustment payments from the central government to local government organizations.

On September 15, MacArthur delivered the full text of the Shoup Report to Prime Minister Yoshida and instructed him to "formulate an appropriate program for effecting the broad principles and objective set forth in Dr. Shoup's recommendations."[50] Upon reviewing the document, Yoshida noted that the recommendations included certain aspects of the Democratic Liberal Party platform, such as the abolition of turnover taxes and the lowering of income tax rates. Thereupon, Yoshida publicly announced that the recommendations would be adopted and implemented.

But others were not so sanguine, notably State Minister Kimura Kozaemon, who was responsible for local finances. While agreeing that the recommendations were theoretically sound, Kimura questioned their suitability to the current economic and social conditions in Japan and the tax-collecting capacity of local governments. Most importantly, Kimura argued, the Shoup Report did not meet the public's most ardent expectations for lower income taxes. The tax program for fiscal 1950 combined a reduction of about 60 billion yen in national taxes with an increase of about 40 billion yen in local taxes, yielding a relatively small net tax break of only 20 billion yen. These figures were to lead to an unanticipated blowback from opposition parties during the Diet debate on the revision of the Local Tax Law.

The Dodge Recession and Reorganization of the Labor Movement

Reorganization of the Labor Movement

Faced with the Dodge Line, the labor movement was time and again forced to retreat, leaving workers to fend for themselves in the midst of a deepening recession. The labor movement remained divided even after the start of 1949 as the pro- and anti-Communist Party labor unions continued to vie for leadership.

The labor movement was also affected by the gathering forces of the Cold War, which was beginning to cast a dark cloud over international labor organizations. In January 1949, the World Federation of Trade Unions (WFTU)—a

---

50 Sodei, *Correspondence between General MacArthur, Prime Minister Yoshida & Other High Japanese Officials [1945–1951]*, p. 149.

postwar umbrella organization for labor unions worldwide—split into a pro-Soviet camp and a pro-U.S. camp over the issue of whether or not to accept the Marshall Plan. Following the split, a number of unions left WFTU, including Britain's TUC, America's CIO (Congress of Industrial Organizations), and the Netherlands' Vergond van Vakverenigingen (NVV). At the end of November, these unions were joined by AFL (American Federation of Labor) in forming the International Confederation of Free Trade Unions (ICFTU). Responding to the widening divisions in international labor organizations, GHQ pushed Japanese labor unions to join ICFTU. In September, the Mindō faction formed the Preparatory Council for Promoting Membership in ICFTU. Throughout this period, GHQ was intent on eliminating the influence of the Communist Party from the labor movement and creating non-communist unions.

As the division in the international labor movement became final, the Mindō faction began to work toward creating a central organization fully capable of competing with the pro-Communist Party Sanbetsu Kaigi. It was in February 1949 that the first steps were taken in pursuit of this goal. Takano Minoru, who had been elected Secretary-General and taken the position of leadership in the third Sōdōmei convention held in October 1948, joined forces with Hosoya Matsuta of Sanbetsu Mindō to form a preparatory committee for establishing the Japanese Trade Union Congress to be centered around Sōdōmei, Sanbetsu Mindō, and the Kokutetsu Mindō. The two thereafter collaborated in bringing together the various branches of the Mindō movement under the philosophy, "Cut off the left (Sanbetsu Kaigi) with a stroke of the sword, and cut off the right (right wing of Sōdōmei) with the next stroke." At the same time, the two agreed to "form a democratic political force around the goal of reconstructing the Socialist Party." They then joined the Socialist Party in quick succession. However, their Japanese Trade Union Congress petered out without ever going beyond Sōdōmei, Sanbetsu Mindō, and the Kokutetsu Mindō.

GHQ's Views on Labor Unions: The Revision of Labor Laws

June witnessed the revision of the Labor Union Law and the Labor Relations Adjustment Law, which was carried out under very strong guidance from GHQ.

Suehiro Izutarō, the University of Tokyo professor who was serving as chairman of the Central Labor Relations Commission after leaving academia, has summarized the views that GHQ subscribed to during this period.[51]

(1) The internal administration of Japan's labor unions is not adequately democratic, and labor unions are at times subject to the dictatorial leadership of small groups of leaders as ordered by their respective political parties.

(2) In many instances, union membership includes employees who obviously should be on the side of management on account of their posts and responsibilities. This tendency has encouraged some unions to become management-controlled "yellow unions."

(3) The full-time staff members of a majority of unions receive their salaries from management, and union expenses are to a significant degree subsidized by management.

GHQ considered the existing conditions to be unsound and therefore altered its approach to the labor movement. Instead of seeking to make gradual improvements by educating workers, GHQ turned its attention to recommending revisions to existing laws.

Among the changes made were the de-unionization of employees in management posts, a ban on payment of salaries to full-time union staff members by management, rejection of acts of violence, a ban on automatic extension of labor agreements, and elimination of the provision for prior approval of the Labor Relations Commission when dismissing an employee on account of participation in labor dispute actions. These legislative revisions were designed to reorient Japan's labor unions, which had developed under the special conditions that existed after the war as "mixed unions" that combined labor and management under the same roof. While these measures strengthened the autonomy of unions, they also stripped them of some of their vested rights and interests and rendered them less capable of resisting the forceful advance of corporate restructuring.

---

51 Suehiro Izutarō, *Nihon rōdō kumiai undō-shi*, [History of Japanese Trade Union Movement], Chūō Kōronsha, 1954, and Ōkōchi and Matsuo, *Nihon rōdō kumiai monogatari sengo-hen, jō,* p. 312.

At around this time, a number of neutral private-industry unions came together to form the Unification Council. The participating unions were the General Federation of Private Railway Workers' Unions (Shitetsu), the All-Japan Metal Miners' Labor Union Federation (Zenkō), the All-Japan Seamen's Union (Kaiin), and the Japan Coal Miners' Union (Tanrō). In November 1949, the three unions of the National Congress of Industrial Unions (Sōdōmei, Shin-sanbetsu, and Kokurō) joined forces with the Unification Council to establish the Preparatory Committee for National Labor Unity. During this same period, the Mindō factions of Kokurō and Zentei had claimed the leadership in their unions by coming out on top in their struggles against pro-Communist Party factions. This development consummated the Mindō movement's anti-Communist Party struggle. With the newly formed Preparatory Committee taking the lead, a preparatory conference was convened in March 1950 for the establishment of the General Council of Trade Unions of Japan (Sōhyō).

Yoshida Shigeru Mounts His Challenge: Reorganizing the Security Organizations

Efforts to Dismiss the Head of the National Rural Police, Saitō Noboru

On June 30, 1949, Yoshida sent a letter to Brigadier General Willoughby, chief of GHQ's G2 Section, urging him to fire the Head of the National Rural Police, Saitō Noboru. At this point, about a year had passed since the establishment of the new police system. Yoshida stated, "Mr. Saitō does not seem to be the right man," and cited such grievances as Saitō's failure to respond speedily to wildcat railway strikes and his generally uncooperative stance on police reform. On the following day, Yoshida sent a second letter to Willoughby recommending Hisayama Hideo as Saitō's replacement.[52]

When the National Rural Police was initially established, the first candidate for its Head was Hisayama, the head of the Bureau of Police and Public Security.

---

52 Sodei, *Correspondence between General MacArthur, Prime Minister Yoshida & Other High Japanese Officials [1945–1951]*, pp. 133–134.

The second candidate was Saitō, Chief Commissioner of the Tokyo Metropolitan Police. However, the Government Section had nixed Hisayama's appointment and the post had ultimately gone to Saitō. From Yoshida's perspective, the problem with Saitō was that he was too close to the Government Section and kept his distance from the Prime Minister. Firing Saitō and replacing him with Hisayama looked to be a smart political move, as Yoshida was anxious to bring the National Rural Police under the direct influence of the Cabinet. Believing the police system to be "one of the Occupation reforms that had been pushed upon us,"[53] Yoshida was now mounting a clear challenge. But one problem remained: the power to dismiss the police chief belonged to the National Public Safety Commission and not the government.

After writing to Willoughby, Yoshida made arrangements to meet with Tsuji Jirō, Director of the National Public Safety Commission. In the meeting that took place on July 4, Yoshida directly requested the removal of Saitō. However, on the following day, the National Public Safety Commission concluded that there were no clear grounds for dismissal, and that Saitō was effectively carrying out his duties in administering the police authorities.

On July 8, the government responded with a statement released by Chief Cabinet Secretary Masuda. The statement announced that the National Public Safety Commission was not acting in harmony with the government, and that it had rejected the Prime Minister's demand for the dismissal of Saitō due to his being unsuitable for the position of responsibility in the National Police. But the National Public Safety Commission held its ground and refused to budge. Political party leaders and the media came out in support of the Commission.

With the Government Section also rejecting dismissal, nothing finally came of Yoshida's endeavors. Frank Rizzo, who by this time had replaced Kades as Deputy Chief of the Government Section, praised the National Public Safety Commission for withstanding government pressure and intimidation to reject Yoshida's demand, and commented that its actions had set a precedent that greatly encouraged other independent government commissions. Furthermore,

---

53 Yoshida, *Kaisō jūnen, vol. 2*, p. 129.

Rizzo expressed his strong support by stating that the actions of the Commission indicated a sound understanding of the requisite principles for the democratic administration of the policy system, and should not be criticized.[54]

On July 22, reports began to circulate that Yoshida was preparing to significantly roll back the purge. Reports claimed that this would be announced on August 15 to mark the passing of four years since the end of the war. The Government Section jumped in to refute the reports by stating that the Occupation forces had "no intention of changing the policy" on the approximately 210,000 wartime leaders that had been purged from public office.

Tug-of-War on Police System

Three weeks had passed since the failed efforts to dismiss Saitō when Yoshida wrote to MacArthur on August 6 requesting him to consider revising the police system. Yoshida's proposal was to disband small-scale autonomous police forces and transition away from a police system centered on local government units to one that would be centered on a robust national police system. Yoshida posited that this would facilitate the integration of politics and the police, and would strengthen the Cabinet's influence over the police.

Chief Whitney of the Government Section responded to these developments with a warning and an expression of concern. "The emergence of a proposal contradicting a SCAP letter is extremely ill-advised. Such irresponsible behavior is embarrassing and will lead to loss of face for the Japanese government, as well as for SCAP."[55]

In the same letter addressed to MacArthur, Yoshida complained about the problems in the new police system by citing the missteps that had been made by the police authorities in the Mitaka Incident and requested that revision of the system be considered. But Yoshida's requests were contrary to the spirit that had been expressed by the GHQ, and there was no possibility that MacArthur would accede to his entreaty.

---

54 Ogura Yūji, ed., *GHQ Minsei-kyoku shiryō, 11*, pp. 109–112.
55 Ibid., p. 117.

On August 8, MacArthur replied to Yoshida in writing, warning of the dangers of returning to a centralized police system and rejecting the Yoshida proposal and recommending that, "the executive control over the exercise of the police power, both on the national and local levels of government, be brought under the restraining influence of public safety commissions composed of representative and responsible citizens appointed by the executive with legislative approval for fixed terms of years."[56] Furthermore, MacArthur went to the trouble of enclosing a copy of his letter of September 16, 1947, addressed to then-Prime Minister Katayama. To this, MacArthur appended the note, "in case the same has not been brought to your personal attention." Thus, MacArthur and the Government Section had made clear that they were not prepared to make any concessions on the two pillars of police reform: democratization and decentralization.

Okinawa as Military Base: The Sheetz Administration

Transformation of the U.S. Military Government: NSC-13/3

NSC-13/3 was finalized and formally approved on May 6, 1949. This document revised NSC-13/2 and clarified the status and treatment of Okinawa. NSC-13/3 stated that the U.S. government would (1) retain on a long-term basis the military facilities on Okinawa, (2) carry out a program on a long-term basis for the economic development of Okinawa, and (3) at a proper time, obtain international sanction for United States long-term strategic control of the Ryūkyū Islands south of latitude 29 degrees north.[57]

The decision to retain Okinawa on a long-term basis was accompanied by a budgetary commitment to the administration of Okinawa, which meant that the United States was accepting responsibility for the well-being of residents. This marked the end of "day-to-day" administration that had heretofore characterized

---

56 Sodei, *Correspondence between General MacArthur, Prime Minister Yoshida & Other High Japanese Officials [1945–1951]*, pp. 140–142.

57 Report by the National Security Council on Recommendations with Respect to United States Policy toward Japan, May 6, 1949, *FRUS*, 1949, The Far East and Australasia, vol. 7, Part 2.

the governance of Okinawa and signaled the inflow of substantially increased economic aid.

In its fiscal 1950 budget, the U.S. Congress allocated 58 million dollars to military bases in Okinawa. This allocation was approved by President Truman on October 28, 1949. The GHQ Public Relations Office thereupon announced that MacArthur had been granted the means to resolve one of his most serious long-standing concerns.[58]

Following these developments, a series of missions were dispatched to Okinawa at the behest of the General Headquarters Far East Command to formulate plans for economic rehabilitation. In April, an investigative mission headed by Chief Dellinger of the Natural Resources Section of GHQ (which later compiled the Report of Temporary Duty in Okinawa) arrived in Okinawa and was followed by an agricultural mission headed by the agricultural econo-mist, Raymond Vickery, that arrived from Washington in mid-September.

In November 1949, the Vickery Mission released a report titled "Agriculture and Economic Reconstruction in the Ryukyus," which would serve as a "manual" for the Okinawa reconstruction plan that was being implemented by General Josef Sheetz. The Vickery Report addressed two sets of problems that obstructed recovery in agricultural productivity: administrative problems and technical problems. The report noted that such administrative concerns as administrative structure, trade, finance, and land ownership were acting as serious obstacles to agricultural recovery. The report went on to make the following recommenda-tions: (1) to establish a central government with adequate financial resources and authority with jurisdiction over all regions of the Ryukyu Islands, (2) to establish an independent agency to cope with food and agricultural problems, (3) to reorganize the Military Administration, and (4) to establish trade channels with Japan and foreign countries, adjust the value of the B-Yen, and establish appropriate prices.

58 Bank of the Ryūkyūs Research Department, ed., *Sengo Okinawa keizai-shi* [The History of the Postwar Okinawan Economy], Ryūkyū Ginkō, 1984, p. 179.

The "Good Government" of General Sheetz

On October 1, 1949, the day of the birth of the People's Republic of China, Major General Josef Sheetz assumed his post as Military Governor of the Ryūkyūs. (He remained at this post until the end of July 1950 when he left due to illness.) In a press conference held immediately after taking office, Sheetz underscored his desire to promote the democratization of Okinawa. "This is what I consider to be desirable. Responsibility for the administration of Okinawa will be gradually transferred to Okinawa, and the U.S. military will remove itself one step at a time from the tasks of administration. Ultimately, the U.S. military will act as something like an adviser to the people of Okinawa."

As one of his first acts, Sheetz abolished the four military governments that had separately administered the four islands chains of Okinawa, Miyako, Yaeyama, and Amami. In their place, Sheetz established a single General Headquarters of the Military Government of the Ryūkyū Islands in a move that was designed to strengthen the administrative capacity of the military government. He next tackled the problem of morale that provided a source of constant friction with residents, dismissing members of the military and civilian personnel, whose morale was reputed to be the "worst of any U.S. occupation force in the world."[59] On the economic front, Sheetz announced a fifty percent increase in food rations. To quell another source of dissatisfaction, Sheetz announced that income taxes for fiscal 1949 would not be collected.

In January 1950, Sheetz established the Interim Ryūkyūs Advisory Council and assigned to it the function of investigating and issuing recommendations on matters pertaining to the common interests of the civilian administrations of the four island chains of the Ryūkyūs as referred to it by the military government. Higa Shūhei, the Chief Secretary of the Civil Government, was appointed to head the Council.

---

59 Ibid., p. 185.

Toward a Base-Dependent Economy: Dodge Line for Okinawa

In early September 1949, Under-Secretary of the Army Tracy Voorhees was in Honolulu on his way back from Japan when he stated, "General MacArthur and I discussed the possibility that employing Japanese and Okinawan labor in Army and Air Force construction projects could have a positive impact on the economies of the two regions."[60] Sheetz echoed this sentiment, estimating that some 25,000 islanders could be employed in U.S. military projects. This, he explained, would have a major positive effect on constructing a self-sufficient Okinawa economy.[61] The situation was particularly dire at this time due to the powerful typhoons that had hit Okinawa during 1948 and 1949. Almost all of the temporary facilities that had been constructed during the war had been flattened or seriously damaged by these enormous typhoons.

Construction work on military projects was to be assigned to enterprises located both in Okinawa and the Japanese mainland, and necessary materials were to be imported from the mainland. As for labor needs, the policy at this time was to give preference to the hiring of Okinawa residents. A group of nine major construction companies including Shimizu Corporation arrived in Okinawa in late November 1949 to investigate business opportunities in Okinawa.

The U.S. government hoped that the injection of dollars in base construction projects would have a "double impact." First, the infusion of cash would promote economic recovery in Okinawa. Second, the dollars spent in Okinawa would be used to import materials from the Japanese mainland, thus assisting Japan's recovery also.[62] In April 1950, the Ryūkyū Reconstruction Finance Fund was established. Over 1949 and 1950, funds from these sources were used in establishing private businesses in such key industries as transportation, food, and gasoline retailing.

Resurgent economic activities naturally encouraged local residents to relocate to the vicinities of U.S. military bases. Okinawa's prewar (1940) population

---

60 Nakano Yoshio and Arasaki Moriteru, *Okinawa Sengo-shi* [Postwar History of Okinawa], Iwanami Shoten, 1976.
61 Bank of the Ryūkyūs Research Department, *Sengo Okinawa keizai-shi*, p. 185.
62 Ibid., pp. 87–88.

distribution by industry was 74.2 percent in agricultural and forestry, 7.55 percent in manufacturing, 6.9 percent in commerce, 3.8 percent in civil service and self-employed, and 2.1 percent in fisheries. However, by 1950, the breakdown had changed to 58.1 percent in agriculture and forestry, 15.1 percent in military-related work, 3.5 percent in commerce, 3.4 percent in manufacturing, 2.6 percent in fisheries, and 2.3 percent in construction. Okinawa was well on the way to transitioning from an agricultural society to a "base-dependent economy" that relied significantly on U.S. military bases and the provision of related economic services to these facilities.

In January 1950, a fixed exchange rate of 120 B-Yen per dollar was established, representing a significant revaluation of the currency. This had come eight months after the introduction of a fixed rate on the Japanese mainland. The difference, however, was that the currency had been substantially devalued in Japan to promote exports. But Okinawa had hardly anything to export, and the dollar revenue generated from the U.S. bases led Okinawa in the direction of becoming an import-oriented economy.

Military base construction marked the "dawn of the Okinawa economy," helped strengthen its ties to the Japanese mainland which had been suffering the recessionary consequences of the Dodge Line. The two regions had now been fitted into America's grand strategy for East Asia and were being integrated in occupational terms. On the other hand, their administrative separation was now finalized.

CHAPTER 5

The San Francisco Peace Treaty:
End of the Occupation

1. Road to the Peace Treaty: An Overall Peace or Separate Peace

Intensification of the Cold War and the "Four Hurdles"

The Cold War in Asia

The North Atlantic Treaty Organization (NATO) was established in April 1949 and the Soviet Union lifted its blockade of Berlin in May, thus averting the first Cold War crisis. The Federal Republic of Germany (West Germany) came into being in May, followed by the formation of the German Democratic Republic (East Germany) in October. This completed the process of dividing Europe into two opposing Eastern and Western Blocs. Among the historical events that marked this period, of particular note was the Soviet Union's announcement in September that it had successfully tested an atomic bomb. This dramatically ended the monopoly that the United States had enjoyed in the development and deployment of nuclear weapons. As Europe began to move toward relative political and military stability, the problems of the Cold War moved to Asia.

In East Asia, the Korean Peninsula had been divided into north and south by the middle of 1948. In China, the Chinese Red Army under Mao Zedong had defeated the Chinese Nationalist Troops of the Kuomintang, leading to the establishment of the People's Republic of China in October 1948. By February of the following year, the newly formed republic had entered into the Sino-Soviet Treaty of Friendship, Alliance and Mutual Assistance. The treaty stated, "In the event of one of the contracting parties being attacked by Japan or any state allied with it and thus being involved in a state of war, the other contracting party shall immediately render military and other assistance by all means at its disposal." It was obvious that this was a military alliance that targeted Japan and the United States.

During this same period, Southeast Asia had become a battlefield pitting the old colonial powers against the various independence movements that were emerging among local populations. Vietnam was divided into north and south. With French support, the Bao Dai regime ruled the south and faced off with the Ho Chi Minh regime in the north, which was supported by China and the Soviet Union. Indochina's national liberation movement had thus taken on the character of a proxy war between East and West.

Restarting the Movement toward Peace: The Four Hurdles

The deepening of the Cold War in Asia prompted the United States to re-examine Japan's geopolitical position. The United States became increasingly concerned about what path Japan would take after regaining its independence. Having already lost China, the United States simply could not allow Japan to leave the Western Bloc. Worried about the negative political effects of a prolonged Occupation, the State Department took the initiative to accelerate the pace of peace negotiations with Japan.

In a meeting held in Washington on September 13, 1949, Secretary of State Dean Acheson and British Foreign Minister Ernest Bevin agreed that the peace treaty with Japan should go forward even without Soviet participation. The following day, September 14, Acheson also extracted the consent of French Foreign Minister Robert Schuman on this matter and cemented a tripartite front. Progress toward peace had been stalled since early 1948, but the stage was now set for regaining momentum. In November, the State Department announced that it was "preparing a draft peace treaty with Japan."

However, there were "four hurdles" that stood in Acheson's path toward a peace agreement. The first was the hurdle posed by the communists and communism (the Soviet Union). The second and third hurdles were the Pentagon and the allied countries (most notably Australia and other members of the British Commonwealth). Finally, the fourth hurdle was the former enemy (Japan). Among these four, the strongest and longest lasting opposition to peace negotiations came from the Pentagon.[1]

---

1   Acheson, Dean, *Achison kaikoroku* [Present at the Creation: My Years in the State Department], Yoshizawa Seijirō, trans., Kōbunsha, 1979, p. 135.

The Pentagon's negative stance on concluding a peace treaty with Japan was based on its Soviet strategies. Nervous about the future of the region, the Pentagon remained unenthusiastic throughout the entire negotiating process. After losing China, the Pentagon had become increasingly aware of the strategic importance of Japan and was anxious to prolong the Occupation, allowing it to make free use of the military bases located not only in Okinawa but also on the Japanese mainland. If China and the Soviet Union were to participate in peace negotiations, it was unlikely that they would approve of U.S. forces remaining in an independent Japan. Thus, the Pentagon's position was that talks of an agreement with Japan were premature until such time as China and the Soviet Union were willing to accept or at least tolerate an American presence in Japan. Any observer could see that the Pentagon had set an almost impossible precondition.

The Acheson Statement: Accelerating the Peace Process

On December 30, 1949, the U.S. National Security Council approved "The Position of the United States with Respect to Asia (NSC-48/2)." The document set the course for an early conclusion of a peace agreement with Japan and restructured U.S. strategies for Asia. It defined the first basic objective of U.S. policies on Asia to be the "development of the nations and peoples of Asia on a stable and self-sustaining basis." This was followed by the twin objectives of developing "sufficient military power in selected non-Communist nations of Asia to maintain internal security and to prevent further encroachment by communism," and the "gradual reduction and eventual elimination of the preponderant power and influence of the U.S.S.R. in Asia." Various specific steps were outlined for achieving these objectives. Among these were to "improve the United States position with respect to Japan, the Ryukyus and the Philippines" and to develop "sufficient military power to prevent further encroachment by communism."[2]

On January 5, 1950, President Truman announced that the United States

---

2 Memorandum by the Executive Secretary of the National Security Council (Souers) to the National Security Council, December 30, 1949, *FRUS*, 1949, The Far East and Australasia, vol. 7, Part 2, Document 387.

and Britain would move forward on negotiations even without the participation of the Soviet Union. On January 12, Secretary of State Acheson stated that Japan would be rebuilt as the hub of the democratic camp in Asia and would be given a degree of influence in a democratic Far East. Defining America's defensive perimeter in the Pacific as running along the Aleutians to Japan and then to the Ryūkyūs and the Philippine Islands, Acheson avowed that the United States would assume the military defense of Japan so as long as required. This Acheson Statement had failed to mention Taiwan and the Korean Peninsula, and this exclusion would later be criticized in Congress as a contributing cause of the Korean War.

Referring to these developments, William Macmahon Ball, the former British Commonwealth representative to the Allied Council for Japan, wrote, "It is unusual for a defeated nation to be given an important role so soon after its defeat."[3] As implied by Ball, the United States was investing Japan with a stabilizing role in the Far East and was moving to treat it as a friend.

The Dilemma of Opting for an Overall Peace or Separate Peace

The State Department's November 1949 announcement that it was "preparing a draft peace agreement with Japan" created an atmosphere of expectation in Japan that a peace treaty with the Allied Powers was not far away. But it was clear that a peace issue would force Japan not only to confront the issue of how it would rejoin the international community but also to wade into the stormy seas of international politics.

A peace treaty may be seen as an agreement between a defeated nation and all the victor nations for the final settlement of hostilities and the establishment of peace. That being the case, it is beneficial to the defeated nation to enter into a single treaty with all of the victor nations in an overall peace. However, when and how it enters into negotiations is in the hands of the victor nations. It is the victors who must take the initiative.

3　Ball, W. Macmahon, *Nihon: Teki ka mikata ka* [Japan: Enemy or Ally?], Nakayama Rippei and Uchiyama Kenichi, trans., Chikuma Shobō, 1953, p. 135.

For Japan, overall peace implied an agreement that would include the Soviet Union and other nations of the Communist Bloc. On the other hand, separate peace (one-sided peace or majority peace) implied an agreement that would exclude these nations. Both formally and effectively, separate peace would place Japan in the Western Bloc and restrict its pursuit of neutrality. Moreover, the path toward separate peace would deprive Japan of the possibility of joining the United Nations.

On November 8, Prime Minister Yoshida addressed sessions of each house of the Diet, delivering his policy statement and declaring in the opening moments of his speeches, "We desire the conclusion of a peace treaty to be moved forward." Responding to a question put to him in the House of Councillors on November 11, Yoshida stated that the choice between overall and separate peace would be determined on the basis of international relations and was not a matter on which Japan possessed the freedom of choice. He then went on to state, "A peace entered into with a small number of nations is preferable to no peace at all, and how much more so if such a peace serves as a path to an overall peace. Therefore, I believe we should happily accept such a settlement." Yoshida's idea was to regain independence through separate peace negotiations, and to later enter into peace treaties with any countries that had been left out.

MacArthur's Concept of a "Neutral Japan"

The U.S. government had once again started to move toward concluding a peace with Japan. For MacArthur, this was good news. In his annual New Year's message released in January 1950, MacArthur looked back on 1949 and commented "the year has witnessed progressive and far-reaching relaxation of Occupation control" and pointed out that a "we internally have virtually arrived at a de facto peace" between Japan and the United States. MacArthur took this opportunity to emphasize Japan's military neutrality.

Some contemporary cynics deride as visionary Japan's constitutional renunciation of the concept of belligerency and armed security. Be not overly concerned by such detractors. A product of Japanese thought, this provision is based upon highest of moral ideals, and yet no constitutional provision was ever more fundamentally sound and practical.[4]

As part of this same message, MacArthur made an extremely important statement. Regarding Article 9 of the Constitution of Japan, he explained, "while by no sophistry of reasoning can it be interpreted as complete negation of the inalienable right of self-defense against unprovoked attack, it is a ringing affirmation by people laid prostrate by the sword, of faith in the ultimate triumph of international morality and justice without resort to the sword."

Perhaps Yoshida was echoing MacArthur's words when he stated in his policy speech of January 23, "The Constitution solemnly proclaims that this nation forever renounces war and the means of war. The keystone of our national security is none other than the determination of the people to contribute to world peace, culture and prosperity in strict conformity with the spirit of this proclamation and with the support of the views held by the peace-loving nations of the world." Yoshida then added, "Strict conformity with the principle of the renunciation of war however does not by any means imply the abandonment of the right of self-defense." Both MacArthur and Yoshida were clearly moving away from the renunciation of the right of self-defense that they had earlier subscribed to in the process of enacting the constitution.

Voices Favoring an Overall Peace: The Intelligentsia, the Japanese Communist Party, and Conservatives

Peace Problems Council and "Overall Peace"

Prime Minister Yoshida chose his words very carefully when speaking on the subject of the peace agreement, but that did not stop the public from engaging in heated discussions on such matters as whether the peace would be overall or separate, and what would be done to ensure national security.

---

4 General MacArthur's New Year's Day Statement, January 1, 1950, Statements by MacArthur, Box No. 2195, Folder 22, GHQ/SCAP Records, Government Section, National Diet Library, Originals in U.S. National Archives & Records Administration, RG331.

The strongest support for an overall peace came from the Peace Problems Council (*Heiwa mondai danwa kai*). This association traced its roots to the Peace Study Group (*Heiwa mondai tōgi kai*) that had been formed following the publication of the Joint Statement on Peace, which had been drawn up by eight scientists and published by UNESCO at a time when the Berlin blockade was pushing the East-West confrontation toward a dangerous climax.

The Peace Study Group was organized by Yoshino Genzaburō of the publishing house Iwanami Shoten. Membership included such so-called "old liberals" as Abe Yoshishige, Watsuji Tetsurō, Tanaka Kōtarō, Takagi Yasaka, and Rōyama Masamichi. But the group also attracted the labor-farmer school of Marxist thinkers (Rōnō-ha), such as Ōuchi Hyōe, Arisawa Hiromi, and Wakimura Yoshitarō. Finally, Yanaihara Tadao and a group of young researchers were drawn to its fold, including Maruyama Masao, Nakano Yoshio, and Tsuru Shigeto. The Peace Study group was committed to rising above political and ideological differences to investigate matters related to peace. Responding to the UNESCO statement released on January 13, 1949, the group announced that it "fundamentally agreed" with the statement. The Peace Problems Council was formed by absorbing the members of its antecedent organization and shortly thereafter released the "Statement on Issues Related to the Peace" on January 15, 1950.

The statement proposed to take the "democratic foundation and stimulus" generated under the Occupation and further develop it through the "responsibility and creativity of the Japanese people." The statement then argued that to advance this process and ensure the continued development of democracy in Japan, it was absolutely essential for an agreement to be entered into "to establish relations of free exchange and sincere cooperation with all the peoples of the world."

Having established this framework, the statement first made the case against a separate peace by arguing that given the intensification of the Cold War, Japan would not be able to contribute to world peace in the spirit of pacifism laid down in the Constitution if it were to enter into a separate peace with the United States, which stood as one of the poles of hostility in the Cold War. The statement warned, "Even if this were to be no more than a nominal peace, the truth is that such a peace would only increase the risks and dangers of a new war." The Peace

Problems Council stood for a neutral Japan and for membership in the United Nations and expressed its clear opposition to "entering into a military treaty with any specific country or providing military bases to any specific country."

As its second point, the statement argued that a separate peace would entrap the Japanese economy in a "position of utter dependence and servitude to a specific country," which in turn would obstruct and undermine Japan's political independence. In order to accelerate the achievement of economic self-sufficiency, the statement declared, it was essential for Japan to engage in free and close trade with Asian countries in general and with China in particular. This comprised the second leg of the group's advocacy for an overall peace.[5]

In March, President of the University of Tokyo Nanbara Shigeru advocated these positions in his commencement address at the university. Prime Minister Yoshida responded angrily in May with the criticism that the fact that President Nanbara had stepped into the realm of politicians to express his opinion constituted nothing other than a "scholar's dream (*Kyokugaku asei no to*)."

The Peace Problems Council continued to push for an overall peace through the monthly journal *Sekai* and other forums. In June 1950, the group submitted a letter addressed to John Foster Dulles who was visiting Japan as a special envoy. The group would eventually come out in support of the Japan Socialist Party.

The Socialist Party and the "Three Peace Principles"

Among all the political parties, it was the Socialist Party that stood for an overall peace based on the principle of neutrality. On December 4, 1949, the left wing and right wing of the Socialist Party's Central Executive Committee came together to unanimously adopt the "General Attitude towards the Peace Issue" drafted by Sone Eki of the party's right wing. The General Attitude set out the so-called "three peace principles" which consisted of the pursuit of an overall peace, maintaining neutrality, and opposing the establishment of military bases. The General Attitude claimed that the Constitution's renunciation of war and espousal of disarmament "meant not only that we ourselves renounce war

---

5　*Sekai*, March issue, Iwanami Shoten, 1950.

but that Japan naturally must maintain neutrality in international conflicts," and closed with the statement, "We fear that if Japan were to enter into a so-called separate peace with one of the camps, its relations with the other camp would be rendered extremely sensitive. Therefore, we strongly demand an overall peace."

While the Central Executive Committee had come to a unanimous agreement, this did not mean that the majority of the Socialist Party stood squarely behind an overall peace at this time. For instance, Suzuki Mosaburō from the left wing of the party commented, "I cannot say anything for sure now, but the Socialist Party is hoping for an overall peace and will settle for a separate peace if nothing else works out. However, what I would like to see is the British and Americans cooperating and making the greatest possible effort to pull the Soviets into an overall peace." There were others who remained unconvinced. Among these were Arahata Kanson and Yamakawa Hitoshi, the prewar socialist and party elder who was now considered the brain of the left wing. The position taken by Arahata and Yamakawa was that "overall peace was unavoidable."[6]

The Socialist Party went into its fifth party convention in January 1950 without being able to resolve the ambiguity that surrounded the question of the peace. When the convention was called to order, the party was quickly torn apart on the issue of the Independent Youth League (Dokuritsu Seinen Dōmei) in an argument that pitted the left and right wings of the party against each other (the first schism). The ambiguity that existed within the party became even less tenable with the conclusion of the Sino-Soviet alliance in February. The party was increasingly pressured to take a clear and unified stance on international developments and the peace issue.

On February 17, the Socialist Party issued a statement in the name of the Central Executive Committee. Entitled "An appeal to all party members on the conclusion of the Sino-Soviet alliance," the document warned that Japan was becoming the focal point of confrontation between the U.S. and the U.S.S.R. in East Asia and that divisions were appearing within Japan between pro-American and pro-Soviet groups. The statement then declared that Japan must avoid becoming embroiled in war by standing firm as a "third force" that belonged

---

6   *Yomiuri Shinbun*, November 19–23, 1949.

to neither the U.S. nor the Soviet camp. Japan, it argued, must resolutely stand by the principle of "overall peace" and ensure its security through an attitude of strict and uncompromising neutrality.

Because the schism that had emerged in the January party convention did not extend to the party's local organizations, the party managed to reunite its left and right wings in its extraordinary sixth convention held in April. Thereupon, the three peace principles that had been adopted in December of the previous year were again formally adopted as the party's official position. However, the party was unable to define any specific policies that it would pursue in line with the three peace principles.

Formation of the People's Democratic Party and MacArthur's "Conversion"

In February 1950, the Democratic Party was hit by massive defections involving Inukai Takeru, Hori Shigeru, and other members of the party's coalition faction. In the following month, the defectors joined the Democratic Liberal Party, at which time the party went back to calling itself the Liberal Party. In the process of hammering out this union, it is reported that Prime Minister Yoshida endeavored to convince Hori with his view of the historical importance of the moment on hand. "To get to a peace settlement, we absolutely need a unified conservative party that can take responsibility. For the sake of the destiny of the Japanese people over the coming century, we need a framework that can take upon itself the entire burden of whatever success or failure ensues."[7]

The opposition faction that was left behind in the Democratic Party joined forces with the People's Cooperative Party to form the People's Democratic Party on April 28. Boasting 67 members in the House of Representatives, the newly formed party elected Tomabechi Gizō to the post of chairman of the supreme committee and adopted the following platform.

---

7   Hori Shigeru, *Sengo seiji no oboegaki* [Memorandum on Postwar Politics], Mainichi Shinbunsha, 1970, pp. 45–48.

1. Devoting ourselves to the high ideals of love for humanity, we shall pursue permanent world peace and the complete independence of the Japanese people.
2. Bringing together a broad coalition of progressive forces among the people, we shall establish a purely democratic political system.
3. Based on the principle of social solidarity and the spirit of cooperation, we shall coordinate the demands of a free and unfettered system of production and assurances for the livelihood of the people to establish a balanced national economic structure.
4. Standing on a rich foundation of knowledge and rational thought, we shall respect fundamental human rights, promote the spirit of diligent labor, and realize a welfare society.

The formation of the People's Democratic Party was one expression of the concept of a "central party" that would stand somewhere between the Liberal Party on the right and the Socialist Party on the left. It was with this in mind that the new entity identified itself as an amalgamating agent for the "progressive forces among the people." The People's Democratic Party was critical of the position that Yoshida and his Liberal Party had taken on the peace issue and vociferously objected to what it called a "reckless rush toward a separate peace" that "absolutely cannot be tolerated and must be blocked in the name of the people." Thus, the new party came out unambiguously in favor of overall peace. At the same time, it advocated an aggressive pursuit of expanded trade with Southeast Asian countries and the promotion of trade with China.[8]

On April 25, all opposition parties with the exception of the Communist Party came together to form the Joint Foreign Policy Council. On April 26, the Council released a joint statement advocating the principles of peace, neutrality and overall peace, and came out in support of MacArthur's policy for making Japan the Switzerland of Asia. On the following day, a U.S. government official commented that "neutrality is idealistic."

On May 1, Chairman Tomabechi of the People's Democratic Party proposed

---

8　Nakakita Kōji, *Keizai fukkō to sengo seiji* [Economic Recovery and Postwar Politics], University of Tokyo Press, 1998, p. 281.

a non-partisan approach to foreign affairs that would not make diplomatic matters fodder for political battles. Tomabechi explained that he wanted to ensure that the will of the people and their hopes would be properly reflected in the peace treaty.

Six months had passed since his New Year's message when MacArthur communicated with Secretary of Defense Louis Johnson on June 14 in a memorandum that the Allied Powers should remain in various parts of Japan as long as "irresponsible militarism [communism]" exists in the world to threaten Japan's peace, security, and justice. By replacing militarism as addressed in the Potsdam Declaration with the threat of the Cold War, MacArthur too was undergoing a conversion toward allowing the large-scale use of Japan as a military base for U.S. forces.[9]

The Soviet Offensive: The Cominform Critique

In January 1950, Yakov Malik, the Soviet delegate to the United Nations, began his boycott of the Security Council to register his opposition to the U.N. membership of the Taiwan government instead of the Beijing government. Concurrently, the Soviet Union absented itself from the Far Eastern Commission for the same reason, effectively removing itself from the stage of international political negotiations. Parallel to these developments, the Soviet Union was turning the focus of its attention from Europe to Asia, as was the United States.

On January 6, 1950, a controversial article appeared in the pages of the Cominform newspaper, *For Lasting Peace, For a People's Democracy*. Entitled "Concerning the Situation in Japan," the article attacked Nosaka Sanzō's idea of a "peaceful and democratic revolution under the Occupation" as a false doctrine that was deceiving the people and lauding Japan's imperialistic occupiers (that is, American imperialism). The article also hinted at the need for a violent revolution in what came to be known as the "Cominform critique."

Two days later, on January 8, the Communist Party rejected the Cominform

---

9 Igarashi Takeshi, *Sengo Nichibei kankei no keisei* [American-Japanese Peace-Making and the Cold War], Kōdansha, 1995, p. 249.

critique as an act of enemy provocation aimed at undermining party unity. On January 13, the Communist Party published an official response written by Nosaka entitled "Remarks on 'Concerning the Situation in Japan'" (hereinafter, Remarks). This, however, elicited scathing criticism from the Chinese Communist Party that appeared in the *People's Daily* on the 17th. In this way, the Japanese Communist Party found itself being simultaneously criticized by the Chinese and Soviet Communist Parties.

On January 19, the Japanese Communist Party came out in support of an overall peace by adding this to its long-standing platform that included full implementation of the Potsdam Declaration, economic recovery by the people, and the realization of Japan's complete independence. The January 19 statement meant that the Communist Party was rejecting a separate peace agreement and criticizing it as a sure path to war. Conversely, it supported an overall peace as an effective guarantee of peace that would be backed by harmonious relations among major powers. On the question of the Sino-Soviet alliance, the party declared, "We support this as a mighty force promoting overall peace and the immediate conclusion of a fair and democratic peace."

The criticism leveled against it by the Chinese and Soviet Communist Parties had the effect of deepening a rift within the Japanese Communist Party. On one side was the mainstream faction (Remarks faction) of Tokuda Kyūichi and others who supported Nosaka, and on the other side was the anti-mainstream faction (International faction) of Shiga Yoshio, Miyamoto Kenji, and others who were sympathetic to Cominform.

GHQ Responses to the Communist Party

In March 1950, William Sebald, Chief of GHQ's Diplomatic Section, filed a report on the activities of the Japanese Communist Party with John Allison, Director of the State Department's Office of Northeast Asian Affairs. Sebald emphasized that the Japanese Communist Party was "anti-American and anti-Occupation in character" and that its activities had come to "conform perfectly with the over-all Soviet objective in the Far East of undermining the position of the United States." As such, Sebald argued, "We can no longer ignore the elementary fact that the Japanese Communist Party is not a bona fide Japanese organization which should be accorded the status of a Japanese political party, but is an agency for implementing Soviet policy in Japan."[10]

Allison responded to Sebald with a note of caution. Given the fierce policy debates that were raging among the leaders of the party, Allison argued that outlawing the Japanese Communist Party carried the risk of driving the party toward an armed struggle, which ultimately would have the effect of strengthening the unity of the party and resolving the conflicts that existed within its leadership. Furthermore, Allison argued, the party would deepen its ties with the Kremlin and reinforce its position.

GHQ was becoming increasingly alarmed by the anti-American character and activities of the Japanese Communist Party. It was against this backdrop that MacArthur criticized the party in a statement made on May 3, labeling the Communist Party, "avowed satellite of an international predatory force."[11] On May 30, a pro-Communist Party demonstration held in front of the Imperial Palace clashed with U.S. military forces, leading to the arrest of eight demonstrators accused of assaulting U.S. soldiers. On June 3, the accused were referred to a military court and sentenced to five years or more of imprisonment with hard labor. The incident was reported as the "first case of public violence against Occupation forces." Seizing on the events of this day, U.S. newspapers reported that the honeymoon has ended for the Occupation of Japan and that the incident was an expression of "inevitable antagonism against Occupation authorities resulting from an occupation that had already continued for too long."

---

10 The Acting United States Political Adviser for Japan (Sebald) to the Director of the Office of Northeast Asian Affairs (Allison), March 24, 1950, *FRUS*, 1950, East Asia and the Pacific, vol. 6, Document 698.

11 General MacArthur's Statement on the Third Anniversary of the Japanese Constitution, May 3, 1950, Statements by MacArthur, Box No. 2195, Folder 22, GHQ/SCAP Records, Government Section, National Diet Library, Originals in U.S. National Archives & Records Administration, RG331.

The Red Purge and the Move to Outlaw the Communist Party

Immediately following the May 30 incident, Chief Willoughby of the G2 Section urged MacArthur to outlaw the Communist Party. However, Whitney, Chief of the Government Section, opposed this line of action, arguing that this was a matter for the Diet to determine. While MacArthur agreed that some form of action had to be taken to counter the Japanese Communist Party's attitude of open opposition to the Occupation forces, he did not support outlawing the party. Ultimately, MacArthur ruled against a ban and overt suppression of the party and instead opted for action that paralleled the purging of undesirable elements from public office. What followed was an effort to divide the Communist Party into separate legal and illegal entities.[12]

On June 6, MacArthur ordered the purge of 24 members of the Central Committee of the Communist Party, including Tokuda and Nosaka. This was followed by a shutdown of *Akahata*, the party's newspaper, on June 26. Tokuda and other mainstream faction members who had been purged went underground in order to continue their activities.

On the other hand, speaking shortly after the May 30 incident, Prime Minister Yoshida explained, "We are left with no choice but to consider outlawing the Communist Party." On June 8, Yoshida wrote to MacArthur outlining his thoughts on applying the Organizations Control Order to the Communist Party, "I wish to [have] your prior approval so that the Order may be invoked anytime at the discretion of the government."[13] Yoshida also considered submitting the question of outlawing the Communist Party to the Diet but ultimately did not move forward with the idea. The Socialist Party put up stiff resistance, claiming the action was unconstitutional, while the People's Democratic Party remained circumspect throughout the process.

---

12 Ogura Yūji, "Makkāsā to Kyōsantō" [MacArthur and the Communist Party] in *Nenpō Nihon gendaishi dai 4-kan* [MacArthur and the Japan Communist Party (Annual Report on Modern Japanese History)], Gendai Shiryō Shuppankai, 1999, p. 164.
13 Sodei Rinjirō, ed., and trans., *Correspondence between General MacArthur, Prime Minister Yoshida & Other High Japanese Officials [1945–1952]*, Hōsei Daigaku Shuppankyoku, 2000, pp. 200–201.

The Dodge Recession: Opposition Parties on the Offensive

Finance Minister Ikeda's "Gaffe"

Diet discussions of the peace treaty began in the sixth extraordinary session of October 1949 and extended through the seventh ordinary session that convened in December of the same year. However, the most pressing issues facing the Diet continued to be economic questions in general and formulating the national budget for fiscal 1950 in particular.

Deflation and economic stagnation triggered by the Dodge Line showed no signs of abating even in early 1950. Growing unemployment was sowing the seeds of social unrest, financial conditions were tightening, and businesses were facing increasingly harsh conditions. Miyazawa Kiichi has described the prevailing situation in this passage.

The Dodge Line had begun in Japan the year before and inflation, which had plagued Japan for much of the postwar, came to an end. However, on the other hand, the stoppage in money flow and salary rises became severe. Economists warned of businesses about to go under, exclaiming a "mini-depression." There was a growing feeling around this time that the Dodge Line should be gradually eased. Moreover, the impression was widely held among the people of Japan that this recession was the result of an occupation by an uncaring foreigner, Dodge. The economic struggle in their daily lives began to turn the people of Japan against the Occupation.[14]

In February, Yoshida wrote to Finance Minister Ikeda to sound him out on a visit to the United States. Yoshida's comment that a "telegram has been received from Mr. Dulles" points to the second purpose for Ikeda's visit that is discussed in detail below.[15]

It was against this backdrop that Finance Minister Ikeda made a highly

---

14 Miyazawa Kiichi, *Secret Talks between Tokyo and Washington*, Rowman & Littlefield Publishers, 2007, p. 15.
15 Yoshida Shigeru to Ikeda Hayato, (February 4, 1950), Yoshida Shigeru Kinen Zaidan, ed., *Yoshida Shigeru shokan* [Letters of Yoshida Shigeru], Chūō Kōronsha, 1994, p. 37.

embarrassing gaffe in a press conference held on March 1, while the Diet was in the midst of its seventh ordinary session. Ikeda said, "In the face of such a critical policy as disinflation, we should not allow the bankruptcy or suicide of five or ten owners of small businesses to deter us. These things cannot be helped because we are now in the midst of a major transformation that is called the Dodge Line.... Having lost the war, this is an ordeal that cannot be avoided if we are to go forward on the reconstruction of the Japanese economy."

Responding to this statement, the opposition parties called for a "non-confidence vote on Finance Minister Ikeda" in the plenary session of the House of Representatives. But the motion was defeated with a single comment from Yoshida that united the ruling party behind the beleaguered finance minister.

Notwithstanding the finance minister's embarrassing statement, the fiscal 1950 budget was adopted in the House of Representatives by a majority vote on March 10. In the House of Councillors where the opposition parties held a majority, however, the opposition parties pushed through a different resolution on a wage hike for government employees. Due to this inconsistency, the budget was not enacted until April 1, leaving a three-day period during which the government was left without a budget.

Rejection of the Proposed Local Tax Law: The Limits of GHQ

The opposition parties again went on the offensive when the revision of the Local Tax Law came up for debate in the Diet. The proposed revisions, based on the Shoup Report, were designed to redistribute prefectural and municipal taxes, first of all, and increase tax revenues by increasing value-added prefectural taxes and property-based municipal taxes. The opposition parties rallied around the cry of protecting the livelihood of the people and made the House of Councillors their platform for attacking the government.[16]

The bill for the revision of the Local Tax Law was presented to the Cabinet for approval in January 1950, but became stalled when various government

---

16 Amakawa Akira, *Senryōka no Nihon* [Japan under the Occupation], Gendai Shiryō Shuppan, 2014, p. 217.

ministries representing the interests of the business community argued in favor of a net reduction in taxes. The Cabinet itself was eager to cut taxes in preparation for the approaching upper house election. This reflected the groundswell of voices demanding an easing of the Dodge Line, a sentiment that had by now also spread to the government and ruling party. Finance Minister Ikeda negotiated with GHQ on lowering tax rates, but was rebuffed. GHQ viewed the Shoup recommendations to be part and parcel of the Dodge Line and was not prepared to make any concessions on taxes.

On March 18, Yoshida wrote to MacArthur requesting a revision in property tax rates. MacArthur rejected the request and wrote back, "It is imperative that the revised local tax laws become effective as of April 1, 1950."[17] Left with no alternative, Yoshida submitted the bill for the revision of the Local Tax Law to the Diet on March 23. Furthermore, acting on MacArthur's directive, the government and ruling Liberal Party pushed the bill through the House of Representative's Committee on Local Administration on April 20 in the absence of opposition members. Thereafter, the bill was pushed through the plenary session of the House of Representatives and sent to the House of Councillors.

With 74 seats under its control, the largest political group in the House of Councillors at this point was the Green Breeze Society (Ryokufūkai). Yoshida's Liberal Party was second with 52 seats. The bill was rejected in the Upper House's Committee on Local Administration by a vote of five to eight, and was similarly defeated in the plenary session by a vote of 73 in favor and 102 against. The government was left with two options. One was to carry the bill in the House of Representatives with a two-thirds majority, and the other was to convene a joint committee of houses. Yoshida failed to obtain a two-thirds majority in the House of Representatives, and no compromise could be reached between the two sides in the joint committee. Consequently, the bill was tabled on May 2. The failure to pass the revised Local Tax Law stands as one of the rare cases in which support and pressure from GHQ was not enough to obtain the desired outcome.

---

17 Sodei, *Correspondence between General MacArthur, Prime Minister Yoshida & Other High Japanese Officials [1945–1952]*, pp. 173–175, (March 18, 1950).

With the exception of the Communist Party, all of the opposition parties came together to lambast the government, stating, "This bill, which embodied one of the government's highest priority policies, failed to gain the support of the public and the cooperation of the Diet. Therefore, the Cabinet should immediately resign en masse and apologize to the public for its wrongdoings."

On May 1, 1950, the opposition parties (again with the exception of the Communist Party) jointly called for a non-confidence motion on the Yoshida Cabinet in the House of Representatives. The motion claimed that the Yoshida Cabinet had failed to take an independent and responsible approach to political affairs, the complaint started. The Cabinet had resorted to the tyranny of the majority to create a crisis in parliamentary politics and party politics. In fiscal and economic policies, the Cabinet had brought about an unprecedented deflationary crisis that had pushed small and medium-sized businesses, farmers and workers into the abyss of dire distress. Moreover, on matters concerning the peace negotiations, the Cabinet had deeply divided the public by opting for separate peace and abandoning the principle of neutrality.[18]

At this point, the People's Democratic Party, the Socialist Party, and other opposition parties (again with the exception of the Communist Party) were in agreement in supporting an "overall peace." The opposition was now in a strong position to strengthen its criticism of the Yoshida Cabinet.

Dilemma in Democratic Procedures

The failed revision of the Local Tax Law undermined the Dodge Line. Moreover, the failure had caused MacArthur to lose face. With a "furious" expression on his face, MacArthur convened a meeting of related section chiefs on May 2 to demand an explanation of what had gone wrong. Those called included Chief Whitney of the Government Section, Chief William Marquat of the Economic and Scientific Section, and Deputy Chief Frank Rizzo of the Government Section. One of the participants in the meeting, Justin Williams, the head of the Government Section's Parliamentary and Political Division, has described this

---

18 *Yomiuri Shinbun*, May 1, 1950.

session in the following words:

> Instead of telling him [MacArthur] the unvarnished truth of which he was already aware, that the uncompromising inflexibility of two of his staff sections was the root cause of the trouble, I told him that sooner or later his enlightened policy of encouraging the national assembly to become in fact as well as in theory the highest organ of state power made inevitable a negative vote in the Diet.[19]

In Williams' view, the rejection of the revised Local Tax Law was the result of the conflicting "political and economic objectives of the Occupation." If the Economic Stabilization Program were to be given priority, this would imply making light of the deliberative functions and powers of the Diet. On the other hand, if the decision of the Diet were to be respected, proper implementation of the Economic Stabilization Program could not be guaranteed in certain instances. Williams concluded that the role of GHQ was to explain a bill to opposition leaders before its adoption and to give ear to their views and opinions.

MacArthur's statement on the rejection of the bill was released on May 3, 1950. The "legislative stalemate which resulted was not unusual under the democratic process in comparable situations." But MacArthur went on to demand that the Diet "proceed 'with resolution, statesmanship and unity of purpose' to discharge its attendant responsibility in implementation of this phase of the Economic Stabilization Program designed to insure 'stability in public finance as reciprocal warrant for American economic aid'" after the election of the House of Councillors.[20]

The Local Tax Law was finally enacted on July 31 after undergoing some revisions in the eighth session of the Diet. Passage of the law was helped by the fact that the Korean War had started by this time and the attention of both GHQ

---

19 William, Justin, *Japan's Political Revolution under MacArthur: A Participant's Account*, University of Georgia Press, 1979, p. 224.
20 General MacArthur's Statement on Local Tax Law Revision Bill, May 3, 1950, Statements by MacArthur, Box No. 2195, Folder 22, GHQ/SCAP Records, Government Section, National Diet Library, Originals in U.S. National Archives & Records Administration, RG331.

and the Japanese public had turned to the situation on the Korean Peninsula. A compromise was hammered out in the shadow of the war, with the ruling Liberal Party and the People's Democratic Party coming together over a revision proposed by the latter to lower the tax rate from 1.7 percent to 1.5 percent.

Ikeda's U.S. Visit and the June 1950 Election of the House of Councillors

In April 1950, Finance Minister Ikeda visited the United States on the pretext that he was inspecting matters related to government finance in an advanced economy. However, the real purpose of his visit was elsewhere. Ikeda had been entrusted with two missions. First, he was to meet with Joseph Dodge on behalf of the government and the ruling party and to extract a promise regarding the easing of austerity measures ahead of the upper house election scheduled for June. His second mission was to convey an "important message"[21] from Yoshida on the peace negotiations and to gauge the American reaction. The second task will be discussed in a later section.

Ikeda succeeded in extracting some concessions on raising the salaries of government workers and lowering taxes, and was also able to discuss peace issues with Dodge. GHQ reacted furiously to this development as it felt that Ikeda had gone over its head to negotiate directly with Washington. On May 22, Chief Marquat of the Economic and Scientific Section and Chief Whitney of the Government Section jointly issued a statement calling Ikeda to task and warning him not to "use the easing of the Dodge Line as a political campaign." For a period thereafter, Ikeda was banned from visiting GHQ. This whole affair came to be known as the "the incident over the present from the U.S. trip."[22]

The election of the House of Councillors was held on June 4, 1950. While the peace issue stood among the principal issues that were debated during the election campaign, its relative weight in the election campaign was light. While Yoshida made a point of mentioning the issue in all of his campaign speeches, the opposition parties remained focused on the economic policies of the ruling

---

21 Ikeda Hayato, *Kinkō zaisei* [Fiscal Balance], Chūō Kōron Shinsha, 1999, p. 231.
22 Miyazawa, *Secret Talks between Tokyo and Washington*, p. 25.

Liberal Party and the infamous Ikeda gaffe.

In the election, the Liberal Party won 52 seats (totaling 76 seats including seats not up for re-election), the Socialist Party took 36 seats (totaling 61), the People's Democratic Party took nine seats (totaling 29), Ryokufūkai took nine seats (totaling 61), the Communist Party took two seats (totaling 4), and other parties took 24 seats (totaling 30). The Liberal Party and the Socialist Party increased their number of seats. While the Liberal Party overtook Ryokufūkai to become the top party in the upper house, it fell far short of claiming a majority.

Dulles' Visit to Japan and the Outbreak of the Korean War: Launching the National Police Reserve Forces

Dulles' Views on the Peace Issue

Following the establishment of the People's Republic of China, the Truman Administration came under vicious attack from congressional Republicans for the failure of its China policy. In February 1950, Republican Senator Joseph McCarthy launched his campaign of accusations against "communists and communist sympathizers" in the State Department. McCarthy singled out for criticism Philip Jessup, U.S. special envoy and author of "The China White Paper," and U.S. diplomat John Service, whom he accused of being saboteurs who had sold China out to the communists. The hysterical anti-communism that characterized McCarthyism marked the beginning of the so-called Red Scare.

In April 1950, President Truman took the first step toward rebuilding a non-partisan diplomatic initiative by appointing the Republican John F. Dulles as senior adviser to the Secretary of State. In the following month, Truman formally appointed Dulles to represent the United States in the peace negotiations with Japan.

Dulles is best known as an anti-communist ideologue and as the hawkish Secretary of State who formed and led U.S. Cold War diplomacy. But during this earlier period, Dulles played the role of a tough negotiator pitted against the State Department, the military, MacArthur, and the nations of the Allied Powers.

Dulles was convinced that the punitive peace settlement at Versailles had not been conducive to long-term peace and stability but had instead led to the rise of Nazi Germany and the outbreak of World War II. Dulles respected the democratization policies that had been implemented in the early stages of the Occupation and expected that the Japanese people would come to share the basic Western values, which he described as "peace-loving" and "respecting fundamental human rights through practice." It was his hope that as a member of the "free world," Japan would serve as a model of pro-Americanism and resistance to communism for other Asian countries.[23]

Dulles' Visit to Japan and MacArthur's Abandonment of Neutrality

In mid-June, two American missions arrived in Japan. The first was the Dulles mission representing the State Department. Landing in Haneda on June 17, Dulles went directly to South Korea and returned to Tokyo on June 21. The second mission, which arrived on June 18, represented the U.S. military and was led by Secretary of Defense Louis Johnson and General Omar Bradley, chairman of the Joint Chiefs of Staff. Unlike Dulles, the second mission was firmly against an early peace and had been sent to convince MacArthur not to support it. In effect, this mission carried "the gap between the State and the Defense Department."[24]

The purpose of the Dulles visit was to meet with MacArthur and other key individuals and to gather information on the viability of a peace treaty. To fulfill his purpose, Dulles met with leading political figures such as Prime Minister Yoshida, Tomabechi Gizō, and Asanuma Inejirō. But he also met with business and labor leaders as well as intellectuals and leaders of thought. Throughout these meetings, Dulles emphasized the need for non-partisan diplomacy and listened intently to the views on national security held by his interviewees.

In his meeting with Dulles, Prime Minister Yoshida argued that economic recovery was more important than rearmament and that priority should be assigned to achieving Japan's domestic stability. Throughout their exchange,

---

23 Igarashi, *Sengo Nichibei kankei no keisei*, p. 245.
24 Sebald, William J., *With MacArthur in Japan: A Personal History of the Occupation*, W.W. Norton, 1965, pp. 254–255.

John Foster Dulles (1888–1959) U.S. politician. After joining the State Department in April 1950 as senior adviser to the Secretary of State, in the following month he was made responsible for negotiating the peace agreement with Japan. Dulles made three visits to Japan. He called for the rearmament of Japan during the Korean War and set the course for Japan's independence by combining the peace treaty with the U.S.-Japan Security Treaty.

Yoshida took pains to avoid committing to the "important message" that he had entrusted to Ikeda on his visit to the United States. Dulles had no patience for small talk and was taken aback by Yoshida's circuitous and ambiguous choice of words. After the meeting, Dulles turned to William Sebald, Chief of the Diplomatic Section, to express his distaste. "It was much like Alice in Wonderland," he complained.[25]

The People's Democratic Party's Tomabechi used his meeting with Dulles to express his support for an overall peace and U.N. membership for Japan. However, he did concede that he would not oppose a peace treaty in the event that the Soviet Union refused to become a signatory to the peace treaty. Thus, he effectively signaled his acceptance of a separate peace. The Socialist Party's Asanuma argued that an overall peace was necessary for the purpose of maintaining Japan's neutrality. He then went on to outline his position on U.N. membership as a means to ensure Japan's national security, his position to providing military bases and entering into military agreements with any specific country, and the need to promote trade with Asia as a means of achieving economic self-sufficiency for Japan.

On June 23 Dulles met with MacArthur. In the course of the meeting, MacArthur confirmed his support for the placement of U.S. military bases throughout the Japanese mainland and providing U.S. forces with "unlimited freedom of action." For all intents and purposes, this meeting marked the abandonment of Japan's military neutrality. Dulles came away from the meeting armed with the materials he needed to convince the military on maintaining U.S. bases in Japan.

---

25 Ibid., p. 257.

Outbreak of the Korean War

The Korean War broke out on June 25 as the North Korean army crossed the 38th parallel to invade South Korea. It was just four days after Dulles had arrived in Japan. The North Korean leader, Kim Il-sung, had obtained the prior consent of Stalin and Mao Zedong in his bid to unify the two Koreas through military force. The war that ravaged the Korean Peninsula overturned the conventional wisdom that the front lines of the Cold War were situated on the European continent.

On the same day, June 25, the United Nations Security Council held an emergency meeting at the request of the United States. With the Soviet Union absent from this emergency meeting, the Security Council adopted a resolution determining that the "armed attack on the Republic of Korea by forces from North Korea... constitutes a breach of peace" and calling on "North Korea to withdraw forthwith their armed forces to the 38th parallel." On June 27, the Security Council adopted a second resolution recommending members of the United Nations to "furnish such assistance to the Republic of Korea as may be necessary to repel the armed attack."[26] At the same time, President Truman ordered the dispatch of U.S. naval and air forces to South Korea, while the Seventh Fleet was dispatched to the Taiwan Strait to forestall a Chinese invasion of Taiwan. On July 7, the Security Council adopted a resolution for the creation of a U.N. Force. The following day, Truman appointed MacArthur to lead the U.N. Force as Commander-in-Chief of the U.N. Command.

Although it contained elements of British, Canadian, and Australian military forces, the U.N. Force was principally manned by the U.S. and South Korean militaries. The North Korean military had made extensive plans and preparations for the invasion and was able to push southward without pause. By the third day of hostilities, North Korean forces had occupied the capital city of Seoul. As the southward thrust of the invasion continued, by September, the U.S. and South Korean forces had been pushed back to Busan in the southern reaches of the Peninsula.

---

26 Resolution Adopted by the United Nations Security Council, June 27, 1950, *FRUS*, Korea, vol. 7, Document 130.

Establishment of the National Police Reserve Forces: Toward Limited Rearmament

Now tasked with leading the U.N. Command in rebuffing the North Korean invasion, MacArthur wrote to Prime Minister Yoshida on July 8 authorizing the creation of a national police reserve of 75,000 men to exist alongside current autonomous and national rural police forces with combined personnel of 125,000. The same message also instructed the addition of 8,000 personnel to the Maritime Safety Board. MacArthur explained in his letter that police forces needed to be reinforced to fill the vacuum left by the redeployment of Occupation Forces to the Korean Peninsula.[27]

Also on July 8, Chief Whitney of the Government Section communicated with Chief Cabinet Secretary Okazaki Katsuo to instruct the government on the implementation of MacArthur's orders. Whitney's instructions contained two salient points. First, the National Police Reserve was to be placed under the direct jurisdiction of the government as a separate organization from the national rural police force. Second, the National Police Reserve was to be established through the issuance of a Potsdam Cabinet Order. Whitney added that GHQ did not intend to change the spirit that had animated the reformation of the police system. Furthermore, in his meeting with the National Public Safety Commission, Deputy Chief Frank Rizzo of the Government Section explained that the character of the National Police Reserve was neither that of an army nor a police force, and that it was similar to the American organization of state troopers in that it could be called on for deployment in emergency situations. These explanations aside, the important point was that, faced with the southward march of the North Korean army, MacArthur had opened the door to the rearmament of Japan, albeit in a limited way.

Yoshida and the Japanese government had already been keen on strengthening the nation's police forces from the perspective of maintaining public order, and welcomed MacArthur's instructions as a golden opportunity to move

---

27 Sodei, *Correspondence between General MacArthur, Prime Minister Yoshida & Other High Japanese Officials [1945–1952]*, pp. 203–204.

forward on their plans. On August 10, the National Police Reserve Order was promulgated under Potsdam Cabinet Order No. 260.

The newly formed National Police Reserve Force was placed under the jurisdiction of the G2's Public Safety Division, leaving limited room for intervention by the Government Section. However, in one exceptional case, Whitney stepped in to exercise his veto. Given the shortage of higher echelon officers available for service in the National Police Reserve Force, a movement emerged for lifting the purge of former officers of the Imperial Army. However, Whitney blocked this by citing the decisions of the Far Eastern Commission. Whitney went on to demand that all executive appointments be submitted to the Government Section for prior approval and continued to enforce the exclusion of purged former military officers and former members of the Special Police from executive posts in the National Police Reserve Force.

Reforming the Police System: The Conflicting Aims of GHQ, Yoshida, and the Police

In December 1950, MacArthur advised the Japanese government that he was prepared to approve the reform of the police system in light of the need to strengthen internal security in Japan. Proposals for reform were immediately drafted (December 28 draft) and submitted to the Government Section. The speedy response points to the preparations that the government had already made behind the scenes. The main points of the government proposal were: (1) expansion of the powers and authority of the National Rural Police, (2) mutual cooperation and assistance between national rural police and autonomous police, and (3) dissolution of autonomous police forces in small and medium-sized municipalities. Deputy Chief Rizzo of the Government Section contended that the proposed dissolution of some autonomous police organizations was contrary to the development of local autonomy, one of the principal objectives and policies of the Occupation.

On the Japanese side, views and positions on reforming the police system were not necessarily united. In addition to strengthening the National Rural Police, Yoshida was anxious to restrict the independence of the National Public

Safety Commission. On the other hand, the National Rural Police Headquarters supported the expansion of its powers and authority, but was interested in preserving the independence of the National Public Safety Commission and shielding it from government intervention and pressure. Finally, autonomous police organizations including the Tokyo Metropolitan Police were uncomfortable with the prospect of a National Rural Police organization armed with enhanced powers and authority.

Within GHQ, the Government Section and G2 agreed on the need to uphold the fundamental spirit outlined in MacArthur's 1947 note, which stipulated the independence of the police from political forces and advocated the principal of local autonomy. Based on this consensus, both sections remained critical of any changes that would expand the powers of the National Rural Police and the Cabinet.

In consultations held in January 1951, GHQ informed the Japanese government that, subject to two conditions, it was prepared to accept the dissolution of certain autonomous police organizations. First, the scope of dissolution would be limited to the autonomous police forces of towns and villages. Second, dissolution would be predicated on the outcome of local referendums. The National Rural Police lobbied for the removal of the referendum requirement, but G2 refused to step back on this point on the grounds that it would not sanction any reform that was disadvantageous to local autonomy and local government organizations.

2. Approval for Stationing U.S. Forces in Japan and Intensification of the Korean War

Impact of the Korean War on Political Parties

The Yoshida Message

As previously mentioned, Prime Minister Yoshida had entrusted his "important message" to Finance Minister Ikeda on his visit to the United States. The "important message" outlined Yoshida's belief that the call for an overall peace was primarily intended as a means for attacking his government. Yoshida further speculated in his message that public opinion would side with an early treaty if the terms of the treaty were reasonable. Miyazawa Kiichi, Personal Secretary to the Minister of Finance, who accompanied Ikeda on his trip, has described the conveyance of Yoshida's message in his memoirs.

> The Japanese government desires the earliest possible treaty. Even after such a peace treaty is signed, U.S. forces will probably be necessary for the security of Japan and the Asian region. If the U.S. government is unable to make such a request, the Japanese government can study the way in which to make such an offer.[28]

The idea of ensuring Japan's post-Occupation national security by stationing U.S. forces had already been suggested in the "Ashida Memo" of the summer of 1947, and Prime Minister Yoshida made a point of emphasizing the linkage between his proposal and that of Foreign Minister Ashida. However, there

---

28 Miyazawa, *Secret Talks between Tokyo and Washington*, pp. 22–23.

was one critical difference between the two proposals. Whereas Ashida only advocated "emergency stationing," the Yoshida proposal accepted the concept of "continuous stationing" of U.S. forces in Japan. To further press his point, the Yoshida message conveyed by Ikeda was accompanied by the prime minister's assurance that the stationing of U.S. forces in Japan did not contravene the Constitution.

But Yoshida took a different tack in public debate and did not reveal the content of his message to the U.S. government. Responding to a question put to him by the Socialist Party's Kaneko Yōbun in a session of the Committee on Foreign Affairs, House of Councillors, held in July 1950, Yoshida is recorded to have said, "My thinking is that I do not want to lease military bases."

In any case, Yoshida had made up his mind to seek an early peace treaty and pay for it by providing military bases to U.S. forces. As for the defense of Japan, Yoshida's plan was to pursue military cooperation with the United States based on a formal security agreement. The fact of the matter is that these plans had already gelled in Yoshida's mind before the outbreak of the Korean War. Yoshida's "important message" was presented in turn to William Butterworth, Director of the Office of Far Eastern Affairs, Dulles and later to MacArthur. Butterworth penned the following comments after receiving the Yoshida proposal. "This conversation is regarded as significant because it is the first expression we have had at an official level of the attitude of the Japanese government on the peace treaty and related questions."[29]

Yoshida and the Korean War: Choosing between a Liberal-Democratic Alliance and a Liberal-Democratic-Socialist Alliance

In a report filed with his home government dated July 13, or three weeks after the outbreak of war in Korea, the British ambassador in Tokyo wrote, "Yoshida did not seem displeased with, or anxious about, the Korean issue, which he appeared to think might go against Japan's economy on the short term."[30] The

---

29 Finn, Richard B., *Winners in Peace: MacArthur, Yoshida, and Postwar Japan*, University of California Press, 1992, p. 250.
30 Ibid., p. 262.

fact is that the Korean War saved the third Yoshida Cabinet. "All the discussions on easing the Dodge Line and correcting the disinflation policy were transformed by the turning point marked by the start of the Korean conflict."[31] As U.S. military purchase orders began to pour into Japan for a broad range of goods and services, a national economy that was suffering the consequences of anemic demand suddenly perked up.

On June 26, one day after the outbreak of hostilities, Yoshida met with Ashida of the People's Democratic Party to request his cooperation. "We want an early peace treaty, but domestically this cannot be helped. You and I and Mr. Shidehara have our diplomatic careers in common. Therefore, I believe that you can appreciate our diplomatic challenges. In whatever way possible, I wish to enter into a cooperative relation with the Democratic Party." Ashida replied that it was undesirable for the country to be divided into two camps and suggested that "In the very least, I would like to win the support of the right wing of the Socialist Party."[32]

While Yoshida was eager to enter into an alliance with the People's Democratic Party, he had no interest in teaming up with the Socialist Party because in his eyes, the Socialist Party, particularly its left wing, was no different from the Communist Party. Ashida took a very different approach based on his recent experiences with coalition governments and coalitions among opposition parties. In light of prevailing conditions within the People's Democratic Party, Ashida judged that a successful coalition government needed a three-party coalition that at least included the right wing of the Socialist Party. Moreover, Ashida subscribed to the position that excluding the Socialist Party from the coalition government would drive it into the arms of the Communist Party. Reorganizing the political landscape and launching a supra-partisan diplomatic initiative was proving more difficult than expected due to conflicting party interests and differences that existed within the respective parties.

---

31 Yoshida Shigeru, *Kaisō jūnen, dai 3-kan* [A Memoir of Ten Years, vol. 3], Shinchōsha, 1957, p. 23.
32 Shindō Eichi and Shimokōbe Motoharu, eds., *Ashida Hitoshi nikki* [Ashida Hitoshi Diary], Iwanami Shoten, 1986, (June 26, 1950).

Meeting on July 8, the Central Committee of the Socialist Party acknowledged that the Korean War had been instigated by North Korea's military invasion of the South and adopted a position critical of the North. The party announced, "We lend our moral support to the United Nations in its efforts to maintain law and order," but pressed for Japan's neutrality in the conflict by stating, "Standing under the new Constitution that renounces all forms of war, we oppose the intervention of the Japanese people in this conflict." The Central Committee concluded by saying, "The Korean situation is proof of the attendant dangers of a hurried pursuit of an incomplete peace treaty," and therefore the "Socialist Party shall remain true to its established policies in moving forward on matters related to the peace."[33] Firmly believing that neutrality and an overall peace were the best means available to Japan for "avoiding becoming entangled in war," the Socialist Party was signaling that it would not abandon its "three peace principles" at any time in the foreseeable future.

The Socialist Party held that there were "unresolved issues in Asia," including the recognition of the Beijing government, the situation on the Korean Peninsula, and the problems of Taiwan and Indochina. The party claimed that, given that Japan belonged to the Asian region, an overall peace treaty needed to be considered also from the perspective of how such a resolution would contribute to peace throughout Asia.

The Socialist Party found encouragement in the statements of Prime Minister Nehru of India in which he criticized North Korea for its aggression, argued for the containment and localization of the Korean conflict and advocated that the Korean people themselves had to find a solution to their problems. The Socialist Party supported Nehru's positions and proclaimed, "Japan, India, China, and the other East Asian nations must stand united in preventing the spread of war in East Asia," claiming that the East-West confrontation could be surmounted through Asian solidarity.[34]

---

33 Nihon Shakaitō Kettō Yonjushūnen Kinen Shuppan Kankō Kinen Iinkai, ed., "Chōsen sensō to shakaitō no taido [Attitudes of the Socialist Party toward the Korean War]" in *Shiryō: Shakaitō yonjū nenshi* [Document: Forty-Year History of the Socialist Party], Shakaitō Chūō Honbu, 1986, pp. 89–90.
34 Igarashi, *Sengo Nichibei kankei no keisei*, pp. 199–200.

Formation of the General Council of Trade Unions and the Korean War

Shortly after the start of the Korean War, the General Council of Trade Unions of Japan (Sōhyō) was formed on July 11, 1950. Sōhyō claimed 3.76 million members, which was equivalent to more than half of all the nation's workers. Immediately after its formation, Sōhyō was pressed to clarify its stance on the Korean War and chose a position similar to that of the Socialist Party. That is, it acknowledged that the war had been caused by North Korean aggression. Furthermore, it adopted a cooperative stance toward the Occupation forces.

For instance, Takano Minoru, who was in charge of organizing for Sōhyō, has left the following analysis. Starting with the disclaimer that "American imperialism is not invasive imperialism," Takano stepped beyond the confines of the Socialist Party platform to state, "The American military is fighting for the development of worldwide democracy because it has no other choice. The present war can be characterized as the war of democracy against North Korean aggression. From this perspective also, it is necessary to abide by orders issued by the Occupation forces." In later years, it was Takano who picked up the mantle of anti-Americanism and played a leading role in redirecting Sōhyō to the left. But at this time, Takano supported a separate peace and the rearmament of Japan.[35]

Sōhyō and the Socialist Party were enmeshed in an ongoing argument over how Japan should support the United Nations. Finally, at the end of August, the Socialist Party organized a discussion meeting with various labor unions —including the National Railways Workers' Union (Kokurō), the National Federation of Industrial Unions (Shin Sanbetsu), the Japan Postal Workers' Union, the All Japan Communication Workers' Union (Zentei), the Council of Japanese Government and Public Workers Unions (Kankōrō), and the All Japan Seamen's Union (Kaiin)—in the course of which a compromise was hammered out on the question of U.N. cooperation. "We have confirmed that there is absolutely no contradiction between the Socialist Party's policy on moral support

---

35 Minami Tadashi, *Nihon no jinmyaku* [Japan's Personal Networks], Nikkan Rōdō Shinbunsha, 1973, pp. 235–238.

and the real economic cooperation that labor unions are providing in that both are predicated on United Nations police actions that aim to protect law and order and build peace."[36]

The People's Democratic Party: The Ashida Initiative

On July 12, the People's Democratic Party held a parliament assembly of its Diet members and voted to abandon its policy of neutrality. The transition was led by Ashida Hitoshi who was on trial at this time for involvement in the Shōwa Denkō scandal. Ashida had long been suspicious of policies of neutrality and overall peace, and his diary entry for this day boasts of "obliterating" the policy of neutrality.[37]

On July 18, Ashida met with Nishio Suehiro to explore the possibility of an alliance with the Socialist Party. Nishio, who at this time had lost his Diet seat and had been expelled from the party, is reported to have said, "The battle has already been joined," and "I think of nothing else all day and night." Nishio continued, "The Socialist Party has a very important role to play, and for this reason I want to put something together. But I have no leads to follow. Yet, I believe that I can accomplish this. I would first talk to Wada Hiroo of the left wing. I would follow this with meetings with Asanuma and Miyake Shōichi, centrists in the party. I would also consult Mr. Katayama. But I have been expelled from the party and have nothing to go on." On his part, Ashida was able to confirm that he shared Nishio's sense of urgency and concluded, "There is no question that Nishio is the best the Socialist Party has."[38]

Be that as it may, the start of the Korean War had pushed the People's Democratic Party to shift its position from overall peace to support for a separate peace.

---

36 *Yomiuri Shinbun*, August 31, 1950.
37 Shindō and Shimokōbe, *Ashida Hitoshi nikki*, (July 12, 1950).
38 Ibid., (July 18, 1950).

The Issue of U.N. Cooperation: Fissure among Political Parties

On July 14, Prime Minister Yoshida delivered his policy speech to the eighth extraordinary session of the Diet. In it, Yoshida mentioned that North Korea had invaded the Southen Korea and that the threat of communism was now at Japan's doorstep, but explained that Japan was in no position to actively participate in the war or to support the activities of the U.N. forces. However, Yoshida emphasized that it was necessary for Japan to cooperate with these efforts within possible limits, and criticized support for an overall peace treaty and permanent neutrality as being nothing more than an empty theory. "This is a form of idealism fraught with danger that would lead the nation straight into the communist stratagem."

On August 19, the Ministry of Foreign Affair Information Department released a statement titled "The Upheaval of the Korean War and Our Position," which argued that the communist world sought to achieve "peace" by destroying the peace of the democratic world. Therefore, the document averred, remaining neutral between the two worlds was impossible and Japan had no means to ensure its security other than to join the community of democratic nations and to actively cooperate with U.N. forces.

The question of U.N. cooperation created a deep fissure among political parties. The People's Democratic Party accepted the Foreign Ministry statement as being justified and advocated active cooperation within the limits allowed under the Constitution. The Socialist Party took the opposite position. A statement released by Katsumata Seiichi, Chairman of the Party's Policy Committee, strongly criticized the position taken by the Foreign Ministry as being arbitrary, dogmatic and wrongheadedly leading the nation into the jaws of international conflict.

At its Fifth National Party Convention held in October 1950, the Communist Party adopted a clearly "anti-American position" and laid out a policy supporting democratic national liberation fronts. Having characterized the international situation in terms of a face-off between "imperialism and the socialist and democratic forces of anti-imperialism," the party argued for the immediate conclusion of an overall peace that included China and the Soviet Union and called for the formation of a "united domestic and international anti-imperialism front." In doing so, the Communist Party abandoned its stance on neutrality and came out in favor of joining forces with China and the Soviet Union. By committing to violent revolution, the party was preparing to take up its role as a player in the International Communist Movement.

In December, acting on a GHQ request, Ashida submitted a position paper on the development of domestic institutions and mechanisms for responding to the Korean War. In it, Ashida underscored the need for rearming Japan. Meeting on December 26, the Special Committee on Foreign Affairs of the People's Democratic Party echoed the Ashida position paper and outlined a treaty negotiating policy that featured the strengthening of Japan's autonomous defense capabilities and preserving national security through the United Nations.[39]

The People's Democratic Party Conference was convened at the end of December. The party agreed to support a separate peace as a means to achieving an early peace treaty, and put together a new party platform that set out policies including joining the United Nations and establishing a collective security system, enhancing police powers for self-defense purposes, achieving economic self-sufficiency, the pursuit of non-partisan diplomacy, and the return of territories acknowledged to be integral to Japan on ethnic, historical, and cartographical grounds (Chishima [the Kurile Islands], the Ryūkyū Islands, and the Ogasawara Islands). Within the party, there was growing support for strengthening Japan's own defenses, the first step of which would be to expand the National Police Reserve Force to 200,000 members.[40]

Intellectuals and Public Opinion

The Peace Problems Council and "On Peace for the Third Time"

The outbreak of the Korean War shocked the intellectuals gathered in the Peace Problems Council and prompted them to write a rebuttal to the Foreign Ministry

---

39 Ōtake Hideo, *Saigunbi to nashonarizumu* [Rearmament and Nationalism], Chūō Kōronsha, 1988, pp. 133–135.
40 Igarashi, *Sengo Nichibei kankei no keisei*, p.161.

statement of August 19. Entitled "On Peace for the Third Time," the statement was published in December 1950.[41]

The Council's statement argued that in an age when war had lost its meaning as a practical measure, the idea of depending on arms for national security was illusory, and that policies based on the renunciation of war and disarmament as stipulated under the Constitution were far more realistic. Furthermore, the statement posited that the ideological confrontation between liberalism and communism did not immediately imply war and that the superpower standoff between the United States and the Soviet Union had created a shared awareness that there would be no winner in a third world war. The statement closed with the argument that insofar as world peace and the happiness of the people constituted the nation's highest aspiration, neutrality was not a policy of convenience affected by the international situation but rather a fundamental position that Japan should subscribe to as a matter of principle.

The Council's statement would later provide those who would become the main supporters of the left wing of the Socialist Party—youth, women, and organized labor—with a theoretical framework for opposing Japan's rearmament.

Public Opinion: Peace Settlement and Rearmament

Where did public opinion stand on "overall peace treaty" versus "separate peace treaties" at a time when this question had split the world of domestic politics into two distinct camps? Answers can be found in a series of public opinion polls conducted between the end of 1949 and 1951 by three of Japan's major newspapers—*Asahi Shinbun*, *Mainichi Shinbun*, and *Yomiuri Shinbun* (Table 5-1).

The first of these polls was conducted by *Mainichi Shinbun* in November 1949 and showed that 45.2 percent of the public supported a separate peace versus 33 percent who favored overall peace. *Asahi Shinbun* conducted its poll in November 1950, a few months after the start of the Korean War. The *Asahi* poll showed that twice as many people favored a separate peace (45.6 percent) than an overall peace (21.4 percent). In January 1951, *Mainichi Shinbun* conducted

---

41 *Sekai*, December issue, Iwanami Shoten, 1950.

its second survey, which indicated that support for a separate peace had risen sharply to 66.3 percent, equivalent to a 21-point gain. Conversely, support for an overall peace had dropped precipitously to 14.3 percent. On the same day, *Yomiuri Shinbun* conducted a poll where it posed the question, "Is an overall peace treaty possible?" Because of the difference in the way the question was formulated, the results of the Yomiuri survey are not directly comparable to the other three polls. Nevertheless, 64.5 percent of the respondents said that an overall peace was not possible versus 7.1 percent who believed it was possible. A stunning nine-fold gap separated the two positions. These results clearly indicate how the U.S.-U.S.S.R. confrontation and the Korean War prompted the public to lean preponderantly toward a separate peace treaty.

The three newspapers also polled the public on the issue of Japan's rearmament. In all instances, those in favor of rearmament widely outnumbered those opposed. In two *Asahi Shinbun* polls conducted in November 1950 and September 1951, those in favor of rearmament were in the majority on both occasions. However, during the ten months that separated the two polls, those in favor had increased by nearly 20 points while those opposed had decreased by 10 points. *Mainichi Shinbun* also conducted two similar polls in January and March 1951. In both instances, those in favor of rearmament exceeded 60 percent of the respondents. It is interesting to note, however, that those opposed to rearmament also increased by 3 points between the two polls.

Yomiuri Shinbun conducted a number of polls on the question of stationing U.S. troops in Japan. The results of a poll taken in August 1949 showed that 46.4 percent supported the stationing of troops. While support declined by four points to 42.5 percent with the start of the Korean War, it bounced sharply back up to 62.8 percent in August 1951. A 1950 poll conducted by *Asahi Shinbun* on the question of U.S. military bases in Japan indicated that those opposed to U.S. military bases outnumbered those in favor by a margin of 37.5 percent to 29.9 percent. However, in a similar poll conducted by *Yomiuri Shinbun* in 1951, more than half of the respondents said that they favored the presence of U.S. military bases.

Table 5-1 Public Opinion Polls Conducted by Three Major National Newspapers (%)

	Date conducted	Form of Peace Treaty			Stationing U.S. Troops in Japan			U.S. Military Bases in Japan			Rearmament		
		Overall	Separate	Don't know	Approve	Dis-approve	Don't know	Approve	Dis-approve	Don't know	Approve	Dis-approve	Don't know
Mainichi	Nov. 21, 1949	33	45.2	21.8									
Yomiuri	Aug. 15, 1949	--	--	--	46.4	35.8	17.8						
Asahi	Nov. 15, 1950	21.4	45.6	33				29.9	37.5	32.6	53.8	27.6	18.6
Yomiuri	Dec. 22, 1950										43.8	38.7	17.5
Mainichi	Jan. 3, 1951	14.3	66.3	19.4	41.2	38.4	20.4				65.8	16.5	17.7
Yomiuri	Jan. 3, 1951	7.1	64.5	28.4	42.5	41.2	16.3						
Mainichi	Mar. 3, 1951				62.8	18.5	18.7				63	19.5	17.5
Yomiuri	Aug. 15, 1951							51.9	29	19.1	50.8	31.5	17.7
Asahi	Sept. 20, 1951										71	16	13

Note: Results from the August 15, 1949 survey conducted by *Yomiuri Shinbun* indicated 73.4 percent were in favor of "permanent neutrality" and 16.6 percent in favor of "collective security."

Source: Compiled by the author from Kanda Fuhito, *Shōwa no Rekishi 8: Senryō to minshu-shugi*, [Shōwa History 8: Occupation and Democracy] (Shogakukan, 1989).

Announcement of the Seven Principles of the Peace with Japan

Seven Principles of the Peace with Japan

The Korean War was a dark cloud that cast a shadow over a peace treaty with Japan. Following the start of hostilities, the U.S. military went back to adopting a negative stance on peace with Japan. On the other hand, judging that war on the Korean Peninsula had awakened the Japanese public from its idyllic fantasy perpetrated by Article 9 of the Constitution, Dulles urged the U.S. government to speed the process of peace negotiations.

Working on the assumption that Japan would join the United Nations at some time in the future, Dulles proposed to the military that the stationing of U.S. troops in Japan would be a "tentative measure" that would remain in place until Japan joined the U.N. and world peace was achieved through collective security under the auspices of the U.N.

In August 1950, the U.S. Joint Chiefs of Staff took the position that a peace treaty should not be allowed to go into effect until a favorable resolution to the Korean War had been reached. On the other hand, the Joint Chiefs of Staff rescinded its previous condition regarding the participation of China and the Soviet Union and consented to pursuing an early and separate peace treaty with Japan.

Responding to this development, on September 11, 1950, the State Department prepared an internal draft of a 26-article peace treaty with Japan. This was distilled into the following Seven Principles of the Peace with Japan, which were released by the State Department on November 24.[42]

1. Parties. Any or all nations at war with Japan which are willing to make peace on the basis proposed and as may be agreed.
2. United Nations. Membership by Japan would be contemplated.
3. Territory. Japan would (a) recognize the independence of Korea; (b) agree to U.N. trusteeship, with the U.S. as administering authority of the Ryukyu and Bonin Islands and (c) accept the future decision of the U.K., U.S.S.R.,

---

42 Unsigned Memorandum Prepared in the Department of State, September 11, 1950, *FRUS*, 1950, East Asia and the Pacific, vol. 6, Document 757.

China, and U.S. with reference to the status of Formosa, Pescadores, South Sakhalin, and the Kuriles. In the event of no decision within a year after the treaty came into effect, the U.N. General Assembly would decide. Special rights and interests in China would be renounced.

4. Security. The Treaty would contemplate that, pending satisfactory alternative security arrangements such as U.N. assumption of effective responsibility, there would be continuing cooperative responsibility between Japanese facilities and U.S. and perhaps other forces for the maintenance of international peace and security in the Japan area.

5. Political and Commercial Arrangements. Japan would agree to adhere to multilateral treaties dealing with narcotics and fishing. Prewar bilateral treaties could be revived by mutual agreement. Pending the conclusion of new commercial treaties, Japan would extend most-favored-nation treatment, subject to normal exceptions.

6. Claims. All parties would waive claims arising out of war acts prior to September 2, 1945, except that (a) the Allied Powers would, in general, hold Japanese property within their territory and (b) Japan would restore allied property or, if not restorable intact, provide yen to compensate for an agreed percentage of lost value.

7. Disputes. Claims disputes would be settled by a special neutral tribunal to be set up by the President of the International Court of Justice. Other disputes would be referred either to diplomatic settlement, or to the International Court of Justice.

On September 14, President Truman announced the start of preliminary negotiations on peace with Japan.

Different Reactions Among U.N. Members

The Soviet Union and China immediately reacted to the announcement of the Seven Principles.

The Soviet Union first raised the question of participation in the peace treaty. Would all or only some of the four Allied Powers consisting of the U.S., Britain,

China, and the Soviet Union participate? Next, the Soviet Union pointed out that matters related to Taiwan and the Pescadores had already been resolved by the Cairo and Potsdam Declarations, and that the question of returning the southern part of Sakhalin Island and handing over the Kurile Islands had been decided in the Yalta Agreement. In this connection, the Soviet Union questioned what reason there was to seek a new decision on these matters by the four countries. The Soviet questions continued. What was the basis for placing the Ryūkyū and Bonin Islands under U.N. trusteeship and U.S. administration? In connection with cooperative responsibility for the maintenance of international peace and security in the Japan area, did this imply the creation of a Japanese army, a Japanese navy, and a Japanese air force, as well as the corresponding Japanese staffs? Did "joint responsibility" mean that even after the conclusion of a peace treaty with Japan, American army, naval, and air force bases would be maintained on the territory of Japan?

China (the Beijing government) claimed that any peace treaty not attended by China was "unlawful and void." Beyond that, China took the same position as the Soviet Union and argued that there was no reason to re-examine matters related to Taiwan, the Pescadores Islands, the southern part of Sakhalin Island, and the Kuriles because these had already been decided by the Cairo Declaration and the Yalta Agreement. As to the trusteeship of the Ryūkyū and Bonin Islands, China claimed that this proposal revealed America's intent to maintain long-term occupation of these territories. Finally, China criticized the rearmament of Japan as an attempt to make Japan a colony of the United States and to enlist it as tool of American aggression against Asian nations.[43]

Britain, the Netherlands, and France took a generally favorable stance toward a "soft peace." However, Britain was critical of Japan's re-emergence as a competitor in Asian markets and unhappy with the fact that the Seven Principles contained no provisions for restraining Japan's economic activities.

Australia, New Zealand, and the Philippines opposed Japan's rearmament and strongly resisted any "soft peace" that would not be accompanied by strict guarantees against future Japanese aggression. Lastly, the Philippines and Burma strongly opposed the cancellation of reparations.

---

43 *Asahi Shinbun*, December 6, 1950.

From the Incheon Landing Operation to Entry of the Chinese People's Volunteer Army

On September 15, 1950, a day after the Truman statement, a critical turning point came in the Korean War. Mobilizing the U.N. forces that had retreated to the area around Busan, MacArthur set in motion a grand counterattack by boldly landing his forces in Incheon near the capital city of Seoul. This surprise attack succeeded in taking back Seoul by September 28. Attacked from behind, the North Korean Army collapsed and was forced into a disorganized retreat. At this point, Truman allowed MacArthur to cross over the 38th parallel in pursuit of North Korean forces, subject to certain conditions. First, the Army, Navy, and Air Force were barred from crossing the borders of China and the Soviet Union. Second, only South Korean forces were to be deployed in areas abutting these borders.

On October 1, the U.N. Forces crossed the 38th parallel and continued to advance northward to take Pyongyang by October 19. During this period, China continued to issue warnings that the crossing of the 38th parallel by U.N. Forces constituted a serious threat to China's security. Finally, upon confirming the advance of U.S. forces to its borders, China sent the Chinese People's Voluntary Army into the war. The conflict had now taken on the dimension of the "United States and South Korea" versus "China and North Korea."

The People's Voluntary Army pushed the U.N. Forces back to around the 38th parallel and on January 4, 1951 Seoul was once again occupied by the North Korean Army. Thereafter, the U.N. Forces regrouped and pushed back. By June, the war had reached a stalemate.

Okinawa in Japan's Peace Treaty

The Korean War and Okinawa

At the start of the Korean War, the U.S. military was in the midst of a major construction rush to build up its bases in Okinawa. Hostilities on the Korean Peninsula placed huge demands on U.S. military forces in Okinawa, and the island's military bases were quickly drawn into the war effort as critically important forward bases. Among the people of Okinawa, blackouts and air-raid drills revived the dreadful memories of the Battle of Okinawa that had been fought five years earlier.

On June 30, Okinawa Governor Shikiya Kōshin released a statement to the public saying, "Let us avoid unnecessary disorder, and let us redouble our efforts toward reconstruction." On July 3, Military Governor Josef Sheetz reassured the public that normality would be maintained throughout the Ryūkyū Islands. "The United States is not at war. As a member of the United Nations, it is merely engaged in police actions aimed at resisting the wrongful invasion of the South Korean republic by the criminal forces of North Korea."[44]

It should be noted that postwar histories of Okinawa contain limited references to the period of the Korean War, making it difficult to ascertain what exactly was happening in Okinawa and how the people were living during this period.

Uruma Shinpō, a local Okinawa newspaper, carried a large number of articles touching on the Korean War, but also gave substantial space to reports related to local elections taking place throughout the Ryūkyū Islands. Particularly noteworthy, however, are a series of articles that appeared at the end of August and the end of October 1950. The earlier period coincided with U.S. military efforts to reinforce police organizations throughout the Ryūkyū Islands, and the latter with the formation of the Ryukyuan Special Police Battalion. Coming two and a half months after MacArthur's order to create the National Police Reserve Force, the Ryukuan Special Police Battalion was in effect the Okinawa version of the same initiative.

On December 1, 1950, the U.S. military government issued an order to the governors of the Ryūkyū Islands concerning the "Special Police Force." Although it is difficult to follow the developments that ensued, what is clear is that a police reserve force ultimately was not established in Okinawa.

---

44 *Okinawa Times*, July 4, 1950.

Governors and Assembly Elections

Governor and regional assembly elections in the four island chains of Okinawa, Miyako, Yaeyama, and Amami were held over September and October 1950.

In the election for governor of Okinawa, the first candidate to declare was Matsuoka Seiho, Director of the Engineering Department of the Okinawa civilian government. Matsuoka derived his power from controlling the recovery and reconstruction budget that drew its funds from U.S. economic assistance. The second candidate was Taira Tatsuo, director of the Ryūkyū Ministry of Agriculture and Forestry, who was supported by farming and fishing interests, the youth, and teachers. Senaga Kamejirō, president of the People's Party, was the third candidate. There were no major differences in policy among the candidates, and the three made no effort to clarify their positions on Okinawa's future international status or the presence of U.S. military bases.[45] In later years, Taira explained this omission saying, "This was when it was taboo to even mention reversion to Japan." With nearly 160,000 votes, Taira won the election in a landslide, garnering more than twice the number of votes cast for Matsuoka. The other winners in the gubernatorial races were Nishihara Gaichi (Miyako), Asato Tsumichiyo (Yaeyama), and Nakae Sanetaka (Amami).

On November 4, 1950, five years after the end of the war, for the first time the government of the four islands chains were launched headed by governors who had been elected in direct public elections.

One week later, elections were held for the regional assemblies of the four island chains. Okinawa and its proximate islands were divided into ten electoral districts and assigned two representatives each. A total of 43 candidates vied for these seats. (The People's Party and the Democratic Alliance had nominated four and three candidates, respectively, while all other candidates ran as independents.) The election registered an 86 percent turnout. One member of the People's Party gained victory in the election, and political parties were unable to exert much influence.

---

45 Higa Mikio, *Okinawa: Seiji to seitō* [Okinawa: Politics and Political Parties], Chūō Kōronsha, 1965, p. 234.

Formation of the Okinawa Social Mass Party

The election results triggered a series of changes in Okinawa's political world. Having failed to win any seats in the election, the Democratic Alliance dissolved itself in October 1950 and merged with the Republican Party that had been formed by groups that supported Matsuoka. In its platform, the Republican Party called for the creation of a unified government for all of the Ryūkyū Islands and advocated the political independence of Okinawa.

On the other hand, Taira and his supporters took to actively criticizing the existing political parties—the Democratic Alliance, the People's Party, and the Okinawa Social Party—which they attacked in turn as "a party too intent on finding fault with the Civil Administration, a party that is beginning to oppose the positions of the United States, or a party that is obsessed with the issue of the trusteeship of Okinawa." After the election, the Taira group started to work toward establishing a new political party that would "contribute to building a new Ryūkyū." The idea was to create a party based on the support of "farmers, fishermen, medium-sized manufacturing enterprises, and workers in general" that would win wide popular support.

The Social Mass Party was founded on October 31 with Governor Taira Tatsuo as its chairman. In its party platform, the newly created entity proclaimed the following three positions: (1) awareness and responsibility for politics of the people and for the people, (2) creating a people's party based on the values of humanism, and (3) uniting the powers of the masses to build a new Ryūkyū. Nowhere did the party platform mention reversion to Japan. By enrolling fifteen of the twenty local assembly members, the Social Mass Party emerged as the ruling party led by the governor.[46]

---

46 Okinawa Social Mass Party Historical Materials Committee, ed., *Okinawa shakai taishū-tō shi* [History of the Okinawa Social Mass Party], 1981, pp. 215–217.

FEC Directive: Establishment of the Ryūkyū Provisional Central Government

In December 1950, the Far Eastern Command issued its "Directive for the United States Civil Administration of the Ryukyu Islands." Pursuant to the directive, the military government was renamed the United States Civil Administration of the Ryūkyū Islands (USCAR), but no change was made in the fact that all administrative agencies remained under the control of USCAR. USCAR was placed under the authority of MacArthur as the Supreme Commander of the Far East Command, while its actual operations were commanded by the Deputy Commander for Military Government, a post that was assigned to the commander of the Ryukyuan Command. The "fundamental democratic freedoms" of the population were guaranteed only within "such limits as do not hamper the military occupation."

Initially, USCAR considered creating a "federal system" by establishing a "central government" that would sit atop the regional governments of the four island chains (Okinawa, Amami, Miyako, and Yaeyama).

In March 1951, USCAR issued Proclamation No. 3, which was followed on April 1 with the formation of a provisional central government. Higa Shūhei, chairman of the Interim Ryūkyūs Advisory Council and member of the Okinawa Social Mass Party, was appointed to head the provisional central government. To achieve geographic balance, Izumi Arihira of the Amami Islands was appointed his deputy. However, sufficient efforts were not made to differentiate the powers and functions of the provisional central government and the governments of the four island chains. This ambiguity would later invite a dispute that would split Okinawa politics in two.

Homeland Reversion Movement Hits a Snag

The announcement of the State Department's Seven Principles of the peace with Japan at the end of 1950 had the effect of setting off a heated debate on the future of Okinawa.

In February 1951, the People's Party invited Okinawa's other political parties to a non-partisan four-party discussion on the future status of Okinawa.

The Social Mass Party and the People's Party advocated an immediate reversion to Japan. However, the Republican Party stood for independence and the Social Party favored trusteeship administration by the United States. Thus, no consensus could be reached. In March, the Social Mass Party and the People's Party held party conventions and formally committed to the reversion movement. On March 19, following a lengthy debate, the regional assembly of Okinawa adopted a resolution for reversion. Pushing aside the opposition of three Republican assembly members who advocated independence, the resolution was passed with a vote count of seventeen to three.

On April 29, the Association for the Return of Okinawa to Japan was formed around the two parties favoring this course of action. Concurrently, a signature drive was launched by the Okinawa Youth Federation and Shinshinkai, literally the New Frontier Society, the youth arm of the Okinawa Social Mass Party targeting local councils and residents above the age of twenty. Within three months, the campaign had collected 195,000 signatures, which represented 72.1 percent of the target population. The signatures were then sent to Prime Minister Yoshida and Special Envoy Dulles.

However, this did not mean that Okinawa was united in seeking reversion. As mentioned, the Republican Party advocated independence, arguing that the "greatest cause of Okinawa's poverty" was the Japanese rule that began with the establishment of the Ryūkyū Domain. The Republican case for independence was predicated on the continuation of U.S. support and assistance.

In June, Higa Shūhei, the head of the Ryūkyū Provisional Government, commented that talk of reversion was "premature." In his statement, Higa said, "I do believe that Okinawa will eventually be returned to Japan. However, we need to take a closer look at the present reality. With Japan, Okinawa cannot hope for economic reconstruction, which leaves us with nowhere to turn to other than American assistance. Taking this into consideration, a period of trusteeship is both necessary and inevitable."[47] Higa's statement enraged the Shinshinkai and split the Social Mass Party.

---

47 Toriyama Atsushi, *Okinawa kichi shakai no kigen to sōkoku* [Origins and Conflicts in Okinawa's Military-Base Society], Keisō Shobō, 2013, p. 146.

3. Toward the Conclusion of Two Treaties: The Peace Treaty and the Japan-U.S. Security Treaty

Dulles Returns to Japan: Demands for Rearmament

State-Defense Disagreements during the Korean War

The entry of the Chinese People's Volunteer Army into the Korean War on October 25, 1950, placed the U.N. Forces at an extreme disadvantage, prompting MacArthur to plead with the U.S. government for reinforcements. But the Joint Chiefs of Staff took a negative stance on sending reinforcements and began instead to consider the withdrawal of U.S. forces from the Korean Peninsula. The Joint Chiefs considered the Chinese military fully capable of driving the U.N. Forces out of the Peninsula and were leaning toward prioritizing the security of Japan. MacArthur criticized the U.S. government's talk of retreating and proposed a counterattack on China led by the Chinese Nationalist troops of the Kuomintang that had escaped to Taiwan. The chasm between Washington and the front lines of the war began to widen when the MacArthur proposal was rejected.

Even as the war situation continued to worsen for the U.N. Forces, Dulles continued to actively pursue a peace treaty with Japan. Against the backdrop of unfavorable developments on the Korean Peninsula, on December 8, Dulles reported to Secretary of State Acheson that the U.S. should be prepared to pay a certain price to push negotiations with Japan forward in order to ensure that Japan would join the Free World.

In response to the Dulles recommendation, Acheson decided that given the new situation, peace with Japan should be pursued according to new conditions and he became involved in the negotiations via a memorandum to Secretary of Defense Marshall. Dated December 13, this memorandum marked the start of

State Department negotiations with the Joint Chiefs of Staff and other elements of the U.S. military.[48]

1. Seeking an early conclusion of a peace settlement with Japan without awaiting a favorable outcome of the situation in Korea.
2. Discussing the peace treaty with the assumption that the United States intends to commit substantial armed forces to the defense of the island chains close to the Asian continent.
3. Leaving Okinawa and the Bonin Islands under Japanese sovereignty.
4. Exploration at this time of a possible Pacific Pact.

Acheson received a response on December 28. The military was not prepared to make any concessions on a "favorable outcome of the situation in Korea" as a precondition for seeking an early peace treaty with Japan. Moreover, it countered the idea of defending the island chains adjoining the Asian continent on the grounds that this would sabotage Japan's rearmament efforts. Finally, on the question of Okinawa and the Bonin Islands, the military stated that there was no reason to make "such a concession for nothing." Furthermore, the military was passive in regard to the idea of a Pacific Pact, which could be described as an Asian version of NATO.

At around this time, the U.S. military was preparing for an all-out war with China and was even considering the possibility of a world war. Given that Japan was not equipped to cope with even domestic riots and disturbances, the military was strongly opposed to concluding a peace treaty with Japan "until the constitution is revised and the nation rearms." The military was even opposed to Dulles returning to Japan to negotiate the peace treaty on the grounds that this could stimulate the Soviet Union to launch a resistance movement.

Responding to the military's aggressive push back, Dulles lodged a rebuttal on January 3, 1951, by arguing that postponing negotiations would raise anxiety in Japan and that the United States could be beaten to a treaty by Britain. With

---

48 The Secretary of State to the Secretary of Defense (Marshall), December 13, 1950, *FRUS*, 1950, East Asia and the Pacific, vol. 6, Document 790.

these arguments on the table, Dulles succeeded in winning some concessions from the military. First, the military agreed to defend the island chains along the Asian continent and to support the idea of a Pacific Pact. Concerning Okinawa and the Bonin Islands, the military agreed to leave these under U.S. strategic administration. However, it was left undecided as to whether the peace treaty with Japan should be concluded before the end of the Korean War. It was also unclear whether the pursuit of an early peace agreement with Japan might lead to the dangerous situation of a military response from the Soviet Union, in particular one aimed at the occupation of Hokkaido.

On January 4, Seoul once again came under the control of the North Korean Army, which prompted the issuance of certain contingency orders on January 9. First, the U.S. would continue to fight while assigning top priority to the safety of its troops and to the defense of Japan. Second, if at any time withdrawal from the Korean Peninsula were to be deemed unavoidable, U.S. troops would retreat to Japan.

Under these extremely tense conditions, President Truman reached a decision on January 10 to proceed with the Japan peace agreement without waiting for a favorable outcome in the Korean War. Thereupon, Dulles got the green light to travel to Japan. However, in consideration of the position taken by military authorities, Truman indicated that separate consideration would be given to the timing at which the peace treaty would come into effect.

The Japanese Government Prepares for the Peace Treaty: The Four Proposals

Immediately following President Truman's September 1950 announcement of the start of preliminary negotiations on peace with Japan, the Ministry of Foreign Affairs began working on relevant proposals to be submitted to the prime minister. Between September and the end of 1950, four scenarios for negotiating with the United States were formulated within the ministry under the leadership of Director of the Treaties Bureau Nishimura Kumao. These came to be known under the names of Operation A, Operation B, Operation C, and Operation D.

Completed on October 5, the output of Operation A comprised four documents concerning the following: Assessment of conditions pertaining to the peace agreement, principles of the U.S. draft of the peace treaty, Japan's requests corresponding to the principles of the U.S. draft of the peace treaty, and a statement of appeal to the United States. The four documents embodied Japan's thinking on the peace treaty in general and represented one of the conclusions reached by the Ministry of Foreign Affairs.[49]

Operation A was predicated on the signing of a separate peace and advocated "cooperation with the democratic countries based on the full restoration of sovereignty and equality." On territorial issues, Operation A did not oppose the independence of Korea and the abandonment of all claims and rights in Taiwan and the Pescadores Islands. On the other hand, it called for retaining the Kuriles and not handing them over to the Soviet Union, and sought explicit confirmation that the Ryūkyū and Bonin Islands constituted the territory of Japan. On the question of stationing U.S. troops in Japan, Operation A posited that this would not be based on the special relations that existed between Japan and the United States, and instead sought to relate the matter to the United Nations by claiming that the defense of Japan by U.S. military forces "embodies the functions and responsibilities" of the United Nations. Based on the restrictions of the framework, Operation A took the position that U.S. forces "would be deployed in Japan in response to certain proposals from the Japanese side." First, U.S. forces were to be stationed in Japan for a "specific duration of time (to be as short as possible)." Second, such forces would be "stationed as far as possible from the central parts of Japan." Finally, the cost of stationing such forces would be "borne by the United States."

Operation A opposed the rearmament of Japan, arguing that rearmament would "unquestionably" lead to the bankruptcy of the nation and that incomplete rearmament would have the opposite effect of inviting the aggression of other countries. "Defenselessness is the surest source of security," it averred.

On October 11, Prime Minister Yoshida criticized the Operation A

---

49 Ministry of Foreign Affairs of Japan, ed., *Nihon gaikō bunsho: Heiwa jōyaku no teiketsu ni kansuru chōsho, dai 1 satsu,* [Papers on Japanese Foreign Policy: Records Related to the Conclusion of Peace with Japan, vol. 1] (hereinafter *Papers on the Peace Treaty*), Ministry of Foreign Affairs, 2002.

documents and sent them back to be reformulated. "These are merely and primarily observations made on objective conditions and are short on policy responses." "These documents are composed in the style of an opposition party and are not worthy of any discussion. They need to be re-examined from the perspective of statesmanship."[50] Commenting on the prime minister's scathing criticism, Director Nishimura of the Treaties Bureau later wrote, "At this time, the officers in charge had not yet been able to completely free themselves of the previously existing assumptions of an overall peace treaty. For them, these were terribly sharp words of criticism. However, at the same time, these were also words of silent encouragement."[51]

On the same day, October 11, Operation B completed its draft of matters related to Japan's post-peace treaty security arrangements. Operation B further underscored the importance of Japan's ties to the United Nations by subscribing to the fundamental proposition that the provision of military bases to the United States accorded with the "right of individual or collective self-defense" as provided for under the U.N. Charter.

Created at the request of Yoshida, Operation C put together a proposal for creating a demilitarized Northeast Asia. The concept was to involve six countries (Japan and South Korea, plus the United States, Britain, the Soviet Union, and Taiwan) in demilitarizing the Korean Peninsula and Japan. Predicated on the recognition of the governments of South Korea and Taiwan as the legitimate governments of their territories, the proposal had little chance of being realized.

Operation D was organized by the Foreign Ministry in response to Yoshida's unforgiving criticism of the output of Operation A and was a realistic proposal that had been drafted by "placing themselves in the position of the negotiators and channeling the wisdom and insight of statesmen."

The document produced by Operation D was predicated on the assumption that "Japan must persistently resist the forces of communism and must resolve to cooperate with the democratic countries in maintaining world peace and security" and advocated the following basic principles: (1) While the peace treaty

---

50 *Papers on the Peace Treaty,* vol. 1, p. 572.
51 Nishimura Kumao, *Nihon Gaikōshi 27: Sanfuranshisuko Heiwa Jōyaku* [Diplomatic History of Japan 27: The San Francisco Peace Treaty], Kashima Shuppan kai, 1971, p. 81.

is likely to be entered into with multiple nations, in the event that this proves impossible, Japan should undertake a separate peace with the United States alone. (2) A bilateral Japan-U.S. security treaty should be concluded. This treaty should be separate from the peace treaty and should be entered into on an equal footing with the United States. (3) Japan should permit the stationing of U.S. forces in Japan. (4) For the foreseeable future, Japan should continue to reject rearmament. The fundamental concept was that the United States would be expected to take responsibility for defending Japan because peace and security in Japan and the Pacific region was indispensable to the peace and security of the United States itself.

The Rearmament Exchange: Dulles Returns to Japan

On January 25, 1951, Dulles arrived in Japan on his second visit. On January 26, the Japanese side was handed a memorandum on the seven principles of the peace with Japan plus a list of subjects for discussion. These covered such areas as Japan's territories, national security, and rearmament. Following this exchange, Dulles held his first meeting with Prime Minister Yoshida on January 29.

Dulles: If an agreement had been concluded three years ago, the terms and conditions would have been much more unfavorable for Japan than today. We are not here today to craft and impose the victor's peace on the defeated. We are discussing a peace treaty as friendly nations.

Yoshida: Japan desires the crafting of a treaty that it can accept without damaging its *amour-propre* (self-respect). We hope to regain our independence through a peace treaty. We wish to firmly establish democracy in Japan. We hope to become a self-supporting country. Having achieved these objectives, we hope then to cooperate in strengthening the Free World.

Dulles: Japan talks only about regaining its independence. If Japan desires to regain its independence and become a member of the Free World, how is Japan prepared to contribute to strengthening the Free World? The United States is now fighting for the freedom of the world. As a member of the Free World, how does Japan propose to contribute to this fight?

Yoshida: You ask what contribution we can make, and I suspect you want to know our position on rearmament. Japan today is solely focused on regaining its independence. At this point, the question of how we can cooperate is premature.[52]

From the outset, an uneasy atmosphere pervaded the discussions due to differences over the issue of rearmament.

Citing the following reasons, Yoshida would not budge from this negative stance on rearmament: (1) Japan had not yet recovered to the point where it can withstand the financial burdens of rearmament. (2) Rearmament might expose Japan to the danger of being once again dominated by militarists. (3) Rearmament could create social unrest and open up opportunities for communists. (4) Rearmament could cause a reaction among neighboring countries. It is reported the Dulles seemed quite displeased as Yoshida went over his points. William Sebald, Chief of GHQ's Diplomatic Section, later wrote that Yoshida gave the impression that he "was unprepared to discuss even broad principles" and was there only to sound out his counterpart.[53]

The same evening, Yoshida and Dulles met again in MacArthur's office. MacArthur stepped in to mediate between the two saying, "What the Free World needs from Japan is not military power. That is not practical. Japan has capacity for military production. It has manpower for labor. By supplying materials to Japan, its production capacity can be used to increase the strength of the Free World."[54] Yoshida had gained a trump card in MacArthur's disapproval of Japan's rearmament.

---

52 *Papers on the Peace Treaty,* vol. 2, pp. 19–20.
53 Sebald, *With MacArthur in Japan*, p. 262.
54 Finn, *Winners in Peace*, p. 276.

Yoshida's Decision to Rearm: Toward the Japan-U.S. Security Treaty

On January 30, the Japanese government handed to the American side a document it called "Our View," which was based on the output of Operation D. "Our View" contained several salient points. Japan said that it would ensure its own domestic security but would call on the cooperation of the United Nations and the United States for its international security. Apart from the peace treaty, Japan proposed to enter a bilateral agreement with the United States that would be based on an equal partnership. On the question of rearmament, Japan clearly indicated that rearmament was impossible for the time being.

On the following day, January 31, Yoshida met with Dulles for the second time. As before, Yoshida avoided making any definitive statements on national security but said, "Japan does intend to play a positive role." Finally, Yoshida added that he wished to know what "contribution" the United States wanted Japan to make in the area of joint defense. On the same day, Yoshida brought up the question of the status of the Ryūkyū Islands and made an appeal for maintaining Japanese sovereignty, asking whether Japan and the United States could jointly administer the Ryukyus under the trusteeship of the U.N. Alternatively, Yoshida asked whether the Bermuda pattern be invoked for leasing the Ryūkyūs for a period of 99 years. Dulles shocked Yoshida with his blunt rejection of these proposals saying, "All these matters have already been settled."

The two did not meet again until February 6, during which time bilateral working-level meetings continued. On February 1, the Japanese government submitted a document based on the output of Operation B that was entitled "Proposal for a Japan-U.S. Treaty on Mutual Security." The American side noted its dissatisfaction with the document, which argued that cooperation in the form of a police force and manufacturing capacity was insufficient and that cooperation should also include "ground forces," and hinted at the need to amend the constitution to open the way to rearmament. The following day, the American side countered with a document entitled "Agreement Concerning U.S.-Japan Cooperation for Mutual Security," which contained provisions related to military bases in Japan. The gist of the U.S. proposal reflected the wish of the U.S. military, which was that it should be allowed to "place whatever number of troops deemed necessary in any place in Japan for any period of time deemed necessary." Director Nishimura of the Treaties Bureau later complained of the proposal, "It was of such a character that one could not help but be pained from even a single reading."[55]

Faced with persistent U.S. demands for Japan's rearmament, Yoshida found no choice but to propose the establishment of "security forces," Yoshida's proposal submitted on February 3 suggested creating a land and maritime force of 50,000 men. The American side proposed moving forward on two parallel tracks—a formal security treaty plus an administrative agreement that would not require ratification by the Diet.

On February 5, Dulles made two significant pledges to the Japanese government: that the peace treaty would not contain any provisions or conditions related to rearmament and that Japan would not be forced to rearm itself. Having made these two pledges, Dulles handed to the Japanese side a provisional draft of the peace treaty that had been formulated on the basis of the seven principles. While the provisional draft placed the Ryūkyū and Bonin Islands under U.S. administration, Japan's right to self-defense was recognized and all war reparations had been eliminated. These provisions prompted Director Nishimura of the Treaties Bureau to note, "With a single reading, I was deeply touched by the magnanimity and fairness of the document... and was inspired with fresh courage."[56] The Security issue had turned the corner.

In his meeting with MacArthur on February 6, Yoshida touched on why he had brought up territorial issues in his earlier meeting with Dulles. Yoshida explained that given the strong interest of the Japanese people in territorial matters, he had no choice but to bring them up as the leader of the government, but that he was well aware that territorial matters had already been settled. Well aware of MacArthur's position on U.S. possession of Okinawa, Yoshida went out of his way to reassure MacArthur that his comments to Dulles did not hide a deeper intent.

On the same day, Dulles met with Hatoyama Ichirō, Ishibashi Tanzan, and others, and was handed a proposal favoring rearmament.

---

55 Nishimura, *Nihon gaikōshi 27*, p. 92.
56 *Papers on the Peace Treaty*, vol. 2, p. 88.

A final agreement was reached between the U.S. and Japan on February 9. The following day, Dulles met with the Emperor and asked for and received his support for the peace treaty.

Using the Socialist Party as a Negotiating Card

The October 1950 entry of China into the Korean War reignited the simmering conflict between the left and right wings of the Socialist Party on the question of the peace treaty. The right wing began to lean toward accepting a separate peace on the grounds that the Korean War had finalized the split between the U.S. and U.S.S.R.

The seventh convention of the Socialist Party held in January 1951 was dominated by the left wing of the party. It was against this backdrop that a right-wing resolution labeling separate peace unavoidable and implying that rearmament should not be opposed in principle was roundly rejected in a lopsided vote of 342 to 82. Thereupon, the convention adopted a resolution on "four principles" that consisted of the "three principles on peace" plus an additional provision opposing rearmament. The left wing maintained its superior position by electing Suzuki Mosaburō to the post of chairman. The iconic phrase that Suzuki uttered at the convention would later evolve into a widely repeated anti-war slogan: "Youth, do not take up arms. Husbands, never shoulder the soldier's backpack."

During this period, Yoshida was communicating with the Socialist Party's Katsumata Seiichi and Suzuki Mosaburō through his aides, Takemi Tarō and his son-in-law, Asō Takakichi, to request and encourage the Socialist Party to mount a campaign against rearmament.[57] Yoshida was planning to use the Socialist Party's arguments against rearmament as a negotiating card in his discussions with the American side. The ploy can be viewed as a collaborative effort between the Liberal and Socialist Parties.

Encouraged by Yoshida's request, Suzuki further determined to meet with Dulles on February 1 accompanied by the party's Secretary-General Asanuma Inejirō. Suzuki used the meeting to reiterate his opposition to rearming the nation

---

57 Igarashi, *Sengo Nichibei kankei no keisei*, pp. 203–206.

and to communicate requests for (1) realization of Japan's economic self-suffi-ciency, (2) recognition of Japanese sovereignty over southern Sakhalin Island, the Kurile Islands, the Ryūkyūs, and the Bonin Islands, (3) ensuring Japan's security through membership in the United Nations, and (4) Japan's need as an Asian nation for the cooperation of China and India. Suzuki also posed a number of questions. Specifically, he wanted to know how the Soviet Union and the China-U.S.S.R. alliance would be treated in case of a separate peace treaty, and what measures the United States was prepared to take on this matter. Suzuki closed with a repeated request for an overall peace.

Commenting on the position of "positive neutrality" that was repeated by the two representatives of the Socialist Party in their meeting with Dulles, William Sebald, Chief of the Diplomatic Section, wrote that the positions taken by Suzuki and Asanuma demonstrated that "they lacked practical understanding of the world situation and the complexities in negotiating formal peace." With obvious distaste, Sebald characterized the meeting as the "longest and most unsatisfactory" encounter engaged in by Dulles.[58]

When Dulles visited Japan for the third time in April 1951, Suzuki and Asanuma delivered a list of requests based on the "Four Peace Principles." Dulles, however, immediately brushed it aside. In the previous month, Yakov Malik, the Soviet delegate to the United Nations, had announced the suspension of talks with Dulles on subject of peace with Japan. Coming after this development, Dulles declared that the overall peace advocated by the Socialist Party was impossible and that the repeated advocacy of an overall peace was either intended as a criti-cism of the government or was an indication of a desire to prevent a peace.

Transformation of Sōhyō: Opposing Separate Peace in Favor of an Overall Peace

Just as the Korean War had exacerbated the division between the left and right wings of the Socialist Party on the question of the peace treaty, so too was Sōhyō pushed into internal turmoil. During this period, Valeri Burati, Chief

---

58 Sebald, *With MacArthur in Japan*, p. 261.

of the Labor Division of the Economic and Scientific Section, was lobbying the Sōhyō leadership to come out in support of a separate peace. Finally, in January 1951, Sōhyō's Chairman Mutō Takeo and Takano Minoru, Chief of the Organization Section responded that Sōhyō was ready to support a separate peace if two conditions were met. These consisted of assurances that democratic norms and institutions introduced under the Occupation would be maintained, and a pledge of continued U.S. economic assistance, which Sōhyō believed to be indispensable to maintaining working conditions and thereby preventing the infiltration of communists.

At the same time, the two Sōhyō leaders indicated their stance on territorial issues. Specifically, while they demanded the reversion of the Kurile Islands by the Soviet Union, they accepted the leasing of Okinawa to the United States on the condition that Japan's sovereignty would be maintained. It should be noted that Takano expressed opposition to Japan's rearmament.[59]

However, all of this was overturned in the Second Sōhyō Convention held in March when the convention adopted the Socialist Party's "four principles" (support for overall peace and neutrality, and opposition to U.S. military bases and rearmament). While it is unclear what changes were taking place within Sōhyō at this time, what is very clear is that the union council had broken out of its original commitment to anti-communism and was also distancing itself from the framework of the International Confederation of Free Trade Unions to eventually reinvent itself along the ideological lines of neutrality and anti-Americanism. GHQ clearly found the transformation of Sōhyō to be undesirable.

It was at this Second Sōhyō Convention that Takano Minoru, who represented the left wing of the Japanese Federation of Trade Union (Sōdōmei), was elected secretary-general of the organization, and it was under the leadership of Takano that Sōhyō became increasingly combative and anti-establishment in both its economic and political positions. Inevitably, the right wing of Sōdōmei reacted angrily to these developments and the convention held in March 1951

---

59 Nakakita Kōji, *Nihon rōdō seiji no kokusai kankei shi* [History of International Relations of Japan's Labor Politics], Iwanami Shoten, 2008, p. 72.

for dissolving Sōdōmei became a battleground for the two wings of the movement. Subsequently, the right wing called a convention in June for relaunching Sōdōmei, which culminated in April 1954 with the formation of the All-Japan Trade Union Congress, the antecedent to Japan Confederation of Labor (Dōmei).

The International Environment Surrounding the Peace: Responses of Nations other than the United States

The Allied Powers and the Peace

On February 11, Dulles left for the Philippines and Australia to build up Allied support for the peace treaty. Both countries were known for favoring a "hard peace" with Japan. Although it was true that the United States had taken the initiative throughout the peace negotiations, this did not change the fact that the Occupation of Japan was an Allied occupation. Because of that, now that China and the Soviet Union had adopted a hostile stance, it was critically important for the United States to gain the consent and cooperation of the other Allied Powers.[60]

For the United Kingdom, the peace treaty with Japan was essentially a "peripheral" issue. The reconstruction of Germany and the anti-British movements that were gaining force in Iran, Egypt, and Malaya (present-day Malaysia) left little room for Britain to involve itself in the peace with Japan. The most important issue for Britain was how to avoid a retreat from Asia. In this context, Britain, as a major trading nation, saw the recovery of Japan in the Asian region as a major concern.

In comparison, the countries of the Pacific region were home to far more aggressive anti-Japanese sentiments. Among these countries, Australia and New Zealand had made clear that they were adamantly opposed to a "soft peace" that did not contain compelling guarantees against future Japanese aggression. In particular, a deep-seated sense of distrust and wariness toward Japan existed

---

60 This section draws on Watanabe Akio and Miyazato Seigen, eds., *Sanfuranshisuko kōwa* [San Francisco Peace], University of Tokyo Press, 1986, and Hosoya Chihiro, *Sanfuranshisuko kōwa e no michi* [The Road to the San Francisco Peace Treaty], Chūō Kōronsha, 1984.

in Australia. Not only had certain parts of the country experienced Japanese aerial bombings, but Australian soldiers had fought directly against the Japanese military as part of the British Commonwealth forces. Australian public opinion calling for a "hard peace" created a level of pressure that simply could not be ignored. For Australians, it was a question not of how Japan could be protected but of how they would be protected from Japan. For this reason, Australia continued to make stern demands for restricting Japan's rearmament and economic resurgence.

The same was basically true for the Philippines where 1.1 million lives had been lost during the war. In addition to opposing a soft peace, the Philippines was deeply dissatisfied with the changes that had occurred in U.S. Occupation policies beginning in 1948. Throughout this period, the Philippines maintained the position that continued efforts should be made to move the processes of economic, social, and political democratization forward in Japan and was deeply concerned by the possibilities of the rebirth of Japan as an industrial and military power. Naturally, the Philippines did not wish to forgo its claims on Japan for the payment of reparations.

It was India that manifested a forgiving and flexible attitude toward Japan. Under the leadership of Prime Minister Nehru, India subscribed to the view that Japan's economic recovery would benefit the whole of Asia and supported a series of policies and measures that would speed Japan's reconstruction and its re-entry into the international community. Furthermore, India opposed the placement of any restrictions on the Japanese economy and expressed the hope that Japanese technology and other forms of aid would flow to it. During this period, India was searching for a "third power" that stood apart from both the United States and the Soviet Union, and it was also anxious to find a way to bring lasting peace to Asia and the Far East. In August 1951, India announced that it was prepared to end the state of war and enter into a peace treaty with Japan. Ultimately, however, India did not participate in the peace conference due to its dissatisfaction with the stationing of U.S. forces in Japan and a series of territorial issues pertaining to the Ryūkyū and Bonin Islands, Taiwan, the Kurile Islands, and the southern part of Sakhalin Island.

The Pacific Pact: A Failed Attempt at Creating an Asian Version of NATO

Differences in attitudes toward Japan and the peace treaty among the Allied Powers generated growing disharmony on the issue of security in the Pacific region.

In May 1950, President Quirino of the Philippines proposed the creation of a Pacific Pact modeled after NATO. The idea was to establish an anti-communist regional organization that, among others, would include Japan and the government of Taiwan. Although anti-Japanese sentiment was strong in the Philippines and President Quirino's own wife and children had been killed by the Japanese army, Quirino concluded that his Pacific Pact would rekindle the interest of the United States in the region while also serving to counter any future threat from Japan. However, Australia and New Zealand expressed strong reservations about the membership of not only Japan but also the Taiwan government. Their argument was that the proposed composition of the Pacific Pact could very easily draw them into conflicts arising in the northern Pacific region.

In September 1950, Australian Foreign Minister Percy Spender conveyed to Dulles that Australia had a strong interest in matters related to the rearmament of Japan and security arrangements designed to counter any future Japanese aggression. Spender followed this with a proposal for creating an expansive regional alliance covering Australia, New Zealand, the Philippines, the United States, Canada, and the Pacific coast countries of South America. The United States responded that Soviet expansionism posed the greatest present threat and sought to incorporate Japan into the policy of "Soviet containment" as a bulwark against Soviet expansion. In effect, the United States viewed Spender's proposed alliance as a collective defense framework that was indispensable to countering the Soviet threat. On the other hand, the greatest threat for Australia remained the "revival of Japanese military power." Stranded on these differences in perception, the alliance failed to materialize.

At the end of 1950, the idea of a Pacific Pact re-emerged within the U.S. State Department as U.N. Forces were beating a hasty retreat southward on the Korean Peninsula. In this iteration, the Pacific Pact would include five countries: Japan, the United States, the Philippines, Australia, and New Zealand. (Canada was initially included.) The primary objective of the alliance would be to defend Japan and to prevent its absorption into the communist camp. It was argued that the rearmament of Japan was absolutely necessary. Japan's land forces would be rebuilt and operate in tandem with U.S. naval and air support to defend the Japanese homeland.

Britain reacted strongly and negatively to a Pacific security framework that did not include it, and Australia claimed that its national security demanded the application of certain restrictions on Japan's rearmament.

Faced with opposition from Britain and negative reaction from Australia, the United States abandoned its hope for a multilateral Pacific Pact and instead moved to conclude mutual defense security pacts with the countries of the region. The first of these mutual security treaties was concluded between the U.S. and the Philippines in August 1951, followed by the signing of the ANZUS Security Treaty with Australia and New Zealand in September.

Dismissal of MacArthur

Yoshida Requests Changes in Occupation Policy

On April 9, 1951, Yoshida wrote to MacArthur requesting the review and revision of various policies implemented under the Occupation in a letter titled "Laws and ordinances promulgated under the Occupation whose revision or abolition are desirable."

The scope of Yoshida's proposed review and revision was extremely broad and included the local government system (strengthening the supervisory powers of the Cabinet), the family system (legislating the head-of-household status, reinstating primogeniture), the police system (police centralization for more efficient cooperation between national rural police and autonomous police forces), the education system (abolishing the independent status of boards of education, revising the six-three school system), economic laws (easing the Antimonopoly Law), the Code of Criminal Procedure (restricting the rights of defendants and suspects), labor laws (easing regulations to correspond to the Labor Standards Law), and the reorganization of administrative agencies (abolishing administrative committees). The proposed changes spoke to the very essence of the reforms that had been implemented by GHQ.[61]

However, the letter did not reach MacArthur due to his sudden dismissal. Against the backdrop of the stalemate in the Korean War, MacArthur had on March 24, 1951, referred to the possibility of expanding the war to China's "coastal areas and interior bases." This was enough for President Truman to dismiss MacArthur on April 11. Lieutenant General Matthew Ridgway, who until then was commanding the ground forces in Korea, was appointed to succeed MacArthur on the following day, April 12.

Informed of MacArthur's dismissal, Chief Sebald of GHQ's Diplomatic Section rushed to the prime minister's residence to convey a message received from the State Department. Of his late night meeting with Yoshida, Sebald writes, "Yoshida was visibly shaken."[62] The message conveyed by Sebald was intended to assure the Japanese government that the "change in commanders in Japan in no manner signified any change in United States policy toward Japan, the impending peace treaty, or the Far East."[63]

The following day, all the major newspapers carried front-page headlines that screamed, "MacArthur Dismissed," while the editorial columns uniformly wrote that MacArthur's departure was "regrettable." For instance, *Yomiuri Shinbun* wrote, "At least for us, the dismissal of General MacArthur comes as a complete surprise and is a source of great sorrow." The column continued with a eulogy. "General MacArthur was a soldier, but at the same time he was the most understanding leader for postwar Japan.... The Japanese nation, destroyed and standing in ruins because of the outrageous actions of the Japanese military, was rebuilt by a soldier of the former enemy—General MacArthur. What is more, this soldier worked assiduously and never failed to encourage the democratization of the Japanese people. Who is there to object to the expression of gratitude to General MacArthur as the benefactor of Japan's rebirth?"

On April 15, the Emperor visited MacArthur at the American Embassy to

---

61 Sodei, *Correspondence between General MacArthur, Prime Minister Yoshida & Other High Japanese Officials [1945-1951]*, pp. 213–221.
62 Sebald, *With MacArthur in Japan*, p. 229.
63 Ibid., p. 228.

say farewell. Early the next morning, April 16, MacArthur left Japan. Chief Whitney of the Government Section also left to return home. Miyazawa Kiichi describes the events of that day in the following passage of his memoirs.

In any case, within GHQ and around Japan, there was a general feeling that MacArthur was being crucified. The send-off for him was huge. People lined the streets from Tokyo's Hibiya district to Haneda airport on both sides, something not seen before or after.... In any case, the people who came to bid farewell [the prime minister, members of the cabinet, and their aides], unlike the ordinary people, were those who had suffered in some way directly at the hands of the Occupation. Even if we were personally grateful to MacArthur, there were likely few people who were truly sorry to see him go. Although there was an eerie silence throughout the farewells, as soon as MacArthur got on the top landing of the stairs to go inside the plane, one of the Cabinet Ministers screamed out, 'General MacArthur, Banzai!' and everyone raised their arms. If someone who looked the other way and did not do this, he would have been labeled a serious 'resister,' I imagine. This label was something that was feared at the time in Occupied Japan.[64]

The Diet was in recess when MacArthur left Japan, but in the afternoon of the same day, the two houses convened in plenary sessions to unanimously adopt a resolution of gratitude. On the same evening, April 16, Dulles arrived in Tokyo on his third visit to Japan.

Frank Rizzo Appointed Chief of the Government Section

Following Whitney's departure, Frank Rizzo was promoted from his deputy post to head the Government Section on April 17. With the signing of the peace treaty close at hand, there was very little left for the Government Section to do.

Soon after his appointment, Rizzo sent a memorandum to Far East

---

64 Miyazawa, *Secret Talks between Tokyo and Washington*, pp. 37–38.

Command Assistant Chief of Staff, Lieutenant General Doyle Hickey. Dated April 21 and titled "Reorganization of the Government Section," the memorandum outlined plans for revamping the Government Section and reducing its personnel. Regarding the responsibilities of the Government Section, Rizzo proposed that the raison d'etre of the Government Section would be "to advise concerning the progressive relaxation of Occupation supervision and control of the Japanese Government in order that dangers of political vacuum, uncertainty, and possible crisis upon the elimination of the SCAP [Supreme Commander of Allied Powers] authority is minimized."[65]

Within the Government Section, the functions of the Public Affairs Division were absorbed into the Parliamentary and Political Division during April, followed by the dissolution of the Civil Service Division on June 30. This left the Government Section with only three divisions—the Administrative, Public Administration, and the Parliamentary and Political Divisions.

On April 19, just two days after being appointed chief of the Government Section, Rizzo responded to Chief of Staff Hickey regarding the contents of Yoshida's April 9 letter to MacArthur. Referring to the letter outlining Yoshida's proposals for reviewing and revising Occupation policies, Rizzo wrote that wide-ranging revisions to the laws and systems adopted under the Occupation could give the impression that democratic reforms were being abandoned and could consequently obstruct the conclusion of the peace treaty.[66] On April 23, Rizzo summoned Chief Cabinet Secretary Okazaki Katsuo to GHQ to convey GHQ's opposition to revising Occupation policies.

It should be noted that shortly before this meeting, Yoshida had met with Dulles and Ridgway on April 18 and had directly appealed to them on the revision of Occupation policies, stating that he was submitting the proposals with MacArthur's agreement in principle and "with the full knowledge of Mr. Dulles."

---

65 Fukunaga, *GHQ Minsei-kyoku shiryō, bekkan*, p. 29.
66 "Letter from the Prime Minister to General MacArthur," (April 19, 1951), Ogura, ed., in *GHQ Minsei-kyoku shiryō, 11*, pp. 27–28.

Ridgway's Statement: Depurge

In a statement released on May 1, 1951 to coincide with the fourth anniversary of the promulgation of the Constitution of Japan, General Ridgway announced that authority to re-examine the laws and ordinances enacted under the Occupation would be transferred to the Japanese government. Acting on this announcement, Yoshida appointed an Ordinances Review Committee within the office of the prime minister and launched a wide-ranging review and revision of laws and policies adopted under the Occupation.

Membership of the Ordinances Review Committee consisted of Kimura Tokutarō (former Minister of Justice), Nakayama Ichirō (Hitotsubashi University professor), Maeda Tamon (former Minister of Education), Obama Toshie (senior adviser to *Nihon Keizai Shinbun*), Ishizaka Taizō (president of Toshiba Corporation), Itakura Taizō (president of Jiji Shinpōsha), and Hara Yasusaburō (president of Nippon Kayaku). Later, Maeda was replaced by Tanaka Jirō (University of Tokyo professor) and Ishibashi Tanzan (former Minister of Finance) was added to the committee when his purge was lifted.

The committee convened for the first time on May 14 and established that the "spirit of the directives issued by General Headquarters shall be preserved" and the "democratic direction shall be resolutely upheld." The committee would re-examine issues of a depurge, administrative agencies and organizations, the education system, anti-monopoly laws, laws and regulations on labor relations, and the police system.

The government immediately moved to end the purge upon receiving the recommendations of the committee. Subsequently, on June 20, the purge was lifted on approximately 3,000 individuals, including Ishibashi Tanzan, Miki Bukichi, and Kōno Ichirō. Phase two was announced on August 6 covering about 14,000 individuals. This second depurge affected a number of key political figures, including Hatoyama Ichirō, Matsumoto Jiichirō, Ōhasa Tadao, Kawakami Jōtarō, Kōno Mitsu, and Ogata Taketora.

After holding a total of 31 meetings, the Ordinance Reviews Committee was suddenly dissolved on March 12, 1952. Appearing before the committee, Prime Minister Yoshida announced, "The committee has already fulfilled its mission and is now dissolved." Remarking on this unexpected denouement, Ishibashi wrote in his diary, "Although I was not against dissolving the committee, I was a little surprised at the sudden dissolution order."[67]

What truly surprised Ishibashi was that this dissolution had come only a month after the committee had "generally agreed" to the proposal that Ishibashi had submitted to the committee suggesting that its agenda should include the examination of constitutional revision. Prime Minister Yoshida was anxious to avoid any discussion of constitutional revision ahead of the approaching peace conference.

Origins of "Reverse Course"

The formation of the Ordinance Review Committee and the beginning of the easing of the purge triggered a wave of criticism against the phenomenon of "reverse course" in the process of Japan's democratization.

For instance, during the one month between November 2 and December 2 of 1950, the *Yomiuri Shinbun* published a special 25-part series of articles that for the first time used the term "reverse course." The first installment contained the passage, "It is as if we are living now in the age of 'reverse course.' The start of the resurrection of many prewar things informs us that the lifting of the purge is not a privilege limited to people."

In its list of "prewar things" making a comeback, the article mentions such things as the Warship March, samurai swordplay films (*chanbara*), Yasukuni Shrine, high-handed policemen, the Organizations Control Order, and the Imperial Rescript on Education (*kyōiku chokugo*). Midway through the series, the paper analyzed "reverse course" in an editorial underscoring the serious misgivings that the editors had. "As we look to recent social developments, we see numerous strange phenomena and a frightening relapse that holds no kinship to the spirit of reform that permeated the nation just a few years ago when the new Constitution of Japan was going into effect. It would be truly tragic if this process were to move forward without eliciting the surprise of the members of society."[68]

---

67 Ishibashi Tan'ichi and Itō Takashi, eds., *Ishibashi Tanzan nikki* [Diary of Ishibashi Tanzan], Misuzu Shobō, 2010, (March 12, 1952).
68 *Yomiuri Shinbun*, November 15, 1950.

The San Francisco Peace Conference

Anglo-American Confrontation over China

By the end of 1950, the British government had finished putting together its basic paper on the peace treaty with Japan. However, a firm consensus had yet to be formed among the members of the British Commonwealth. India, Pakistan, and Ceylon (present-day Sri Lanka) supported a "soft peace," while Australia and New Zealand insisted on a "hard peace" that would restrict Japan's industrial recovery and rearmament.

The British proposal contained the following points on the contents of the peace treaty. (1) Regarding territorial issues, explicit provisions should be made for the return of Taiwan and the Pescadores Islands to "China." (2) China (the Beijing government) should be invited to participate in the peace conference. (3) The stationing of U.S. forces in Japan and the conclusion of a Japan-U.S. security agreement should be accepted. (4) Regarding economic matters, restrictions should be placed on Japan's shipbuilding capacity. The British proposal contained no mention of Japan's rearmament.

In March 1951, the United States conveyed its draft of the peace agreement to a group of fifteen nations consisting of the member states of the Far Eastern Commission plus South Korea, Indonesia, and Ceylon. The draft was based on the "Seven Principles of the Peace with Japan" and comprised a total of eight chapters covering such matters as terminating the state of war, the reinstatement of sovereignty, the territory of Japan, and Japan's national security. The same draft agreement was handed to the Japanese government on March 27.

During April and May, the United States and Britain engaged in extensive consultations on the contents of the draft. The most important point of contention between the two countries was the issue of China for which no easy compromise could be found. Britain had already recognized the Beijing government in January of the previous year and held fast to its position that Taiwan and the Pescadores Islands should be returned to "China" and that the Beijing government should be invited to participate in the peace conference. The British position was that Japan had traditionally maintained close economic ties with the Asian continent and that it was unwise to sever these ties by seating the

Taiwan government at the peace conference.

Dulles countered that the United States had not recognized the Beijing government and therefore could not invite it to participate in the peace negotiations. On territorial issues, Dulles pointed out that the Cairo Declaration stated, "Manchuria, Formosa, and the Pescadores shall be restored to 'the Republic of China'" and contained no mention of ceding Taiwan to the People's Republic of China. The "Seven Principles of the Peace with Japan" posited that the status of Taiwan, Pescadores, South Sakhalin, and the Kuriles would be settled under a single "future decision" reached by the United States, Britain, the Soviet Union, and China, and that "Japan would accept" this decision. Based on this, Dulles argued that the peace treaty should go no further than to affirm that Japan had abandoned all rights, titles, and claims to Taiwan and the Pescadores Islands.

Ultimately, the United States and Britain agreed that neither of the two Chinese governments would sign the peace treaty. In other words, neither would be invited to participate in the peace conference, and Japan would be allowed to decide which of the two Chinese governments it would choose to conclude a peace treaty with.

South Korea had announced its intent to participate in the peace conference and that its name at one point appeared in the list of prospective signatories. However, the United States rejected its participation on the grounds that "South Korea had never been in a state of war with Japan and was not a signatory to the Joint Declaration by the United Nations."

Having obtained the prior consent of Britain, the United States released the draft of the full text of the peace treaty on July 12.

On July 16, after comparing the contents of this draft with the Allied peace treaty that had been concluded with Italy, February 1947, the Ministry of Foreign Affairs welcomed the draft as being conciliatory. For instance, the treaty with Italy contained a war responsibility clause and was predicated on Italy's unconditional surrender and the "unconditional" character of the surrender. By comparison, the treaty with Japan declared, "The Allied Powers and Japan are resolved that henceforth their relations shall be those of nations which, as sovereign equals, cooperate in friendly association." Whereas the peace with Italy provided for the supervision of Italy by the Allied Powers for a "period not to exceed eighteen months from the coming into force of the present Treaty," the treaty with Japan did not contain any supervisory provision.

On July 20, the United States and Britain issued formal letters of invitation to a peace conference to be held in San Francisco beginning on September 4. The recipients were 49 countries that had declared war on Japan. Following this, the final American draft of the Japan-U.S. Security Treaty was received on August 14.

The San Francisco Peace Conference

The San Francisco Peace Conference opened on September 4, 1951 with 52 participating countries including Japan. Six years had passed since the signing of the Instrument of Surrender on board the USS *Missouri* anchored in Tokyo Bay. Neither the Beijing government nor the Taiwan government had been invited to represent China. Three non-aligned nations—India, Burma, and Yugoslavia—declined to attend. Japan was represented by Prime Minister Yoshida as chief delegate and plenipotentiary. Ikeda Hayato and Hoshijima Nirō of the Liberal Party accompanied Yoshida as plenipotentiary delegates, as did Tomabechi Gizō, Chairman of the People's Democratic Party. Two other Japanese plenipotentiary delegates were in attendance—lower house member Tokugawa Muneyoshi of the Ryokufūkai and Governor of the Bank of Japan Ichimada Hisato.

The United States and Britain could not hide their shock at seeing an "uninvited guest," the Soviet Union, at the conference. The next day, the United States and the Soviet Union immediately clashed over rules of procedure. This was followed by speeches given by the chief delegates of the U.S., Britain, and the Soviet Union.

Dulles, the chief U.S. delegate, touched on the developments leading to the conclusion of the peace treaty and prefaced his explanation of the provisions of the treaty with this statement. "The treaty remains, as first agreed, a non-punitive, non-discriminatory treaty, which will restore Japan to dignity, equality, and opportunity in the family of nations."

Next to take the podium was Kenneth Younger, the chief delegate of Britain. "The peoples of Britain and the Commonwealth have not forgotten the cruel atrocities that accompanied Japanese invasions. The people of Malay and Hong

Kong have not forgotten what they directly experienced under Japanese occupation. However, we all agree—and India is with us on this point—that hatred and thoughts of revenge must be sublimated into peaceful settlement. We must turn our eyes to the future and not ruminate over the past."[69] Moreover, the chief delegates of the United States and Britain did not fail to mention Japan's residual sovereignty in Okinawa.

The chief Soviet delegate, Andrei Gromyko, took the podium to denounce the treaty at length. First, the treaty contained nothing to block the resurgence of Japanese militarism, nor did it contain any guarantee that the Occupation forces would leave Japan. On the question of territory, Gromyko argued, there were no explicit provisions concerning Chinese sovereignty over Taiwan and the Pescadores Islands, and no explicit provisions for the return and transfer of Sakhalin and the Kurile Islands to the Soviet Union. Gromyko concluded that this stood in violation of international treaties, and broadly criticized the treaty as not being a peace treaty at all but instead a device to prepare for a new war in the Far East.

Yoshida took the podium on September 7 to affirm the "treaty's fairness and magnanimity unparalleled in history." Averring that the treaty "contains no punitive or retaliatory clauses" and that it was an "instrument of reconciliation" and trust, Yoshida announced that the "Japanese Delegation gladly accepts this fair and soft peace." On territorial issues, Yoshida expressed the hope that the administration of the islands of Amami, Ryūkyū, and Bonin would be put back in Japanese hands. He drew attention to the fact that the islands of Etorofu and Kunashiri comprised the territory of Japan and that the islands of Habomai and Shikotan constituted a part of Hokkaido. Finally, he sought the assistance and cooperation of all Allied Powers for the speedy repatriation of Japanese nationals remaining in foreign lands.

The peace treaty was signed on September 8 in the absence of the Soviet Union, Poland, and Czechoslovakia. For the Japanese side, six plenipotentiary delegates signed the instrument. The Treaty of Mutual Cooperation and Security

---

69 Kanda Fumito, *Shōwa no rekishi 8: Senryō to minshu-shugi* [History of Shōwa vol. 8: The Occupation and Democracy], Shogakukan, 1994, p. 438.

Prime Minister Yoshida signs the San Francisco Peace Treaty (morning of September 8, 1951)
The plenipotentiaries of the Japanese delegation—Ichimada Hisato (Governor of the Bank of
Japan), Tokugawa Muneyoshi (Chairperson, General Assembly of Ryokofū kai Members of the
House of Councillors), Hoshijima Nirō (General Affairs Board of the Liberal Party), Tomabechi
Gizō (Supreme Chairman of the People's Democratic Party), and Finance Minister Ikeda Hayato—
gather on the stage awaiting their turn to sign the instrument.

Prime Minister Yoshida signs the Japan-U.S. Security Treaty (evening of September 8, 1951)
Only Yoshida signed the instrument. Yoshida is surrounded by three plenipotentiary delegates
(from left): Ikeda Hayato, Hoshijima Nirō, Ichimada Hisato, and two deputy delegates, Ōnogi
Hidejirō and Yoshitake Eichi.

between the United States of America and Japan (Japan-U.S. Security Treaty), which was inseparable from the peace treaty, was signed the same evening at the Sixth Army command at the Presidio located outside of San Francisco. This second instrument was signed by Yoshida alone in a perfunctory ceremony that is reported to have taken no more than fifteen minutes to complete.

The San Francisco Peace Treaty ended the state of war between Japan and the Allied Powers and allowed Japan to emerge from the Occupation as a sovereign and independent nation.

The treaty comprised a total of twenty-seven articles. Under its terms, Japan recognized the independence of Korea and renounced all right, title, and claim to Formosa, the Pescadores Islands, the Kurile Islands, and Southern Sakhalin. Moreover, Japan accepted U.S. trusteeship of Okinawa and the Bonin Islands (Article 3), the stationing of U.S. forces in Japan, and the judgments of the International Military Tribunal for the Far East (Tokyo Tribunal). On the issue of reparations, it was confirmed that in principle, reparation claims would not be made.

As for the Japan-U.S. Security Treaty, the document stated that, "Japan desires a Security Treaty with the United States" "because irresponsible militarism [Communism] has not yet been driven from the world" and because Japan "has been disarmed." Moreover, the treaty affirmed that "Japan grants, and the United States of America accepts, the right to dispose United States land, air, and sea forces in and about Japan." As for the disposal of these armed forces, the treaty affirmed that specific conditions "shall be determined by administrative agreements between the two Governments."

Public support for the Cabinet dropped from 43.1 percent in October 1949 to 31 percent in April 1950. However, it rose sharply to 58 percent in September 1951. Miyazawa Kiichi, a member of Yoshida's entourage in San Francisco, later commented on the day of the signing of the San Francisco Peace Treaty and the Japan-U.S. Security Treaty in these words. "That night, I was overcome by a vague feeling that the next twenty years or so were going to be a sort of 'tightrope act' for Japan."[70]

---

70 Uchida Kenzō, *Sengo Nihon no hoshu seiji* [Postwar Japan's Conservative Politics], Iwanami Shoten, 1969, pp. 3–4.

Ratification of the Two Treaties: Division of the Socialist Party

The two treaties had now been signed, but the Socialist Party found itself in internal conflict and turmoil over the Peace Treaty and the Japan-U.S. Security Treaty. This was because the right wing and the centrists had come together in favor of separate peace and were now taking a far more confrontational stance toward the left wing, which remained wedded to the concept of an overall peace. The Central Executive Committee at this time consisted of fourteen left-wing members plus a combined sixteen right-wing and centrist members. To prevent an irreparable schism in the party, Secretary-General Asanuma Inejirō and Mizutani Chōzaburō from the center of the party mediated between the two wings by proposing the idea of "yes to the peace treaty and no to the security treaty." It is said that this scheme was suggested to the two by Justin Williams, Chief of the Parliamentary and Political Division of the Government Section.[71]

The two sides of the party clashed in the meeting of the Central Executive Committee held on October 5. Arguing that the two treaties were separable, the right wing and centrists rallied around "yes to the peace treaty and no to the security treaty" (the so-called "white and blue" position), while the left wing opposed both treaties (the so-called "blue and blue" position). With Chairman Suzuki abstaining, the Central Executive Committee adopted colored ballots for voting—white for agreement and blue for opposition—for submission to the party convention. However, the left wing later turned the tables on their opponents and managed to have "white and blue voting" rejected in the party convention held on October 24.

Once again, the Socialist Party stood divided. (The left wing nominated Suzuki Mosaburō for chairman and demanded that the post of secretary-general be left unfilled. The right wing nominated Asanuma Inejirō for secretary-general and demanded that the post of chairman be left unfilled.) At this juncture, the right wing held 29 seats in the House of Representatives compared to 16 seats for the left wing. In the House of Councillors, the right wing and left wing held 30 and 31 seats, respectively.

---

71 Igarashi, *Sengo Nichibei kankei no keisei*, p. 208.

In the time leading up to the division, the left wing was being constantly pressured and goaded by its local organizations and labor unions. Pressure from Sōhyō was particularly strong, with much of it coming from the Workers' Comrade Group (Rōdōsha Dōshikai) of the left wing of Sōhyō. Hinting that they were prepared to form a "new workers party" and rallying around the battle cry of "Don't fear division. Remain loyal to the principles of a socialist political party!" These activist groups peppered the left wing of the Socialist Party with a combination of reproof and encouragement. Working under the slogan, "Never again send your students to war," it was around this time that the Japan Teachers' Union (Nikkyōso) announced its support for the Socialist Party's "four principles of peace." Soon, Kokurō, Zentei, the General Federation of Private Railway Workers' Unions (Shitetsu), the All-Japan Federation of Metal Mining Workers' Unions (Zenkō), the All-Japan Express Workers' Union (Zennittsu), and other labor organizations followed.

On October 26, the Peace Treaty and the Security Treaty were put before the plenary session of the House of Representatives. The Peace Treaty was approved with a vote of 307 in favor and 47 against. Opposition to the treaty came from 22 members of the Communist Party, sixteen members of the Left-wing Socialist Party, four members of the Party for Workers and Farmers, three members from the People's Democratic Party, and two independents. Next, the Japan-U.S. Security Treaty was approved with a vote of 289 in favor and 71 against. The two treaties were then submitted to the House of Councillors on November 18, where the Peace Treaty was carried with a vote of 174 to 45 and the Security Treaty was carried with a vote of 147 to 76. On the following day, November 19, ratification procedures were completed for the two treaties.

After the Peace Conference: Toward Independence

Emergence of Anti-Yoshida Forces: Hatoyama's Return to the Liberal Party and Formation of the Progressive Party

The San Francisco Peace Treaty was considered to be Yoshida's greatest "diplomatic masterpiece" and he was now overcome by a sense of mission—the belief that it was his duty to prepare and create domestic conditions that would be worthy of his masterpiece. On the other hand, contrary to his expectations, public support for the Yoshida Cabinet was beginning to wane. Whereas public support for the Cabinet at the signing of the Peace Treaty stood at 58 percent, it had dropped to 33 percent by March 1952.

Against this backdrop, politicians who were now depurged were moving to create new political parties with an eye to an independent Japan. It was in this environment that the Progressive Party (Kaishintō) was established in February 1952 through the merger of the Peoples' Democratic Party and the New Politics Club (Shinseikai), which itself had been formed with about 120 members, including Matsumura Kenzō, Ōasa Tadao, and others from the former Constitutional Democratic Party whose purge had been recently lifted. The Progressive Party did not initially elect a president and instead elected a roster of officers who included Miki Takeo as secretary-general and Matsumura Kenzō as chairman of the standing committee. (Shigemitsu Mamoru assumed the post of party president on June 13.) The newly formed party included 67 lower house members and sixteen upper house members.

Calling itself the "vanguard of progressive popular forces," the Progressive Party aimed to create a powerful political party that, as a viable opponent of the Liberal Party, would be fully capable of taking the reins of government. The Progressive Party confronted the Liberal Party with such policy prescriptions as "create a democratic self-defense force commensurate with the capacity of the nation" and "eliminate the waste of laissez-faire economics and make the transition to a self-sufficient manufacturing economy based on comprehensive economic planning." The declaration of the party's founding convention contained the following statement. "To correct the ill-effects of capitalism, we shall resolutely incorporate socialistic policies and contribute to realizing the welfare of the nation's masses."

During the summer of 1951, Hatoyama Ichirō, Kōno Ichirō, Ishibashi Tanzan, Miki Bukichi, and others rejoined the Liberal Party. These were people who did "not think or wish to believe that Japan completely changed with its defeat."[72]

---

72 Miyazawa, *Secret Talks between Tokyo and Washington*, p. 62.

In that sense, these were politicians who believed in negating and not protecting or preserving the reforms implemented during the Occupation. Putting constitutional revision and rearmament front and center, Hatoyama and his group began to challenge Yoshida from within the Liberal Party. Thus, adding to the criticism that came from the Progressive Party and the Socialist Party, Yoshida now had to contend with newly empowered challengers within his own party.

Government Section's Last Report

On March 31, 1952, Chief Rizzo filed the Government Section's last briefing report with the Chief of Staff. Filed a month before the San Francisco Peace Treaty was to come into force on April 28, Rizzo's report analyzed the constitutional and legal basis of Japan's political system as follows:

(1) The basis was "a peace settlement which would not create a sense of oppression, inferiority and hopelessness in the collective Japanese mind," (2) "Japan's economic order would be integrated with the international economic order so as to afford its eighty million inhabitants an adequate standard of living," and (3) "time must elapse for the toughness of the new laws, new customs and new institutions to be demonstrated."[73]

Rizzo also reported on the suspicions that were being voiced in both American and Japanese media as to whether the postwar reforms were real and permanent. The Japanese government and Diet "are in the process of revising many Occupation-inspired laws and reforms, some of them substantially." However, Rizzo noted, this did not imply that Japan was reverting to the old order.

In assessing the strength and durability of Japan's new laws, practices, and institutions under point (3), Rizzo referred to the three basic principles of popular sovereignty, local autonomy, and respect for the value and dignity of individuals that had been incorporated into the new constitutional system. He followed this with an examination of recent developments pertaining to these basic principles.

---

73 Weekly SCAP Briefing on Current Political Development in Japan by Frank Rizzo, Government Section, March 31, 1952, Box No. 2187, Folder 18, General Headquarters/Supreme Commander for Allied Powers, National Diet Library, Originals in U.S. National Archives & Records Administration, RG331.

On the subject of popular sovereignty, Rizzo noted that there was no move-ment in Japan to restore the sovereignty of the Emperor. On local autonomy, Rizzo touched on the reform of the police system and explained that the aboli-tion of national rural police and autonomous police forces in towns and villages had occurred due to fiscal difficulties and had been implemented independently based on the outcome of local referendums. Moreover, he noted, there was persistent opposition to the abolition of autonomous police forces in cities.

Finally, on the subject of respect for the value and dignity of individuals, Rizzo wrote that the Japanese people had overcome the strictures of feudal tradi-tions and were well aware of the difference between democracy and communism. Rizzo also touched on the recent movement for the enactment of a Subversive Activities Prevention Law and proposal of the guideline on ethics based on a program for moral education advocated by Education Minister Amano Teiyū, and noted that strong opposition to both of these were seen in not only the media but also in the Diet. Rizzo concluded with the comment that while Japan was currently undergoing a process of "readjustment," it was continuing its battle for the respect of fundamental human rights.

The Price of the Peace Treaty (1): The "Yoshida Letter"

On the other hand, Yoshida was made to pay a price in exchange for concluding the Peace Treaty and the Security Treaty. Signing a separate peace treaty meant that peace with the Eastern Bloc had been pushed far into the future. In regard to China, in particular, Japan had little choice but to treat the Nationalist govern-ment in Taiwan as China due to strong pressure from the U.S. government.

Yoshida has commented on the developments that were taking place at the time.

After the signing of the peace treaty, would an independent Japan choose Beijing or Taiwan? This was a matter of extreme concern and interest for the United States. What if Japan, enticed by trade and other economic benefits, were to enter into some form of friendly relation with Beijing? Such a development would seriously undermine America's anti-communist policies. Thus, the United States decided to extract a commitment from Japan on establishing diplomatic relations with only the Nationalist government in Taiwan, and this had to be done before the Peace Treaty and other treaties were ratified by the Senate. In other words, the Senate would not ratify the treaties unless and until convincing proof had been obtained that Japan would choose the Nationalist government.[74]

On December 24, 1951, Yoshida reluctantly wrote to Dulles informing him that, "Japan shall conclude a peace with the Nationalist Government in Taiwan prior to America's ratification of the peace treaty."[75] (This letter was not made public until January 16, 1952.) Restoration of diplomatic relations with the People's Republic of China had to wait another twenty years until normalization was achieved in 1972, and the signing of a peace treaty was further delayed until 1978.

The Price of the Peace Treaty (2): Administrative Agreement on U.S. Military Bases

The Japan-U.S. Security Treaty was predicated on a very fundamental relationship. That is to say, the United States would accept responsibility for ensuring Japan's security, in exchange for which Japan would provide the United States with military bases. Some of the other aspects of the agreement were unusual for a treaty that supposedly had been concluded between equals. For instance, the treaty provided for the deployment of U.S. military in maintaining law and order within Japan. Moreover, the treaty did not specify an expiration date. The soft peace had been realized in tandem with a set of demanding conditions that governed the stationing of U.S. forces in Japan.

The Administrative Agreement under Article III of the Security Treaty between Japan and the United States of America (Japan-U.S. Administrative

---

74 Yoshida, *Kaiso jūnen, dai 3-kan*, pp. 71–72.
75 "Kokumin seifu to Kōwa ni kansuru Yoshida shokan" [Yoshida Letter on China], (December 24, 1951), Kashima Heiwa Kenkyusho, ed., in *Nihon gaikō shuyō bunsho, Nenpyō*, [Principal Documents on Japanese Diplomacy: Chronology].

Agreement) was signed on February 28, 1952, giving the U.S. military the right to request the placement of a military base anywhere in Japan. This provision seriously compromised Japan's sovereignty. As one witness and participant in these developments, Miyazawa Kiichi later wrote, "The formula was unavoidable in regaining independence." Moreover, he wrote, "I do not believe that the formula itself is to blame for the situation that emerged. I am disappointed by the numerous mistakes made in realizing the formula."[76]

At the time of the signing, there were 733 U.S. military bases and installations throughout Japan. These occupied an area of more than 140,000 *chōbu* (1,388 square kilometers), equivalent to 75 percent of the total area of Osaka Prefecture.

Advancing Toward Independence: Attitudes of Political Parties

The San Francisco Peace Treaty came into effect on April 28, 1952, thus ending the Occupation that had continued for six years and eight months. On the same day, Japan concluded the Peace Treaty between Japan and the Republic of China (Sino-Japanese Peace Treaty) with the Nationalist Government in Taiwan. The various political parties responded in different ways to the long-awaited day of Japan's independence.

The Liberal Party, the Progressive Party, and the Right-wing Socialist Party announced that they joyfully welcomed independence and released the following statements.

Speaking on behalf of the Liberal Party, Secretary-General Masuda Kaneshichi said, "The international situation is extremely delicate, and the path of independence and self-defense will no doubt be fraught with challenges. Domestically, Japan must seek to establish a fair and equitable system of parliamentary government and to make improvements in domestic affairs in general. Internationally, Japan must value the faith that has been placed in us and must cooperate closely with friendly democratic nations in order to contribute to the advance of democracy and peace throughout the world and to thereby respond to the trust and expectations of the people. We sincerely desire to honor and

---

76 Miyazawa, *Secret Talks between Tokyo and Washington*, p. 60.

reciprocate the trust placed in us by friendly nations."

Secretary-General Miki Takeo of the Progressive Party stated that his party would tread the correct path of democracy. "It will not be easy for Japan to achieve economic self-sufficiency after finally rejoining the international community and while contributing to preserving world peace.... We must brace ourselves for the winds of international criticism, and there is no doubt that domestic conflicts of interest will be intensified."

The Right-wing Socialist Party took the following position: "In the future, our party shall work toward realizing the conditions concerning national security, territory, reparations, and four other conditions that we have submitted concerning the peace treaty. What we need to achieve to buttress true independence is economic self-sufficiency and the stabilization of the lives of the people." The party went on to emphasize that the protection of democracy required battling the growing forces of totalitarianism on both the left and right.

The Left-wing Socialist Party expressed its interpretation of Japan's independence in the following terms: "The independence that Japan has gained hardly differs from the Occupation that preceded it. Moreover, the Japanese people were made to pay far too exorbitant a price for this independence. Japan's newly gained position is the position of an American forward base in the Far East. Japan has been forced down into an unstable and untenable situation where it not only has no peace treaty with the Soviet Union and China, but also has no peace with India and other major Asian countries. Instead of democracy, the people are hemmed in by the forces of reverse course. Instead of freedom, the people are facing the forces of repression. And now, the Peace Constitution is on the verge of being ignored. Our party is committed to fighting to win true freedom and independence, and for this purpose we shall promote a wide range of movements under the banner of social democracy."

The Communist Party released the following statement. "Having arrived on the day on which the Peace Treaty comes into force, we together with all patriots stow our boiling indignation deep inside our chests and stand up with renewed determination to fight for the abrogation of the traitorous peace treaty, the removal of all foreign military forces, the liberation of the Japanese people, and for world peace."

The Price of the Peace Treaty (3): Okinawa

Under the San Francisco Peace Treaty, Okinawa was formally separated from Japan and placed under continued U.S. administration.

Shortly after the signing of the peace treaty, the U.S. Civilian Administration made a series of announcements in November 1951. First, it released its guidelines on the establishment of a "central government." Next, it announced that a "Basic Law," which would serve as a constitution for Okinawa, would be voted on and enacted by freely elected representatives, and that heads of local government bodies would be elected through public elections. This was followed in February 29, 1952 with the promulgation of the United States Civil Administration of the Ryūkyū Islands (USCAR) Proclamation 13, which formally established the Government of the Ryūkyū Islands.

The Government of the Ryūkyū Islands was supposedly invested with full powers to govern the political and administrative structures of the Ryūkyū Islands. In reality, however, it had to obey all proclamations, ordinances, and directives issued by USCAR. The legislative functions of the Government of the Ryūkyū Islands were assigned to a legislature comprised of publicly elected representatives. However, the post of Chief Executive held by Higa Shūhei would not be an elected office. Instead, the office holder was to be appointed by the Governor of USCAR. (In practice, this appointment would be made by the Supreme Commander of the Far East Command.) This signified a regression from the arrangements that existed under the Okinawa Civilian Administration.

Elections for the legislature were held in March. Thereupon, Chief Executive Higa announced that it was not necessary for the legislature to enact a Basic Law because the functions and powers of the Legislature of the Government of the Ryūkyū Islands had already been determined by USCAR Ordinance No. 68 (Provisions of the Government of the Ryūkyū Islands). In accordance with the provisions of Proclamation 68, it was understood that the Government of the Ryūkyū Islands was henceforth empowered to govern all political matters in the Ryūkyū Islands subject to the rigid constraints placed on it of having to "obey the proclamations, ordinances, and directives of the United States Civil Administration of the Ryūkyū Islands."

In an Okinawa formally separated from Japan, the day on which the San Francisco Peace Treaty came into force—April 28, 1951—would long be remembered as the "Day of Disgrace."

Final Chapter

The Occupation and Postwar Japan

Two Occupations: The Mainland and Okinawa

Having accepted the Potsdam Declaration as an international pledge entered into with the Allied Powers, Japan surrendered and came under the Occupation of the Allied Powers. The Allied Powers demanded Japan's implementation of the various terms and conditions contained in the Potsdam Declaration, and Japan accepted that it was its obligation to faithfully carry these out.

The Occupation of the Japanese mainland began under the authority of General MacArthur as Supreme Commander for the Allied Powers. This fact and a series of related developments determined that the Occupation of Japan would effectively be an American occupation. That is to say, not only had the United States played an overwhelmingly important role in the war with Japan, but MacArthur had firmly ensconced himself in Japan well before the various agencies of the Allied Powers were established, most notably the Far Eastern Commission and the Allied Council for Japan. The principal mission of the Occupation was to ensure that Japan would never again pose a threat to the United States and the rest of the world. Specific policies and measures for the realization of this objective would be informed by the pursuit of the demilitarization and democratization of Japan. In devising and implementing his Occupation policies, MacArthur was fundamentally guided by the Initial Post-Surrender Policy, the Basic Initial Post-Surrender Directive and other directives received from the U.S. government. Throughout this process, the Occupation opted for methods of "indirect rule" that used the Japanese government to execute its decisions and policies.

The occupation of Okinawa began before the Occupation of the Japanese mainland and took shape before the end of hostilities. Moreover, the occupation of Okinawa was not integrated into the occupation of the mainland even after the surrender. In January 1946, Okinawa was effectively separated from Japan and placed under the continued and direct rule of the U.S. military government.

For Okinawa, this signified a start from zero. The administrative authority of the Japanese government did not extend to postwar Okinawa; the prefectural and agency offices that could have filled the vacuum had been completely destroyed in the war; and no vestiges of government organizations remained that could be used to govern. Priority was given to political restoration through the establishment of political agencies and institutions "ordered from above" by the military government. This process began with the formation of the Okinawa Advisory Council and led up to the creation of the Okinawa Civilian Administration. To add to the general confusion, the commander of the military government went through frequent changes and the chain of command on the U.S. side remained poorly defined. Consequently, until 1948, Okinawa remained a "forgotten island" for both the United States and Japan. The occupation of Okinawa was beset by yet another problem. After the initial plan to use Okinawa as a forward base for the invasion of the Japanese mainland was rendered moot by the surrender of Japan, the United States was unable to formulate a clear vision for what to do with the island and left the matter in a state of limbo.

Thus, the separation of Okinawa from the Japanese mainland was further deepened by the time lag in the start of their respective occupations, dissimilarities in the structures of their occupation, and differences in the purposes of their occupation.

Enactment of the Constitution of Japan: Demilitarization and Democratization

GHQ policies for demilitarizing Japan were implemented with great speed at the start of the Occupation and were more or less completed by the end of 1945. Specific measures taken included the dissolution of the Japanese military, arrest of war criminals, issuance of the Civil Liberties Directive, issuance of the directive on the Five Major Reforms, zaibatsu dissolution, and the separation of Shinto from the government. The purge of undesirable elements from public office that was ordered in January of the following year can be viewed to represent the culmination of the entire demilitarization process.

As the vanquished side, Japan joined the processes of demilitarization and democratization to speed the nation's transition from a wartime footing to peacetime systems. For the Japanese, this signified a clear and irreversible break from the war years.

What Japan initially imagined "democratization" to be was a return to the political system that existed in Japan before the Manchurian Incident of 1931 and the resurrection of what Shidehara Kijūrō referred to as the "Japanese model of democracy." However, the Japanese government took the initiative in implementing various early reforms, which included the granting of women's suffrage, enactment of the Labor Union Law, and the first phase of the Farmland Reform. While these reforms contained various inadequacies, they went well beyond the confines of "Japan before the Manchurian Incident" and presented an alternate vision for postwar Japan. The Civil Liberties Directive that ordered the freedom of speech and the liberation of political prisoners, and the purge that removed militarists from politics and public office drove home the significance of the Occupation to the Japanese public and swept away any illusion that the nation would be permitted to simply return to its prewar state.

The divergent postwar visions entertained by the United States and Japan first came to the fore in the discussions held in early 1946 between GHQ and the Japanese government on revising the constitution. What the Japanese side had in mind was to strengthen the powers of the Diet by restricting or eliminating some of the Emperor's Prerogative, and to guarantee certain fundamental human rights.

However, as far as GHQ was concerned, the limited revisions that were being considered by the Japanese government were unsatisfactory. Moreover, GHQ had position of having to prevent and rebuff the stern demands made on Japan by countries such as the Soviet Union and Australia within the Far Eastern Commission. Without even bothering to consult Washington, MacArthur put together an outline for a new constitution based on the so-called "MacArthur's Three Basic Points," which consisted of the principles of popular sovereignty, the renunciation of war, and respect for fundamental human rights. In the ensuing deliberations, the Emperor system was allowed to continue in the form of the "Emperor as symbol" in exchange for the inclusion of a clause on the renunciation of war. It can be said that this solution was accepted precisely because the continuation of the Emperor system constituted the most fervent desire of then-Prime Minister Shidehara and Foreign Minister Yoshida.

The promulgation of the constitution created a balance between democratization and the Emperor system, and defined the epoch of Japan's "postwar." Led by Whitney and Kades, the Government Section of GHQ played a major role in drafting the constitution, and in doing so reinforced the Government Section's standing as MacArthur's "political brain." Thereafter, the Government Section pushed forward with various reforms, such as the Five Major Reforms, that pursued political democratization in line with the principles enunciated in the Constitution of Japan. Simultaneously, the Government Section sought to establish a "middle-of-the-road" government that excluded both the extreme left and the extreme right, and pinned its hopes on the Socialist Party to shoulder the role of creating such a government.

From Demilitarization and Democratization to Economic Recovery

Economic reconstruction, which specifically meant ensuring people's access to the basic necessities of clothing, food, and shelter, confronted the Japanese government as a high hurdle from the earliest days of the postwar period. Given the serious food shortages, high inflation, and dire economic conditions, rumors were rife that ten million would die of starvation. The unfolding crisis most seriously impacted the lives of the nation's workers. As they battled for jobs and wages, workers quickly organized into labor unions. Thereafter, the focus of the emergent labor movement rapidly evolved and moved from the arena of economic struggle to that of political struggle. While the expansion of the labor movement was buttressed by the democratization policies that GHQ was pursuing, widespread poverty and economic difficulties posed a formidable challenge to the goal of democratization. It was against this backdrop that the labor unions began hurtling toward the general strike of February 1, 1947.

MacArthur interpreted the February 1 general strike to be an uncontrolled explosion of the labor movement and stepped in to order its cancellation. In the following month, March 1947, MacArthur advocated an early peace treaty and identified "economic recovery" as one of the objectives of the Occupation. The adoption of MacArthur's new objective did not signify the end of demilitarization and democratization, and instead was a measure that complemented the earlier goals.

For the Japanese side, economic recovery was an absolute necessity. Standing under the banners of the completion of democratization, installation of a planned economy and labor participation in management, the successive Cabinets of Katayama Tetsu and Ashida Hitoshi sought to achieve economic recovery through labor-capital cooperation. This position symbolized the consummation of the "alliance of reformists" that stretched across the U.S. and Japanese sides, an alliance made possible by Japan's honeymoon with the Government Section.

However, with the start of the Cold War, Washington grew increasingly dissatisfied with MacArthur's Occupation policies. By this time, Washington had come to place greater emphasis on economic recovery as the path to Japan's independence, with more urgency than MacArthur. In Washington, William Draper was pushing the "logic of the American taxpayer" and promoting economic recovery as a means to reducing the cost of the Occupation. At the same time, George Kennan was arguing for promoting the economic recovery of Japan and Germany from the perspective of "Cold War logic." The two had come to view the occupations of Japan and Germany through the same lens.

The Dodge Line: From MacArthur's Occupation to an American Occupation

By early 1948, the food crisis had been significantly eased and economic output had recovered to about 60 percent of prewar levels. Issued in October 1948, NSC-13/2 ("Recommendations with Respect to United States Policy Toward Japan") formally shifted the focus of Occupation policies from democratization to economic recovery and advocated the speedy realization of economic self-sufficiency. MacArthur resisted the new policy direction on the grounds that it negated the economic recovery measures that were being implemented by the Japanese government and GHQ, and that this would undermine the middle-of-the-road government that he had been supporting. Washington responded to this resistance by aggressively intervening in the Occupation and issuing the

"Nine Principles for Economic Stabilization" in the form of an interim directive.

Meanwhile in Okinawa, an election of municipal heads and assembly members was held in early 1948, which had the effect of prompting citizens to demand autonomy. At around the same time in Washington, a broad consensus was reached between the State Department and the Department of the Army on the occupation of Okinawa.

Joseph Dodge arrived in Japan for the first time in February 1949 in a visit that signified the transfer of power in determining the direction of Japan's economic policies to the U.S. government. The Dodge Line that he rendered featured fiscal austerity and a super-balanced budget that sought to promote economic recovery through a "shock approach" that would stabilize the economy in an accelerated manner. These policies, which had been initiated by Draper, were not by any means punitive in character. Instead, they were presented as an unavoidable ordeal that the nation had to weather for the sake of realizing the rebirth and resurgence of Japan in the long run. However, in the short run, these polices exacted a heavy toll on the general public and the nation's workers in particular. It seemed that the heavy clouds of chaos and turmoil were closing in on the horizons of the Japanese economy.

Yoshida Shigeru returned to the post of Prime Minister in October 1948 with the hope of realizing a "virtual peace treaty" through the full implementation of the nine principles program for economic stabilization. After his return to power, Yoshida began to seek out direct channels of communication with Washington that would effectively bypass MacArthur.

Concurrent to changes made in Occupation policies for Japan, the U.S. government began to move forward on its policies for Okinawa. NSC-13/3 outlined a path for combining the occupation of Okinawa with its transformation into a military base. In other words, predicated on the assumption that Okinawa would henceforth be separated politically from the Japanese mainland, the occupation took on the challenge of realizing the economic reconstruction and recovery of Okinawa. In this way, the United States advanced toward integrating Okinawa and the Japanese mainland into its strategies for the Asian region. In a certain respect, this meant that Okinawa was being used as a form of "collateral" in allowing Japan to strive toward political and economic independence.

Peace Treaty and Outbreak of the Korean War

Motivated by the desire to bring Japan into the Western Bloc and to position it firmly in its Asian strategies, the United States accelerated the process of finalizing the peace with Japan as the Cold War grew in intensity. While Japan had been ordered out of the international community, this did not mean that it was free and unaffected by ongoing changes in the international situation. Thus, for a while thereafter, Japan would be pressed to make the choice between "overall peace" and "separate peace."

In light of the Cold War that pitted the United States and the Soviet Union against each other, Yoshida and his Liberal Party concluded that separate peace was the realistic and unavoidable choice, and hence opted for joining the "Free World." On the other hand, the Socialist Party and the People's Democratic Party initially came together to form a united front supporting an overall peace and neutrality and opposing the placement of U.S. military bases in Japan. In this way, the policies of the two political camps began to move in opposite directions.

The Korean War had a profound effect on Japan. The start of hostilities helped Japan escape the dire economic conditions that had long troubled it and also accelerated its move into orbit of the Western Bloc. However, these developments also served to polarize Japan's political environment. Before long, the People's Democratic Party abandoned its advocacy for neutrality, switched to supporting a separate peace, and adopted an even more aggressive stance than Yoshida on the issue of strengthening Japan's defense capabilities. The Socialist Party, however, maintained its existing platform and expanded its "three peace principles" to include opposition to rearmament.

For Yoshida, the highest priority was the realization of economic independence, and he agreed to the stationing of U.S. forces in Japan for the sake of national security. However, in his negotiations with Dulles, Yoshida continued to resist the rearmament of Japan out of concern in the face of apprehensions of the countries of Asia.

The Liberal Party and the People's Democratic Party came to cooperate on the peace issue and national security but opposed each other on rearmament. In contrast, the Liberal Party and Socialist Party adopted opposing positions on the peace issue and national security, but were close to each other on the question of rearmament. To complicate matters further, the left and right wings of the Socialist Party were deeply divided on the peace and security treaties.

Japan brought the Occupation to an end and returned to the international community by concluding a peace treaty in which Okinawa was used as collateral. Walking along two different paths, the mainland and Okinawa had come together in the process of "reconstruction and recovery," but were once again separated by the peace treaty and Japan's independence. Meanwhile, Okinawa would remain under U.S. administration.

Balance Sheet for the Occupation

What would a balance sheet for the Occupation look like? In considering this question, attention should be paid to the fact that the Yoshida proposals that came at the end of the Occupation for correcting the excesses of earlier reforms did not contain any hint of constitutional revision. Instead, Yoshida's corrections concentrated on "reforms that did not suit the conditions in Japan" and were limited to such matters as the revision of the Police Law, the Anti-Monopoly Law, and the system of the board of education, and the reorganization of government administration. From this, it can be concluded that Yoshida was unable to turn back the clock on reforms that addressed problems that had been out of sync with real conditions since the prewar years. Ultimately, there was no way of rolling back any reforms that already had some kind of fertile soil for acceptance on the Japanese side. It is interesting to note that Yoshida would in later years comment that, in the final analysis, the reforms implemented by the Occupation garnered considerable success. Yoshida would go on to conclude that the Occupation's idealistic reforms provided hope to the Japanese people at a time when they were caught in the confusion and despair of the postwar years.[1]

In the preface to the Japanese edition of *Winners in Peace: MacArthur, Yoshida and Postwar Japan*, Richard Finn wrote of the Occupation as follows.

---

[1] Yoshida Shigeru, *Japan's Decisive Century*, Frederick A. Praeger, 1967.

Of the Occupation, Americans in general believe that General MacArthur singlehandedly reformed Japan and reconstructed its economy. Thus, many overlook the contributions made by the Japanese themselves. Also, many people have misunderstood what was happening in Japan at the time.

Finn arrived in Japan in 1945 as a naval officer and later worked for nearly two years in Washington for the Far Eastern Commission. In 1948, Finn returned to Japan as a diplomat and served in Japan for the next seven years. The central theme of Finn's book, *Winners in Peace: MacArthur, Yoshida and Postwar Japan*, is the question of why and how postwar Japan was able to succeed. Looking back on the Occupation, Finn wrote, "There are winners and losers in war, but all are winners in peace."

Theodore Cohen, who served as Chief of the Labor Division of the Economic and Scientific Section and wrote *Remaking Japan: The American Occupation as New Deal*, named the final chapter of this book "Balance Sheet" and added the subtitle, "Stabilization, Economic Miracle and Interrupted Dialogue" to his chapter title. As in the case of Finn, Cohen focused on the economic miracle to describe Japan as the "winner of the peace." As a researcher of Japan's labor movements, however, Cohen also pointed to the negative legacy of Japan and the United States by describing the "interrupted dialogue" between labor unions and the U.S. government.

What Was the Occupation? The Occupation and Postwar Politics

The Japanese postwar starts with the Occupation. As mentioned in the Preface, the Occupation provided Japan with a preparatory period for returning to the international community.

The "Constitution of Japan system" symbolizes the reforms of the early years of the Occupation, while the "Security Treaty system" born of the San Francisco Peace Treaty and the Japan-U.S. Security Treaty encapsulates the latter years of the Occupation. To return to the international community, Japan accepted both of these systems and underwent a subtle reincarnation that transformed it from a "Meiji nation" into a "postwar nation." The Yoshida line of light rearmament and prioritizing the economy sought to balance the Constitution and the Japan-U.S. Security Treaty while resisting full-scale rearmament. From the perspective of any normal sovereign nation, this balancing act must have seemed strange and unstable. Moreover, like it or not, this balancing act meant that the slightest tilting toward either the "Constitution" or the "Security Treaty" would later rend Japanese politics into opposing camps of conservatives and progressives.

The Socialist Party accepted and valued the "democratization" reforms implemented under the Occupation and swore to protect the Constitution as the pinnacle of these reforms. On the other hand, the Liberal-Democratic Party used the lever of "Japan-U.S. security" that came to the fore in the closing years of the Occupation to reinterpret the Constitution and bring it to where it stands today. Needless to say, this was never a straight and uninterrupted path. During the 1950s, Hatoyama Ichirō, Kishi Nobusuke and others challenged Yoshida by lobbying to correct the excesses of Occupation policies, calling for the revision of Article 9 and other aspects of the Constitution, and advocating the rearmament of Japan. The tumultuous 1960 campaign against the Japan-U.S. Security Treaty emerged as an arena where conservatives and progressives clashed sharply.

At the same time, the tumult pressured the conservatives to make certain adjustments. As a result, the conservative politics that existed under the Meiji Constitution gave birth to the conservative politics that would persist under the postwar Constitution of Japan. This would come to be called the conservative mainstream. By standing against constitutional revision and by supporting the Japan-U.S. Security Treaty, the conservative mainstream pitted itself against two camps. One consisted of a group within the Liberal-Democratic Party— that stood for constitutional revision and rearmament. The second encompassed the opposition parties that universally opposed all changes to the Constitution but also stridently opposed the Japan-U.S. Security Treaty.

Seventy years after the end of the war, more than sixty years since the San Francisco Peace Treaty and the independence of Japan and a quarter of a century since the end of the Cold War, Japan has now arrived at a critical crossroads. The politics of postwar Japan unfolded within an elliptical space with two foci that would never come together: "constitution" and "security." Once again today,

Japan faces the question of how to interact with the international community. This inevitably poses the additional question of what it meant for Okinawa to be torn away from Japan to experience its own version of the "postwar."

Afterword

Some fifteen years have passed since I published *Senryō-ka chūdō seiken no keisei to hōkai: Minsei-kyoku to Nihon Shakaitō* [Formation and Collapse of Middle-of-the-Road Governments under the Occupation: Government Section and the Japan Socialist Party], in which I depicted the interaction between GHQ and Japan's various political parties. After finishing that book, I found myself increasingly drawn to the question: What did the Occupation bequeath to Japan and the Japanese people? The present book considers these latter years culminating in the end of the Occupation.

The present book takes on two challenges. One is to evaluate the two principal legacies that the Occupation bequeathed to postwar Japan—the Constitution of Japan and the Japan-U.S. Security Treaty. The second is to address the gnawing discomfort that I feel about arguments that posit that the Occupation somehow ruined Japan. Were Japan and the Japanese so frail and indolent as to be ruined by an Occupation that lasted six years and eight months? Wouldn't that be a masochistic view of history?

Yotarō Senki [Yotarō's war stories], written by Shunpū-tei Ryūshō, the traditional *rakugo* raconteur, offers an interesting perspective on this issue. Having received news of the end of the war while recovering in an army hospital in Qingdao, the author writes of the emotions that swept over him to learn of Japan's defeat. "I was relieved to think that I had survived. But at the same time, there was an indescribable feeling of overwhelming sorrow. It was a complex vortex of emotions." In the ship that carried him back to Japan, the author penned the following thoughts on his future and the future of Japan,

"What does the future hold for Japan? Will they flood Japan with foreign entertainment and render the Japanese spineless?" I thought to myself. In fact, this was what some were already saying. Will all place names be expunged and all building names erased and replaced with English names?

Would they go so far as to strip us of our Japanese language? These thoughts raced through my mind...

I liked *rakugo* and was thinking of pursuing a career as a *rakugo* raconteur. But then, what would be the use if the Japanese language were fated to disappear? No one would be left to understand those old stories about 'Hattsan and Kuma-san.' What about doing *rakugo* in English? 'Hello, Mr. Hattsan and Mr. Kuma-san calling.' No, that just would not work. But then I said to myself, 'Wait a second,' and thought the matter over. Wasn't China occupied by the Japanese military? But that didn't stop the people from wearing Chinese clothes and speaking Chinese.

The pride of a people and a nation cannot be destroyed so easily. Even if America takes over the country and forces its language on us, that would only reinforce the people's fondness and attachment to the Japanese language. That would mean that *rakugo* would become even more popular.

In this passage, the author touches on two occupations, one in which he was part of the occupying force and the other in which he would stand among the occupied. At the same time, the passage speaks of the will to live and the indomitability of the human spirit that draws its strength from the needs of everyday life.

A dozen or so years ago, I was given the opportunity to speak to two visiting groups of African parliamentarians on the subject of Japanese politics under the Occupation. In what I saw to be a reminder of prewar colonial rule, the first group was from the Anglophone regions of Africa and the second from the Francophone. All of the parliamentarians were keenly interested in two matters: Japan as a model for "democratization" and Japan's success in economic reconstruction. Many questions were brought up in both sessions, and these questions themselves contained numerous extremely interesting points. What these sessions drove home to me was that the experience of the Occupation needs to be recounted in various forms and from various perspectives.

Due to the space limitations, I was unable to touch on such subjects as educational reform and the occupation of the outlying Amami, Miyako, and Yaeyama Islands of Okinawa. Nevertheless, this book represents the culmination of my research on the Occupation. I earnestly hope that the book can provide readers with a life-size image of the Occupation and serve as a starting point in examining the course of postwar Japan.

*　*　*

I am indebted to numerous people for their support and assistance. When I began researching the Occupation, Professor Iokibe Makoto, my teacher and mentor, instructed me from the very basics. Not only was I guided by his strict and unsparing advice, I also gained much from the warmth of his instruction. Professor Amakawa Akira provided me with valuable advice at critical points in my research and generously shared sources and materials. I take this opportunity to express my special gratitude to these two scholars.

Finally, I express my thanks to Mr. Shirato Naohito of Chuokoron-Shinsha who patiently waited for the manuscript and favored me with his encouragement throughout the writing of this book.

Fukunaga Fumio
November 30, 2014

Bibliography

Amakawa Akira, Hoshi Kenichi, and Fukunaga Fumio, eds. *GHQ Minsei-kyoku shiryō: Senryō kaikaku, zen 12-kan* [GHQ Government Section Materials: Reforms of the Occupation, Vols. 1–12]. Tokyo: Maruzen, 1997–2001.

Amakawa Akira. *Senryōka no gikai to kanryō* [Diet and Bureaucracy under the Occupation]. Tokyo: Gendai Shiryō Shuppan, 2014.

——. *Senryōka no Nihon: Kokusai kankyō to kokusai taisei* [Japan under the Occupation]. Tokyo: Gendai Shiryō Shuppan, 2014.

Amemiya Shōichi. *Senryō to kaikaku* [Occupation and Reform]. Tokyo: Iwanami Shoten, 2008.

Andō Yoshio, ed. *Shōwa seiji keizai-shi e no shōgen, ge* [Testimonies on Shōwa Political and Economic History, Vol. 2]. Tokyo: Mainichi Shinbunsha, 1966.

Asai Yoshio. *Sengo kaikaku to minshu-shugi: Keizai fukkō kara kōdo seichō e* [Postwar Reform and Democracy: From Economic Recovery to Growth]. Tokyo: Yoshikawa Kōbunkan, 2001.

Ara Takashi. *Nihon senryō-shi kenkyū josetsu* [Introduction to Research on the History of the Occupation of Japan]. Tokyo: Kashiwa Shobō, 1994.

Baerwald, Hans H. *The Purge of Japanese Leaders under the Occupation.* Berkeley: University of California Press, 1959.

Bank of the Ryūkyūs Research Department, ed. *Sengo Okinawa keizai-shi* [Postwar Economic History of Okinawa]. Naha: Ryūkyū Ginkō, 1984.

Bisson, Thomas A. *Nihon senryō kaisōki* [Reform Years in Japan, 1945–47: An Occupation Memoir]. Tokyo: Sanseidō, 1983.

Borton, Hugh. *Spanning Japan's Modern Century: The Memoirs of Hugh Borton.* Lanham: Lexington Books, 2002.

Cohen, Theodore. *Remaking Japan: The American Occupation as New Deal.* Free Press, 1987.

Hunter-Chester, David. *Creating Japan's Ground Self-Defense Force, 1945–2015: A Sword Well Made.* Lanham: Lexington Books, 2016.

Dower, John W. *Embracing Defeat: Japan in the Wake of World War II.* New York: W.W. Norton and the New Press, 1999.

——. *Empire and Aftermath: Yoshida Shigeru and the Japanese Experience, 1878–1954.* Cambridge: Council on East Asian Studies, Harvard University, 1979.

Economic Planning Agency, ed. *Sengo keizai fukkō to keizai antei honbu* [Postwar Economic Reconstruction and the Economic Stabilization Board] in *Tsuru Shigeto nisshi* [Diary of Tsuru Shigeto]. National Printing Bureau, 1988.

Eldridge, Robert D. *The Origins of the Bilateral Okinawa Problem: Okinawa in Postwar U.S.-Japan Relations, 1945–1952.* New York: Routledge, 2013.

Etō Jun, ed. *Senryō shiroku, zen 4-kan* [Historical Records of the Occupation, Vols. 1–4]. Kōdansha, 1989.

Finn, Richard B. *Winners in Peace: MacArthur, Yoshida, and Postwar Japan.* Berkeley: University of California Press, 1992.

Fujita Hisanori. *Jijū-chō no kaisō* [Memoirs of a Grand Chamberlain]. Tokyo: Chūō Kōronsha, 1987.

Fukunaga Fumio. *Sengo Nihon no saisei* [Rebirth of Postwar Japan]. Tokyo: Maruzen, 2003.

——. *Senryō-ka chūdō seiken no keisei to hōkai: Minsei-kyoku to Nihon Shakaitō* [Formation and Collapse of Middle-of-the-Road Governments under the Occupation: Government Section and the Japan Socialist Party]. Tokyo: Iwanami Shoten, 1997.

Geselbracht, Raymond H, ed. *The Memoirs of Harry S. Truman: A Reader's Edition*, Baltimore: Johns Hopkins University Press, 2019

Gikai Seiji Kenkyū-kai, ed. *Seitō nenkan: Shōwa 22–24 nen* [Almanac of Political Parties: Shōwa 22–24 (1947–1949)]. Tokyo: Nyūsu-sha, 1947–1948.

Hasegawa Tsuyoshi. *Antō: Sutārin, Torūman to Nihon kōfuku* [Secret Battle: Stalin and Truman, Japan's Defeat]. Chūō Kōron Shinsha, 2006.

Hata Ikuhiko. *Shōwa zaiseishi shūsen kōwa 3: Amerika no tai-nichi senryō seisaku* [Fiscal History of the Shōwa Era, from the End of the War to the Peace Treaty 3: America's Policies for the Occupation of Japan]. Tokyo: Tōyō Keizai Shinpōsha, 1976.

Hatoyama Ichirō. *Hatoyama Ichirō kaikoroku* [Memoirs of Hatoyama Ichirō]. Tokyo: Bungei Shunjū Shinsha, 1957.

Higa Mikio. *Okinawa: Seiji to seitō* [Okinawa: Politics and Political Parties]. Tokyo: Chūō Kōronsha, 1965.

Higashikuni Naruhiko. *Ichi kōzoku no sensō nikki* [Wartime Diary of an Imperial Prince]. Tokyo: Nihon Shūhōsha, 1957.

——. *Watashi no kiroku* [My Personal Records]. Tōhō Shobō, 1947.

Hori Shigeru. *Sengo seiji no oboegaki* [Memorandum on Postwar Politics]. Tokyo: Mainichi Shinbunsha, 1970.

Hosokawa Morisada. *Hosokawa nikki, ge* [Hosokawa Diary, Vol. 2]. Tokyo: Chūō Kōronsha, 1979.

Hosoya Chihiro. *Sanfuranshisuko kōwa e no michi* [The Road to the San Francisco Peace Treaty]. Tokyo: Chūō Kōronsha, 1984.

Igarashi Takeshi. *Sengo Nichibei kankei no keisei* [American-Japanese Peace-Making and the Cold War]. Tokyo: Kōdansha, 1995.

Ikeda Hayato. *Kinkō zaisei* [Fiscal Balance]. Tokyo: Chūō Kōron Shinsha, 1999.

Inoki Masamichi. *Hyōden Yoshida Shigeru, zen 3-kan* [Critical Biography of Yoshida Shigeru, Vols. 1–3]. Tokyo: Yomiuri Shinbunsha, 1981.

Iokibe Makoto. *Senryō-ki* [Occupation Era]. Tokyo: Yomiuri Shinbunsha, 1997.

Ishibashi Tan'ichi and Itō Takashi, eds. *Ishibashi Tanzan nikki* [Diary of Ishibashi Tanzan]. Tokyo: Misuzu Shobō, 2010.

Ishii Osamu. *Kokusai seiji-shi to shite no nijū seiki* [Twentieth Century International Political History]. Tokyo: Yūshindō, 2000.

Itō Takashi and Suetake Yoshiya, eds. *Hatoyama Ichirō to Kaoru nikki, jō* [Diary of Hatoyama Ichirō and Kaoru, Vol. 1]. Tokyo: Chūō Kōronsha, 1999.

Itō Takashi and Watanabe Ikuo, eds. *Shigemitsu Mamoru shuki* [Memoirs of Shigemitsu Mamoru]. Tokyo: Chūō Kōronsha, 1986.

Katayama Naikaku Kiroku Kankō-kai, ed. *Katayama Naikaku* [The Katayama Cabinet]. Tokyo: 1980.

Katayama Tetsu. *Kaiko to tenbō* [Recollections and Outlook]. Tokyo: Fukumura Shuppan, 1967.

Kayō Yasuharu. *Okinawa minsei-fu* [Okinawa Civilian Administration]. Tokyo: Kume Shobō, 1986.

Kennan, George F. *Memoirs, 1925–1950.* New York: Atlantic Monthly (Little, Brown), 1967.

Kōno Yasuko. *Nihon no rekishi 24: Sengo to kōdo seichō no shūen* [History of Japan 24: The Postwar Period and the End of Rapid Economic Growth]. Tokyo: Kōdansha, 2002.

Koseki Shōichi, ed. *Teikoku kenpō kaisean iin shoiinkai sokkiroku, dai 90 teikoku gikai shūgiin* [History of Trade and Industry Policies, Vol. 2, 1992, "Stenographic records of the sub-committee of the Imperial Constitution Revision Drafting Committee–House of Representatives of the 90th session of the Imperial Diet]. Tokyo: Gendai Shiryō Shuppan, 2005.

Koseki Shōichi. *Nihon-koku kenpō no tanjō* [Birth of the Constitution of Japan]. Tokyo: Iwanami Shoten, 2009.

Kusunoki Ayako. *Gendai Nihon seiji-shi 1: Senryo kara dokuritsu e* [Contemporary Political History of Japan 1: From the Occupation to Independence]. Tokyo: Yoshikawa Kōbunkan, 2013.

——. *Yoshida Shigeru to anzen hoshō seisaku no keisei* [Yoshida Shigeru and the Formation of National Security Policies]. Kyoto: Minerva Shobō, 2009.

Local Government Research and Data Center, ed. *Sengo jichi-shi* [History of Postwar Local Governance]. Tokyo: Bunsei Shoin, 1977.

MacArthur, Douglas. *Reminiscences.* New York: McGraw-Hill, 1964.

Manchester, William. *American Caesar: Douglas MacArthur 1880–1964.* New York: Little, Brown, 1978.

Masamura Kimihiro. *Sengoshi, jō* [Postwar History, Vol. 1]. Tokyo: Chikuma Shobō, 1985.

Masuda Hiroshi. *Kōshoku tsuihōron* [Theory of Purging of Public Officials]. Tokyo: Iwanami Shoten, 1998.

——. *Makkāsā* [MacArthur]. Tokyo: Chūō Kōron Shinsha, 2009.

Masumi Junnosuke. *Sengo seiji, jō-ge* [Postwar Politics, Vol. 1–2]. Tokyo: University of Tokyo Press, 1983.

Matsumura Kenzō. *Sandai kaikoroku* [Memoirs of Three Generations]. Tokyo: Tōyō Keizai Shinpōsha, 1964.

Minami Tadashi. *Nihon no jinmyaku* [Japan's Personal Networks]. Tokyo: Nikkan Rōdō Shinbunsha, 1973.

Ministry of Finance, Fiscal History Section, ed. *Tai senryō-gun kōshō hiroku: Watanabe Takeshi nikki* [Confidential Records of Negotiations with Occupation Forces: Watanabe Takeshi Diary]. Tokyo: Tōyō Keizai Shinpōsha, 1983.

Ministry of Foreign Affairs, ed. *Nihon gaikō bunsho: Heiwa Jōyaku no teiketsu ni kansuru chōsho, zen go satsu* [Survey Report on Conclusion of the Peace Treaty, Vols. 1–5]. Tokyo: 2002.

Ministry of International Trade and Industry, ed. *Tūshō sangyō seisaku-shi, dai 2-kan*, 1992.

Miyazawa Kiichi. *Secret Talks between Tokyo and Washington.* Lanham: Rowman & Littlefield Publishers, 2007.

Nakakita Kōji. *Keizai fukkō to sengo seiji* [Economic Recovery and Postwar Politics]. Tokyo: University of Tokyo Press, 1998.

——. *Nihon rōdō seiji no kokusai kankei shi* [History of International Relations of Japan's Labor Politics]. Tokyo: Iwanami Shoten, 2008.

Nakamura Masanori et al., eds. *Sengo Nihon: senryō to kaikaku, zen 6-kan* [Postwar Japan: Occupation and Reform, Vols. 1–6]. Tokyo: Iwanami Shoten, 1995.

Nakamura Masanori, ed. *Kindai Nihon no kiseki 6: Senryō to sengo kaikaku* [Trajectory of Modern Japan 6: The Occupation and Postwar Reform]. Tokyo: Yoshikawa Kōbunkan, 1994.

Nakamura Takafusa, ed. *Senryoki Nihon no keizai to seiji* [Japan's Economy and Politics during the Occupation]. Tokyo: University of Tokyo Press, 1979.

——. *Shōwa-shi II* [History of the Shōwa Era II]. Tokyo: Tōyō Keizai Shinposha, 1993.

Nakano Yoshio and Arasaki Moriteru. *Okinawa sengoshi* [Postwar History of Okinawa]. Tokyo: Iwanami Shoten, 1976.

Narahashi Wataru. *Gekiryū ni sao sashite* [Riding the Rapid Currents]. Tokyo: Tsubasa Shoin, 1968.

Nishimura Kumao. *Nihon Gaikōshi 27: Sanhuranshisuko Heiwa Jōyaku* [Diplomatic History of Japan 27: The San Francisco Peace Treaty]. Tokyo: Kashima Shuppan kai, 1971.

Nishio Suehiro. *Nishio Suehiro no seiji oboegaki* [Political Memorandums by Nishio Suehiro]. Tokyo: Mainichi Shinbunsha, 1968.

Ogura Yūji. *Makkāsā to Nihon Kyōsan-tō (Nenpō Nihon gendai-shi–dai 4-kan)* [MacArthur and the Japan Communist Party (Annual Report of Contemporary Japanese History, Vol. 4)]. Tokyo: Gendai Shiryō Shuppan, 1998.

Okinawa Prefectural Library, Historical Materials Department, ed. *Okinawa-ken shiryō: Sengo*

2 *Okinawa minsei-fu kiroku 1–2* [Okinawa Prefecture Historical Documents–Postwar 2: Records of the Civil Administration of the Ryukyu Islands 1–2]. Naha: Okinawa Prefecture Board of Education, 1988, 1990.

Okinawa Prefecture, Bunka shinkō-kai kōbunsho kanri-bu shiryō henshū-shitsu, ed. *Okinawa ken-shi shiryō-hen 14: Ryūkyū rettō no gunsei 1945–1950 gendai 2 (Wayaku-hen)* [Okinawa Prefecture Historical Documents 14: Military Government of the Ryukyus 1945–1950 Contemporary 2 (Japanese translations)]. Naha: Okinawa Prefecture Board of Education, 2002.

Okinawa Prefecture, Okinawa Historical Materials Section, ed. *Okinawa-ken shiryō: Sengo 1 Okinawa shijun-kai kiroku* [Okinawa Prefecture Historical Documents: Postwar 1 Records of the Okinawa Advisory Council]. Naha: Okinawa Prefecture Board of Education, 1986.

Okinawa Social Mass Party Historical Materials Committee, ed. *Okinawa shakai taishū-tō shi* [History of the Okinawa Social Mass Party]. Naha, 1981.

Ōkōchi Kazuo and Matsuo Hiroshi. *Nihon rōdō kumiai monogatari sengo-hen, jō-ge* [Tale of Japan's Labor Unions: The Postwar Period, Vols. 1–2]. Tokyo: Chikuma Shobō, 1973.

Oppler, Alfred C. *Legal Reform in Occupied Japan: A Participant Looks Back.* New Jersey: Princeton University Press, 1976.

Ōta Kenichi et al., eds. *Tsugita Daizaburō nikki* [Diary of Tsugita Daizaburō]. Okayama: Sanyō Shinbunsha, 1991.

Ōtake Hideo. *Saigunbi to nashonarizumu* [Rearmament and Nationalism]. Tokyo: Chūō Kōronsha, 1988.

Ōtake Hideo, ed. *Sengo Nihon bōei mondai shiryōshū, dai 1-kan* [Documents of Japan's Postwar Defense Issues, Vol. 1]. Tokyo: Sanichi Shobō, 1991–1992.

Rix, Alan, ed. *Intermittent Diplomat: The Japan and Batavia diaries of W. Macmahon Ball,* Melbourne University Press, 1988.

Sakamoto Yoshikazu and Robert E. Ward, eds. *Nihon senryō no kenkyū* [Research on the Occupation of Japan]. Tokyo: University of Tokyo Press, 1987.

Satō Tatsuo. *Nihonkoku kenpō tanjōki* [Record of Establishment of the Constitution of Japan]. Tokyo: Chūō Kōron Shinsha, 1999.

Schonberger, Howard B. *Aftermath of the War: Americans and the Remaking of Japan, 1945–1952.* Kent: Kent State University Press, 1989.

Sebald, William J. *With MacArthur in Japan: A Personal History of the Occupation.* New York: W.W. Norton, 1965.

Schaller, Michael. *The American Occupation of Japan: The Origins of the Cold War in Asia.* Oxford University Press, 1985.

Shibata Shinichi, ed. *Yoshida Shigeru shokan, tsuiho* [Letters of Yoshida Shigeru, appendix]. Tokyo: Chūō Kōron Shinsha, 2011.

Shidehara Peace Foundation, ed. *Shidehara Kijūrō* [Shidehara Kijūrō]. Tokyo: Shidehara Peace Foundation, 1955.

Shindō Eiichi and Shimokōbe Motoharu, eds. *Ashida Hitoshi nikki, zen 7-kan* [Ashida Hitoshi Diary, Vols. 1–7]. Tokyo: Iwanami Shoten, 1986.

Shinobu Seizaburō. *Sengo Nihon seijishi, zen 4-kan* [Political History of Postwar Japan, Vols. 1–4]. Tokyo: Keisō Shobō, 1965–1967.

Sodei Rinjirō, ed. and trans. *Correspondence between General MacArthur, Prime Minister Yoshida Shigeru & Other High Japanese Officials [1945-1951].* Tokyo: Hōsei Daigaku Shuppankyoku, 2000.

Sodei Rinjirō. *Makkāsā no nisennichi* [MacArthur's Two Thousand Days]. Tokyo: Chūō Kōronsha, 1974.

———. *Senryō shita mono sareta mono* [The Occupiers and the Occupied]. Tokyo: Simul Press, 1986.

Suzuki Mosaburō. *Aru shakaishugisha no hansei* [The Reflections of a Socialist]. Tokyo: Bungei

Shunjū Shinsha, 1958.

Suzuki Tetsuzō. *Katayama naikaku to Suzuki Mosaburō* [Katayama Cabinet and Suzuki Mosaburō]. Tokyo: Kashiwa Shobō, 1990.

Taikakai Henshū Iinkai, ed. *Naimushō shi, dai 3-kan* [History of the Ministry of Home Affairs, Vol. 3]. Tokyo: Taikakai, 1970.

Taira Tatsuo. *Taira Tatsuo kaisōroku* [Memoirs of Taira Tatsuo], Naha: Nanpō-sha, 1963.

Taira Yoshitoshi. *Sengo Okinawa to Beigun kichi: "Juyō" to "kyozetsu" no hazama de 1945-1972-nen* [Postwar Okinawa and U.S. Military Bases, 1945-1972]. Tokyo: Hōsei University Press, 2012.

Takahashi Hiroshi. *Shōwa Tennō 1945-1948* [Emperor Shōwa 1945-1948]. Tokyo: Iwanami Shoten, 2008.

Takashima Kikuo. *Sengo rōdō undō shishi, dai 1-kan* [Personal History of Postwar Labor Movements, Vol. 1]. Tokyo: Daisan Shokan, 1991.

Takayanagi Kenzō et al., *Nihonkoku kenpō seitei no katei, 1-2* [Formation Process of the Constitution of Japan, 1-2]. Tokyo: Yūhikaku Publishing, 1972.

Takemae Eiji and Okabe Fuminobu. *Nihonkoku kenpō kenshō dai 1-kan: Kenpō seiteishi* [Verifying the Constitution of Japan, Vol. 1: History of the Drafting of the Constitution of Japan].Tokyo: Shōgakukan, 2000.

Takemae Eiji. *Nihon senryō: GHQ kōkan no shōgen* [The Occupation as Told by Senior GHQ Officials]. Tokyo: Chūō Kōronsha, 1988.

——. *Senryō sengo-shi* [History of the Occupation and the Postwar Era]. Tokyo: Iwanami Shoten, 1992.

——. *The Allied Occupation of Japan*. New York: Continuum, 2003.

Toyoshita Narahiko. *Nihon senryō kanri taisei no seiritsu* [Formation of the Administrative System of the Occupation of Japan]. Tokyo: Iwanami Shoten, 1992.

Toriyama Atsushi. *Okinawa kichi shakai no kigen to sōkoku* [Origins and Conflicts in Okinawa's Military Base Society]. Tokyo: Keisō Shobō, 2013.

Uchida Kenzo. *Sengo Nihon no hoshu seiji* [Postwar Japan's Conservative Politics]. Tokyo: Iwanami Shoten, 1969.

Wada Haruki. *Rekishi toshite no Nosaka Sanzō* [Nosaka Sanzō as History]. Tokyo: Heibonsha, 1995.

Ward, Eric E. *Land Reform in Japan 1946-1950: The Allied Role.* Tokyo: Nobunkyo, 1990.

Watanabe Akio and Miyazato Seigen, eds. *Sanfuranshisuko kōwa* [San Francisco Peace Treaty]. Tokyo: University of Tokyo Press, 1986.

Watanabe Akio, ed. *Sengo Nihon no saishōtachi* [Prime Ministers of Postwar Japan]. Tokyo: Chūō Kōronsha, 1995.

Williams, Justin. *Japan's Political Revolution under MacArthur: A Participants Account.* Athens, GA: University of Georgia Press, 1979.

Willoughby, Charles A. *Shirarezaru Nihon senryō* [The Unknown Occupation of Japan] (Yong Yan, trans.). Tokyo: Banchō Shobō, 1973.

Yamagiwa Akira and Nakamura Masanori, eds. *Shiryō Nihon senryō 1: Tennō-sei* [Documents on the Occupation of Japan 1: Emperor System]. Tokyo: Ōtsuki Shoten, 1999.

Yamazaki Hiroshi. *Nihon shakaitō jūnenshi* [Ten-Year History of the Socialist Party of Japan]. Tokyo: Taibunkan, 1956.

Yoshida Shigeru Kinen Zaidan, ed. *Yoshida Shigeru shokan* [Letters of Yoshida Shigeru]. Tokyo: Chūō Kōronsha, 1994.

Yoshida Shigeru. *Gekidō no Hyakunenshi: Waga ketsudan to kiseki no tankan* [History of a turbulent hundred years]. Kyoto: Shirakawa Shoin, 1978.

——. *Kaisō jūnen, zen 4-kan* [Memoirs of Ten Years, Vols. 1-4]. Tokyo: Shinchōsha, 1957.

——. *Japan's Decisive Century 1867-1967*. New York: Frederick A. Praeger, 1967.

* Many of the quotations from Etō Jun's *Senryō shiroku* regarding the establishment of Japan's Constitution can be found on the National Diet Library's online database "The Birth of the Constitution."
  URL: https://www.ndl.go.jp/constitution/e/index.html

* Sources quoted and referenced in Sodei Rinjirō's *Correspondence between General MacArthur, Prime Minister Yoshida & Other High Japanese Officials [1945-1951]* can be found in the National Diet Library's digital collection under the section title "GHQ/SCAP Records, Government Section (GS)."
  URL: https://rnavi.ndl.go.jp/kensei/entry/GS.php

Illustration Sources

Alinari/Aflo: 42
The Asahi Shinbun: 267
Kyodo News: 63, 108, 175, 362 (above and below)
Library of Congress: 231
The National Archives: 45, 57
National Diet Library, Japan: 40, 136, 176, 208, 227
The U.S. Senate Historical Office: 312

Development of Postwar Political Parties (1945 – 1955)

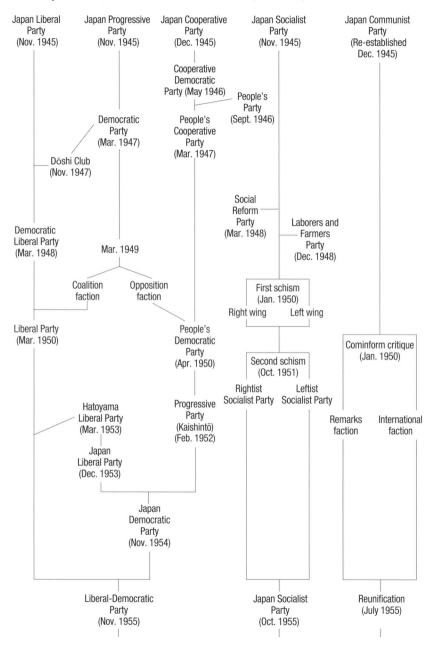

Chronology of the Occupation of Japan

Date	Event
1944 (Shōwa 19)	
Jul. 7	Saipan falls
Jul. 18	Tōjō Hideki Cabinet resigns en masse
Jul. 22	Koiso Kuniaki Cabinet formed
Oct. 10	U.S. forces bomb Okinawa
Oct. 20	MacArthur lands on Leyte Island
1945 (Shōwa 20)	
Feb. 4	Yalta Conference (Feb. 4–11)
Apr. 1	U.S. forces land on main island of Okinawa
Apr. 5	Koiso Kuniaki Cabinet resigns en masse
Apr. 7	Suzuki Kantarō Cabinet formed
Jun. 8	Imperial Conference meeting decides on "decisive battle on mainland"
Jun. 23	Battle of Okinawa effectively ends
Jul. 26	Potsdam Declaration issued
Aug. 6	Atomic bomb dropped on Hiroshima
Aug. 8	Soviet Union declares war on Japan
Aug. 9	Atomic bomb dropped on Nagasaki; meeting of Supreme Council for the Direction of the War; "imperial decision"
Aug. 14	Emperor makes decision to surrender
Aug. 15	War ends, Suzuki Kantarō Cabinet resigns en masse
Aug. 17	Higashikuni Naruhiko Cabinet formed
Aug. 20	Okinawa Advisory Council formed
Aug. 30	MacArthur lands at Atsugi Airfield
Sept. 2	Signing of surrender instrument
Sept. 22	U.S. government announces Initial Post-Surrender Policy
Sept. 27	Shōwa Emperor visits MacArthur
Oct. 2	GHQ established
Oct. 4	Civil Liberties Directive issued; Konoe visits MacArthur
Oct. 5	Higashikuni Naruhiko Cabinet resigns en masse

Oct. 9	Shidehara Kijūrō Cabinet formed
Oct. 11	Directive on Five Major Reforms issued
Oct. 24	United Nations established
Nov. 2	Japan Socialist Party formed (Katayama Tetsu elected secretary-general)
Nov. 3	U.S. government issues Basic Initial Post-Surrender Directive to MacArthur
Nov. 6	GHQ issues directive on zaibatsu dissolution
Nov. 9	Japan Liberal Party formed (Hatoyama Ichirō elected president)
Nov. 16	Japan Progressive Party (Shinpotō) formed (Tsurumi Yusuke elected secretary-general)
Dec. 8	"Four Matsumoto principles" announced
Dec. 9	GHQ announces Memorandum on Farmland Reform
Dec. 16	U.S., U.K., and Soviet foreign ministers' meeting (decision to form Far Eastern Commission and Allied Council for Japan)
Dec. 17	Revised House of Representatives Election Law promulgated
Dec. 22	Labor Union Law promulgated

1946 (Shōwa 21)

Jan. 1	Emperor's "Declaration of Humanity"
Jan. 4	GHQ issues first directive on public offices purge
Jan. 11	SWNCC-228 received
Jan. 24	Prime Minister Shidehara visits MacArthur
Jan. 25	MacArthur cables Washington on retaining Emperor system
Jan. 29	GHQ directs administrative separation of Amami Ōshima and islands south of 30 degrees north latitude
Feb. 1	*Mainichi Shinbun* scoops Matsumoto Committee's draft constitution
Feb. 3	MacArthur's "three basic points"
Feb. 13	GHQ hands constitutional revision draft to Japanese government
Feb. 26	First meeting of Far Eastern Commission
Mar. 6	Japanese government announces Outline of a Draft for a Revised Constitution
Apr. 10	22nd general election of House of Representatives

Apr. 22	Shidehara Kijūrō Cabinet resigns en masse
May 3	International Military Tribunal for the Far East opens
May 4	GHQ purges Hatoyama Ichirō
May 19	Food May Day
May 22	First Yoshida Shigeru Cabinet formed
Oct. 21	Second Farmland Reform launched
Nov. 3	Constitution of Japan promulgated
Dec. 17	People's Meeting for Bringing Down the Yoshida Cabinet
Dec. 27	Cabinet adopts "priority production system"

1947 (Shōwa 22)

Jan. 4	GHQ issues second directive on public offices purge
Jan. 18	Joint Struggle Committee of All Government and Municipal Workers' Union announces "February 1 Strike"
Jan. 31	MacArthur orders cessation of "February 1 Strike"
Mar. 8	People's Cooperative Party formed (Miki Takeo elected secretary-general)
Mar. 12	Truman Doctrine announced
Mar. 17	MacArthur statement on early peace treaty
Mar. 31	Democratic Party formed (Ashida Hitoshi elected president, May 18)
Apr. 20	1st election of House of Councillors
Apr. 25	23rd general election of House of Representatives
May 3	Constitution of Japan takes effect
Jun. 1	Katayama Tetsu Cabinet formed
Jun. 5	Marshall Plan announced
Dec. 18	Law for the Elimination of Excessive Concentration of Economic Power promulgated
Dec. 22	Revised Civil Code promulgated (family system abolished)
Dec. 31	Ministry of Home Affairs dissolved

1948 (Shōwa 23)

Jan. 6	U.S. Secretary of the Army Royall delivers speech on Japan as anti-communist bulwark
Feb. 10	Katayama Tetsu Cabinet resigns en masse
Mar. 10	Ashida Hitoshi Cabinet formed
Mar. 15	Democratic Liberal Party formed (Yoshida Shigeru elected president)

Mar. 20	Draper mission on reparations arrives in Japan
Jun. 23	President of Shōwa Denkō arrested on bribery charges (Shōwa Denkō Incident)
Jun. 24	Berlin blockade begins (continuing through May 1949)
Jul. 31	Cabinet Order No. 201 issued
Aug. 15	Republic of Korea established
Sept. 9	Democratic People's Republic of Korea established
Oct. 7	Approval of NSC-13/2 finalizes new Occupation policies; Ashida Hitoshi Cabinet resigns en masse
Oct. 19	Second Yoshida Cabinet formed
Dec. 18	Nine Principles for Economic Stabilization announced

1949 (Shōwa 24)

Jan. 23	24th general election of House of Representatives (Democratic Liberal Party becomes majority party)
Feb. 1	Joseph Dodge arrives in Japan
Feb. 3	Premier Yoshida Shigeru moves to approve rearmament
Feb. 16	Third Yoshida Shigeru Cabinet formed
Mar. 1	Dodge orders adoption of balanced budget
May 6	U.S. government adopts NSC-13/3 (decision on long-term administration of Okinawa)
Sept.	Red Purge starts; foreign ministers of U.K., U.S., and France agree to move forward on peace treaty with Japan
Oct. 1	People's Republic of China established

1950 (Shōwa 25)

Jan. 1	MacArthur affirms "right of self-defense" in New Year's message
Jan. 6	Cominform criticizes Communist Party
Jan. 15	Peace Problems Council releases "Statement on Issues Related to the Peace"
Jan. 19	Left and right wings of Socialist Party split (first schism)
Jun. 6	MacArthur orders purge of Communist Party Central Committee members
Jun. 21	Dulles arrives in Japan
Jun. 25	Korean War starts
Aug. 10	Directive issued on formation of National Police Reserve

Sept. 14	President Truman announces "Seven Principles of the Peace with Japan"
Sept.–Oct.	Elections held in Okinawa archipelago
Dec.	Peace Problems Council releases "On Peace for the Third Time"

1951 (Shōwa 26)

Jan. 21	Socialist Party adopts "four principles on peace"
Jan. 25	Dulles returns to Japan
Feb. 23	Communist Party proposal on armed struggle
Apr. 1	Ryukyu Provisional Central Government established
Apr. 11	MacArthur dismissed
May 1	Ridgway statement issued
Sept. 4	San Francisco Peace Conference (Sept. 4–8)
Sept. 8	Signing of San Francisco Peace Treaty Conclusion of U.S.–Japan Security Treaty
Oct. 24	Left and right wings of Socialist Party split over Peace Treaty and Security Treaty (second schism)

1952 (Shōwa 27)

Jan. 16	Yoshida letter indicating intent to conclude peace treaty with The Nationalist government in Taiwan released
Feb. 8	Progressive Party (Kaishintō) formed (Miki Takeo elected secretary-general)
Feb. 28	Signing of Japan-U.S. Administrative Agreement
Feb. 29	U.S. Civil Administration of the Ryukyu Islands issues USCAR Proclamation 13 establishing Government of the Ryukyu Islands
Apr. 28	Peace Treaty between Japan and the Republic of China concluded; San Francisco Peace Treaty takes effect

Index

Note: Page numbers in *italics* refer to photographs or diagrams. The abbreviation 't' refers to tables.

revision of Occupation policies 205–6, *207*, 208, 209, 211, 212, 218

Draper-Johnston Report (May 1948) 242–44

freedom of the press 60
Fukuda Takeo 252, 253
Funada Naka 74
Fundamental Policy for the Conduct of the
War 30

G

G2 Section (Public Safety Division) *49*, 58,
124, 126, 199, 213, 253, 279
Government Section and 181–82, 183
peace treaty 303, 315, 316
GARIOA *see* Government Appropriation for
Relief in Occupied Area Fund (United
States)
Gayn, Mark 124
General Affairs Bureau (Foreign Ministry)
119, 202
General Council of Trade Unions of Japan
(Sōhyō) 279, 321, 347–48, 365
General Election (April 1947) 130–31, 157,
170–77
General Election (January 1949) 261–63
General Federation of National Railways
Workers' Unions (Kokutetsu) 152, 160,
271, 277
General Federation of Private Railway
Workers' Unions (Shitetsu) 279, 365
General Headquarters of the Army Forces in
the Pacific (GHQ-AFPAC) 47
General Headquarters of the Military
Government of the Ryūkyū Islands 284
General Headquarters, Supreme Commander
for the Allied Powers (GHQ/SCAP)
assessment of political parties 74–75
establishment of 15, 16–17, 19, 47–48
organization chart *49*
General Procurement Agent *49*, 183
General Strike (1947) 151–52, 159–60, 161,
165, 166, 234, 271, 380
GHQ-AFPAC *see* General Headquarters of the
Army Forces in the Pacific
GHQ/SCAP *see* General Headquarters,
Supreme Commander for the Allied
Powers
"Government and Administrative Separation
of Certain Outlying Areas from Japan"
(SCAPIN-677) 81
Government Appropriation for Relief in
Occupied Area Fund (GARIOA Fund)

(United States) 185, 233
Government of the Ryūkyū Islands 372
Government Section (GS) 29, 81, 177, 183,
184, 208, 213, 314, 315
appointment of Frank Rizzo as Chief
354–55
Ashida Cabinet 226–27, 228, 236, 245
Constitution of Japan 139, 141, 145, 380
Dodge Line 307, 309
downsizing of 218–20, 381
establishment of 48, 49, 55–56, *57*, 58
G2 Section and 181–82, 183
last report 367–68
Ministry of Home Affairs 201–3
Nine Days of Secrecy 106–14, *115*,
116–21
Okinawa 186, 189, 192
political parties 153, 157, 158, 160, 161,
170–71, 198, 199
purge of public officials 124, 125–26, 303
reorganization 218–20
revison of election laws 126–27, 186
Whitney appointed as Head 56, *57*, 58,
354
Yoshida Shigeru and 146–47, 253–56,
263, 269, 280, 281, 282, 315–16
Great Britain *see* United Kingdom
Great Japan Patriotic Industrial Association
69, 76
Great Japan Political Association 59, 67, 72,
131, 172
Green Breeze Society (Ryokufūkai) 173, 306,
310, 360
Grew, Joseph 50, 206–7
Gromyko, Andrei 361

H

Hague Laws of Land Warfare Respecting the
Laws and Customs of War on Land 26,
89
Hara Hyō 68
Hara Yasusaburō 356
"hard peace guys" 50, 349, 350, 358
Hatano Kanae 200
Hatoyama Ichirō 37, 103, 345, 356, 386
postwar politics 67, 68, 71, 75
purge of 126, 130, 132–35
return to Liberal Party 365–67
Hays, Frank *115*, 219

Local Government Division (Government
Section) 186, 219
Local Public Finance Committee 203
Local Tax Law 276, 305–7, 308
Lovett, Robert 208

M

MacArthur, Douglas 23, 30, 77, 87, 127, 131,
136–137, 217–18, 303, 384–85
Ashida Cabinet 237, 245, 252
"Bataan boys" 56
"blue-eyed tycoon" 43–44
"Neutral Japan" 293–294, 311–12
Constitution of Japan 96, 98–99, 100, *115*
"Conversion" 298–300, 302
democratization 60–61, 63, 70–71, 75, 79,
158, 159
directive on general elections 165–66,
171, 174, 177
dismissal of 352–57
Dodge Line 269, 275, 285, 307–8,
381–382
economic recovery 241, 242, 243, 244,
245, 246, 252, 256, 258, 259, 380
establishment of headquarters 47–48, *49*,
50–51, 53
Far Eastern Commission and 54, 121–22,
123, 139, 141
farmland reform 143–44
Five Major Reforms directive 82, 98,
378, 380
Instrument of Surrender 44, *45*, 46, 47,
377
Katayama Cabinet 196, 197, 207, 211
Korean War 313, 314, 318, 331, 337
Okinawa 150–51, 186, 190, 191, 192,
250, 283, 285, 335, 345
Operation Blacklist 29–30
peace settlement 168–70, 310–11
plans for reformation of Japan 5, 6, 15,
16, 17
pledge to return 24–25
police reform 181–82, 185, 281, 314, 315,
316, 332
profile 41, *42*
revision of Occupation policies 205, 206,
207, 209–10, 211, 212, 213, 218,
234
Shidehara Cabinet 63, 65–66, 98–99

State Department (U.S.) and 209–10, 229,
230, 231, 246
Three Basic Points 106–14, *115*, 116–21,
379
"Two Hats" 40, *41*, 42
visit by Emperor 60–61, 62
Whitney and 57–58, 171, 204
Yoshida Shigeru 60, 146–147, 165–66,
176, 238, 253, 254, 255, 261, 262,
281–82, 306, 343
McCarthy, Joseph 310
McCoy, Frank R. 122, 123, 218
Machida, Chūji 73, 135
Maeda, Tamon 128, 356
Maeo Shigesaburō 262
Mainichi Shinbun 62, 111–13, 119, 274, 325,
326
Maintenance of Public Order Law 62
Manchurian Incident (1931) 74, 85, 99, 227,
379
March Offensive 233–34
Marcum, Carlos 219
Marquat, William F. 159, 234, 241, 244, 266,
307, 309
Marshall, George 167, 192, 209, 210, 337
Marshall Plan (1947) 167, 169, 207, 209, 258,
259, 277
Marshall, Richard 45
Maruyama Masao 295
Masuda Kaneshichi 253, 265, 274, 280, 370
Matsudaira Tsuneo 135
Matsudaira Yasumasa 35
Matsukawa Incident (1949) 275
Matsumoto Jiichirō 356
Matsumoto Jōji 100
Matsumura Kenzō 65, 83, 128, 366
Matsuoka Komakichi 38, 68, 76, 82, 152, 254
Matsuoka Seiho 333, 334
Matsuoka Yōsuke 261
Meeting on Wage Stabilizing Measures 242
Meiji Constitution 95, 96, 99, 101, 107, 386
Metropolitan Police 62
Metropolitan Public Security Ordinance 272
Miki Bukichi 356, 366
Miki Takeo 138, 171, 178, 221, 237, 238, 253,
366, 371
militarism 5, 15, 18, 32, 60, 169, 300, 361,
363
"Military Government Proclamation No.

22." *see* Law for the Election of Local
Government Heads (1947)
Military Government of the Ryūkyū Islands
250–51, 284
Military Government Sections/Units 29, 48,
189, 250–51, 269
Minister of the Army 30–31
Ministry of Agriculture and Forestry 17, 65,
74, 82, 83, 128, 137, 155, 178, 333
removal of Minister Hirano 199–201, 220
see also farmland reform
Ministry of Commerce and Industry 79, 178,
252, 270
Ministry of Education 239
Ministry of Finance 202, 209, 222, 252
Ministry of Foreign Affairs 61, 65, 78, 79, 96,
263–64, 323, 339–40, 359
Ministry of Home Affairs 82, 181, 201–3, 219
Ministry of International Trade and Industry
194, 270
Ministry of Justice 179
Ministry of Labor 82, 220
Ministry of Public Administration 202
Minobe Tatsukichi 71, 103
Mitaka Incident (1949) 274–75, 281
Mitsuchi Chūzō 117
Miwa Jusō 76
Miyake Shōichi 68, 70, 322
Miyako Islands 24, 91–92, 189, 249, 250, 284,
333, 335, 389
Miyamoto Kenji 301
Miyazawa Kiichi 266, 304, 317, 354, 363, 370
Miyazawa Toshiyoshi 71, 112
Mizutani Chōzaburō 38, 69, 178, 364
Molotov, Vyacheslav 31
Morito Tatsuo 103, 106, 270
Moscow Agreement (1945) 108, 258
Municipal Elections (February 1948) 248–49
Murofuse, Kōshin 106
Murray, Colonel 87
Mutō Takeo 348
mutual security treaties 344, 352

N

Nagano Osami 261
Nagano Shigeo 195, 228
Nakae Sanetaka 333
Nakagawa Zennosuke 179
Nakajima Chikuhei 77, 85

Nakano Yoshio 295
Nakayama Ichirō 78, 356
Nanbara Shigeru 296
Nansei Shotō 24, 26, 91–92
Narahashi Wataru 117, 132, 172
Nashimoto Morimasa 77
National Civil Service Law (October 1947)
204
National Congress of Industrial Unions 279
National Council of Government 244
National Council of Labor Unions (Zenrōkon)
153
National Farmers Union 220
National Federation of Chambers of
Commerce and Industry 85
National Federation of Commerce and
Industry Cooperatives 85
National Federation of Industrial Unions (Shin
Sanbetsu) 321
National Government Division (Government
Section) 219, 226
National Land Bureau 203
National Police Reserve Force 314–15, 324,
332
National Police Reserve Order (Potsdam
Cabinet Order No. 260) 314–15
national polity 30, 34, 35, 60, 105t 136, 140
postwar politics 71, 72, 73, 74
National Public Safety Commission 280, 314,
315, 316
National Public Service Law (1947) 203–4,
244, 245, 255, 256
National Rural Police 181, 182, 279–81, 314,
315–16, 352, 368
National Security Council (NSC) (United
States) 257, 291
NATO *see* North Atlantic Treaty Organization
Natural Resources Section (NRS) (GHQ) *49*,
84, 143, 183, 283
New Frontier Society (Shinshinkai) 336
New Politics Association (Shinseikai) 366
Nimitz, Chester 23, 24, 25, 26
Nimitz Proclamation (U.S. Navy Military
Government Proclamation No. 1) 26
"Nine Principles for Economic Stabilization"
258–259, 260t, 261–62, 265, 266, 267,
268, 269, 272, 381, 382
Nishihara Gaichi 333
Nishimura Kumao 339, 341, 345

About the Author

Fukunaga Fumio, Ph.D., was born in 1953 in Hyogo Prefecture, graduated from Kobe University Faculty of Law in 1976, and completed a doctorate at Kobe University Graduate School of Law in 1985. Beginning in 1987, he taught at Himeji Dokkyo University successively as a lecturer, associate professor, and professor before joining Dokkyo University as a professor in 2001. He specializes in political science and the political and diplomatic history of Japan and is the author of numerous works including *Senryō-ka chūdō seiken no keisei to hōkai: Minsei-kyoku to Nihon Shakaitō* [Formation and Collapse of Middle-of-the-Road Governments under the Occupation: Government Section and the Japan Socialist Party] (Iwanami Shoten, 1997) and *Ōhira Masayoshi: "Sengo hoshu" towa nanika* [Ōhira Masayoshi: What Is Postwar Conservatism?] (Chūō Kōron Shinsha, 2008). He co-authored *Sengo towa nanika, jōgekan* [Defining the Postwar Period, Vol. 1–2] (Maruzen, 2014), and co-edited *Sengo Nihon dai 2-kan: Senryō to kaikaku* [Postwar Japan Vol. 2: Occupation and Reform] (Iwanami Shoten, 1995), *Sengo Nihon no saishōtachi* [Prime Ministers of Postwar Japan] (Chūō Kōronsha, 1995), and *Daini no "sengo" no keisei katei: 1970-nendai Nihon no seijiteki, gaikōteki saihen* [Japan's Postwar History Revisited: Politics and Diplomacy in the 1970s] (Yūhikaku Publishing, 2015).

（英文版）日本占領史1945–1952：東京・ワシントン・沖縄
The Occupation of Japan 1945–1952: Tokyo, Washington, and Okinawa

2021年3月27日　第1刷発行

著　者　　福永文夫
英　訳　　公益財団法人日本国際問題研究所
発行所　　一般財団法人出版文化産業振興財団
　　　　　〒101-0051 東京都千代田区神田神保町2-2-30
　　　　　電話　03-5211-7283
　　　　　ホームページ　https://www.jpic.or.jp/

印刷・製本所　　大日本印刷株式会社